SINGER

AND HIS CRITICS

PHILOSOPHERS AND THEIR CRITICS

General Editor: Ernest Lepore

Philosophy is an interactive enterprise. Much of it is carried out in dialogue as theories and ideas are presented and subsequently refined in the crucible of close scrutiny. The purpose of this series is to reconstruct this vital interplay among thinkers. Each book consists of a contemporary assessment of an important living philosopher's work. A collection of essays written by an interdisciplinary group of critics addressing the substantial theses of the philosopher's corpus opens each volume. In the last section, the philosopher responds to his or her critics, clarifies crucial points of the discussion, or updates his or her doctrines.

SINGER

AND HIS CRITICS

Edited by

Dale Jamieson

BLACKWELL
Publishers

Copyright © Blackwell Publishers Ltd 1999

First published 1999
Reprinted 2000

Blackwell Publishers Ltd
108 Cowley Road
Oxford OX4 1JF
UK

Blackwell Publishers Inc.
350 Main Street
Malden, Massachusetts 02148
USA

British Library Cataloguing in Publication Data

A CIP catalogue record for this book is available from the British Library.

Library of Congress Cataloging-in-Publication Data

Singer and his critics / edited by Dale Jamieson.
p.   cm.—(Philosophers and their critics ; 8)
Includes bibliographical references and index.
ISBN 1–55786–908–1 (hardcover : alk. paper).—ISBN 1–55786–909–X (pbk. : alk. paper)
  1. Singer, Peter—Ethics. I. Jamieson, Dale. II. Series
B5704.S554S56   1999
170'.92—dc21   98–42231
                                                                                   CIP

Typeset in 10 on 12 pt Times
By Pure Tech India Ltd, Pondicherry
http://www.puretech.com
Printed in Great Britain by MPG Books Ltd, Bodmin, Cornwall

This book is printed on acid-free paper

Contents

Notes on Contributors

RICHARD J. ARNESON is Professor of Philosophy at the University of California at San Diego, 9500 Gilman Drive, La Jolla, CA 92093-0119. He is the author of many articles on contemporary theories of justice. He can be reached on the Internet at rarneson@ucsd.edu.

ROGER CRISP is Fellow and Tutor in Philosophy at St Anne's College, Oxford OX2 6HS. He is the author of *Mill on Utilitarianism*, the editor of the journal *Utilitas* and a member of the *Analysis* Committee. He can be reached on the Internet at roger.crisp@st-annes.ox.ac.uk.

LORI GRUEN teaches in the Department of Philosophy at Stanford University, Building 90, Stanford, CA 94305, where she is also affiliated with the Ethics in Society Program. She is the co-editor of *Sex, Morality and the Law*, and has published articles on human relations with non-human animals and ecofeminist philosophy. She can be reached on the Internet at gruen@csli.stanford.edu.

R. M. HARE is formerly White's Professor of Philosophy in the University of Oxford and is Professor of Philosophy Emeritus at the University of Florida. His most recent book is *Sorting Out Ethics*.

RICHARD HOLTON is Lecturer in the Department of Philosophy at the University of Sheffield, Arts Tower, Sheffield, England S10 2TN. His work is mainly in philosophy of language and moral psychology.

FRANK JACKSON is Director of the Institute of Advanced Studies and Professor of Philosophy in the Institute of Advanced Studies, Australian National University, Canberra, ACT 0200. His most recent book is *From Metaphysics to Ethics: a Defence of Conceptual Analysis*. He can be reached on the Internet at frank.jackson@anu.edu.au. His home page is http://coombs.anu.edu.au/Depts/RSSS/Philosophy/People/Jackson/index.html.

DALE JAMIESON is Henry R. Luce Professor in Human Dimensions of Global Change at Carleton College, Northfield, MN 55057. He is the author of many articles in environmental philosophy, moral philosophy and philosophy of biology and mind. He can be reached on the Internet at djamieso@carleton.edu. His home page is http://dir.ucar.edu/esig/HP_dale.html.

F. M. KAMM is Professor of Philosophy and Adjunct Professor of Law at New York University, 55 Main Building, 100 Washington Square East, New York, NY 10003; and Visiting Professor of Philosophy at UCLA. Her most recent book is *Morality, Mortality, Volume 2: Rights, Duties, and Status.* She can be reached on the Internet at fmkl@is4.nyu.edu.

RAE LANGTON is Lecturer in the Department of Philosophy at the University of Sheffield, Arts Tower, Sheffield, England S10 2TN. She is the author of *Kantian Humility.*

COLIN MCGINN is Professor of Philosophy at Rutgers University, PO Box 270, New Brunswick, NJ 08903-0273. His most recent book is *Ethics, Evil, and Fiction.* He can be reached on the Internet at cmcginn@mail.msn.com

HOLMES ROLSTON III is University Distinguished Professor and Professor of Philosophy at Colorado State University, Fort Collins, CO 80523. He is the author of *Conserving Natural Value* and the Associate Editor of the journal *Environmental Ethics.* He can be reached on the internet at rolston@lamar.colostate.edu. His homepage is http://lamar.colostate.edu/~rolston/.

PETER SINGER is Professor of Philosophy, on secondment to the Centre for Human Bioethics, at Monash University, Clayton, Victoria 3168, Australia. His most recent book is *Ethics into Action: Henry Spira and the Animal Rights Movement.* In the autumn of 1998 he became the Ira W. De Camp Professor of Bioethics at Princeton University.

MICHAEL SMITH is Professor of Philosophy and Head of the Philosophy Program in the Research School of Social Sciences at the Australian National University, Canberra ACT 0200. He is the author of *The Moral Problem.* He can be reached on the Internet at msmith@coombs.anu.edu.au.

ROBERT C. SOLOMON is the Quincy Lee Centennial and Distinguished Teaching Professor of Philosophy at the University of Texas, WAG 316 (203), Austin, TX 78712. His most recent book is *A Short History of Philosophy* (with Kathleen Higgins).

Preface

This book is a celebration of the work of Peter Singer. Since philosophers honor people by criticizing them, Singer's writings on a wide array of topics come in for analysis and appraisal in this volume. Singer's metaethical views, his normative theory, and his substantive positions on such matters as the moral status of animals, the sancity of human life, and famine relief are all subjected to scrutiny. Singer's replies to his critics importantly supplement what he has previously written on these issues and will be essential reading for anyone who wants to fully understand his views.

Many people helped to make the present volume possible. It was Ernie Lapore's enthusiastic invitation and Steve Smith's steady support that got the project going and sustained it. Carleton College in conjunction with the Henry R. Luce Foundation provided funds for research and staff support, and the Environmental Impacts Group of the National Center for Atmospheric Research (NCAR) was my home while the book was being completed. Kelly Knutsen and Paula Lackey provided support at Carleton, and Baat Enosh performed various electronic miracles at NCAR. I am indebted to Baat for both her competence and her good humor. I also thank John Taylor for his good and patient copy-editing. Finally, Peter Singer was unfailingly helpful in making his papers available and discussing his work with me. The entire Singer family has my gratitude for their hospitality during my visit to Melbourne.

Since most of us produce so few books and there are so many worthy people to acknowledge, I believe that all books should have dedications. This book is dedicated to all those who believe that philosophy is not just an academic exercise or a way of making a living, but also an instrument for improving ourselves and making the world better. In particular this book is dedicated to those who look at themselves and others and wonder, "Why not the best?"

Dale Jamieson
Northfield, Minnesota

1
Singer and the Practical Ethics Movement

DALE JAMIESON

Peter Singer is one of the most influential philosophers of the twentieth century. While other philosophers have been more important in the development of the discipline, none has changed more lives. *Newsweek* magazine observed that "the modern [animal rights] movement may be dated to the publication of *Animal Liberation*."[1] For many years this book was given away by People for the Ethical Treatment of Animals, one of the organizations founded in the wake of *Animal Liberation* and now one of the largest and most effective animal rights organizations in the world. On Paul McCartney's 1993 world tour copies of *Animal Liberation* were sold alongside T-shirts. Thus far *Animal Liberation* has sold more than 400,000 copies in nine languages. Altogether Singer is responsible in whole or part for producing twenty-seven books, most of which sell significantly better than books by other philosophers. *Practical Ethics*, for example, has sold over 100,000 copies in ten languages. Singer has also authored a vast number of articles and reviews that have appeared in journals ranging from *The Philosophical Review* to the *New York Times*.

Peter Singer was born in Melbourne, Australia, on July 6, 1946. His parents were Viennese Jews who escaped in 1938, shortly after the *Anschluss* incorporated Austria into the German Reich. They fled to Australia because that was the only country that would accept them, sponsored by a man whom Peter's mother had met only once through a mutual acquaintance when he was a tourist in Vienna. By the time Peter was born, his father was a successful importer of coffee and tea and his mother was practicing medicine, a profession for which she had trained in Austria. Eager to integrate their children into Australian society, the Singers spoke only English at home and sent Peter to a prestigious Protestant school. He went on to Melbourne University, where as an undergraduate he studied law, history, and philosophy. In 1969 he received an MA in philosophy, writing a thesis on "Why should I be moral?" A scholarship allowed Singer to complete his graduate studies in Oxford, where he received his BPhil in 1971 and served as Radcliffe lecturer from 1971 to 1973.

In 1972, Singer published "Famine, affluence and morality" in the first volume of a new journal, *Philosophy and Public Affairs*. This article, which has been reprinted more than two dozen times, is important for several reasons. In style it was an unconventional philosophical essay in that it was written in simple, direct prose, with few references to philosophical texts. Rather than beginning from Kant, Aristotle, or a hypothetical moral question, it addressed events that were occurring as Singer was writing. The article began with these words: "As I write this, in November 1971, people are dying in East Bengal from lack of food, shelter, and medical care."[2] Singer went on to present his readers with a stark moral challenge. On the basis of some apparently simple, plausible premises, he argued that we ought to transfer our resources to those who are worse off until we reach the point at which further transfers would harm us more than they would benefit others. Singer was asking his readers to give up their opera tickets, their wine cellars, and private schools for their children – the accoutrements of the sophisticated, upper-middle class life favored by many academics. Furthermore, Singer was completely unapologetic about making such demands:

> the whole way we look at moral issues...needs to be altered, and with it, the way of life that has come to be taken for granted in our society...Discussion...is not enough. What is the point of relating philosophy to public (and personal) affairs if we do not take our conclusions seriously? In this instance, taking our conclusion seriously means acting upon it.[3]

Singer was writing these words at a new moment in philosophy. Little more than fifteen years before, in 1956, Peter Laslett had declared political philosophy dead, and moral philosophy clearly was among the walking wounded. In 1960, in *The End of Ideology*, Daniel Bell declared that "ideology, which once was a road to action, has come to be a dead end."[4] In the United States there was widespread agreement that fundamental challenges about how to live and what sort of country to create had largely been resolved by the affluent society of the 1950s.[5] The intellectual problems of the future were in the basic sciences or in devising efficient solutions to problems of rational choice and social organization. Moral and political philosophy were not only dreary subjects, but irrelevant to the modern world.

The convulsions of the 1960s came as a shock to much of the American intellectual establishment. Sparked by the war in Vietnam, the civil rights movement and the rebirth of feminism, the apparent consensus of the 1950s was shattered by student protests and black militancy. In the United States there was a clear "disconnect" between what was going on in the university and what was happening in the streets. This was symbolized by the disruption of John Searle's ethics classes at Berkeley. Searle wanted to lecture on deriving an "ought" from an "is," while students wanted to discuss the war in Vietnam. As an undergraduate at San Francisco State in the late 1960s, I was vividly aware of this split between philosophy and life. Ethics in the classroom was W. D. Ross and P. H. Nowell-Smith but it was Martin Luther King, Che Guevara, and the Black Panthers who dominated our conversations outside of class. In 1968, the year in which student insurrections broke out all over the world, the biggest news in academic philosophy was the growing hegemony of truth-conditional semantics. But the philosophers who made a difference to the events of 1968 were not Quine and Davidson but Marx and Marcuse. The frustration that many of us felt was not merely that Marx and Marcuse were not discussed in classes, but that the very concerns that motivated them seemed to have been banished from academic philosophy. While there is a lot to be said for working in philosophy of language, even during wartime, in retrospect it seems inevitable that the concerns of real life could not forever be excluded from the academy, especially in a discipline that has a long history of concern with substantive normative questions.

By the late 1960s, a group of elite East Coast philosophers, including Thomas Nagel, John Rawls, and Judith Jarvis Thomson, had formed the Society for Ethical and Legal Philosophy and were discussing such topics as racism, abortion, affirmative action, and the morality of war. Soon thereafter a group of philosophers at Rockefeller University launched *Philosophy and Public Affairs*. The practical ethics movement soon swept the country.

The philosophers who were turning their attention to matters of urgent public interest were not exclusively moral and political philosophers. Since the issues that they discussed were of broad interest, yet had largely been ignored by professional philosophers, they were fair game for whoever wanted to take them up. Ironically, just as Russell turned out to be the most politically active major philosopher of the century, so logicians and philosophers of science helped to bring practical ethics back into the discipline. But while Russell considered his political and social writings to be distinct from his philosophical work, these philosophers thought that they were doing philosophy.

Most of the concerns, both substantive and methodological, that would dominate the next twenty-five years of work in practical ethics and political philosophy were on display in the first volume of *Philosophy and Public Affairs*. War and morality was the dominant topic, but articles on Marxism, abortion, suicide, and freedom of expression also appeared. The style of argument was generally intuitive, but in a symposium on the rules of war R. B. Brandt grounded his account in rule-utilitarianism, while R. M. Hare criticized Thomas Nagel for having no theoretical basis for deciding between competing moral considerations.

In 1971, the year in which Singer was writing "Famine, affluence, and morality," John Rawls published *A Theory of Justice*. With the publication of Robert Nozick's *Anarchy, State and Utopia* in 1974 and Gerald Cohen's *Karl Marx's Theory of History: a Defense* in 1978, liberalism, libertarianism, and Marxism were all represented by major works in the analytic tradition. Political philosophy, which had been pronounced dead only fifteen years earlier, was now very much alive. Still, much of this new work in political philosophy was very abstract and surprisingly unworldly. For example, although Rawls explicitly addressed civil disobedience, it was difficult to say exactly how his view applied to particular cases. The practical indeterminacy of Rawls's views led to an explosion of literature and also to increasing differentiation between political philosophy and practical ethics. If there was any concern that was central to practical ethics it was to address specific problems in context. The emerging differences between practical ethics and the new political philosophy were obscured to some extent by the fact that throughout the 1970s much of the important literature in both fields appeared in *Philosophy and Public Affairs*. But with the founding of such journals as the *Journal of Medicine and Philosophy* (1976), *Environmental Ethics* (1979), and the *Journal of Business Ethics* (1982), the differences became increasingly apparent.

Moral and political philosophy in the UK were hardly in better shape than in the United States during the immediate post-Second World War period. However, the fact that PPE (Philosophy, Politics, and Economics) was one of the most popular Oxford courses of study kept philosophy alive and to some extent allied with topics of moral and political concern. Influential senior figures in Oxford such as H. L. A. Hart, Sir Isaiah Berlin, and John Plamenatz, though their appointments were not in the Subfaculty of Philosophy, were interested in a variety of issues at the intersection of philosophy, politics, law, and history. And although he had made his name by applying the techniques of linguistic analysis to metaethical questions, R. M. Hare, White's Professor of Moral Philosophy from 1966 to 1983, was supportive of work in practical ethics. When Peter Singer, a young veteran of the Australian anti-war movement, came to him with a proposal to write a thesis on civil disobedience, Hare was receptive.

In 1973 Singer published his first book, *Democracy and Disobedience*, which was based largely on his thesis. In April of that year, "Animal liberation" appeared in the *New York Review of Books*. The story of how this article came to be written is by now well known. While a student in Oxford, Singer, with his wife Renata, fell in with a group of Canadians who were moral vegetarians, two of whom, Stanley and Roslind God-lovitch, were involved in editing a book called *Animals, Men and Morals*. Unable to resist the Godlovitchs' arguments, the Singers changed their lives. Wanting to do what he could to promote his recently adopted views regarding animals, Singer sent an unsolicited review of *Animals, Men and Morals* to the *New York Review of Books*. Surprisingly, it was accepted. Astonishingly, the review had a major impact, leading to a book contract from New York Review Books.

In autumn 1973 Singer moved to the United States in order to teach at New York University. He was in America only sixteen months, but his visit had a large impact. He wrote most of *Animal Liberation* during his stay, and while working on the book Singer presented draft chapters to philosophy departments around the country. With his Oxford credentials and his connections to Hare, Singer helped to legitimize concerns about animals in the American philosophical community. When *Animal Liberation* was published in 1975, it had an enormous effect in transforming what had been a collection of small, largely invisible animal welfare organizations into a strong and vibrant social movement.

Also during his time in New York, Singer wrote "Philosophers are back on the job" for *The New York Times Magazine* (July 7, 1974). This essay brought the practical ethics movement to the attention of a wide, non-professional audience. Singer began the article by providing an overview of twentieth-century philosophical movements, bringing out what was salutary about both positivism and ordinary language philosophy, but arguing that in the end they failed either to resolve or dissolve traditional philosophical problems. He went on to discuss *A Theory of Justice*, regarding its enthusiastic reception as a sign "of the new strength of moral and political philosophy" (p. 19). But while he granted that the book "has many good things in it" (p. 19), he claimed that it "does not represent moral and political philosophy at its best." Singer went on to criticize Rawls's theory in ways that were emblematic of the division between political philosophy and practical ethics that was already under way, and his objections to Rawls's method of reflective equilibrium foreshadowed fissures that have subsequently opened up within the practical ethics movement itself, and continue to reverberate in this book. Signalling his later interests, Singer identified medical ethics as an area "in need of the clarification and rigor that a philosopher can provide" (p. 20) and concluded that "the entry of philosophers into areas of ethical concern from which they have hitherto excluded themselves is the most stimulating and potentially fruitful of all the recent developments in philosophy" (p. 20).

In 1975 Singer returned to Melbourne, where he has remained, except to take up various visiting appointments in universities around the world. From 1975 to 1977 he was a Senior Lecturer at La Trobe University and since 1977 he has been Professor of Philosophy at Monash University. In the autumn of 1999 he will become the Ira W. DeCamp Professor of Bioethics at Princeton University.

In the early 1980s Singer wrote a series of books that provided some context to his moral and political views. *Marx* appeared in 1980 (since translated into four languages) and *Hegel* was published in 1982 (now translated into seven languages). In 1981 *The Expanding Circle: Ethics and Sociobiology*, Singer's account of the biological foundations of ethics, was published.

Although he produced plenty of work on other topics throughout the 1980s, Singer's attention turned increasingly to medical ethics. In 1983 he founded the Centre for Human Bioethics and served as its Director until 1992. In 1985 with Helga Kuhse he established *Bioethics*, which has become one of the leading bioethics journals in the world. Between 1983 and 1994 Singer produced seven books and monographs on medical ethics, including *Rethinking Life and Death*, published in English in 1994, and subsequently translated into Italian, Dutch, Polish, German, Japanese, and Spanish.

Virtually all of Singer's work exemplifies the following three important characteristics. First, it is revisionary. The point of practical ethics is not simply to understand the world, but to change it. Singer's specific views are well known: that we should stop eating and experimenting on animals; that we should give large portions of our wealth to those who are worse off; that in some cases infanticide is permissible. The concern that practical ethics should make a difference has led him to be skeptical of approaches to moral and political philosophy that rely on our everyday moral beliefs. His main criticism of Rawls in the 1974 *New York Times Magazine* article concerned Rawls's reliance on moral intuitions. According to Singer,

> No conclusions about what we ought to do can validly be drawn from a description of what most people in our society think we ought to do. If we have a soundly based moral theory we ought to be prepared to accept its implications even if they force us to change our moral views on major issues. Once this point is forgotten, moral philosophy loses its capacity to generate radical criticism of prevailing moral standards, and serves only to preserve the status quo. (pp. 19–20)

A second characteristic of Singer's work is that facts matter. Philosophy may begin where facts run out, as Singer wrote in "Philosophers are back on the job," (p. 20), but it is hard to see what philosophy would be for Singer if it didn't start with a vivid appreciation of the way things are. The observation that facts matter might seem platitudinous to most people, even to most academics, but philosophers often pretend that "mere" empirical facts have nothing to do with anything of philosophical significance; and when this conceit becomes difficult to sustain, they often invent facts (under the guise of thought experiments) rather than bothering to discover them. What makes *Animal Liberation* so powerful, even for readers who do not share Singer's utilitarian principles, is the two-thirds of the book that brings to light our treatment of animals and provides practical suggestions for how to change our lives. A reviewer wrote in the *Philosophical Review*, not without admiration, that *Animal Liberation* was the first philosophy book ever to contain recipes.

A third characteristic of Singer's work is the presupposition that individual action can make a difference. As his work has unfolded, Singer has increasingly addressed social policy dimensions of the problems that he considers, but usually he writes as one person in conversation with another. Feminists may have coined the slogan "the personal is the political," but Singer has been telling stories about himself, his family, and his friends as long as he has been doing philosophy. His goal is to change our attitudes and behavior because that is how you change the world. If animals suffer when they are raised for food, then we should stop eating them. If giving 10 percent of our income to Oxfam would save lives without depriving us of any comparable goods, then we should sit down and start writing checks.

What all this adds up to is a conception of practical ethics that is both activist and demanding. It requires us to find out what is going on in the world and to determine how we can change it for the better. It then requires us to act accordingly. This has led Singer to march, demonstrate, and sit in a cage in a city square to publicize the plight of battery hens. He has been enjoined from publicly criticizing or demonstrating against a circus, and arrested for trying to photograph confined sows on a pig farm partly owned by Australia's prime minister. Twice he has stood as a candidate for the Green Party in Australian federal elections.

Not everyone shares Singer's conception of practical ethics. In retrospect, it is easy to see the differences among the contributors to that first volume of *Philosophy and Public Affairs*. In the first sentence of his article on abortion, Wertheimer said that his goal was "to understand an argument"; he wasn't primarily interested in persuading us of particular conclusions.[6] Thomson's defense of abortion, while remarkably inventive and sensitive to feminist rhetoric about the right to control one's body, was a good deal more modest than the position that many people had already embraced and was soon to become law in the United States.[7]

Nagel was excruciatingly sensitive to the nuances and complexities of the ethics of war, but in the end he seemed to embrace the views with which he had begun, only now for reasons that seemed less than compelling in the light of the case that he had made for the difficulty of the issues involved.[8]

Since the 1970s, conservative tendencies in practical ethics have grown in influence. Although there are still those willing to be as revisionist as Singer, he has become increasingly isolated among philosophers in his willingness to argue for unpopular views and to take strong actions.

One reason for the increasing conservatism of practical ethics involves methodological problems at the core of the subject. Singer, following Hare, is hostile to the idea that considered moral judgements can serve as "the data" which moral theory is supposed to systematize. But not many have been convinced of his alternative approach.[9] According to Singer, we should follow moral principles wherever they lead. But if a moral principle conflicts with a deeply held, reflective moral judgement, it is far from clear why the judgement should defer to the principle rather than the principle deferring to the judgement. To put the point another way, whatever approach we take must equilibrate between our principles and our considered moral judgements. As a first approximation, it seems implausible to suppose either that principles should always defer to intuitions or that intuitions should always defer to principles.[10]

In part because he is clearly committed to a principle-driven methodology, Singer has been able to embrace wholeheartedly a particular normative theory: two-level utilitarianism. But most philosophers have a hard time committing themselves to a single moral theory. This sometimes manifests itself in the endorsement of some version of pluralism – a bit of Mill, a dash of Kant, some moralizing about "the virtues," and so on. In other cases it is expressed as an unwillingness to take strong normative positions at all because of refined sensibilities about the difficulty of defending any particular view against all possible objections.

A second reason why practical ethics has become more conservative is that it has become professionalized. A community of professionals examining each other's work in microscopic detail is less likely to produce bold views than a collection of concerned amateurs. Where once practical ethics largely involved the exploration of new territory, often by people who had other areas of primary academic interest, increasingly it has given way to a kind of scholasticism. There are virtues in scholasticism, but a willingness to take risks is not one of them.

Finally, practical ethics has become more conservative as it has become increasingly specialized. It is sometimes said (e.g. by Justin Oakley) that the three central areas of practical ethics are medical ethics, environmental ethics, and business ethics. As these subfields have developed, there is less communication across them. The problems of each subfield increasingly require specialized knowledge even to understand and engage with them. What this means is that to succeed in medical ethics, for example, requires to some extent becoming part of the medical community. A reasonably charitable cynic might say that in order to speak some truth to power one must refrain from speaking too much truth, or one won't be invited to speak to power at all. As practical ethicists move closer to the communities they moralize about, they become increasingly cautious about taking strong stands.

Interestingly, reasons two and three tend to pull in different directions. Reason two requires ethicists to find some distinctive philosophical subject matter in their field so that they can claim to be upstanding members of the philosophical community. This often leads them to focus on what are practically the less important features of an issue and also to try to communicate with philosophers rather than practitioners. The third reason pulls them in the direction of trying to communicate with practitioners at the expense of their philosophical identities. Perhaps practical ethics is becoming more conservative because it is in danger of being pulled apart.

However, practical ethics should not be treated as an undifferentiated field. Environmental philosophy, for example, has thus far has been relatively resistant to the conservatizing tendencies prominent in other areas. Environmental philosophy was late to develop, and its roots were deeper in the counter-culture of the 1960s than those of medical and business ethics. Early on the field was defined (wrongly but still influentially) as involving the search for a new ethic.[11] People who just wanted to apply traditional moral views to the environment (e.g. Passmore) were in effect drummed out of the community. Environmental philosophy has also resisted institutionalization, not because of the moral purity of its practitioners, but because it has had a hard time finding patrons and institutions with which to affiliate. Environmental studies is an ill-defined area, and programs are constantly being born, reformed, and killed off. Since no clear ecosystem has evolved, it is not clear what niche environmental philosophy should occupy. Finally, environmental philosophy is more expansive than other areas of practical ethics. It involves philosophy of science, history of philosophy, and philosophy of religion, to name a few allied areas. Rather than being a subfield of practical ethics which in turn is a subfield of ethics, environmental philosophy is really a new area of philosophy. Since it is a large and untamed field of inquiry, it is difficult to professionalize.

The present volume is not the first to give voice to Singer's critics. As contemporary philosophy's most visible utilitarian, his views have been the target of a wide range of objections. Most of these are versions of textbook objections to utilitarianism: that the theory has no place for justice, no account of the morality of killing, and no respect for moral agency. Some philosophers have complained that utilitarianism is a heartless doctrine which cannot recognize the importance of emotions, much less those dispositions and character traits that constitute the good life. Others have argued that utilitarian morality is too demanding. Indeed, Bernard Williams has written that

> Some utilitarian writers aim to increase a sense of indeterminate guilt in their readers. Peter Singer is an example, and in his book, *Practical Ethics* (New York: Cambridge University Press, 1980), he is evidently more interested in producing that effect than he is in the theoretical basis for it, which gets very cursory treatment.[12]

Although he has written widely, Singer will forever be most closely associated with his defense of animals and his attack on the traditional ethic of the sanctity of human life. On these questions his views are the converse of what most people believe. Although it is highly improbable that we would ever have to make the following forced choices, the character of Singer's views can be brought out by saying that generally he thinks that you are more likely to do something wrong by killing a healthy pig rather than your severely handicapped infant; and if you are choosing between an early abortion and killing an adult cow, you should probably have the abortion.

The agricultural lobby and the scientific establishment have tried to discredit his views about animals, and both right-wing pro-life organizations and leftist defenders of disabled people have mobilized against his views on euthanasia and abortion. In Germany, Singer's lectures have been disrupted and he has been physically assaulted. In the United States, he has been accused of "demonizing" American scientists.[13] No wonder that the profile of Singer published in the Australian edition of *Time Magazine* for November 2, 1989, was entitled "Saintly or satanic?"

What has come to be called the "Singer Affair" began in June 1989 with the cancellation of a long-standing invitation to Singer to lecture in Marburg, Germany, at a European symposium on "Bioengineering, ethics, and mental retardation." The cancellation was in response to protests which were being planned by organizations of disabled people. According to Hans Johann Glock, protesters claimed that "by promoting active euthanasia Singer's *Practical Ethics* condoned 'mass extermination' of the same kind as the euthanasia programme of the Nazis, and that his ideas were 'fascist' and 'murderous'."[14] Eventually the entire meeting was called off, and other scheduled lectures of Singer's were canceled or disrupted. The newspaper *Die Zeit* initially defended Singer's right to speak, but it too came under withering attack. It was forced to back down and, according to two German observers of the Singer Affair, "a vast consensus unified left-leaning and conservative papers, all of which strongly opposed ever again questioning anybody's right to life."[15] Since 1989 Singer has been unable to lecture openly in Germany, Austria, and Switzerland. Courses using the German translation of his book *Practical Ethics* have been disrupted, several major conferences at which he was to have spoken have been moved or canceled, and German supporters of Singer have been discriminated against for university positions. In 1992 more than one hundred people, many of them doctors of theology or medicine, signed a manifesto defending the disruption of Singer's lectures.

Another episode, different in many ways, but also indicative of the reaction Singer sometimes elicits, concerns the publication of an article in the refereed scientific journal, *Proceedings of the Society for Experimental Biology and Medicine*.[16] This article, "A dissection of the chapter 'Tools for research' in Peter Singer's *Animal Liberation*," is perhaps especially egregious, but it is not atypical of how Singer's views are sometimes treated by the scientific establishment. The authors of this article were openly contemptuous of Singer and his views. When they say that Singer documents his case with 138 notes they put both "documents" and "notes" in shudder quotes, as they do the words "evidence" and "scholarship" when they refer to Singer's evidence and scholarship. They say that Singer "supposedly embraces utilitarianism," that he "presents himself as an ethicist and moralist," that he is "anti-science," that he uses the methods of "propagandists," that he "lacks objectivity," and that he relies on "distortion and selective quotation." The list of charges and innuendos goes on. In the version of the article accepted for publication, the authors accuse Singer of fabricating a quotation. This charge was withdrawn in a revision to the original article that was sent to Singer after he was already supposed to have completed his reply. Nine months later yet another revision of the critical article was sent to Singer. Whatever the substance of the charges, it is clear that no scientific journal would publish such an abusive article on any other subject. Nor would the editors of a scientific journal treat other authors who were under attack in such a cavalier way.[17]

It is not surprising that the response to Singer has been so ferocious. In both these cases philosophical argument runs up against serious power embedded in history, culture, politics, and money. The groups that have organized in opposition to Singer are not particularly interested in his arguments. They want publicity for their causes and to intimidate or silence their opponents. A recent opinion piece in the influential right-wing newspaper the *Washington Times* (June 30, 1998, p. A17) amounts to a call for Princeton to rescind Singer's appointment.

What is surprising is the attitude of many philosophers towards these events. In assessing the responses it is perhaps useful to reflect on the fact that professional philosophers whose work is directed towards changing the world have always been rare, and often have been treated as outlaws by the profession. Compare, for example, the fate of Hegel with that of Marx. Singer is in the tradition of Bentham, Mill, and Russell, but only one of them ever held a college job.

Some philosophers have come to Singer's defense but others have come close to endorsing his silencing. In 1992, the Cambridge philosopher Jenny Teichman published an article, entitled "Humanism and personism: the false philosophy of Peter Singer," which began with these words: "I want to argue that false philosophy can be dangerous, and to suggest that, if circumstances prevent its being refuted in print, it is probably all right, in extreme cases, to try to silence it in other ways."[18] Two years later she returned to this subject, and wrote that

> Singer's philosophy... resembles Nazism in some ways but not in others. Here we are faced with a problem which has to do with a borderline... The importance of allowing, or not allowing, the dissemination, in Germany, of Nazi-style opinions, has to do primarily with political and social consequences; and it would seem on the face of it that German citizens are the people best able to predict, and understand, those consequences.[19]

Teichman concluded that Singer's inability to lecture openly in the German-speaking world is analogous to the situation of someone who writes a letter to the editor of a newspaper that does not publish it. In such cases "the authors often feel very indignant indeed about being deprived of access to a public platform," but no serious infringement of freedom of speech has occurred.[20]

Other philosophers seem curiously ambivalent about these episodes. Some people with whom I have discussed these cases express a kind of weary acceptance of the abuse that Singer has suffered, or even a kind of "blame the victim" attitude. "Of course what was done to him was wrong," they say, "but on the other hand, given his views and how he expresses them, what else could he expect?" Indeed, I think many would agree with Teichman when she wrote: "let's remember that Singer was a guest in the protesters' countries, and guests have some obligation to be tactful and circumspect... it is a truism that gross insensitivity is liable to provoke angry reactions. Whether or not the protesters had a right to silence Peter Singer, it is surely not surprising that they wanted to."[21]

What I find both alarming and interesting about these episodes is the challenge that they pose to practical ethics. How can practical ethics be genuinely revisionary, yet still manage to stimulate rational dialogue about controversial issues? To put the question in a different way, "Does revisionary practical ethics inevitably run the risk of provoking its own suppression?" Some would respond by saying that we should give up on the idea that practical ethics should be revisionary. At least two distinct alternatives to revisionary practical ethics might be suggested.

On one alternative, the role of practical ethics is to identify normative judgements about practical issues by extracting them from our prior set of considered moral judgements. On such a conception, the role of practical ethics is to reproduce our everyday moral beliefs and apply them to particular cases. It is certainly true that such an enterprise will not stimulate vocal, public opposition. On the other hand, it is hard to see why such an activity should be thought to be particularly important. Commonsense morality does not require the support of philosophers to maintain its authority. And if all that philosophers can contribute to discussions of practical moral issues is the occasional "hallelujah" in response to expressions of what most people already believe, then they might as well stick to the problem of universals.

A second role for practical ethics would be to clarify various positions on important practical issues and present a cafeteria of options. Clearly there is value in this sort of activity, and anyone who believes in revisionary practical ethics would view these clarificatory activities as steps along the way. But at least when it comes to ethical questions, clarity is not enough. Some views are better than others and it matters what views people hold. It is hard for me to imagine that anyone who would devote his or her life to practical ethics could really be as neutral about morality as this approach suggests.

Some would say that what causes extreme reactions to Singer is not the fact that he does revisionary practical ethics, but the way that he practices his subject. The problem is one of sensitivity. It is not Singer's views that provoke outrage, but the way that he expresses them. Sometimes I think that what it would have taken for Singer to be more sensitive in the Singer Affair is not to have written *Practical Ethics*, or to have saved the protesters some trouble by voluntarily banning himself from Germany. Still, no one who writes or speaks as much as Singer can claim to have always steered clear of insensitive remarks and phrases, and such lapses can be found in Singer's work. Moreover, Singer's direct approach to issues of profound importance may be viewed by some people as confrontational. Yet what I find most striking about Singer's writing is its sobriety and simplicity. Singer is usually clear and direct, without rhetorical flourishes. His books are aimed at his readers' heads rather than their hearts. This just make it all the more ironic that so many of his readers seem to lose their heads when reading him.

One reason for thinking that the problem is the singer rather than the song is that there are prominent philosophers who largely share Singer's views who do not elicit the same vituperative responses. And perhaps there are lessons here for those who do revisionary work in practical ethics. But it may also be the case that other philosophers do not provoke such reactions because their work is not seen as threatening. Perhaps challenges to the reigning orthodoxies are tolerated as long as they are seen as merely "academic" or (what comes to the same thing) ineffectual. Singer is good at what he does. His books change people's lives. Perhaps the attacks that he must endure are the complement to his successes.

Singer himself seems genuinely surprised and hurt that his views sometimes elicit such responses. He is optimistic enough about the possibility of rational thought, even about sensitive subjects, that he could honestly believe that Germans could rationally assess questions of euthanasia despite their history. And he shares the scientific worldview of many of those who have sought to discredit his views about animals. Singer believes in the epistemological privilege of science as much as most scientists, so one of his strategies in discussions of animal experimentation has been to use scientific authority to undermine scientific practices such as the Draize test, the LD_{50} test, and the use of primates in invasive research. Since Singer believes that the scientific outlook both expresses and vindicates such values as cooperation, egalitarianism, freedom of expression, and the objective search for truth, he is constantly confounded by the often hysterical, *ad hominem* attacks which some scientists launch in his direction. At his core Singer is an Enlightenment progressive. Perhaps he would not have seemed as unusual in eighteenth-century France or nineteenth-century England as he does in the United States at the end of the twentieth century. But after the horrors of our century and the rise of relativism and postmodernism, Enlightenment progressives are hard to find.

Singer's recent work has become more introspective and perhaps a bit darker. His Oxford ethics anthology (1994) includes readings by great spiritual teachers such as Buddha and Jesus, as well as by the usual figures who are part of the philosophical canon. It is unusual for texts drawn from religious traditions to appear in textbooks on philosophical ethics. It is especially surprising to find them in a book edited by an analytic philosopher who is non-religious and a utilitarian. In *How Are We to Live?* (1995), Singer returns us to what Socrates considered to be the only really important philosophical question. Singer's answer is that we should live our lives in contribution to a worthy cause even if in the end it does not triumph, for that is what gives life its meaning. This book is also filled with reminiscences about Singer's cultural roots and acknowledges that as well as being a child of the 1960s, he is also a child of the Holocaust, having lost much of his family to the Nazis. His most recent book is about

Henry Spira, a vigorous campaigner for both human rights and animal rights.[22] This book is a homage to a man whom Singer considers to be one of the great activists of our time, and also a meditation on how to bring about social change. Singer is currently preparing a book about his grandfather, who was a legendary teacher in Vienna for nearly thirty years until being dismissed by the Nazis in 1938.

Singer's work ultimately challenges us as both philosophers and moral agents. Although practical ethics continues to be a growth area in terms of job opportunities, it has lost much of its energy and direction. While moral philosophy in general has turned its attention towards an intensive study of its own history and returned to the traditional questions of metaethics, practical ethics has increasingly looked to law or policy studies for guidance. Perhaps the present state of the subject is really just an expression of the larger sense of powerlessness and confusion about what is really right that seems endemic to our culture. While it would be wrong to put too much weight on the importance of any single person, I can't help but wonder if the activist conception of practical ethics would have more influence today on the international philosophical community if Singer had not returned to Australia in 1975. Philosophy, like other subjects, has a history, sociology, and its own centers of power whose influence cannot be denied. It will be interesting to see how the practical ethics movement will be affected by Singer's move to Princeton.

The generation that developed practical ethics came of age in the 1960s and is now well represented in the senior ranks of the profession. But whether practical ethics fades from the scene, burrows more deeply into specialization and professionalization, or experiences a rebirth of creativity and activism will depend largely on those who are now studying philosophy and beginning their careers. Many institutional factors will be important – for example, whether there will be professional homes for those who think of philosophy as a vehicle for social change. But it will also matter how these young philosophers understand those who pioneered the practical ethics movement and how their influence is assimilated. Reading Singer in dialogue with his most sympathetic and acute critics is one way of helping to shape this legacy. That is what I have tried to make possible with this book.[23]

Notes

1 May 23, 1988.
2 "Famine, affluence, and morality," *Philosophy and Public Affairs*, 1, 3 (Spring 1972), p. 229.

3 Ibid., pp. 230, 242.

4 Daniel Bell, *The End of Ideology* (Glencoe, IL: The Free Press, 1960), p. 370.

5 The former television newsman, John Chancellor, has been quoted as saying about the 1950s in the USA that "if you weren't looking for work, black, or getting shot at in Korea, it was a very nice time" (*New York Times*, 20 February 1988, p. B33).

6 Roger Wertheimer, "Understanding the abortion argument," *Philosophy and Public Affairs*, 1, 1 (Fall 1971), p. 67.

7 Judith Jarvis Thomson, "A defense of abortion," *Philosophy and Public Affairs*, 1, 1 (Fall 1971), pp. 47–66.

8 Thomas Nagel, "War and massacre," *Philosophy and Public Affairs*, 1, 2 (Winter 1972), pp. 123–44.

9 Singer's views about methodology are most fully expressed in his "Sidgwick and reflective equilibrium," *The Monist*, 58 (July 1974), pp. 490–517.

10 For more on moral methodology see my "Method and moral theory," in P. Singer (ed.), *A Companion to Ethics* (Oxford: Blackwell, 1991), pp. 476–87; and James Rachels, "Moral philosophy as a subversive activity," in E. Winkler and J. Coombs (eds), *Applied Ethics: a Reader* (Oxford: Blackwell, 1993), pp. 11–130, reprinted in Rachels's *Can Ethics Provide Answers and Other Essays in Moral Philosophy* (Lanham, MD: Rowman and Littlefield, 1997), pp. 1–19.

11 See, for example, Richard Routley, "Is there a need for a new, an environmental, ethics?" in *Proceedings of the XVth World Congress of Philosophy*, no. 1 (Varna, Bulgaria, 1973), pp. 205–10. For further discussion see my "Animal liberation is an environmental ethic," *Environmental Ethics*, 7 (1998), pp. 41–57.

12 *Ethics and the Limits of Philosophy* (New York: Cambridge University Press, 1985), p. 212.

13 See the articles by Sharon M. Russell and Charles S. Nicoll, and Singer's reply, in *Proceedings of the Society for Experimental Biology and Medicine*, 1996.

14 "The euthanasia debate in Germany – what's the fuss?" *Journal of Applied Philosophy*, 11, 2 (1994), p. 213.

15 Bettina Schone-Seifert and Klaus-Peter Rippe, "Silencing the Singer," *Hastings Center Report* (November/December 1991), p. 21.

16 Op. cit., n. 13.

17 The last two statements may overstate the point: "creation scientists" or those who reject the idea that HIV causes AIDS might also come in for such treatment. What is important to see is that in the pages of the *Proceedings of the Society for Experimental Biology and Medicine* Singer is treated as a dangerous crackpot rather than a colleague who holds an unpopular view. While colleagues are to be persuaded, crackpots are to be stopped.

18 *Quadrant* (December 1992), p. 26.

19 Jenny Teichman, "Freedom of speech and the public platform," *Journal of Applied Philosophy*, 11, 1 (1994), p. 101.

20 Ibid., p. 105. Teichman overlooks one obvious and important disanalogy: Singer had been invited by Germans to address Germans, and this was prevented by the actions of third parties.

21 Ibid. On the subject of "gross insensitivity," I cannot help but remark that physical assault is no way to treat a guest, especially when much of the guest's extended family was murdered in your country by your parents and their compatriots.

22 *Ethics into Action: Henry Spira and the Animal Rights Movement* (Lanham, MD: Rowman and Littlefield, 1998).

23 I am grateful to Joel Feinberg for a helpful conversation, and to Susan Jones, Claudia Mills, and especially Peter Singer for comments on an earlier draft. Of course, I alone am responsible for the view expressed in this essay.

2
Non-cognitivism, Validity and Conditionals

FRANK JACKSON

The first chapter of Peter Singer's *Practical Ethics* is called 'About ethics'. It is concerned with certain rather general questions about reasoning in ethics as a preliminary to entering the fray. It contains the following passage:

> So what has to be shown to put practical ethics on a sound basis is that ethical reasoning is possible. Here the temptation is to say simply that the proof of the pudding lies in the eating, and the proof that reasoning is possible in ethics is to be found in the remaining chapters of this book, in which we do reason about ethics; but this is not entirely satisfactory. From a theoretical point of view it is unsatisfactory because we might find ourselves reasoning about ethics without really understanding how this can happen. (p. 8)

In this chapter I am concerned with how to understand ethical inference or reasoning under the assumption of non-cognitivism. I take this to be of particular interest to Singer as he is a non-cognitivist.

By non-cognitivism I mean the view variously expressed as that ethical sentences are not capable of truth, are not truth apt, do not express propositions, do not represent how things are, are expressions of special pro and con attitudes rather than beliefs and are to be classed with prescriptions rather than statements.[1] Non-cognitivism, as I am understanding it, does not hold that ethical judgements cannot be rationally defended and are not cognitive in some wide sense, but it does hold that they are not judgements in the sense of beliefs that may be true or false. The distinction between non-cognitivism and cognitivism cuts across that between subjectivism and objectivism. For instance, the view that 'X is good' in the mouth of S is true iff S approves of X is a (very simple) version of subjectivism and also a version of cognitivism; and the view that 'X is good' is a prescription whose rationality is *a priori* derivable is a version of objectivism and of non-cognitivism.

Unless non-cognitivists are prepared, heroically, to put the distinction between good and bad argument on ethical subjects into the 'don't care' basket, they must offer an account of validity for inferences involving ethical sentences and terms. They must give us an account of validity that can sensibly be applied to arguments like

Either Mary did the wrong thing or John did the wrong thing.

Mary did not do the wrong thing.

Therefore, John did the wrong thing.

and

Gambling is wrong.

If gambling is wrong, then getting other people to gamble is wrong.

Therefore, getting other people to gamble is wrong.

The problem for non-cognitivists is that the validity of these inferences cannot be the question of whether they necessarily preserve truth. The sentences that appear as their premises and conclusions are not in the business of being true or false to start with, according to them. Non-cognitivists need to give us an account of validity that makes good sense when applied to sentences that lack truth values. The same goes for probabilistic reasoning in ethics. Non-cognitivists need to be able to declare

Jones's opinions on matters of public policy are mostly right.

Jones supports compulsory seat belt legislation.

Therefore, compulsory seat belt legislation is right.

inductively good. But if 'compulsory seat belt legislation is right' lacks a truth value, we cannot say that the argument's conclusion is probably *true* given its premises along with agreed background information.

This point has been widely appreciated, and a number of non-cognitivists, most recently Simon Blackburn and Allan Gibbard, have offered accounts of validity, and more generally a logic of attitudes, on behalf of non-cognitivism. What is distinctive about the account I will be defending (apart from the fact that it is being offered by someone who is not, as it happens, a non-cognitivist) is, first, the fact that, as will emerge, it is very simple. The folk make inferences involving ethical terms and sentences all the time, and we should be able to tell a story about what they are doing that can plausibly be supposed to be one they implicitly understand. Second, it derives from a general, and to my mind highly plausible, view about how certain declarative, meaningful sentences – sentences that certainly give the appearance of being truth apt – might nevertheless fail to be truth apt. Finally, the discussion draws at various points on what we learn from discussions of validity for inferences involving conditionals by theorists who hold that conditionals are not truth apt.

Validity for the Non-truth Apt: Three Conditions

There are three conditions that have to be satisfied by any plausible account of validity for inferences involving sentences that are not truth apt. I will call them the meaning constraint, the significance constraint and the intuition constraint.

The meaning constraint requires that any account of validity of inference for the non-truth apt advert to a property intimately connected with the meanings of the sentences involved. When validity is necessary preservation of truth,[2] meaning enters the picture by virtue of the fact that meaning and truth conditions are intimately interconnected. When giving an account of validity of inferences involving the non-truth valued, including ethical sentences according to non-cognitivism, we perforce must bring meaning into the picture in some other way. But we must bring meaning into the picture all the same – validity in the sense we are concerned with is a semantic property.

The significance constraint requires that an account of validity for the non-truth apt make it transparent why it is good to be valid; what the point of being valid is. In the case of inferences that are valid in the classical, truth preserving sense, what is good about validity is that it is good to preserve truth. But we cannot give that answer in the case of inferences that are valid in some other sense.

Finally, the intuition constraint is the requirement that the proffered account delivers as valid the inferences that intuitively seem to be valid.

It is, it seems to me, only by showing that a non-standard account of validity meets these three constraints that we can meet the charge of changing the subject. For it is natural to object, 'Validity *is* necessary truth-preservation, and so to talk of validity for inferences involving sentences that lack truth values is simply to change the subject.'[3] But if we can show that a non-standard account of validity meets all three constraints, we show that it has enough in common with validity as standardly conceived to be called a species, albeit a non-standard species, of validity.

A good example of a non-standard theory that meets these three constraints is Ernest Adams's account of validity for certain inferences involving indicative conditionals. He offers an account that does not presuppose that indicative conditionals have truth values.[4] It can, therefore, serve as a model for non-cognitivists in ethics seeking an account of validity. We will also see that the case of indicative conditionals casts light on other issues surrounding non-cognitivism.

Adams on Validity for Inferences Involving Conditionals

A rough sketch of Adams's account of validity for inferences involving indicative conditionals will serve our purposes here, but even a rough sketch needs a little stage setting.

Although little is common ground in the philosophy of conditionals, one claim is, by the standards that operate in philosophy, close to common ground. It is that there is a class of conditionals – often called indicative conditionals, although there is controversy over whether this is a good name for them – governed by a simple rule of intuitive probability:

(IP) The intuitive probability of $(A \rightarrow B) = P(B/A) =$ by def. $P(AB)/P(A)$, when $P(A) \neq 0$.

When intuitive probability is interpreted as justified assertability, (IP) is often known as (Adams), after the same Adams whose account of validity for indicative conditionals I am about to expound. It seems to me, however, that this interpretation is a mistake. What justifies a person in asserting a conditional, or indeed any sentence, is a matter of the likely consequences of the action of so asserting. Thus, if someone's life depends on my asserting 'If it rains, the match will be cancelled', I would, other things being equal, be justified in asserting it. But it need not be the case that the conditional probability of the match being cancelled given rain is high. Once upon a time I thought that such 'extraneous' sources of justification could be ruled out in some illuminating way. I think this no longer. But I stand by (IP); indeed, I think that (IP) is what those who championed (Adams) in the past were really championing all along.[5]

The appeal of (IP) can be captured in a dartboard analogy. Suppose that I am throwing a dart at a board containing an A region and a B region. What is the intuitive answer to how likely it is that the dart will land in B if it lands in A? The answer is transparent: it is one and the same as the probability that the dart lands in the part of A shared with B, as a fraction of the probability of its landing in A, and this is $P(AB)/P(A)$.

Now, normally, intuitive probability is one and the same as probability; that is, as probability of truth. Thus, it is natural to move from (IP) to what is sometimes called Stalnaker's hypothesis:

(SH) $P(A \rightarrow B) = P(B/A)$.

But we know that (SH) cannot be true. The original proof of this is a *reductio* one due to David Lewis, and since he published his proof in 1976, there have been a number of alternative proofs of the unacceptability of Stalnaker's hypothesis, and Stalnaker himself has repudiated it.[6] In the case of indicative conditionals, intuitive probability is not probability of truth, though for non-conditionals, by the principle of saying what is intuitively plausible except when you are forced not to, intuitive probability is probability of truth.

We can now give the needed rough sketch of Adams's account of validity for inferences involving indicative conditionals: it is in terms of intuitive-probability preservation. The valid inferences are those such that the intuitive probability of their conclusions can be made as close to one as you please by making the intuitive probabilities of their premises sufficiently close enough to one. More precisely, the valid inferences are those such that for any ε, there is a δ such that the intuitive probability of the conclusion is within ε of one for any probability function that makes the intuitive probability of each premise within δ of one. If the premise or conclusion concerned is an indicative conditional, making its intuitive probability close enough to one is a matter of making the conditional probability of the conditional's consequent given its antecedent sufficiently close to one; in the case of non-conditionals it is a matter of making the probability of truth sufficiently close to one. In the case of inferences involving only non-conditional sentences, this definition makes every necessarily truth preserving inference – that is, every inference valid in the classical sense – also valid in the intuitive-probability preserving sense.

Adams satisfies the meaning constraint because the claim that the intuitive probability of a conditional is given by the probability of its consequent given its antecedent is true in virtue of the meaning of indicative conditionals: when you accepted the story I told about the dartboard, you manifested your understanding of indicative conditionals.

Second, Adams's account satisfies the significance constraint. It is transparent why we should value validity in the sense that Adams identifies. If the conclusion of the inference is a categorical sentence, the inference's being a valid inference in Adams's sense amounts to sufficiently intuitively probable premises ensuring high probability of truth, and so is to be valued for the same reason we value high probability of truth. If the conclusion is a conditional 'If A then B', the inference's being a valid inference in Adams's sense amounts to sufficiently intuitively probable premises ensuring high conditional probability of B given A, and this warrants the inferring of B on learning A, and also, in view of the fact that $P(B/A) \leqslant P(A \supset B)$, means that $(A \supset B)$ is highly probable. And both are properties we value.

Finally, Adams's account satisfies the intuition constraint. For it delivers as valid the inferences that seem to be valid when we consider examples. His account in terms of intuitive-probability preservation makes Modus Ponens and Modus Tollens come out valid, and Contraposition, Hypothetical Syllogism and Strengthening the Antecedent come out invalid. And, as has been widely noted, these are the intuitively right results. *Pace* Van McGee, there are no counter-examples to Modus Ponens and Modus Tollens.[7] But there are intuitive counter-examples to Contraposition, Hypothetical Syllogism and Strengthening the Antecedent.[8] Thus Adams's account of validity for inferences involving conditionals meets the intuition constraint.

Indeed, it does this so well that those who hold against Adams that indicative conditionals have truth conditions often appeal to his account of validity in the sense of holding that it best squares with our pre-analytic intuitions about the validity of inferences involving conditionals. Although the Adams account of validity for inferences involving conditionals is motivated by his view that they lack truth values, by his version of the no-truth theory of indicative conditionals, his account does not require that they lack truth values. It is available to those who hold, for instance, that indicative conditionals have the truth conditions of material conditionals (as I do), provided that they agree with Adams about, as we are calling it, the intuitive probability, and, as Adams calls it, the justified assertability, of conditionals. These theorists can distinguish two accounts of validity for inferences involving indicative conditionals: the classical, truth preserving one, and Adams's in terms of intuitive probability preservation, and hold that the latter squares best with intuition.

We will see how non-cognitivists in ethics can satisfy the three constraints and obtain an account of validity satisfactory for their purposes. I will identify a property of ethical sentences intimately related to their meaning according to non-cognitivism, and construct an account of validity for ethical inferences in terms of it which can be shown to satisfy in addition the significance and intuition constraints. As ethical inferences typically contain non-ethical, truth valued sentences as well as ethical ones that lack a truth value on the non-cognitivists' view, we need to identify a property that both the truth valued and the non-truth valued can be held to share. Adams turned the trick for conditionals by using intuitive probability (under, if I am right, the unfortunate name of justified assertability) and giving an account of it that covered both conditionals and non-conditionals. We will turn the trick on behalf of non-cognitivism by noting that ethical and descriptive terms can both be thought of as standing for or picking out properties, though not in the same sense, on the non-cognitivist picture. But, first, I need to say something about what makes truth apt sentences truth apt, as a preliminary to identifying how it might be that ethical sentences *fail* to be truth apt. This is a big issue in its own right; all I can do here is sketch in a rather dogmatic way the answer I favour.

Credo on Truth Aptness

We produce words and sentences for many reasons – to set off alarms, test out sound systems and try out a new pen – but most especially we use language to tell others, and our later selves, how things are. This is why we find a doctor uttering a sentence like 'You have been bitten by a tiger snake' so alarming, and why we are reassured when we hear a sentence like 'There is plenty of anti-venene'. Language is most especially a convention-generated system of physical structures for the communication of information, as Locke said, and as travellers in a foreign country whose language they do not understand are forcibly reminded when they get lost or try to buy something in a shop.

Accordingly, what makes the truth apt sentences truth apt is their role as convention-governed conveyers of putative information, as convention-generated vehicles of representation. But how a sentence represents things as being is an *a posteriori*, contingent matter. The putative information I in fact give by using the sentence 'You have been bitten by a tiger snake' might have been given by the sentence 'Roses are red', much as we might have agreed to drive on the right in Australia.[9] What, then, settles how a sentence represents things as being? The answer is given by the beliefs about how things are that the words and sentences are, under the conventions of the language, used to express. Had 'Roses are red' conveyed the same putative information that 'You have been bitten by a tiger snake' in fact conveys, it would have been because we had settled on the sentence 'Roses are red' as the sentence to use when we believed that you have been bitten by a tiger snake, and wished to convey the content of this belief to you. I am not here disagreeing with the familiar idea that when we think of sentences as truth apt, we think of the sentences as containing terms that stand for things and properties, as having interpretations. 'This is square' gets to have truth conditions, and so to be truth apt, by virtue of the fact that 'this' and 'square' stand for a particular and a property, respectively; and the sentence counts as true just if the particular 'this' stands for has the property 'square' stands for.[10] The point is one about how the words and sentences get to stand for the properties and things that they do stand for – our (unoriginal) answer is via their connection with belief. Thus the word 'square' gets to stand for the property it does stand for by virtue of how speakers use the word to express what they believe. Roughly, 'square' stands for being square in English because the conventions of English imply that the use of the word 'square' expresses beliefs about things being square – the word 'square' is a word to use in English to convey the putative information that things are square. Equally, 'carré' stands for being square in French, because 'carré' is a word to use in French to express the belief that things are square. Likewise, subject terms get to stand for what they do via the way they give the content of beliefs about the things in question.[11]

We can now identify one way that some class of sentences might fail to be truth apt. They might fail by virtue of not having the right connection with belief to enable us to identify how they represent things as being; that is, their truth conditions. This is what many hold concerning indicative conditionals. They ask, how should we settle how 'If P then Q' represents things as being? And answer, by reference to the belief whose degree matches the intuitive probability of 'If P then Q'; that is, that equals the conditional probability of Q given P. But, they then observe, there is no such belief, because the conditional probability of Q given P is not the probability of anything: it is rather a quotient of probabilities. Hence, they conclude, indicative conditionals are not truth apt. In a nutshell, the plausible claim is that the way we use indicative conditionals does not serve to determine truth conditions for them. Of course they appear to be truth apt, but if nothing makes it true that they have one set of truth conditions rather than another, then we must, runs the argument, deny the appearance.

The parallel with one well known argument for non-cognitivism will be obvious. According to this argument, the argument from motivation, as we might call it, there is an internal connection between ethical judgement and motivation which means that ethical judgements are not beliefs, for Hume taught us that beliefs cannot have an internal connection with motivation. Belief is a state designed to record how things are, and is quite distinct from states designed to change how things are. But we produce ethical sentences as expressions of ethical judgements. Thus, runs this argument, the way we use ethical sentences shows that they do not express beliefs. In the case of conditionals, it is the combination of

Lewis and Adams that tells us that we do not use conditional sentences to express beliefs; in the case of ethical sentences, it is the combination of the internal connection to motivation with Humeanism about belief that tells us that we do not use ethical sentences to express beliefs. In neither case are the sentences in question truth apt, because in neither case do their usage patterns determine truth conditions for them. The connection ordinary sentences have to belief, ethical sentences have instead to certain pro and con attitudes. Ethical sentences are generated by conative rather than cognitive attitudes of speakers and writers.

Many questions can be raised about this argument. The two most obvious ones are: is ethical judgement internally connected to motivation (whatever exactly this amounts to); and is Humeanism about belief correct? But our concern is not with whether non-cognitivism is true or false, but with what to say about validity for ethical inferences if non-cognitivism is true. What matters for us is what this argument tells us about non-cognitivism. It tells us that a non-cognitivism arrived at by means of it should be thought of as a doctrine that holds that ethical sentences express conative states rather than beliefs – that the role played by belief for truth apt sentences is played by something of the attitudinal kind for ethical sentences – and that this is why they lack truth values. Now, of course, the argument from motivation is not the only argument non-cognitivists offer us. They also offer us an argument from ethical disagreement, and a version of the open question argument. Nevertheless, I am going to assume that any viable non-cognitivism holds that ethical sentences express attitudes rather than beliefs. My justification is that this is the obvious kind of position for non-cognitivists to hold, independently of whether they reached their non-cognitivism via the argument from motivation. For they must give some account of the meanings of ethical sentences – ethical sentences are not random noises – and they cannot afford to say that they express beliefs, for then they would automatically be truth apt (being true just if the belief they express is true). Moreover, non-cognitivists do in fact typically explain the meaning of ethical sentences via the way they express psychological states that fall, broadly speaking, into the class of conative attitudes.[12]

Digression

Before we return to the question of validity of inference for non-cognitivists in ethics, I should make two remarks in passing. The first concerns the connection of the schematic and dogmatic remarks above to the view on truth aptness advanced in one or another form by Crispin Wright, Paul Boghossian and Paul Horwich.[13] They hold a doctrine sometimes called disciplined syntacticism. On this view, a sentence is truth apt if (a) it has the syntactical marks of truth aptness – it permits the appending of the truth predicate, it may be properly embedded in belief contexts, it may figure in the antecedents and consequents of conditionals, it figures in logical inferences and the like – and (b) it is disciplined in the sense that there are clear standards governing when it is correct and when it is incorrect to use it.[14] If discipline is spelt out in terms of belief – roughly, if for S to be disciplined is for it to be correct to use it just when it is believed that P – then this view is fully compatible with the view I have sketched. But, of course, if discipline is spelt out in some other way, we are in disagreement.

The second concerns how I, *qua* advocate of the view that indicative conditionals are equivalent to material conditionals and so have truth conditions,[15] meet the argument sketched earlier for the no-truth view of conditionals. I meet it by arguing that, although indicative conditionals do not have the standard connection with belief, they have a connection close enough to the standard connection to confer truth aptness. Of course, closeness is a matter of degree, and it is vague how close is close enough to count as conferring truth aptness. Consequently, a position on indicative conditionals that seems to me well worth identifying is that it is indeterminate whether or not they have truth conditions. If someone one day convinces me that indicative conditionals are not equivalent to material conditionals, this is the position I will move to.

Back to the Main Plot

Non-cognitivists cannot say that 'good', 'right', 'bad' and so on stand for properties by virtue of their role in expressing beliefs about things having these properties in assertions of the form 'X is good', 'X is right' and 'X is bad'. Nevertheless, they can link 'good', 'right', 'wrong' and 'bad' and so on to properties, but via a different psychological state. For, on the non-cognitivist view, ethical sentences stand to conative attitudes as factual sentences stand to beliefs. The link that gets made by belief in the case of descriptive terms, they can view as made by certain pro and con attitudes in the case of the ethical terms, the attitudes that we call the attitudes of moral approval and disapproval (however precisely these attitudes should be characterized). They can think of 'right' in English as linked to whatever property the relevant pro attitude is towards when 'X is right' is uttered (and the speaker is following the relevant conventions of English), and 'wrong' as linked to whatever property the relevant con attitude is towards when 'X is wrong' is uttered. For non-cognitivists, it is the relevant conative attitudes that connect ethical terms to features of the world.

We can put the crucial point in terms of how non-cognitivists must understand the notion of sincere assertion. On one interpretation of the words 'sincere assertion', the claim that a sincere assertion corresponds to a belief is a definitional tautology – it follows from the meaning of 'sincere': to be sincere is to say what you believe. But the noncognitivist must give a wider interpretation to the words 'sincere assertion'. There clearly is a distinction between the production of the sentence 'That act is right' to test a sound system or as an example in a tutorial on metaethics, as opposed to what we would naturally call a sincere production of it in response to a request by a friend for honest moral advice; yet the non-cognitivist cannot on pain of self-contradiction say that it counts as sincere precisely when its production is underpinned by the belief that that act is right.

The same point applies to no-truth theories of conditionals. There is a distinction between what we would naturally call the sincere production of the sentence 'If it rains, the match will be cancelled' in response, say, to a question about whether to go to the game, and its production in a tutorial, or in this paper. And no-truth theorists cannot draw the distinction in terms of sincere assertion being underpinned by the belief that if it rains then the match will be cancelled. There is no such belief, properly speaking, according to them. What non-cognitivists in ethics, and no-truth theorists about conditionals alike, must appeal to is the idea of a mental state that a sentence typically serves to express, however precisely this notion of expression is to be analysed. Assertion of a sentence is production of the sentence under the standard convention concerning the mental state that the sentence expresses; *sincere* assertion is production of the sentence under the standard convention concerning the mental state that the sentence expresses when that mental state is in fact present.[16] The no-truth theorist can say that the conditional 'If it rains, then the match will be cancelled' expresses the mental state of giving a high subjective probability to cancellation given rain; and that what happens when the sentence is produced as an example instead of as an assertion is that a signal is given that the conventional connection to this conditional probability is being set aside.[17] Likewise, according to the non-cognitivist, the sentence 'This act is right' expresses a certain pro-attitude, and what makes the production of the sentence on some occasion an assertion is that it is produced in the circumstances in which the convention that connects the sentence to that pro-attitude is in play; and what makes the production count as a sincere assertion is that the speaker has in fact got the pro-attitude in question.

Thus, the mental states the non-cognitivist needs anyway for the elucidation of the notions of assertion and sincere assertion for ethical sentences can be deployed to give sense to interpreting ethical sentences.

Ethical terms are linked to the properties (in the wide sense that includes relations) that the relevant mental states are towards. This means that the non-cognitivist has to suppose that the moral attitudes are primarily to properties, and only to particular actions and happenings *qua* actions and happenings of one or another type. But the universalizability of moral judgements gives us independent reason to hold this. It is common ground between cognitivists and non-cognitivists that ethical judgements, be they judgements proper as cognitivists hold, or expressions of attitude as non-cognitivists hold, are grounded in descriptive nature, and the non-cognitivist can accordingly think of the ethical terms as standing for the grounding properties.

The non-cognitivist must, therefore, distinguish two senses in which adjectives stand for properties: the real McCoy, and a quasi or *q* sense, as we might call it in honour of Simon Blackburn's term 'quasi-realism'.[18] In 'X is square' the word 'square' stands for the property of being square, and 'X is square' is true iff X has the property the word 'square' stands for. In 'X is right' the word 'right' *q*-stands for the (possibly highly disjunctive) property that the word 'right' expresses the relevant pro-attitude towards; and 'X is right' is *q*-true, we can say, iff X has the property that attitude is towards. Likewise, 'X is wrong' is *q*-true iff X has the property 'wrong' expresses the relevant con-attitude towards. Similar accounts will apply to assertions that X is good, bad and so on. Because the properties that ethical terms *q*-stand for depend on the attitudes speakers and writers take to properties, what 'good', for instance, *q*-stands for will be a function of the speaker or writer, just as you would expect on the noncognitivist picture. Thus, 'X is E', for some ethical term 'E', is *q*-true in the mouth or from the pen of Jones if and only if X has the property Jones takes the 'E' attitude towards.

The story just told is for ethical terms in asserted position. What should non-cognitivism say about them in unasserted position? As ethical inferences typically involve ethical terms in both positions, we need to address this problem before we offer an account of validity.

One major consideration that drives noncognitivists to insist that, although ethical terms in a subject's mouth can be thought of as definite descriptions that *q*-pick out possibly highly disjunctive descriptive properties, they cannot be thought of as picking them out in the standard truth-aptness-conferring sense, is (as we saw earlier) the directed nature of moral judgement. The directed nature of moral judgement means, according to non-cognitivists, that it cannot be thought of as judgement proper, as a species of belief; for no belief about how things are, in and of itself, points towards or away from action. But it is only moral judgements expressed by sentences with ethical terms in asserted position that plausibly display this distinctive directedness. Accordingly, non-cognitivists should, it seems to me, hold that ethical terms stand for properties in the standard sense when they occur in unasserted position. For then they follow the good policy of minimizing special cases. This position preserves the distinctive non-cognitivist position on sentences like 'That act is wrong' – it lacks a truth value – while allowing the obvious and familiar account of the contribution that terms like 'right' and 'wrong' make to the meaning of sentences like 'Either George did the wrong thing or Mary did the wrong thing'. In the latter sentence the ethical terms are definite descriptions picking out the properties they q-pick out when, but only when, they appear in asserted position. Thus, when in unasserted position, the term 'right' is simply an abbreviation for 'the property the "rightness" attitude is towards'.

We can now define validity for inferences involving ethical terms and sentences. Say that a sentence is true* if and only if it is true or q-true. Or, equivalently, truth* is truth under the assumption – false according to non-cognitivism – that ethical terms in asserted position are definite descriptions that pick out the properties towards which the relevant attitudes are taken. Truth* is what ethical and truth conditional non-ethical sentences have in common on the non-cognitivist view. We now define a wide notion of validity, validity*, that covers equally: inferences involving ethical sentences alone, those involving non-ethical, truth-valued sentences alone and those involving mixtures of ethical and non-ethical sentences, as necessary preservation of truth*. An inference is valid* if and only if every world where the premises are all true* is a world where the conclusion is true*. In effect, we are simply taking each occurrence of an ethical term E and replacing it with 'the property the E attitude is towards' and ruling the original inference valid* if the new inference is valid in the standard truth preserving sense.[19] As Simon Blackburn pointed out to me, this definition means that if we had treated truth* as truth under the assumption – false according to non-cognitivism – that ethical terms in asserted position are *rigidified* definite descriptions that pick out the properties towards which the relevant attitudes are taken, we would have to count 'X maximizes happiness, therefore, X is right' as valid in the mouth of a non-cognitivist utilitarian. But we avoid this unwelcome result by not rigidifying; alternatively, we could insist that to be valid, the truth* of the conclusion must be *a priori* deducible from all the premises being true*.

This account satisfies the meaning constraint. The story about truth*, and hence about validity* as the preservation of truth*, draws on features of the meanings of descriptive and ethical terms, on the non-cognitivist account. But does the account satisfy the significance constraint; can we show the point of preserving truth*? It seems to me that we can. Preserving truth* ensures a consistency property on what we value that cognitivist and non-cognitivist alike can agree is definitive of the ethical. Independently of whether we think of the ethical vocabulary as standing for, or as q-standing for when in asserted position, properties and relations, we want consistency. We want to rule out inconsistent assignments – or q assignments, but let's take such terms in the wider, disjunctive sense from now on – of properties to the ethical terms. For any person making ethical judgements, it should be possible to match consistently their ethical terms with the descriptive properties that ground their use. Validity* preserves consistency in this sense. It simply tells us which assignments of descriptive properties to the ethical terms (if any) in the conclusion are forced on us by any consistent assignment of descriptive properties to the ethical terms (if any) in the premises.

It might be urged that there is a deeper question to be asked: namely, what is wrong, according to non-cognitivism, with an inconsistent assignment of descriptive properties to the ethical terms? What is wrong, for instance, with judging that an action is right because it has a certain descriptive property, at the same time as judging that another action that is descriptively exactly the same is wrong? To do this would violate universalizability, of course, but the deeper question, it might be urged, is what is wrong with doing precisely that?[20] For non-cognitivists cannot say that what is wrong with inconsistency is that it makes it impossible to get everything right in the sense of having only true ethical judgements. According to them, we cannot have true ethical judgements to start with. However, I am inclined to resist the demand for a deeper reason and justification from the non-cognitivist. Explanations have to stop somewhere. I think that the non-cognitivist can reasonably hold that it is constitutive of the various conative attitudes being moral ones that the same attitude be taken to the same descriptive properties.

The final step is to note that the definition of validity for ethical inferences in terms of validity* gives intuitively correct answers: it satisfies the intuition constraint. Take, for instance, the following, intuitively valid inference.

Either we do not have a person from the moment of conception, or abortion is wrong.

We have a person from the moment of conception.

Therefore, abortion is wrong.[21]

The inference comes out as valid on our account. The reason is that a sufficient condition for the preservation of truth* is the preservation of truth under the assumption – false according to non-cognitivism – that the ethical terms in asserted position behave like normal descriptive predicates that stand for the properties towards which the ethical attitudes are taken. In short, our account of validity* makes every inference that would be valid were ethical terms normal descriptive terms, in particular, were invariably definite descriptions picking out the properties the relevant attitudes are towards, valid* – that is, valid in the sense tailored for ethical inferences on behalf of non-cognitivism. This is the intuitively right result. For the ethical inferences that strike us as intuitively valid are those that would be valid were ethical terms straightforwardly descriptive terms. Thus, our account on behalf of non-cognitivism meets the demand that it makes valid the ethical inferences that intuition rules as valid.

Non-cognitivists have, therefore, a plausible solution to the inference problem. They can do what Adams did for the no-truth theory of indicative conditionals. They can describe a notion of validity that can be regarded as a natural extension of the notion of validity that applies to inferences involving only the truth apt: it turns on the meanings (according to them) of ethical terms; it preserves a property worth preserving; and it makes intuitively valid inferences valid.

The Uniformity Intuition

Our treatment of the embedding problem along the way to offering an account of validity for non-cognitivists goes against what Susan Hurley calls the uniformity intuition.[22] Hurley points out that if we want an argument like

> Either we do not have a person from the moment of conception, or abortion is wrong.
>
> We have a person from the moment of conception.
>
> Therefore, abortion is wrong.

to come out valid, an obvious first step is to give 'wrong' the very same meaning in asserted position in the conclusion as it has in unasserted position in the first premise, thereby honouring the uniformity intuition. However, I think our violation on behalf of non-cognitivism of the uniformity intuition is harmless enough. The word 'wrong' still picks out, via the definite description 'the property towards which the "wrongness" attitude is taken', the same property in both occurrences. The difference is in the mode of picking out; and the variation in this regard is well marked syntactically, and so not something that can be regarded as hard to master by native speakers or as *ad hoc*.[23] Again, the debate over indicative conditionals provides a helpful parallel.

No-truth theorists of conditionals have to see a big difference between

If it rains, the match will be cancelled.

It will rain.

Therefore, the match will be cancelled.

and

Either it will not rain or the match will be cancelled.

It will rain.

Therefore, the match will be cancelled.

The second argument is valid in the standard truth preserving sense; the first argument is valid only in the special, intuitive probability preserving sense. Moreover, despite their evident similarities, the initial premises of the two arguments differ substantially in semantic status: one is truth apt, the other is not; moreover, the contribution that the component clause 'the match will be cancelled' makes to the meanings of the two premises differs. Is this a serious objection to the no-truth theory of indicative conditionals? I don't think so. The crucial point is that the semantic differences are well marked syntactically, so there is no special difficulty about our ability to latch on to them.

Certain cases of embedding call for special treatment. I think that noncognitivists should view 'Mary believes that slavery is wrong' in the same way that no-truth theorists of conditionals view 'Mary believes that if it rains the match will be cancelled'. The latter is strictly false – no one believes conditionals, strictly speaking, according to no-truth theorists – but we count it as true by reading it as a remark about Mary's high conditional subjective probability of cancellation given rain. Likewise, non-cognitivists should (and, I take it, do) view 'Mary believes that slavery is wrong' as ascribing to Mary the relevant distinctive con-attitude towards slavery. As Graham Oppy pointed out to me, this means that they have to tell a special story about an inference like

Mary believes that slavery is wrong.

Mary's belief is true.

Therefore, slavery is wrong.

They will have to see the inference's appeal as amounting to the fact that if Mary has the appropriate con-attitude to slavery and I share it, then I too must have the appropriate con-attitude to slavery. And the same is true of course for no-truth theorists of conditionals. They must tell a 'special case' story for

Mary believes that if it rains, the match will be cancelled.

Mary's belief is true.

Therefore, if it rains, the match will be cancelled.

We now have before us a story as to how non-cognitivists can handle the Frege–Geach problem. I think it raises an obvious general question for noncognitivism. Is the fuss of insisting that ethical terms q-stand for properties when they are in asserted position worth what it buys? The way q-standing for operates in practice is very like the way good old standing for operates. Can we perhaps think of the ethical terms as standing for in the standard sense the descriptive properties that occupy certain functional roles, including of course being the object of the distinctive attitudes that non-cognitivists tell us about? Indeed, I think we can, but that is another story.[24]

Notes

I am indebted to comments from Simon Blackburn, Graham Oppy, Philip Pettit and especially Michael Smith.

1 Here and elsewhere I assume the usual, though dubious, view that prescriptions lack truth values. Nothing turns on this assumption; it is made simply to put matters in a familiar context. Incidentally, 'Jackson is bald' is truth apt even when Jackson's head is such that the sentence lacks a truth value. This is because the failure to be truth-valued comes from the head's being on the borderline between bald and hairy, not from some feature of the sentence's meaning that makes having a truth value impossible. I borrow the term 'truth apt' from Crispin Wright.
2 I mean validity in the wide sense, sometimes referred to as semantic, not in the narrow sense of deducibility in some formal system.
3 Some would phrase the objection by saying that validity is *at least* necessary truth-preservation – perhaps because they do not count 'There is water,

therefore, there is H$_2$O' as valid, in view of its *a posteriori* status, or because they favour certain versions of relevance logic.

4 See, for example, Ernest Adams, *The Logic of Conditionals* (Dordrecht: Reidel, 1975). A similar account was developed independently by Brain Ellis.

5 I discuss this in more detail in 'Postscript on truth conditions and assertability', in Frank Jackson, *Mind, Method, and Conditionals* (London: Routledge, 1998).

6 See David Lewis, 'Probabilities of conditionals and conditional probabilities', *Philosophical Review*, 85 (1976), pp. 297–315, and 'Probabilities of conditionals and conditional probabilities II', *Philosophical Review*, 95 (1986) pp. 581–9; and Robert C. Stalnaker, 'Probability and conditionals', *Philosophy of Science*, 37 (1970) pp. 64–80.

7 Van McGee, 'A counterexample to Modus Ponens', *Journal of Philosophy*, 82 (1985), pp. 462–71, focuses on Modus Ponens but his (nice) examples could easily be redirected to Modus Tollens. For those who know McGee's examples, my short answer to them is that some sentences in English need rewriting to make their logical form clear, or anyway clearer. Thus, the sentence 'You may do A or you may do B' is not really a disjunction, but should be viewed as having the form 'You may do A and you may do B but you may not do A and B'. Likewise, sentences that are of the form 'If A, then if B then C' in English have as their logical form 'If A and B, then C'. In sum, Van McGee's counter-examples to Modus Ponens are no more counter-examples to it than 'You may drive after a small amount of wine, therefore you may drive after a small amount of wine or after a large amount of wine' is a counter-example to Addition, or so I maintain.

8 See, for example, David Lewis, *Counterfactuals* (Oxford: Basil Blackwell, 1973).

9 It may not be contingent and *a posteriori* how 'You have been bitten by a tiger snake' represents things as being in *English*, for it may be that we individuate languages in part by their representational properties. What is then contingent and *a posteriori* is that we, or anyone, speaks English.

10 Of course, there are many different conceptions of particular and property that might be invoked here. As far as I can see, what follows does not depend on controversial assumptions about the relevant notions.

11 In short, I am making the standard, though controversial, Lockean assumption that mental content is conceptually prior to linguistic content, and so the former can serve to fix the latter.

12 See, for example, Allan Gibbard, *Wise Choices, Apt Feelings* (Oxford: Clarendon Press, 1990), pp. 7f, and 84f; A. J. Ayer, *Language, Truth and Logic* (London: Gollancz, 1936), chapter 6; R. M. Hare, *The Language of Morals* (Oxford: Clarendon Press, 1951); and Simon Blackburn, *Spreading the Word* (Oxford: Clarendon Press, 1984), chapter 6. Gibbard talks of expressing systems of norms, Ayer of expressing feelings and sentiments, Hare of expressing preferences and Blackburn of expressing attitudes. There are important differences between these views but, as far as I can see, they do not affect the basic picture I will be putting forward.

13 See, for example, Paul Boghossian, 'The status of content', *Philosophical Review*, 99 (1990), pp. 157–84; Paul Horwich, 'Gibbard's theory of norms', *Philosophy and Public Affairs*, 22 (1993) pp. 67–78; and Crispin Wright, *Truth and Objectivity* (Cambridge, Mass.: Harvard University Press, 1992). I am in this section drawing on some material in Frank Jackson, Graham Oppy and Michael Smith, 'Minimalism and truth aptness', *Mind*, 103 (1994), pp. 287–302.

14 The syntactic part of this story is not, of course, plausibly necessary for truth aptness, whether or not it is part of a sufficient condition for truth aptness. There is no special reason why rather primitive languages that lack, say, the truth predicate and conditional constructions, and so cannot possess the syntactic marks of truth aptness mentioned, should not contain truth apt sentences.

15 In Frank Jackson, *Conditionals* (Oxford: Blackwell, 1987).

16 Or perhaps when it is believed present, but cases of self-deception are the exception and can be set aside here. The same vagueness infects the notion of a sincere assertion in more mundane cases. Is a sincere assertion of 'It will rain' by S an assertion (i) governed by a convention that the sentence is a sign that the S believes that P, and (iia) an assertion underpinned by S's belief that P, or (iib) S's belief that they believe that P?

17 We need, accordingly, to think of mental state in the wide sense of a fact about a subject's psychological profile, so that a fact about the ratio of one degree of belief to another counts.

18 But he should not be held responsible for anything I say in what follows.

19 And noncognitivists who do not agree that we should think of ethical terms in unasserted position as abbreviations for 'the property the relevant ethical attitude is towards' can still use this account of the needed wider notion of validity.

20 This is one of the questions that Simon Blackburn, 'Gibbard on normative logic', *Philosophy and Phenomenological Research*, 52 (1992), pp. 947–52, and Walter Sinnott-Armstrong, 'Some problems for Gibbard's norm-expressivism', *Philosophical Studies*, 69 (1993), pp. 297–313, insist is a compulsory one for Gibbard.

21 I have made the first premise a disjunction rather than the slightly more natural conditional 'If we have a person from the moment of conception, abortion is wrong', so that we are dealing with an example of Disjunctive Syllogism and not Modus Ponens. This avoids having to worry about whether we should use Adams's account of validity for inferences involving conditionals, but the point goes through at the cost of a little complexity if we take the Modus Ponens form of the argument and use Adams's account of validity.

22 Susan Hurley, *Natural Reasons* (New York: Oxford University Press, 1989), pp. 183–5. See also Ralph Wedgwood, 'Noncognitivism, truth and logic', *Philosphical Studies*, 86 (1997), pp. 73–91.

23 Another way of making essentially the same point is to note that the noncognitivist could instead say that 'good' etc. *q*-stand for properties invariably,

and give appropriate rules for deriving truth values (not q-truth values) from compounds containing one or more q-true or q-false components. As far as I can see, this would be only a difference in book keeping. Bob Hale, 'Can there be a logic of attitudes?', in Crispin Wright and John Haldane (eds), *Realism, Value, and Secondary Qualities* (New York: Oxford University Press, 1993), pp. 337–63, §1 notes that noncognitivists can tolerate failures of uniformity.

24 See, for example, Frank Jackson and Philip Pettit, 'Moral functionalism and moral motivation', *Philosophical Quarterly*, 45 (1995), pp. 20–40, and Frank Jackson, *From Metaphysics to Ethics* (Oxford: Clarendon Press, 1998).

3

The Definition of 'Moral'

MICHAEL SMITH

In striking opposition to those who spend their time trying to define 'moral', or arguing over the existence or non-existence of an 'is–ought' gap, Peter Singer argues that such debates are quite trivial.[1] No matter how we define the words 'ought' and 'moral', Singer tells us that the substantive issues remain the same. All that changes is the way in which we use the words 'ought' and 'moral' in describing those issues.

Singer begins his argument for this conclusion by distinguishing between *neutralism* and *descriptivism*, his names for the two very different sorts of view that can be taken about the meanings of 'moral' and 'ought'.

> The neutralist view . . . is that whether a principle is a moral principle for a particular person is determined solely by whether that person allows the principle to override any other principles which he may hold. Any principle at all is capable of being a moral principle for a person, if that person should take it as overriding.[2]

According to descriptivism, by contrast, whether a principle is a moral principle depends crucially on what the principle tells us to do:

> for a principle to be a moral principle, as the descriptivist defines the term, it must satisfy certain criteria of form and content. Thus, to give just one example of the many possible forms of descriptivism, it might be said that moral judgements are logically tied to suffering and happiness, impartially assessed. In other words, a judgement is not a moral judgement unless it is somehow connected to suffering and happiness, and a judgement is also not a moral judgement unless it is an impartial judgement.[3]

Whereas neutralism posits a definitional connection between the moral principles someone accepts and his or her overriding dispositions to action, and is silent as to whether moral principles have a particular form or content, descriptivism says the opposite. It tells us that moral principles must have, by definition, a particular form and content, and is silent as to whether there is any connection between the moral principles someone accepts and his or her overriding dispositions to action.

Despite these differences between neutralism and descriptivism, however, Singer argues that the two views differ not at all on the substantive issue of 'how statements of fact are connected with reasons for action in general (and not just moral reasons for acting)'.[4]

> To go from the statement of fact: 'Giving to famine relief will reduce suffering and increase happiness to a greater extent than spending money on a more expensive car' to the practical conclusion of giving the money away is neither easier nor more difficult if we adopt one position rather than another. The arguments which we might use are, in fact, substantially the same in either case, although the way we express them may differ. Thus if a person accepts, on the basis of an argument from a descriptivist definition of morality, that morally he ought to give to famine relief, but asks what reason there is for taking notice of morality, we may answer by appealing to the feelings of sympathy and benevolence which, in common with most of mankind, he probably has to some extent. We may talk of the fulfilment and real happiness that can come through knowing that one has done what one can to make the world a little better, and contrast this with the disappointments and ultimate sense of futility that are likely to come from a self-centred existence devoted to nothing but selfish concerns... These are just some of the considerations we might mention, and they may or may not be valid reasons for leading a life which the descriptivist would say was morally good. Whether these are valid reasons is not my concern here; it might depend on the person to whom they are addressed. My point is that the neutralist could use exactly the same reasons in an attempt to persuade the man whose overriding, that is, moral, principles take no account of the happiness or suffering of people other than himself, his family, and friends, to widen his area of concern, and so, perhaps, to adopt principles which would involve giving to famine relief.[5]

The upshot, according to Singer, is that opponents in the debates over 'is–ought' and the definition of 'moral' are engaged in a debate which is of no real substance. Who cares how we use the words 'ought' and 'moral' when we can all agree about the only issue of any substance, our reasons for action?

Singer is right, I think, that the only issue of any real substance is what we have reason to do and the relative weights of these reasons *vis-à-vis* each other. He is wrong, however, that this makes the debates over 'is–ought' and the definition of 'moral' trivial. On the contrary, these debates acquire significance precisely *because* the substantive issue concerns our reasons for action. This, at any rate, is to be my argument.

My chapter divides into seven main sections. In the first I explain what the debates over 'is–ought' and the definition of 'moral' are all about. Unsurprisingly, it seems to me that they are about the *nature* of reasons. Because Singer does not conceive of the debates in this way he is led, in his characterization of the two opposing views in these debates, neutralism and descriptivism, to make both views assume something about the nature of reasons which it is the purpose of the debates over 'is–ought' and the definition of 'moral' to call into question. In the six remaining sections of the paper I explore the consequences of rejecting this assumption about the nature of reasons. I argue not only that it can be rejected, but that a satisfactory definition of 'moral' requires its rejection.

What Are the Debates over 'Is–Ought' and the Definition of 'Moral' About?

It is widely held that beliefs in conjunction with desires can play a causal and rationalizing role in the generation of further desires. Suppose I desire to drink some water and believe that I can do so by drinking from the glass in front of me. My belief about this particular means, together with my desire for this particular end, can then both cause and rationalize my having a desire for this particular means: that is, it can both cause and rationalize my having a desire to drink from the glass in front of me. This, in any case, is the widely held belief.

If desire and belief pairs do indeed play a causal and rationalizing role in the generation of further desires, then it follows that there must be at least a sense in which desires in conjunction with facts have the potential to play a causal and rationalizing role in the generation of further desires as well. After all, if my belief that I can drink some water by drinking from the glass in front of me, together with my desire to drink some water, can cause and rationalize my desiring to drink from the glass in front of me, then my desire to drink some water, together with the fact that I can drink some water by drinking from the glass in front of me, has the potential to cause and rationalize my having a desire to drink from the glass in front of me as well. It has that potential because the fact that I can drink some water by drinking from the glass in front of me has the potential to cause and rationalize my acquisition of a corresponding belief.

Many philosophers think that in the justificatory or normative sense of the term 'reason', as opposed to the explanatory or motivating sense of the term, having a reason to act in a certain way is simply a matter of an agent's having desires which, taken together with the facts, have the potential to cause and rationalize their having desires to act in those ways.[6] Let's call normative reasons of the sort these philosophers believe in 'desire-dependent' reasons. Note that the introduction of this terminology is not meant to pre-empt the answers to any important questions. In particular, it is not supposed to pre-empt answering 'no' to the question 'Are normative reasons desire-dependent?' The terminology is meant merely to provide a useful name for a view about the nature of normative reasons prevalent among philosophers. What these philosophers believe is that normative reasons are desire-dependent, and they believe this because they believe that the reasons an agent has depends on the desires she has.

With this particular view about the nature of normative reasons in place, it should be clear that when Singer describes the reasons people have for giving to famine relief, he simply presupposes that normative reasons are one and all desire-dependent. Suppose 'in common with most of mankind' I have certain 'feelings of benevolence', or a desire for 'real happiness', or an aversion to living a life in which there is nothing but 'disappointment' and an 'ultimate sense of futility', and suppose further that I will achieve the things I want and avoid those to which I am averse by giving my money to famine relief. Then, if reasons are desire-dependent, I have a reason to give to famine relief. I have such a reason because the fact that giving to famine relief is a means to the ends that I antecedently desire will be apt to cause and rationalize my having a belief to the effect that giving to famine relief is a means to the ends I desire, and this belief, in conjunction with my antecedent desires, will be apt to cause and rationalize my having a desire to give to famine relief.

It should now be clear why Singer thinks the debates over 'is–ought' and the definition of 'moral' are trivial. He thinks that these debates are trivial because he assumes that the parties to these debates, the neutralists and the descriptivists, will both agree that the substantive question – the question about the reasons that people have – is answered by finding out whether people have antecedent desires that will be satisfied, given the way the facts are. In other words, he assumes that they will agree with him that reasons are desire-dependent. But, as I want now to argue, this is a misrepresentation of what the parties to the debates over 'is–ought' and the definition of 'moral' disagree about. Rather, they disagree about whether reasons are desire-dependent. Consider first the 'is–ought' debate.

Familiarly, those who think there is an 'is–ought' gap believe that we can only derive an 'ought' conclusion from an 'is' premise if there is an additional premise that includes another 'ought'. Their slogan is thus 'No "ought" out without an ought "in"'. But what this slogan means, as I understand it, is that we can only ever cause and rationalize a desire in someone (this is the 'ought' that figures in the conclusion) by getting them to acquire a belief (this is the 'is' that is admitted on both sides to figure as a premise) if they already possess a desire for an end (this is the 'ought' that, according to believers in the 'is–ought' gap, needs to figure as an extra premise) such that the belief in question is a belief about the means to this end. Those who think there is an 'is–ought' gap thus believe that the only relevant norm governing the acquisition of desires is the norm of instrumental rationality. Following Jay Wallace, we can therefore restate their slogan as 'No desire out without a desire in'.[7] The upshot, of course, is that the only desires that can ever be caused and rationalized in someone are desires for means. All reasons are desire-dependent.

By contrast, those who deny there is an 'is–ought' gap say that there are norms which require us to acquire certain desires (this is the 'ought' that figures in the conclusion) simply when we have certain beliefs (this is the 'is' that is admitted on both sides to figure as a premise). They therefore deny the 'No desire out without a desire in' principle. Rather, as they see things, certain beliefs suffice all by themselves to cause and rationalize desires in us. As a consequence, the desires that they think are thus caused and rationalized are desires for ends, not mere desires for means. It therefore follows that there are 'desire-independent' reasons, as we might call them. There are desire-independent reasons because the facts mentioned in the 'is' premise constitute considerations which, once believed, can serve to cause and rationalize desires for ends without the aid of any pre-existing desire. This is what it means to say that we can derive an 'ought' from an 'is.'

Note that Singer's term 'neutralism' is not an inappropriate name for the view that reasons are desire-dependent. If reasons are desire-dependent then it turns out that they can have any old content whatever. The limits on the contents of the reasons are set by the limits on the contents of desires. To the extent that desires are capable of having any content whatever, reasons too can have any content whatever. The theory of reasons itself is therefore *neutral* on questions about the content of the reasons that people can have. Nor is 'descriptivism' an inappropriate name for the view that reasons are desire-independent. If reasons are desire-independent then it turns out that the reasons people have are independent of the contents of their pre-existing desires. The contents of their reasons are fixed instead, in a way specified by the norm, by their circumstances, circumstances that permit a *descriptive* characterisation.

To sum up, then, those who deny that there is an 'is–ought' gap deny that reasons are desire-dependent. They think that reasons are desire-independent. Let's leave to one side whether they are right or wrong about this for the moment. The important point is that the question at issue, 'Are reasons desire-independent?', is a substantive philosophical question if ever there was one. Singer is therefore wrong that the debate over 'is–ought' is trivial. Moreover, and importantly, as I hope to make plain in what follows, this substantive philosophical question must be answered in the affirmative if we want to hold on to some fairly common-sense assumptions about the nature of morality.

In order to see that this is so, imagine being engaged in an argument with someone about the rightness or wrongness of some action – say, abortion – an argument in which we have engaged in order to elicit their compliance with what is morally required. Such an argument has a very different character depending on whether there are, or are not, desire-independent reasons of a particular kind. Suppose, for example, that there are desire-independent reasons of the following kind.

Suppose there is an objective fact of the matter about the rightness or wrongness of abortion – by which I mean a fact equally accessible to all, and about which we might come to form reasonable beliefs by engaging in conversation and argument – and our beliefs about this objective fact are capable of causing and rationalizing corresponding desires and aversions without the aid of any pre-existing desire. If there were such desire-independent reasons then it would be possible for us simultaneously to provide the person with whom we are engaged in argument with reasons for believing that abortion is right or wrong, as the case may be, *and* to rationalize her having a corresponding desire or aversion, independently of the antecedent desires she happens to have. The evidence we provide her with *vis-à-vis* the rightness or wrongness of abortion would be apt to cause and rationalize her having an appropriate moral belief, and then the moral belief would in turn be apt to cause and rationalize her having a corresponding desire or aversion. At a certain level of abstraction, the task of getting someone morally motivated would then be no different to the task of getting her to believe what is true.

But if we now consider the possibility that reasons are desire-dependent, we notice that the argument has a rather different character. If desires can only ever be caused and rationalized if they are caused by a belief about means and a desire for some end – that is, if the only desires that can ever be both caused and rationalized are desires for means – then there is evidently a considerable problem involved in securing the motivation of those who have desires which would not be satisfied by doing what morality requires of them. In order to secure moral motivation, we would have to cause them to have a desire for some relevant end. But, by hypothesis, rational argument is not enough to get them to acquire such a desire. Rational argument can only produce beliefs, in particular beliefs about means to ends, and then, provided they already have desires for some relevant end, desires for means. Desires for ends themselves can be caused but not rationalized. It therefore looks like we could only ever get people to acquire such desires via a process akin to *conversion*. Even though it might look like we are engaged in a rational argument, we would in fact have to use rhetoric, or association, or manipulation of some other kind, in order to get them to acquire desires for suitable ends. At a certain level of abstraction, then, the task of getting people morally motivated would be no different to the task of getting them to buy this or that product as the result of a cleverly devised and manipulative advertising campaign.

Here, then, is the common-sense assumption about the nature of morality that seems to me to get called into question if reasons are desire-dependent. The common-sense assumption is that when we engage in moral argument, and thereby elicit moral motivation from those who do not antecedently have desires for ends which would be satisfied by doing what morality requires of them, we do something quite different from the sort of thing that a clever and manipulative advertising agent does. Getting someone to read Peter Singer's books, and so become a committed vegetarian, differs in a quite fundamental way from getting him to watch advertisements on television, and so become a committed consumer of a particular product. Convincing someone to become morally motivated as a result of moral argument is a *rational* process. So, at any rate, we commonsensically assume. But for this common-sense assumption to be correct it seems that we would have to be able to tell a story about the nature of moral beliefs which makes it plain how it is that they are capable of both causing and rationalizing corresponding desires for ends, a story which makes it plain that the mechanism involved really is much the same as the mechanism involved when we persuade someone to change her beliefs by confronting her with an array of factual evidence.

We can now see where Singer goes wrong in his account of the 'is–ought' debate. He rightly notes that those who oppose the neutralists are descriptivists, theorists who hold that moral beliefs must satisfy certain constraints of form and content. But what he fails to note is that descriptivists have an additional commitment. They hold that, in virtue of their peculiar content, moral beliefs are capable of both causing and rationalizing appropriate desires and aversions all by themselves, without the aid of any pre-existing desire. Descriptivists who oppose the neutralists in the 'is–ought' debate thus believe in the possibility of desire-independent reasons. They deny the view of their neutralist opponents that reasons are desire-dependent. Seen in this light, far from demonstrating that the 'is-ought' debate is trivial, Singer simply teases out the consequences of assuming that one of the views that can be taken in that debate – the view that there is an 'is–ought' gap, and hence that desire-dependent reasons are the only reasons that there are – is the only possible view that anyone could take. But interesting though the consequences of that assumption are, they have no bearing on the outcome of the 'is–ought' debate itself.

In the remainder of this chapter I want to tell a story about the content of our moral beliefs which would vindicate the common-sense assumption described above. I start by giving an example of a belief which, in virtue of its peculiar content, does seem capable of both causing and rationalizing a desire all by itself, without the aid of any pre-existing desire. In other words, I describe a belief which permits the transition from 'is' to 'ought'. Although the belief I describe is not itself a moral belief, as we will see it does provide us with a way of thinking about what a moral belief would have to be like. It provides us with a way of thinking of moral reasons as desire-independent.

An Example of a Belief that Permits the Transition from 'Is' to 'Ought'

Imagine you have promised to help a friend move house on Sunday afternoon, but that come Saturday night you realize how inconvenient it will be. You are having people for dinner the next day, so if you help your friend move house this means that you will have to get up early on Sunday morning to tidy up and prepare the meal. Keeping your promise thus means missing out on your regular Sunday morning sleep-in. As you contemplate the promise you made, and the prospect of having to get up and forgo your sleep-in in order to keep it, you therefore find yourself thoroughly averse to the prospect of keeping your promise. You head off to bed, making sure that the alarm is not set, and you settle yourself down to go to sleep.

At this stage, let's agree that although you believe that you have made a promise, and although you have all sorts of beliefs about what you would need to do in order to keep that promise – that is, all sorts of beliefs about means – you are not in the least inclined to keep your promise, and so your various beliefs about means are causally idle. But let's suppose that you then reflect and try to figure out what you would want yourself to do, in the circumstances you now face, if you had a set of desires that passed the analogue of the sort of reflective equilibrium test that Rawls describes in connection with evaluative beliefs: that is, you try to figure out what you would want yourself to do if you had a set of desires that is maximally informed and coherent and unified.

Note that the question you are asking yourself is what you would want yourself to do in circumstances in which you have absolutely no inclination to help your friend if you had a (potentially) completely different set of inclinations, those that you would have if you had a set of desires that was maximally informed and coherent and unified. If we call the possible world in which you have the inclinations you actually have the 'evaluated'

world, and the possible world in which you have a set of desires that is
maximally informed and coherent and unified the 'evaluating' world, then
the question is not what you, in the evaluating world, want yourself to do
in the *evaluating* world, but rather what you, in the evaluating world,
want yourself to do in the *evaluated* world.

As you try to answer this question, what you will look for is a general
desire which is such that, if only you possessed it, you would be able to
make the best sense of all the more specific desires you actually have.
Among your specific desires is, of course, your aversion to getting up in
the morning, notwithstanding the promise you made to your friend to
help him move house. But let's suppose that you also remember the
resentment you felt when someone who had promised to help you do
something rang at the last moment to say that he wouldn't be able to help
after all, and then provided you with a completely lame excuse which
showed that in fact he just couldn't be bothered. The desire that others
keep the promises that they made to you is thus one of the more specific
desires that needs to be made sense of as well, alongside your aversion to
keeping the promise that you made to your friend.

In the light of this apparent conflict you will therefore need to
ask yourself whether there is an inconsistency involved in your desiring
that others keep their promises to you, even when doing so involves
them giving up their Sunday morning sleep-ins, but your not desiring
that you yourself keep your promises to others, when it involves you
giving up yours. The answer you come up with, let's suppose – and here
we can simply stipulate – is that there is indeed an inconsistency. You
cannot think of any other case in which you desire others to live up to
standards you don't desire yourself to live up to, so this desire looks to be
quite out of keeping with the rest of your desires. It doesn't make any
sense, given what you're like. You therefore conclude that, your actual
aversion to keeping your promise notwithstanding, if you had a maximally informed and coherent and unified desire set, you would want
yourself to keep your promise in the circumstances of action you now
face.

Once it is agreed that you have a belief with this particular content, it
seems to me that there is no difficulty at all in seeing how it could both
cause and rationalize your having a desire to keep your promise. For
consider the pair of psychological states that comprises your belief that
you would desire that you keep your promise in the circumstances of
action that you presently face if you had a maximally informed and
coherent and unified set of desires, and which also comprises the desire
that you keep that promise, and compare this pair of psychological states
with the pair that comprises your belief that you would desire that
you keep your promise in the circumstances of action that you presently

face if you had a maximally informed and coherent and unified set of desires, but which also comprises instead your aversion to keeping that promise. Which of these pairs of psychological states seems to be more coherent?

The answer is plain enough. The first pair is much more coherent than the second. There is a disequilibrium or dissonance or failure of fit involved in believing that you would desire yourself to act in a certain way in certain circumstances if you had a maximally informed and coherent and unified desire set, yet being averse to the prospect of acting in that way. The aversion is, after all, something that you yourself disown. From your perspective it makes no sense, given the rest of your desires. By your own lights it is a state that you would not be in if you were in various ways better than you actually are: more informed, more coherent, more unified in your outlook. Coherence thus seems to be on the side of the pair that comprises both the belief that you would desire yourself to keep your promise in the circumstances of action that you presently face and the desire to keep that promise.

If this is right, however, then it would seem to follow immediately that if you are rational, in the sense of displaying a tendency towards this sort of coherence, then you will end up having a desire that matches your belief about what you would want yourself to do if you had a maximally informed and coherent and unified desire set. In this particular case, if you are rational, in the sense of displaying this sort of tendency, you will therefore end up losing your aversion to keeping your promise, and acquiring a desire to keep it instead.

This, then, is the example of a belief which can both cause and rationalize a desire on which I wish to focus. The belief can cause a corresponding desire when it operates in conjunction with a tendency towards coherence. Because acquiring the desire makes for a more coherent pairing of psychological states, the desire is thus rationalized as well. Moreover, no causal role at all is played by a desire. Provided you are rational, in the sense of having the requisite tendency towards coherence, it thus follows that all we have to do to get you to desire to keep your promise, and so to set the alarm, is to convince you of what is true: namely, that you would indeed desire yourself to do just that if you had a maximally informed and coherent and unified desire set.

Why the Example Works, if It Works at All

If the example works at all, it works because of the dual role played by one and the same tendency towards overall coherence. Let me explain what that dual role is.

Our desires, taken together as a whole, are capable of displaying relations of coherence with one another. Because they are capable of displaying such relations it follows that individual desires are susceptible to rational criticism in so far as they contribute towards the incoherence of a set to which they belong: the individual desire that is saliently responsible for the incoherence of a set of desires to which it belongs is a desire that we rationally shouldn't have, and the individual desire that would be saliently responsible for more coherence in a set of desires, if it were added to it, is a desire that we rationally should have. Those who display a robust tendency towards coherence are therefore people who get rid of the desires that they rationally shouldn't have, and acquire those that they rationally should have. Their desires tend towards reflective equilibrium.

Furthermore, because desires are capable of displaying relations of coherence with one another, and because we can form beliefs about which desires we would have if we were more coherent, there is a further dimension of coherence that can be displayed between desires and these beliefs. The psychology of someone who believes that she would have a certain desire, if she had a maximally coherent desire set, displays more in the way of coherence if it includes that desire than if it lacks it, or includes an aversion instead. Someone who believes that she would not have a certain desire if she had a maximally coherent desire set thus rationally should not have that desire, and someone who believes she would have a certain desire if she had a maximally coherent desire set rationally should have that desire. Those who display a robust tendency towards coherence would therefore get rid of desires that they rationally shouldn't have, and acquire desires that they rationally should.

The reason the example works, if it works at all, then, is because it is so plausible to suppose that a tendency towards overall coherence is constitutive of what it is to be a rational creature. Of course, none of us possesses a tendency towards coherence that is so robust as to ensure that we have all those desires that we believe we would have if our desires were maximally coherent, still less that we have all those desires that are in fact part of the maximally coherent set. But the fact that none of us possesses such a robust tendency towards coherence is neither here nor there. The crucial point is simply that it would suffice for us to acquire such desires that we have a robust tendency towards overall coherence. It is because this is the case that the example is an example of deriving an 'ought' from an 'is': an example of a belief that can both cause and rationalize a desire in much the way in which beliefs cause and rationalize other beliefs.

Let me now turn to consider a variety of objections.

'Desires Do not Exhibit Normatively Significant Relations of Coherence among Themselves'

The first objection attacks the assumption that desires can so much as exhibit normatively significant relations of coherence and unity among themselves: the assumption that our desires tend towards a reflective equilibrium. The objection is Geoffrey Sayre-McCord's.[8]

As it happens, each night when I get home from work I have a desire to drink a glass of wine. But suppose I acquired, in addition, a more general desire to drink alcohol of any kind at any time of the day or night. This desire, once in place, would provide a rationale for my desire to drink wine each night: it would provide a kind of unifying principle in my resultant desire set. Yet it is surely quite implausible to suppose that my desires as a whole would be more rational if I were to acquire such a desire. Notwithstanding the increase in coherence and unity, then, the acquisition of such a desire looks to be completely irrational, an instance of a kind of desire-fetishism. It is therefore wrong to suppose our desires exhibit normatively significant relations of coherence and unity among themselves.

What are we to make of this objection? I agree that the acquisition of a desire to drink alcohol at any time of the day or night, in the circumstances described, would be irrational. But I do not think this shows that desires fail to exhibit normatively significant relations of coherence and unity among themselves. The problem seems to me rather that this particular way of trying to secure more in the way of coherence and unity among my desires – that is, by acquiring the desire to drink alcohol of any kind at any time of the day or night – spectacularly fails to add more in the way of coherence and unity, especially as compared with the coherence and unity that would be secured by adding various obvious alternative desires. And the reason why is plain enough. The desire to drink alcohol of any kind at any time of the day or night does no justice to the rest of the desires that I possess.

When we attempt to secure more in the way of coherence and unity among our desires we must begin by looking at all the different things we desire, and we must then proceed by asking whether there is a more general desire we could add to our overall desire set which is such that, by adding it, our overall set of desires would make more sense. In this case let's assume that I begin with the desire to drink wine each night when I get home from work, to drink coffee in the mornings, to drink mineral water with meals and so on and so forth. I therefore have to ask myself whether there is any more general desire that I could add to my overall desire set which is such that, by adding it, my overall set of desires about what to drink, when, would make more sense.

The answer that seems most plausible is that there is indeed such a desire, and that the desire is most certainly not the desire to drink alcohol of any kind at any time of the day or night. Rather, the desire I should acquire is the desire to drink whatever I enjoy drinking whenever I enjoy drinking it. This is the desire I should acquire because this is the feature that it makes best sense to suppose I see as justifying doing what I desire to do in each case. If I were to add this desire to my overall set of desires then I would ensure that my overall set makes more sense, and so succeed in making it more rational, because by adding the new desire I stop myself being liable to the charge of making arbitrary distinctions. Suppose, for example, that right at the moment I have an aversion to drinking scotch on the rocks when I go to a bar, despite believing that drinking scotch on the rocks when I go to a bar would be enjoyable. This aversion doesn't make any sense at all, given the pattern in the rest of my desires. In order to make sense I therefore really need to acquire the desire to drink scotch on the rocks when I go to a bar, and this is something that becomes possible if I acquire the more general desire to drink whatever I enjoy drinking when I enjoy drinking it.

The example so far considered is fairly trivial, but the point gleaned from it readily generalizes. Imagine someone with certain desires about how people are to be treated. She desires that Adam, Bob and Charlie are not harmed, but she is indifferent to David's being harmed. Is there a more general desire which she could add to her overall desire set which is such that, by adding it, her set of desires, taken together as a whole, would make more sense? When she reflects and tries to extract a feature from Adam's not being harmed, Bob's not being harmed and Charlie's not being harmed which makes the best sense of her desires that none of them gets harmed, we can readily imagine that the feature she extracts is a feature possessed by David too: being a sentient creature whose life prospects are severely diminished if they are harmed, for example. In this way she can come to discover that her desires are not maximally coherent and unified. Reflection can thus lead her to desire that sentient creatures in general not be harmed, and so undermine her indifference to David's being harmed. By trying to make the best sense out of her overall desire set she can in this way be led to see that she had made an arbitrary distinction between David and the others.

I will have more to say about the way in which we are to characterize the normatively significant relations of coherence and unity that our desires exhibit among themselves presently. For the time being, however, it should be clear that, since our desires taken together as a whole can be made to make more or less sense depending on which desires we add to, or subtract from, the set, so considerations of coherence and unity most certainly do get a grip on our desires, just as they can get a grip on our beliefs. Our desires, like our beliefs, should therefore be in reflective equilibrium with each other.[9]

'There Is no Incoherence Involved in Believing that We Would Want Ourselves to Act in One Way if We Had a Maximally Informed and Coherent and Unified Desire Set, Yet Desire to Act in Another'

A second objection attacks the claim that there is any sort of incoherence involved in believing that we would want ourselves to act in one way, if we had a maximally informed and coherent and unified desire set, yet desire to act in another. This objection has been put most forcefully by Christine Korsgaard.[10]

In Korsgaard's view, the claim that there is such incoherence amounts to the 'demand that we should emulate more perfectly rational beings (possibly including our own noumenal selves)'. But she argues that such a demand is without normative force. Why should anyone want to emulate the behaviour of more perfectly rational beings when their lives are so utterly different from ours? Consider a concrete case in order to see the problem.[11]

Suppose I have just suffered a humiliating defeat in a game of squash. I am angry and frustrated, so angry and frustrated that all I want to do is smash my opponent in the face with my squash racquet. Let's suppose further that I know that this is completely irrational. I know that my opponent isn't trying to humiliate me, he isn't gloating and nor is he in any other way behaving inappropriately. He simply beat me, fair and square. In this context, imagine me forming a belief about what I would desire and do in the possible world in which I have a maximally informed and coherent and unified desire set. The belief I come to form, we'll suppose, is that in that possible world I would have and act upon a desire to congratulate my opponent on his fine win by shaking his hand. But the very fact that this is what I would desire and do in that possible world is what makes Korsgaard think that the demand that we emulate perfectly rational beings in our actual, less than perfectly rational, circumstances lacks normative force.

To be sure, there are no grounds for faulting the desires I would have, or the actions I would perform, in that possible world. The desires I would have are part of a maximally informed and coherent and unified set, and so beyond rational reproach. But, impeccable though they might be, they are simply irrelevant when it comes to my deciding what I should desire and do in the circumstances that I actually face. They are irrelevant because in my actual circumstances I have to deal with my completely irrational anger and frustration. Given that the desires I would have and act upon in the possible world in which I have a maximally informed and coherent and unified desire set are formed without regard to such irrational feelings – in that possible world, I have no such feelings to deal with, remember – it follows that they have nothing to teach me about what I am to desire or do in circumstances in which I do have such feelings.

In terms of the earlier distinction between evaluating and evaluated possible worlds, Korsgaard's objection can therefore be put like this. If we imagine the psychology possessed by someone in the evaluated world which comprises, on the one hand, a belief to the effect that in the evaluating world he would desire himself to act in a certain way in the evaluating world, and on the other an aversion to his acting in that way in the evaluated world, then such a psychology, possessed by someone in the evaluated world, isn't in the least incoherent. The desires of someone in the evaluating world about what he is to do in the evaluating world have no rational bearing on the desires of someone in the evaluated world about what he is to do in the evaluated world.

I agree with Korsgaard. But that is no objection to what I have suggested, because my suggestion is different. My suggestion is that there is incoherence involved in a psychology possessed by someone in the evaluated world that comprises, on the one hand, a belief to the effect that in the evaluating world he would desire himself to act in a certain way *in the evaluated world*, and, on the other, an aversion to his acting in that way in the evaluated world. In the language of demands, the demand is not that we emulate the behaviour of our perfectly rational selves, but rather that we follow the advice that they give to us about how we are to act in the circumstances of action that we actually face. Think again about the example.[12]

I am angry and frustrated after suffering a humiliating defeat at squash. I wonder what I should do. I attempt to form a belief about the wants I have in the possible world in which my desires are maximally informed and coherent and unified, but the question I ask myself is not what I would want myself to do in that world, but rather what I would want myself to do in the circumstances I am actually in, circumstances in which I am suffering from irrational anger and frustration. For much the reasons just given, it is quite implausible to suppose that the answer I will come up with, when I attempt to form such a belief, is that I would want myself to emulate the behaviour of a perfectly rational being. After all, I might well have good reason to believe that if I were to try to congratulate my opponent on his fine win by shaking his hand then I would lose control and take the opportunity to smash him in the face with my racquet. It seems plausible to suppose, rather, that I would want myself to do the best I can, given the means available to me. Perhaps

I'd come to the view that I would want myself to close my eyes and take ten deep breaths, or remove myself from the scene immediately in the hopes of calming myself down, or something else along these lines.[13]

Whatever belief I would form, the crucial point is simply this. Since, by hypothesis, that belief represents my best estimation of what someone who is perfectly placed to give me advise would advise me to do in my awful circumstances, it is hard to see how I could ignore that advice without there being some sort of incoherence or disequilibrium in my psychology: hard to see how a failure to desire and act accordingly wouldn't indicate incoherence or disequilibrium. For this reason it seems to me that, properly interpreted, we must suppose that there is indeed incoherence involved in my believing that I would desire myself to do one thing, if I had a maximally informed and coherent and unified desire set, yet my desiring myself to do another. To suppose otherwise is to suppose that I can rationally ignore what I deem to be the most rational advice. Korsgaard's objection therefore misses the mark.

'The Tendency towards Coherence Is a Desire'

A third objection is that when beliefs about what we would want ourselves to do if we had a maximally informed and coherent and unified desire set cause and rationalize our having corresponding desires, they only succeed in doing so because they work in conjunction with further desires. Beliefs about what we would want ourselves to do if we had a maximally informed and coherent and unified desire set are thus incapable of causing and rationalizing corresponding desires all by themselves. This objection comes from Ingmar Persson.[14]

Think again about the psychological transition I described. I suggested that the belief combines with a tendency towards coherence, and that this pair together causes the corresponding desire. But, the objection goes, the state I call a tendency towards coherence is really just a desire to be coherent. The situation is thus one in which I desire to be coherent, and believe that I can be coherent by desiring to keep my promise, and so end up desiring to keep my promise. This is yet another completely straight-forward case of a belief about means combining with a desire for an end to cause a desire for the means. I have therefore failed to describe a case in which a belief both causes and rationalizes a desire in anything other than a means–end way.

How are we to reply to this objection? Although I would prefer not to call the tendency towards coherence a 'desire', I am happy enough to call it that for the purposes of the present objection. The reason is that it is irrelevant what we call it. My claim, remember, is that beliefs about what we would want ourselves to do if we had a maximally informed and coherent and unified desire set are capable of causing and rationalizing corresponding desires in much the same way in which beliefs both cause and rationalize other beliefs. But now think for a moment about the way in which beliefs both cause and rationalize other beliefs.

Suppose I believe that Bill is the man next door, and that I also believe that the man next door rides a motorcycle. Even if it is agreed that these beliefs can both cause and rationalize my believing that Bill rides a motorcycle, note that they do not suffice to explain my coming to believe that Bill rides a motorcycle all by themselves. I could well believe that Bill is the man next door, and that the man next door rides a motorcycle, without ever coming to believe that Bill rides a motorcycle: I might simply fail to make the inference. Something extra is therefore needed in order to explain the causal transition. But what? What is it that corresponds to my disposition to make an inference?

The answer is: the very tendency towards coherence that I described above. For consider the set of psychological states comprised by the belief that Bill is the man next door, the belief that the man next door rides a motorcycle and the belief that Bill rides a motorcycle, and compare this set with that comprised by the belief that Bill is the man next door, the belief that the man next door rides a motorcycle and a complete lack of belief as regards who that man is. Which set of beliefs is more coherent? The first is plainly more coherent than the second. Possession of the same tendency towards coherence is thus once again the needed extra element that explains why, when someone believes that Bill is the man next door and that the man next door rides a motorcycle, they come to acquire the belief that Bill rides a motorcycle. But if this is right, if the tendency towards coherence plays a crucial causal role even in cases in which beliefs both cause and rationalize other beliefs, then the stated objection is no objection at all.

In coming up with a story about the way in which beliefs can both cause and rationalize desires in a way much like the way in which beliefs cause and rationalize other beliefs, there can be no objection whatsoever to our making free appeal to those psychological mechanisms that play a causal role in the belief–belief case, whatever they may be, when we provide our explanation of what happens in the belief–desire case. In effect, this is all we have done. If the objection is right then it turns out that the desire to be coherent plays a crucial causal role in both cases. I would prefer not to call it that – I would prefer to call it a 'tendency towards overall coherence' – but if that's what we're to call it then so be it. The crucial point is that the possession of this desire, or tendency, is partially constitutive of what it is to be a rational creature. Rational creatures just are those who have beliefs and desires that reliably evolve in a coherent way.

Why do I not want to call the tendency towards coherence a desire to be coherent? The problem I see looming is that, since the tendency towards coherence plays a crucial causal role even in means–ends reasoning, so, if we call the tendency a desire, we might set ourselves off on an infinite regress. Imagine someone who desires a certain end, and who believes that acting in a particular way is a way of achieving that end. Her having this desire and belief is not enough to guarantee that she has a desire for the means, because she may be means–end irrational (this is the analogue of inferential failure, as just discussed in the text). Something extra is therefore needed if she is to desire the means. She needs to put the desire and the belief together in the right sort of way. But how does she do this?

The answer, I say, is that she needs to have a tendency towards overall coherence. But if the operation of this tendency itself is thought of on the model of the operation of a desire, then it seems to me irresistible to suppose that it too works in the normal means–end way. In order to desire the means the person we have imagined must first of all desire to be coherent, and then she must form a belief to the effect that, since she desires a certain end and believes that a particular means is a means to that end, so having a desire for that means would achieve coherence, and then . . . And then what? The possession of this desire and belief is not enough to guarantee that the person desires the means either. She needs to put together her desire for coherence and her belief to the effect that desiring the means would achieve coherence in the right sort of way as well. But how does she do this? The answer cannot be that she needs yet another tendency towards overall coherence, or else we are on the path to an infinite regress. For this reason it seems to me best to avoid thinking of the operation of the tendency towards coherence on the model of the operation of a desire. This is why I would prefer not to call the tendency towards coherence a desire at all.

'Moral Facts Do not Entail Facts about the Desires We Would Have if We Had a Maximally Informed and Coherent and Unified Desire Set because Facts about the Latter, Unlike the Former, Are Relative to Our Actual Desires'

So far we have seen no reason to deny that beliefs about what we would want if we had a maximally informed and coherent and unified set of desires are capable of both causing and rationalizing desires in a way analogous to the way in which beliefs both cause and rationalize each other. But how is this supposed to help us understand the way in which moral beliefs can play a similar causal and rationalizing role? The general idea is this.

If facts about the rightness and wrongness of acts *entail* corresponding facts about what we would desire ourselves to do, and be averse to ourselves doing, if we had a maximally informed and coherent and unified desire set, then it follows that the entire transition from evidence, to belief about rightness and wrongness, to belief about what we would desire or be averse to if we had a maximally informed and coherent and unified desire set, and from there to desire or aversion, is a matter of the acquisition of psychological states via processes analogous to the causal processes which are in place when beliefs both cause and rationalize each other. It is the tendency towards coherence that explains the transition in every case. If facts about the rightness and wrongness of acts entail corresponding facts about what we would desire ourselves to do, and be averse to ourselves doing, if we had a maximally informed and coherent and unified desire set, then, it seems, at a certain level of abstraction, the task of getting people to comply with morality is indeed no different to the task of getting them to believe what is true.

Why would facts about the rightness and wrongness of acts entail corresponding facts about what we would desire ourselves to do, and be averse to ourselves doing, if we had a maximally informed and coherent and unified desire set? One answer, the answer I favour, is that facts about rightness and wrongness are analytically equivalent to, and so a subset of, facts about what we would desire ourselves to do, and be averse to ourselves doing, if we had a maximally informed and coherent and unified desire set.[15] Specifically, they are those facts about what we would desire, where the contents of the desires in question satisfy certain loose constraints on form and content: they are desires that in some way or other concern human flourishing, impartially conceived; or they are desires which in some way or other express conceptions of equal concern and respect; or they are desires that satisfy whatever other constraints on form and content get us into the ballpark of the moral, as opposed to the non-moral. (Here I echo the views of Singer's descriptivists.) If we conceive of moral facts along these lines then note two important consequences.

The first is that, since the constraints on form and content are loose, so the distinction between the moral and the non-moral becomes correspondingly vague. Thus, suppose that if I had a maximally informed and coherent and unified desire set then I would have the following two desires: a desire to maximize happiness and minimize the suffering of all sentient creatures, and an independent desire to maximize the happiness and minimize the suffering of my own family members. The first of these desires certainly satisfies the loose constraints on form and content that tell us we are in the ballpark of the moral, as opposed to the non-moral. But what about the second? It seems to me that there is no determinate answer to this question. It all depends on how impartial a desire has to be in order to count as a desire with moral, as opposed to non-moral, content. Nor, as far as I can see, do we gain anything by legislating one way or the other. What matters is the relative strengths of these desires, not whether we label one of them, or both of them, 'moral'. (Here I echo some of Singer's remarks on the significance of the distinction between the moral and the non-moral.)

The second consequence is this. Although, if we conceive of moral facts in this way, it would indeed follow that moral facts provide us with desire-independent reasons for action, it would not follow that those desire-independent reasons ought to be overriding. The desires we would have if we had a maximally informed and coherent and unified desire set may, after all, conflict with each other. The desires that correspond to moral facts might therefore be weaker than some other desire we have. For example, to return to a variation on the case Singer discusses, described at the outset, suppose that if I had a maximally informed and coherent and unified desire set then I would have two desires: a desire of a certain strength that I give to famine relief in circumstances in which I have a spare $20 to spend, and an independent and stronger desire that I spend that spare $20 on myself. In that case, although I do indeed have a moral desire-independent reason to give $20 to famine relief, this desire-independent reason would be outweighed by my non-moral desire-independent reason for spending that $20 on myself. Nothing I have said so far rules out the possibility that moral desire-independent reasons are sometimes outweighed in this way. (Here I echo some of Singer's remarks on the idea that moral reasons are overriding.)

The idea that moral facts are a subset of facts about what we would desire ourselves to do, and be averse to ourselves doing, if we had a maximally informed and coherent and unified desire set is difficult to sustain, however. The problem, at least according to the objection I want to consider here, is that whereas the maximally informed and coherent and unified desire set possessed by one person will be very different from that possessed by another if the two people concerned have very different actual desires to begin with, facts about the rightness and wrongness of our actions are not relative to our actual desires and aversions in this way. There isn't one set of facts about the rightness and wrongness of acts relative to those who actually desire this and that; another set of facts about the rightness and wrongness of acts relative to those who actually desire something else; and so on and so forth. The only conclusion to draw, according to the objection, is that facts about the rightness and wrongness of acts do not entail corresponding facts about what we would desire ourselves to do, and be averse to ourselves doing, if we had a maximally informed and coherent and unified desire set.

Now, as it happens, I agree that facts about the rightness and wrongness of acts are not relative to facts about our actual desires. What is less clear to me, however, is that facts about what we would desire if we had a maximally informed and coherent and unified set of desires are radically relative to our actual desires in this way. Indeed, on the contrary, it seems to me quite plausible to suppose that if we were to reflect on our actual desires, and to come up with a maximally informed and coherent and unified desire set on the basis of such reflection, then we would all converge in the desires that we have.

Don't misunderstand me. My claim is not that everyone who has a maximally informed and coherent and unified desire set will have the same tastes in food, and drink, and clothes, and sports, and careers, and the rest. Those whose desires are maximally informed and coherent and unified are presumably as divergent in their tastes and preferences in these regards as many individuals and groups throughout history have been. My claim is rather that there will be a convergence in that subset of their desires with the following sort of modal content. Suppose we give a total characterization of a possible world in which they must choose to act in one way rather than another, including a characterization of the beliefs and desires they have in that world. As they each reflect on what they want themselves to do in that possible world, my suggestion is that they will all converge on the same desire as regards what is to be done.

It is thus consistent with the convergence thesis that they will sometimes converge on a desire that they act on whatever preference they happen to have in that possible world. In that case, we would expect those whose desires form a maximally informed and coherent and unified set to diverge in these sorts of preferences. This would be a permissible divergence: a divergence sanctioned by the desires upon which they converge. But it is also consistent with the convergence thesis that they will sometimes converge on a desire that they act in a certain way notwithstanding the desires they happen to have in that possible world. If moral facts are a subset of facts about the desires that we would all converge upon if we had a maximally informed and coherent and unified desire set, then presumably the desires in question have this character.

But why should we believe such a convergence thesis? My reasons for believing it are as follows. Given that our actual desires are caused in us by the potentially arbitrary and idiosyncratic processes of enculturation and socialization – socio-economic factors, the media, advertising and the like – it follows that our actual desires too are potentially arbitrary and idiosyncratic in corresponding ways. Our actual desires, taken together as a whole, are thus not guaranteed to be desires to do things that it makes any sense to do whatsoever. But since, when we reflect and try to come up with a maximally informed and coherent and unified set of desires, our task is to come up with a set of desires to do things that it makes sense to do, so it follows that what we must thereby be trying to do is to transcend these potential sources of arbitrariness and idiosyncrasy as much as possible.

If this is right, however, then it surely follows that a convergence in the desires that we would have if we had a maximally informed and coherent and unified desire set – that is, the *complete* transcendence of our arbitrary and idiosyncratic differences – would provide us with a set of desires to do things which are the very best candidates for things that it makes sense for us to do. These must be the very best candidates for things that it makes sense for us to do because nothing arbitrary and idiosyncratic needs to be presupposed in order to give and appreciate the rationale for doing them. The rationale can be given to, and that rationale will be seen to have appeal by, anyone and everyone capable of reflecting on their desires and coming up with a maximally informed and coherent and unified desire set. They aren't just things that will appear to make sense if you arbitrarily and idiosyncratically want this or that; rather they will be things that it makes sense to do *period*.

Now it might be thought that I have just introduced a new idea – the idea of what it makes sense for someone to do *period* – and that I have, in effect, just suggested that we define what it is for a set of desires to be maximally informed and coherent and unified in terms of this idea. It might be agreed that if we had such an independent idea of what it makes sense for people to do period, a standard that didn't just amount to asking what they would want themselves to do if they had a maximally informed and coherent and unified set of desires, given their actual desires as a contingent starting point, then there would indeed (trivially) be a convergence in the desires people would have. But, the objection goes, there is no such independent standard. What it makes sense for people to do *period* is simply what they would want themselves to do if they had a maximally informed and coherent and unified desire set. Because facts about the latter are relative to the actual desires people have to begin with, facts about the former are relative to such facts too.[16]

My reply is that there is a third possibility in between the two just canvassed. We might define what it makes sense for people to do in terms of what they would want themselves to do if they had a maximally informed and coherent and unified desire set, so assigning priority to our independent concepts of coherence and unity. Or we might define what people would want themselves to do if they had a maximally informed and coherent and unified desire set in terms of what it makes sense for them to do, so assigning priority to the independent idea of what it makes sense for them to do. Or we might interdefine both notions, assigning priority to neither. In other words, we might insist that we have no alternative but to achieve some sort of equilibrium between our idea of what people would want if they had a maximally informed and coherent and unified desire set on the one hand, and our idea of what it makes sense for them to do on the other.

This no-priority view is the one that appeals to me. As I see things, it is both the case that in explaining which desires someone would have if he had a maximally informed and coherent and unified desire set we have no choice but to think of him as having desires to do things that it makes sense for him to do period, independently of his antecedent desires, and that in trying to figure out what it makes sense for people to do we have no alternative but to try to figure out what they would want to do if they had a maximally informed and coherent and unified desire set. We give weight to our semi-independent ideas about what it makes sense for people to do period, in so far as we defeasibly assume, at the outset, that it will always make sense for people to desire certain things like pleasure, achievement and the company of their fellows, and that it will never make sense for people to desire things like saucers of mud, the avoidance of pain except on a Tuesday and the destruction of the whole world in preference to scratching their little finger.[17] But we then give weight to our semi-independent idea of what they would want themselves to do if they had a maximally informed and coherent and unified desire set by allowing these assumptions to be defeated if we cannot integrate desires for such things into such a desire set.

If we adopt this sort of no-priority view then it seems to me that the assumption of convergence has some chance of being vindicated. The defeasible assumptions we make about what it makes sense for people to do period give us a non-relative starting point from which we can hope to generate, via the reflective equilibrium process, a non-relative set of facts about the desires we would all have if we had a maximally informed and coherent and unified desire set. Convergence is not guaranteed, of course. Notwithstanding the non-relative starting points, the arguments we give might lead to divergence in desires, rather than convergence. But that is something that we will discover only by giving the arguments and seeing where they lead.

Let me now return to the main line of objection. The objection I have been considering is that facts about the rightness and wrongness of acts do not entail facts about what we would desire or be averse to if we had a maximally informed and coherent and unified desire set, because facts about the former, unlike the latter, are not relative to the actual desires and aversions people have to begin with. As I have just explained, however, it seems to me that the objection is mistaken because it is not the case that facts about what we would desire, or be averse to, if we had a maximally informed and coherent and unified desire set are radically relative to our actual desires and aversions. Such facts, if there are any such facts at all, are non-relative facts, just like facts about the rightness and wrongness of acts. They are facts about the desires we would all converge upon if we had a maximally informed and coherent and unified desire set.

Conclusion

Peter Singer argues that the debates over 'is–ought' and the definition of 'moral' are completely trivial. Against Singer I have tried to argue that these are substantial debates, debates whose aim is to establish whether reasons are desire-dependent or desire-independent. I have also suggested that the resolution of these debates is absolutely crucial to moral philosophy, for it seems that we can only vindicate the common-sense assumption that convincing people to become morally motivated via a moral argument differs in a fundamental way from getting them to acquire desires via a cleverly devised and manipulative advertising campaign if we can demonstrate that moral facts do indeed provide us with such desire-independent reasons for action.

The problem with which I have been concerned for the bulk of this chapter has accordingly been to come up with an account of how there could be desire-independent reasons: an example, in other words, of a belief that can cause and rationalize desires in much the same way that beliefs both cause and rationalize each other, and a story about how a belief of this kind might relate to moral beliefs. My suggestions have been: first, that beliefs about what we would desire ourselves to do if we had a maximally informed and coherent and unified desire set can both cause and rationalize corresponding desires in precisely the way required for the existence of desire-independent reasons; and, second, that moral facts are a subset of facts about what we would desire ourselves to do if we had a maximally informed and coherent and unified desire set.

It thus turns out that there is good reason to suppose both that there are desire-independent reasons for action and that moral facts (if there are any) provide us with such reasons. The common-sense idea that getting people morally motivated differs in a significant way from getting them to acquire desires via an advertising campaign is therefore vindicated, at least in so far as we assume that there are moral facts. On that assumption, the task of getting people morally motivated, unlike the task of getting them to acquire desires via a cleverly devised and manipulative advertising campaign, is simply no different to the task of getting them to believe what is true.[18]

Notes

1 Peter Singer, 'The triviality of the debate over "is-ought" and the definition of "moral"', *American Philosophical Quarterly*, January 1973, pp. 51–56. Singer reiterates his the argument in his recent *How Are We to Live?* (Melbourne: Text Publishing, 1993), p. 248 (footnote 2 to chapter 9).

2 Singer (1973), *op. cit.*, p. 52.

3 Ibid., p. 53.

4 Ibid.

5 Ibid., p. 54.

6 See, especially, Bernard Williams 'Internal reasons,' reprinted in his *Moral Luck* (Cambridge: Cambridge University Press, 1981).

7 The 'No desire out without a desire in' principle is introduced and discussed at some length by Jay Wallace in his 'How to argue about practical reason', *Mind*, 99 (1990), pp. 267–97.

8 Geoffrey Sayre-McCord, 'The meta-ethical problem', *Ethics*, 108 (October 1997), pp. 267–97.

9 This idea is made to do considerable work when we consider issues of freedom and responsibility in the case of both belief and desire. See, especially, Philip Pettit and Michael Smith, 'Freedom in belief and desire', *Journal of Philosophy* (September 1996), pp. 429–49; Michael Smith, 'A theory of freedom and responsibility'. In Garrett Cullity and Berys Gaut (eds), *Ethics and Practical Reason* (Oxford: Oxford University Press, 1997).

10 Christine Korsgaard, 'The normativity of instrumental reason'. In Garrett Cullity and Berys Gaut (eds), *Ethics and Practical Reason* (Oxford: Oxford University Press, 1997).

11 The example that follows come from Gary Watson's 'Free agency', reprinted in Gary Watson (ed.), *Free Will* (Oxford: Oxford University Press, 1982), pp. 96–110.

12 I discuss the difference between following the advice of our perfectly rational selves, and using their behaviour as an example that we should emulate, in my 'Internal reasons', *Philosophy and Phenomenological Research*, 1995, pp. 109–31.

13 Now we can see why my fully rational self's actions are irrelevant as regards what I should do in my circumstances. Whereas I am in circumstances in which the options that are available to me are determined by my irrationality, my fully rational self is evidently never in such circumstances. For further discussion of this point see Pettit and Smith, 'Brandt on self-control'. In Brad Hooker (ed.), *Rationality, Rules and Utility: New Essays on the Moral Philosophy of Richard Brandt* (Boulder, CO: Westview Press, 1993), pp. 33–50.

14 Ingmar Persson, 'Critical notice of Michael Smith's *The Moral Problem*', *Theoria*, 61, 2 (1995), pp. 143–58.

15 Michael Smith, *The Moral Problem* (Oxford: Blackwell, 1994)

16 Consider the biconditional: 'It makes sense to act in a certain way in certain circumstances if and only if we would desire ourselves to act in that way in

those circumstances if we had a set of desires that was maximally informed and coherent and unified.' The distinction just made in the text between assigning the left and right hand sides of this biconditional different orders of priority corresponds to the difference between what Mark Johnston calls reading the biconditional 'right to left' and reading it 'left to right.' See Mark Johnston, 'Objectivity refigured: pragmatism without verificationism'. In John Haldane and Crispin Wright (eds), *Reality, Representation and Projection* (Oxford: Oxford University Press, 1993), pp. 121–6.

17 For discussion of these sorts of example see James Griffin, *Well-Being* (Oxford: Clarendon Press, 1986) pp. 56–60; Susan Hurley, *Natural Reasons* (Oxford: Oxford University Press, 1989), chapters 5 and 6; G. E. M. Anscombe, *Intention* (Oxford: Blackwell, 1976) p. 70; Derek Parfit, *Reasons and Persons* (Oxford: Clarendon Press, 1984), pp. 120–6; and David Hume, *A Treatise of Human Nature* (Oxford: Clarendon Press, 1968), book 2, part 3, section 3.

18 Earlier versions of this chapter were read at the University of Wisconsin at Madison; the Research School of Social Sciences, Australian National University; the Central Division Meetings of the American Philosophical Association in Pittsburgh, April 1997; and the annual Australasian Association of Philosophy conference in Auckland, July 1997. I would like to thank my commentator at the APA, Candace Vogler, for her very helpful remarks. John Bishop, Simon Blackburn, Stephen Darwall, Brian Garrett, Richard Holton, Rae Langton, Philip Pettit, Denis Robinson and Natalie Stoljar also gave me useful comments. A very sceptical set of questions from the editor of this volume, Dale Jamieson, saved me from several errors at the last moment.

4

Peter Singer's Expanding Circle: Compassion and the Liberation of Ethics

ROBERT C. SOLOMON

Philosophy should not try to produce ethical theory . . . A good deal of moral philosophy engages unblinkingly in this activity, for no obvious reason except that it has been going on for a very long time. (Bernard Williams, *Ethics and the Limits of Philosophy*)[1]

The only critique of a philosophy that . . . proves something, mainly trying to see whether one can live in accordance with it, has never been taught at universities: all that has ever been taught is a critique of words by means of other words. (Nietzsche, *Schopenhauer as Educator*, §8)

It is not my intention to be one of Singer's "critics," although there are obvious areas of disagreement. Nor is it my intention to take him on in that arena where he has made the greatest contributions and has inspired the most criticism, indeed, sometimes, the most venom – the practical arena of abortion, euthanasia, and "animal liberation." Perhaps that is because I so rarely disagree with him. I will have something to say about animals, however, but even that only on the way to making some general observations about the methods and approach of Singer's work, including what he calls his "utilitarianism." (The scare quotes are intended to indicate both my doubts about ethical theory in general and Singer's status as a bona fide utilitarian in practice.) What I would like to explore is that difficult conjunction (it is sometimes a confrontation) between Nature and Reason, which together give us ethics. By capitalizing these terms, I hope that it is obvious that I am not glorifying so much as satirizing them, aping the fashion of some Teutonically inspired meta-physicians. I find the split, in a word or two, both unnatural and unreasonable. In this essay, I would like to look at the role of compassion in (or rather, underlying) Singer's work, and, in particular Singer's book, *The Expanding Circle*. In it, Singer outlines what one might take to be the theoretical underpinnings of his many hard-hitting and consequently controversial case studies and policy recommendations. But theory, I suggest, is not what makes Singer such an important philosopher.

A Pack of Hyenas, a Porcine Tragedy: the Two Lives of Peter Singer

The pack of hyenas encircles the panic-stricken mother warthog. One after another of the scruffy, snarling bitches lunges after one then another of the terrified and bewildered little hoglettes until, in total confusion, Mother Warthog is running in four directions at once, inevitably leaving vulnerable one of her squealing babies. With a victorious growl one of the hyenas scoops up and crushes the baby in her powerful jaws and proudly parades it across the veldt, as Mother gives brief and futile chase.

This was the most poignant scene I saw on television last year. Without commenting on the competition, I would say that no other program, including the alleged news and any number of "made for television" movies, brought me so close to tears. But why was this? Warthogs, even baby warthogs, are not the most endearing of creatures. (Then again, neither is a hyena.) It is not as if I had gotten to "know" them after seeing them for seven minutes on TV. It is not as if they reminded me of warthogs – or for that matter any variety of other hogs – that I once knew. Accordingly, one might argue that I was just being "sentimental," in that dismissive sense that remains so *au courant* among the sophisticated and the callous. Or, perhaps, it could be argued that such a response is "unnatural," merely cultivated, "put on" in line with current emotional fashion. But such charges raise important questions, namely whether any such responses are "natural," whether (and how) they can be cultivated, encouraged and strengthened, and what is meant by "emotional fashion."

By way of contrast, there is this tiresomely repetitive biblical image, often reproduced for Christmas cards, depicting "the lion lying down and feeding with the lamb." Saccharine imagery and cynicism aside, the obvious query here is, "What did the lion eat?" Lions don't feed with lambs, but they will, we know, happily feed on lambs.[2] This is a matter of biology. One can dimly imagine a natural order and an animal kingdom in which there was no "food chain," only a (more or less) inexhaustible fresh supply of nutritious and possibly even tasty food, descending "like manna from heaven" or, alternatively, self-manufactured from raw materials, as most plants do. But the fact is, like it or not, that the world is a rough place. Even the well-edited field studies on *National Geographic* and *Nature* depict the inevitable harshness of a world defined, in part, by the rule "eat or be eaten – or starve."

With this bit of naturalistic reasoning, my initial response to the mother warthog and her offspring is put in its proper place. The world is, after all, not designed to suit our civilized, Saran-wrapped tastes. Baby hyenas have to eat too. Reason thus provides a bit of distance from our immediate emotional reactions. And, from that distance, one doesn't have to be a population biologist to understand that "culling" (that is, killing) is necessary, no matter how "cute" or innocent the "culled" might be. We now understand the catastrophe that awaits any species that is overprotected (or too competitive) in the checks-and-balances world of Darwinian nature. So, too, with our own species. One only has to travel to Mexico City, Bombay or Los Angeles to get a glimpse of what overpopulation and bad politics promise for the future. I monitor my own little suburb of West Lake Hills outside of Austin, where the city council debates the fate of the exploding white-tailed deer population with the ferocity that NATO debates the future of the Bosnians. Our heart goes out to the individual deer who are our natural neighbors. Our reason plots the fate of the species. And as for those "natural" sentimental responses, "It is nature," snits the Katherine Hepburn character to Humphrey Bogart in *The African Queen*, "that we are put on this earth to rise above." And what allows us to do that is reason.

I begin with this conflicted meditation on compassion and biology because this is the stuff of Peter Singer's ethics. He is not, in the usual, tedious sense, an ethical theorist. Although a thoroughgoing utilitarian, he has little patience for many of the niceties of the ethical debates and overly prissy qualifications surrounding that ethical theory. Challenged, for example, about the differences between interests and preferences, "happiness," pleasure and pain, Singer might well answer, "Oh yes, there are all of those questions" with a wave of his hand, indicating that there are more important things to talk about and to do. And he does them. *Animal Liberation*, the book that shot him into the rare celebrity status that very few philosophers now enjoy (or suffer), would have been nothing but an exercise in hypocrisy if its author did not live and act – sometimes at considerable risk – on behalf of its argument. And, indeed, that is what an argument is for Singer. It is not an academic exercise. It is, first of all, a practice, an attitude, a set of guidelines for a proper life.

But what moves Peter Singer, I believe, is not his arguments. He may be a champion of reason, and very good at it too, but one sees beneath his clear and occasionally abrasive prose a very different sensibility from that portrayed so persuasively on the page. Talking to Peter, watching Peter with his family and his students, reading between the lines (and looking at the pictures) of *Animal Liberation,* one recognizes a very different response than that of the hard-headed utilitarian weighing up harms and benefits. This is the compassionate Peter Singer. He emerges clearly from the descriptions and the photographs of animals (and elsewhere people) suffering. He appeals not to reason (narrowly defined as argument) but to the sentiments. The compassionate Peter Singer is often at odds with the utilitarian Peter Singer (which is not to say, however, that compassion and utilitarianism are incompatible). The utilitarian Peter Singer, following David Hume, observes that compassion (or what Hume called "sympathy") quickly diminishes with "distance," so that one should not expect to be moved by a stranger as one is moved by one's kin. (Nor will one be so moved by a warthog or a cow as he or she will be by another human being, a child, especially one's own child.) The utilitarian Peter Singer will not succumb to innocent mawkishness. He defends his "humanitarian" vision, not in terms of compassion or sympathy but as "altruism," that vacuous coinage of suspicious ethicists and sociobiologists referring to "other-directed" behavior. We have a "natural" response to our own kin, Singer allows, but that diminishes exponentially (inverse square) with genetic distance. What must quickly take its place, if we are not to be purely selfish, is reason. But it is the compassionate Peter Singer who pushes us beyond this way of thinking.

The "Hard Work" of Philosophy: Nature, Reason, Combat and Compassion

I have long been an admirer and defender of Peter Singer's work. There are those who still insist that it is "not philosophy," to which I can only say, too bad for philosophy. He invites *ad hominem* arguments. Opponents (carnivores, most of them) look for tell-tale conflicts between theory and practice. (The Singer cat, properly fed an all-vegetarian diet, is nevertheless one of the best mousers in the world.) But, of all the moralists and social reformers I know, Peter Singer is the least vulnerable to these. To be sure, he has had to face conflicts and contradictions in his life, but what else gives rise to ethical concerns? (We can exclude petty professionalism and the esoteric theory wars as a source of moral concern.) Most of the attacks on Peter's work, I believe, are just so much denial (of the persuasiveness of his theses), not to mention *ressentiment* and envy and a bit of *mauvaise foi.*

Singer is my candidate for our best living examplar of what Nietzsche celebrated (but did not himself display) as "the philosopher as example." Many philosophers do not even like to use examples, lest the taint of particularity pollute the process of pure ideas. Thus I am sometimes tempted to compare Singer's work to the work of John Rawls, whose *Theory of Justice* has now defined the field of social and political philosophy (in the USA, at least) for the final part of the twentieth century. That book founded a philosophical industry, launching a thousand dissertations. But after two and a half decades in which the gap between the rich and the poor (both nationally – in the USA and Australia – and globally) has increased faster than ever before, the Justice Industry rarely deigns to analyze a concrete issue. And as for policy, we learn mainly that the Right has priority over the Good, and, yes, that the rich should not get richer without the poor getting somewhat richer as well. Singer, by contrast, rarely strays more than a page without a concrete, real-life problem in mind, and some (usually controversial) advice on what, exactly, to do about it.

Now, just to be fair, my friend and colleague Tom Donaldson has credited Rawls's work as being the definitive influence on the late twentieth-century proliferation of "applied ethics" (i.e. ethics), to which Rawls has reportedly responded, "if that's so, then that's the best thing that anyone could say about it." Nevertheless, even if Rawls is the definitive influence, it is Peter Singer who has provided the substance. Despite the self-aggrandizing claims of the ethical theorists, the hard part of ethics is not providing the framework within which practical ethics can establish itself on a serious philosophical footing. The hard part of ethics is facing up to the issues, dealing with the politics and the often violent passions that they provoke. The hard part is getting into the dirty emotional fray, facing a hissing crowd in Germany rather than refuting a deontological rebuttal at Australasian Association of Philosophy meetings. It is the hard part that the whole of philosophy has tried to avoid, ever since Plato's final retreat from Syracuse and Aristotle's insistence that the Athenians would not sin twice against philosophy.

Nevertheless, there are overriding theoretical issues in Singer's work, although not those of the *a priori* and merely conceptual sort that usually pass as ethical theory. The overriding concepts in his philosophy are those of reason and rationality, which are quickly cashed out in terms of utilitarian calculations and arguments and the weighing of needs and interests. The needs are indisputably "natural" – hunger and health, for example. (This is why Singer, unlike many contemporary utilitarians, spends so little time worrying about mere "preferences.") The weighing of needs is indisputably the business of rationality.[3] So, too, is the constraining of desires, on the behalf of the larger and more long-term good. Thus the interplay of Nature and Rationality that drives much of Singer's work. It is a dialectic that, in his hands as well as in a long tradition he does not always share, constitutes the subject matter of ethics. On the one hand, there is psychobiology, natural needs and drives, pleasure and pain, and the powerful emotions of attachment, love and loss. There is also sickness and death. On the other hand, there are those peculiar human beliefs and expectations that are sometimes summarized under the problematic rubric "morality" – concerns for propriety, for social and personal well-being, for public as well as personal "flourishing," for rules and their obediance, for institutions and their respect, for the dignity of individuals and the recognition of their fears and preferences, among them the hatred of pain, the avoidance of humiliation, the fear of death. And then, too, there is the new technology, the ability to keep people alive long after either Nature or they themselves see any reason for doing so, the ability to stop population growth without Malthusian measures, the ability to manufacture food, not, perhaps, as "manna from heaven" but, at least, as tofu from soy beans, with enough shapes, textures, tastes and varieties to keep us (and perhaps those lions) entertained as well as fed for a lifetime. Put all of these together, and you have a stewpot of ethical dilemmas, both old and new, many of them faced daily by millions of people around the globe, some faced only in the rare, headline grabbing exceptional case. Some are as straightforward as the starvation or malnutrition of millions of children or the slaughter of hundreds of thousands of animals. Some are as exotic as the destiny of an infant bred outside of its mother's womb, or another baby born with extremely disabling difficulties, or the desire of a wealthy eighty-year-old to have a new heart and kidney.

As intelligent and sensitive human beings, we can acknowledge the harshness of the world, and yet not accept it at all. We are not merely at the top of the food chain. We are, in an important sense, *above* the food chain. We, as opposed to all the other creatures in nature, are rational. We have what is uncritically called "free will." We are able to reflect and choose our food, our habits, our breeding patterns. As for the saccharine quality of those Christmas greetings and that biblical fantasy, we can understand that, too, as an expression of a certain sentimentality as well as a Christian allegory.[4] Our strange compassion for other species is not a "natural" projection of our more immediate concerns but something learned and cultivated, part of culture rather than nature, the result of so many cuddly teddy bears and puppies when we were children, and aggressive campaigns on the behalf of sensitivity (such as Peter's) when we became adults. But compassion, too, involves a certain distance. It, too, one could argue, is not opposed to but a consequence of reason. Indeed, one wonders what one would reason about – apart from one's own immediate interests – if this were not so. It was Hume, after all, who wrote that "Tis not contrary to reason to prefer the destruction of the whole world to the scratching of my finger."[5]

The Expanding Circle and the Rise of Reciprocal Altruism

When a person (or an animal) increases the fitness of another at the expense of his own fitness, he can be said to have performed an act of altruism. Self-sacrifice for the benefit of off-spring is altruism in the conventional sense but not in the strict genetic sense, because individual fitness is measured by the number of surviving offspring. But self-sacrifice on behalf of second cousins is true altruism at both levels; and when directed at total strangers such abnegating behavior is so surprising (that is "noble") as to demand some sort of theoretical explanation. (E. O. Wilson, *Sociobiology*, p. 55)

In 1981, Singer wrote a book – I personally find it one of his best – taking on sociobiology. It is called *The Expanding Circle*,[6] and, like most of Singer's works, it was greeted upon publication with howls of misunderstanding and misdirected protest. Singer's argument, which seems uncontrovertible, is that biology has something to do with our attitudes and our behavior. More specifically, biology dictates concern for the survival of one's genotype. But such concerns take us only so far, and it is not very far at all. One is deeply concerned with one's offspring ("children" seems overly personal in this context), one is less concerned with one's sibling's offspring, and one is decreasingly concerned at all with the offspring of another family, another tribe, another species. Thus the familiar paradox – the "good" man or woman who is wholly devoted to his or her family and friends but oblivious to the rest of the world. Ethics, however, cannot be so limited, and it is against this too cosy restricted picture of personal goodness that the abstractions and theories of reason offer a more global balance. Ethics is neither personal in the too limited sense nor is it abstract in the global sense, but it is rather a process of enlarged awareness that Peter Singer (following W. E. H. Lecky) calls "the expanding circle." The inner rings of the circle consist of our natural feelings for our kin and our closest friends, but as the circle grows it comes to include acquaintances, neighbors, colleagues, countrymen, foreigners, and other species. What allows the circle to grow, according to Singer, is reason, but this is where I will want to part company with his argument.

Altruism, the biological impulse to care for "one's own," gives us the opening wedge in that age-old but nevertheless perverse and mistaken theory of human nature – that people (and animals) are basically selfish. But this is surely inadequate, one might object, for no one would say that people are ethical if they care only for their own children, and in terms of self-interest, it can be argued that we have only "expanded the circle" slightly, from individual selfishness to a selfishness that includes "one's own." But our opening wedge shows the way to a further expansion, to include friends and extended family and, eventually, communities, even total strangers whom one recognizes as "kin" just by virtue of being human or intelligently sentient. (It is hard to overestimate the significance of such moving political terms as "*fraternité*," "sisterhood," and "the family of man.") Altruism is not selfish but it is certainly not selfless either, and if we are to understand justice we cannot take the "pure" phenomenon of self-sacrifice as our model. The warthog saves her hoglette because it is, in some sense, part of her, but so too we care about people because humanity is, in the relevant sense, part of us. Moreover, altruism is not by itself sufficient (though it certainly is necessary) to account for our natural moral promptings. What more is needed is an understanding of altruism as contextual and contingent. In simple non-scientific language, we tend to be nice to other people because they are nice to us. Altruism, in other words, is not just concerned with how we perceive and treat other people. It is, first of all, concerned with *relationships*. The origins of ethics and of justice in particular lie not in altruism as such but in *reciprocal altruism*, our natural tendency to help and care for *each other*, but, when necessary, to punish one another as well.

How does the circle expand, from strict kinship relations to more distant relations to community to all humanity and beyond? I think that Rousseau (and many other philosophers) had it right when he pointed to *resemblance* as the key to sympathy; we feel "closest" to those who are (or seem to be) most like us. In terms of molecular biology, that means shared genes, but in terms of a larger biology that includes all the phenomena of perception and intelligence that resemblance gets recognized in everything from a familiar smell to an abstract principle of human equality. We may owe our first allegiance to our "blood" kin, but we early learn to recognize that we have much in common with our neighbors, our heroes, our pets, even our gods. Familiarity breeds reciprocity (whether or not it sometimes breeds contempt), and the circle expands as we learn to recognize and reciprocally bring out the similarities we share with all of our countrymen and women and many of the "beasts" that we live with. Reason no doubt can play a role in this expansion, but the primary ingredients of this growing awareness are perception, sympathy, and reciprocity. The expanding circle does not require a leap of reason but rather an open mind and (a bit of bad biology) a receptive heart.

Kinship may be genetic but our phenomenology knows little of genes. (The fact that we want to know whose genes we share is an intellectual and cultural overlay, not a natural inclination.) What we do recognize is proximity and familiarity, and our sense of kin is defined first of all not by our knowledge of genetics but by being raised together and sharing a life. When two siblings long separated find out that they are "blood relations," it is, not surprisingly, a bit of a shock and a source of considerable confusion. For most of us now, in our mobile, rapidly changing urban societies, proximity and familiarity refer to often distant friends, correspondents, and colleagues. With television, the Internet and inexpensive jet travel, the circle of our phenomenological "kin" is enormous indeed. We recognize how many features we share with millions of people around the globe. It is still an open question how far the circle can be expanded, whether we want to join Singer and Lecky in enlarging the circle to include "a nation, a coalition of nations, then all humanity, and finally ... the animal world."[7] But the point is that the altruism identified by the sociobiologists in every parent's concern for its offspring is by no means limited to actual genetic kinship. As the world becomes more proximate and familiar to us, that concern will expand as well. The danger, of course, is that sibling rivalry (and "familiarity breeds contempt") will nurture not the altruistic aspects of ethics but rather its defensiveness and antipathies. But the first move is expanding the circle and moving beyond the myth of natural selfishness.

If the circle is to be expanded, I would want to argue that it must be first of all through just this sense of kinship and shared humanity (and not just "humanity"). I want to be very cautious about joining Peter Singer in the invocation of reason as the means of building on our natural impulses. The danger is that reason, instead of building on our natural impulses, may instead undermine them. If the basis of ethics is personal feeling for those we care about, there is the very real danger that, in over-enlarging the circle to include everyone and everything or in turning from the personal to the impersonality of reason, we will lose precisely that dimension of the personal that produces ethics in the first place. But I want to be equally cautious about premature enthusiasm for those universal feelings of love, called *agape*, which have been defended by some of the great (and not-so-great) religious thinkers of the world. There is the very familiar danger that such feelings, however noble their object or intent, will degenerate into a diffuse and ultimately pointless sentimentality, or worse, that form of hypocrisy that (as has often been said of such "lovers of humanity" as Rousseau and Marx) adores the species but deplores almost every individual of it. The natural sensibility that is at issue here is nothing so lofty as love or even universal care, but rather a kind of kinship or fellow-feeling, which may well produce much caring and many kindnesses but will also provoke rivalry and competition. The basic biological sense we seek, in other words, is not so much a particular attitude or emotion as it is a sense of belonging, the social sense as such.

That social sense can best be summed up in the realm of genetics and evolutionary biology as the phenomenon that Darwin described and that has since been named "reciprocal altruism." Reciprocity is extremely important in all intelligent social life, for it provides the *quid pro quo* or "tit-for-tat" that is the basis of every ethical system larger than the family (though it is obviously central to dealings within the family as well), and which is the foundation metaphor of justice. (It is worth noting that much of ethics and current theories of justice dismiss such "tit-for-tat" dealings as sufficiently personal (or insufficiently impersonal) and sufficiently self-interested (or insufficiently disinterested) to be irrelevant or at least inadequate.) But this presupposes an enormous leap in genetic development, not just in terms of intelligence as such but in terms of *strategy*. One can have enormous intelligence (idiots savant) but shockingly little of that interpersonal sense that is required for even the simplest strategic exchange.

It is not necessarily thinking or negotiating that are essential here. Successful traders and businessmen often claim (truthfully) that they don't "think" about what they are doing. They "just know" what to do. So, too, animals display a remarkable array of strategic behaviors – mother birds pretending to have broken wings to lead predators away from the nest, monkeys fooling one another by uttering a misleading cry to distract the others – without any need on our part to postulate Pentagon-like tactical mentality behind their behavior. In such cases, even Darwin himself seems to have erred in giving too much credit here to the role of "reason" and not enough to heredity, but to attribute strategic skill to heredity is not to relegate it to merely automatic behavior. Good game players usually describe their own skill in non-intellectual terms. A good billiards or pool player simply "sees" the shot, she doesn't calculate it. A good poker player doesn't sit skimming a mathematical odds book on the one hand and a psychology of facial expressions text on the other. Of course, one must (to some extent) acquire such skills but it doesn't follow that such skills are not also (or may not alternatively be) genetically engineered or that the general capacity for strategic behavior – the tit-for-tat attitude as such – must not be so engineered.

Reciprocal altruism, in summary, is the readiness of an individual (or a group) to aid another individual (or group), with the expectation that it will be helped in return. The usual but by no means most dramatic example is that of mutual grooming among apes and monkeys. (Cats, by contrast, do not seem to have this ability or these expectations. Mother cats groom their kittens, and occasionally groom one another. All cats, of course, groom themselves, but there seems to be little evidence of reciprocity.) Monkey A grooms monkey B with the expectation that he will be groomed in turn. But the key to reciprocal altruism is not just this hopeful expectation. It is the reaction in turn when the expectation is not fulfilled. It is a reaction of resentment, a reaction of hostility, perhaps even a reaction of vengeance. Here again is the old cynical question: what if one monkey finds that he can get groomed by everyone without doing any grooming in return? And what if others perceive his strategy and follow it in turn? The answer to this question is that there can be no altruism (except in isolated cases) unless there is also a keen sense and expectation of *punishment*.

The strategically selfish monkey must "learn his lesson," and so do other monkeys too. The selfish monkey suddenly finds himself without groomers, perhaps he is even snubbed or exiled from the group. If failure to fulfill the terms of reciprocity were not punished there would be an obvious advantage (one familiar to us in large, impersonal urban societies) to being a cheater, a dead-beat, to taking without giving. Punishment is both deterrence and reform, but it is also something more. It is *retribution*, not in an abstract sense determined by law but in the most gut-level sense imaginable. We feel the need to punish wrong-doers because that is the precondition of any successful scheme of mutual cooperation. That knowledge is built right into our genes, and it manifests itself in some of our most powerful motives and emotions. Punishment deters and it is intended to deter, but punishment is not just a matter of calculated deterrence. It is also revenge, and any adequate discussion of our natural propensities and sense of justice must include not only the "nice" feelings of kinship and altruism but their necessarily "nasty" correlates.

The example of mutual grooming may seem unimportant and inessential to the life (as opposed to the comfort) of the animals, but part of my point here is to emphasize the essentially social (as opposed to survival) instincts and inclinations of animals. And how many of our activities, from "common courtesies" to getting along at the office or "bucking for promotion," are just so many variations on mutual grooming? (It is not even hard to find an analog to picking body lice in much of our social behavior.) Sometimes, however, the success of reciprocal altruism can be a straightforward matter of life or death. Birds and antelopes acting as "scouts," for example, often risk their own lives warning their respective flocks and herds of impending attack. It is expected that others will do the same in return. When a group of zebras is attacked by lions some zebras will risk (or lose) their lives by fighting off their attackers. (If enough zebras fight, a victory is likely; if only a few fight, the outcome is sure to be disastrous for them.) Again, it is expected that others will do the same in return.

Animals acting in concert can be very effective in warding off predators who could easily kill an isolated member. Animals in groups who practice "every beast for itself," on the other hand, have to have a very large reproduction rate for the group to survive, for many will perish to predators. But in life and death matters, especially, reciprocal altruism requires harsh punishment for those who fail to reciprocate. The bird or beast who does not warn the group when danger approaches will be ignored or abandoned. The zebra who hides from a fight and allows his fellows to be killed must be taught that the risk in battling lions is less than the certainty of being punished by the group. This may sound overly rational and calculating, but the fact is that it goes on in nature all the time, without either reason or calculation. The genetic mechanisms are obviously complicated but the results are quite clear. Reciprocal altruism, including the demand for punishment, gives an obvious genetic advantage to those in the group and condemns those who do not comply. It thus becomes a powerful force for group cohesion as well as a competitive advantage in competition with other groups. It also explains, in no uncertain terms, the need for hostility and punishment within otherwise amiable groups, and why ethics cannot ignore the role of the negative emotions, not as obstacles to justice but as one of its driving forces.

Rethinking the Expanded Circle: Compassion and "Distance"

My argument, in a sentence, is that Singer, in his emphasis on reason (and consequently, on the role of normative ethical theory) underestimates the power of compassion. An adequate sense of ethics requires not only reason but concern and curiosity, a need to know about the state of the world and the plight of people outside of one's own limited domain. Reason, according to Singer, adds universal principles to the promptings of our biologically inherited feelings. The danger, however, is that reason will also leave those feelings behind, as evidenced by any number of philosophers who simply "talk a good game." Thus, I want to argue that what allows the circle to expand is not reason (in the technical sense of calculation on the basis of abstract principles) but rather know-ledge and understanding in the sense of coming to appreciate the situa-tions and the circumstances in which other people and creatures find themselves. This requires what many theorists now call "empathy" or "feeling with" (which Hume and Adam Smith called "sympathy" and which might more accurately be called "fellow-feeling"), and it requires care and concern, the emotional sense that what happens to others *matters*. According to this "moral sentiment" view, there is no "line" to be drawn between ethics and benevolence, no place in our experience where affect and affection leave off and some new faculty called "reason" kicks in and takes over. Rather, our emotions get more and more expan-sive and better educated and new perspectives join with the old to enlarge our world and embrace new populations in it. This is the role of "emo-tional fashion," which once we get beyond the hint of conformity and mere transience should be recognized as the vital force in ethics. We *learn* to empathize with others, and we *learn* to care about what happens to children we never meet thousands of miles (or, in our large cities, feet) away. We *learn* to perceive chickens, cows, and warthogs as sentient beings with real emotions, and we *learn* to conceive of our uses of animals as a moral choice, not, first of all, because of any rational principles but because of our cultivated and expanded emotional awareness. And, like most learning, we learn this by way of social practice, imitating others, sharing their feelings and thus expanding our limited repertoire of moral sensibilities.

David Hume, like Singer and the sociobiologists, argued that there are limits to how far our concern and benevolence toward others can reach, that the problem with any conception of justice based on personal feelings is the "distance" between us. This seems to me to be much overblown. It may be a fact that it is more difficult to feel compassion for a person whom we do not know and will never meet than for someone we know and already care about, but this problem of "distance" is much more often a matter of ignorance or hard-heartedness than it is a simple function of our feelings. The problem of the homeless in the USA, for example, is not one of distance, but the very opposite; it is a problem of proximity. The homeless are not unknown to us. We can and do get a personal picture of them on television nightly and, for example, through such moving books as Jonathan Kozol's *Rachel and Her Children*.[8] They are not different but rather frighteningly like us, with much the same backgrounds, with much the same personal histories. They are not just, in some abstract sense, "fellow Americans." They came from similar families, with similar skills, similar aspirations, before a financial catastrophe, or a disastrous divorce, or a bout of mental illness, or simply skyrocketing rents or the closing of an industrial plant ended their "normal" lives and dumped them on to the streets. What I want to argue is that our sympathy for them (and, one hopes, the resultant urgency to do something about the problem) is a natural reaction, and it is this reaction – not the pursuit of some abstract system of policy (which may and certainly should follow as a means) – that constitutes the heart of ethics.

In place of the Hume and Singer Precipitous slide, I suggest the much gentler Held-Slote Slope. Virginia Held, in a recent work, and Michael Slote, in a recent essay, have suggested that, while compassion and caring certainly do diminish with distance, it is a mistake to conclude that they thereby drop out of sight or do no motivational work.[9] To the contrary, the drop-off is not exponential (except, perhaps, in the transition from immediate family to everyone else). It is a slope, indeed, almost a horizontal, which extends as far as our informed perceptions.

It is our hard-heartedness, not our compassion, that is unnatural. The sameness of the homeless stirs our sympathies, but it also stimulates our defenses. The homeless man who speaks our language, who may have gone to the same school or, years before, rented an apartment in the same complex, terrifies us. "There but for the Grace of God" is not just an abstract phrase of cosmic gratitude but a very real recognition of the real contingencies that threaten us all. And some of us build a defensive (and willfully uninformed) ideology: "It's their own fault." "They should get a job." (Many of the homeless already have one.) "They should get off the bottle" (as if that were the universal explanation for wretchedness, rather than an easily affordable tranquilizer); "They should see somebody about their depression" (as if public mental health were so readily available, and as if being homeless were not itself a more than sufficient cause for depression). Instead of sympathy for someone in a plight, we supply a context in which the homeless instead are failures, or (even better) on the streets by choice ("a lifestyle," in one of the more obscene phrases of the decade). By intentionally misunderstanding and misappropriating the tragedy we may manage to "distance" the problem, but distance itself is not the problem, nor is numbness of feeling. The problem is that we let our beliefs – even our reason – get in the way of our feelings.

The Pathology of Theory

[In civilization] one's fellow man can be killed with impunity underneath his window. He has merely to place his hands over his ears and argue with himself a little in order to prevent nature, which rebels within him, from identifying him with the man being assassinated. Savage man does not have this admirable talent, and for lack of wisdom and reason he is always seen thoughtlessly giving in to the first sentiment of humanity. (Jean-Jacques Rousseau, *Discourse on the Origins of Inequality*)

An intellectual without an ideology is defenseless. (Irving Kristol, *The Public Interest*)

In an innocent sense, of course, beliefs are essential to life, to emotion and to ethics; one has to know about the world to live and feel in the world. Ethics presupposes not just a good heart but a good amount of intelligence and knowledge, what Lorraine Code has called our "epistemic responsibility."[10] But there is another kind of belief that is not just personal knowledge of the world but a self-righteous, impersonal moral stance toward the world that parades as knowledge and blocks emotion – even as it generates outrage and indignation on its own behalf. It is this kind of belief – or ideology – that is the enemy of ethics, and this may have little to do with whether the beliefs in question are conservative, liberal, libertarian, Marxist, or anarchist in orientation. I would like to suggest that much of what passes for "ethical theory" is better seen as ideology, and this would include utilitarianism as well as Rawlsian "fairness." (Rawls is pretty clear about the "liberal" significance of his theories, as Bentham and Mill were years ago.) There is an obvious sense in which dwelling in the abstractions of theory not only postpones but blocks ethical action, but sometimes, I would argue, this may be the very point of the theory, or rather, the theorizing. Indeed, I have often thought that one of the curious by-products of the evolution of the huge human cerebellum is our ability to distance ourselves from our lives and our emotions and falsify them in spectacular ways. Philosophy should provide edification and concern, but it too often encourages escape through rationalization.

Ethics requires intelligence as well as sensitivity, but theories of ethics may impose blinders as well as insight and argument. The blinders are those ideologies through which we interpret ideas and information that ought to stimulate our concern and instead turn them into abstract but righteous condemnation. In his book *Quandaries and Virtues*, Edmund Pincoffs writes: "I will argue that the structures known as ethical theories are more threats to moral sanity and balance than instruments for their attainment... They restrict and warp moral reflection."[11] So, too, I want to argue that ideologies and so-called moral theories may not be the primrose pathway to ethics but rather its primary obstacle. Pincoffs adds, "an unjust person could be an authority on the justice of social practices" and, indeed, we are well aware that the most articulate ideologues are often those with the most dangerous axe to grind. The authors of the quasi-utilitarian, pseudo-sociobiological treatise *The Bell Curve* provide one among too many cases in point.[12] The most sophisticated thinking about social policy and ethics may be a refusal to feel compassion.

This is what worries me about Singer's utilitarianism: not Singer's use of it but the abuses to which it can be subjected. Utilitarianism and overly abstract calculations of "the greatest good for the greatest number" can too easily serve as rationalizations for the most unethical policies and behavior. Usually such arguments are put in the language of rights and their violation, but my concern is a very different one. Thinking about "the greatest good for the greatest number" – even apart from the infinity-grabbing polemics of the philosophers – can too easily dull one's sensibilities. My friend and colleague Paul Woodruff, who served in Cambodia in the sixties, told me that, under his command, the soldiers who were not college educated, who were not versed in the wiles and ways of "reason," typically remained sensitive to and repulsed by the war crimes that had by then become a daily feature, if not an inevitability, of the war. The college educated recruits and officers, on the other hand, were able to rationalize these handily, using familiar utilitarian arguments, thus cutting themselves off quite effectively not only from guilt and shame but from the human tragedies they caused and witnessed. Reason as rationalization can sometimes be inversely proportional to justice.

I am not denying that ethics necessitates some systematic thinking. There are no non-policy solutions to the most glaring problems of ethics and social justice, from "crack" motivated crime in urban streets to the dire poverty of hundreds of millions. What requires defense and articulation is the centrality of the moral sentiments, rather than ethical theory, in ethics. The problem is well illustrated in a parenthetical aside by Robert Nozick, in a discussion of the rights of animals. Arguing against those who insist that animals have no rights, Nozick comments: "Animals count for something... It is difficult to prove this. (It is also difficult to prove that people count for something!)"[13] Difficult, indeed! But do people or animals need to be "proven" to "count for something"? Or is the entire project of philosophy and social theory gone awry when such a demand can even arise? Ethical theory alone, no matter how well articulated, supported or demonstrated, cannot give us even the beginnings of a sense of care and concern. We must rather *begin* with an emotional awareness that people (and animals) "count for something," before the cumbersome apparatus of proof and demonstration is rolled on to the podium. It is that emotional awareness, not the impetus of practical reason, that makes ethics possible, and Peter Singer demonstrates this, even though he does not argue it, throughout his philosophy.

It is not that ethical theory and ideology have nothing to do with feelings. Debates about ethical theory generate intense controversy, and not just because ethical egos are on the line. Ideology obviously generates its own feelings, feelings of identification, especially pride, a sense of being in the right, and of being threatened personally when one's beliefs are challenged. But that is much of the problem, that one's ego is on the line *instead of* the issues. The last idea I would want to suggest is that feelings and beliefs are antagonistic to one another. Indeed, one might confront that view with a challenge: "Are not the moral sentiments determined by our beliefs and judgments?" Yes, but it is not as if any emotion is as good as any other. Our ethics is in part an "ethics of emotion" ("resentment is nasty, love is beautiful"); there are right and wrong emotions, and emotions can be right or wrong depending on the context and the conditions. When people are starving in Africa, jealous pride in the status of one's political beliefs is the wrong emotion. It is in the shadow of such unfeeling opinions and the actions and policies that follow from them that beliefs, especially political beliefs, are getting more and more suspicious. Having the "right" beliefs may make it harder, rather than easier, to become a good and just person. Ethical theories and ideology, in the last analysis, may just be powerful feelings that refuse to see themselves as feelings.

What worries me is what I believe worried Plato, when he attacked the mere "opinions" of his sophist friends and acquaintances. The problem was not that such opinions might be false; in fact, it did not matter that an opinion might be correct. Truth and falsity were not the issue. The problem was rather that such opinions were "second-hand," merely borrowed, the product of persuasion rather than thinking. (Of course, Plato worried that the persuasive force might be passion rather than reason, but his central concern was that the opinions so derived were not, in an important sense, "one's own.") In this sense, Plato argued, opinions were worthless even if, for all appearances, they seemed to be well thought out, supported by all sorts of reasons and arguments and ready with all sorts of replies to objections and counter-examples. So too Sextus Empiricus rejected "belief" as worthless, as "too intense" and as a falsification of life. Needless to say, neither Plato nor the ancient Skeptics rejected opinion and belief in the ordinary practical sense, as guidelines for getting through daily life. But when it came to the grand arguments and theories about life and the cosmos, about justice in particular, the solidarity of opinion and belief interfered with rather than came to the aid of ethics. Ethical theories may merely reflect undisclosed personal prejudices, projected as objective and often insensitive truths about the world. Peter Singer, happily, wears his prejudices on his sleeve.

A Plea for Compassion: Another Way of Reading Singer

No man is devoid of a heart sensitive to the sufferings of others...whoever is devoid of the heart of compassion is not human. (Mencius, 372–289 BCE)[14]

What is ethics, and what is an ethicist to do? Part of the problem, I think, is as old as (Western) philosophy itself, perhaps permanently traumatized by the execution of Socrates. Socrates was an activist – and he spent little time developing an ethical "theory." Plato was more prudent, and Aristotle after him as well. They were advocates of reason, and in the shadow of reason their concrete concerns and proposals tended to pale. Ever since, philosophers have tended to contrast reason and active engagement, occasionally holding out for "*praxis*," perhaps, but concentrating their energies on the theory of *praxis*, not practice, none the less. It is in this context, too, that we can perhaps understand the long-standing competition between reason and the emotions, although, to be sure, not every emotion leads to action. But when philosophers portray themselves as lovers of reason, it is important to see what too easily gets lost. By implication, at least, philosophy tends to display a contempt for action

and passion. "Appeal to the emotions" gets listed in almost every introductory logic text and ethics book as an "informal" fallacy, something to
avoid, not at all costs, perhaps, but at least in term papers. "Sentimentality" is viewed with disdain. Philosophy gets (re)defined as the formulation
and criticism of argument, the exclusive domain of reason. "Heated"
argument, though not uncommon, is considered inappropriate. Dispas-
sionate analysis is encouraged, but passionate advocacy is not. In such a
context, it is not hard to appreciate why a passionate advocate like Peter
Singer feels compelled to promote the former while not sacrificing the
latter.

Compassion does not necessarily lead to action, but it is the motivational seed from which all ethical action emerges. Thus, when philosophers marginalize or dismiss the emotions from ethics, they leave
ethics without its motivational core. Thus when Hume defends the sentiments against the excessive claims of reason, the result too easily leads to
moral skepticism. When he insisted that "reason is and ought to be the
slave of the passions," he did not mean to demean or dismiss the moral
significance of the passions. Quite the contrary. But Hume at least implied
and certainly set the stage for others to argue that morals were beyond the
grasp of reason and in some essential sense unarguable. I think that it is
not coincidental that Hume was politically extremely conservative. His
activism was largely confined to bars and billiards. In juxtaposing reason
and the sentiments, Hume fit all too well into a long line of philosophers
who also set them off against one another and separated sentimentality
from rationality. Descartes and his compatriot Malebranche analyzed
emotions in terms of physiological "animal spirits," distinctively inferior
parts of the psyche insofar as they were to be counted as parts of the
psyche at all. Leibniz thought of emotions as "confused perceptions" and
Kant rather famously dismissed what he called "pathological love" (i.e.
love as an emotion) from the love more properly commanded by the
Scriptures and practical reason. Kant may have been an enthusiast
(from a very safe distance) of the French Revolution, and he also may
have said that "nothing great is ever accomplished without passion" (a
comment usually attributed to Hegel), but it is clear that passion and
activism play at best modest roles in his grand "critique" of the higher
human faculties.

The suspicion concerning all things emotional continues to dominate
ethics. In his presidential address to the American Philosophical Association (Pacific Division), Joel Feinberg asks, "What relevance, if any, do
appeals to sentiment have for issues in practical ethics?"[15] He begins with
the usual answer: "The abrupt way with the question is to respond 'none;
sentiment is one thing and argument is another, and nothing fogs the
mind as thoroughly as emotion'." Feinberg rejects this "abrupt" answer,

but his conclusion is far less than an enthusiastic endorsement; he acknowledges that feelings may be "relevant" or at least not irrelevant to ethics, and he concludes that he "finds no unmanageable conflict between effective humanitarianism and the maintenance, under flexible control, of the essential human sentiments." He adds, as if this is not already sufficiently cautious, "I hope that conclusion is not too optimistic."[16] His analysis of the place of sentiment in ethics calls attention to the extreme caution and defensiveness a sensitive social phlosopher feels compelled to adopt in presenting an "optimistic" thesis – that sentiment may not be wholly irrelevant to ethical considerations. In considering the abortion issue, for instance, Feinberg agonizes over the rational relevance of those horrid photographs of aborted fetuses, depicting unmistakably baby-like corpses, mutilated and discarded. But now let us remember those upsetting pictorial inserts in Singer's *Animal Liberation*. These were no mere "illustrations." We should remind ourselves of their impact – compared with the ethereally controversial utilitarian attack on "speciesism" that accompanied them. One can imagine oneself faced with an argument about "justice" in the wild, coming to terms with Mother Warthog and her loss or the justifiable *ressentiment* of the lambs in their not-so-peaceful encounter with the lions. Those arguments would no doubt be seen as a joke, or, perhaps, a *reductio ad absurdum*. But nothing is so powerful as *being there, seeing that*, or otherwise being prompted by compassion and, perhaps, horror. One might well hesitate, with Feinberg, to call such pictures "arguments," but the weight of our ethical judgments is largely determined by them.[17]

I hope this explains my admiration for Singer. I suspect that many philosophers – and no doubt Peter himself – will feel offended by such shoving aside of the traditional emphasis on ethical argument and what must surely seem like a vulgar emphasis on photojournalism. But what I find moving about Singer's work is surely not the arguments – most of them undeniably valid – that provide his philosophical skeleton. It is rather the passion of his convictions, the passion that drives those arguments, indeed, at risk of seeming paradoxical, his passionate insistence on "rationality." But I believe that ethics is first of all a matter of emotion, to be cultivated from our natural inclinations of fellow-feeling ("kinship") and molded into a durable state of character. What Singer has done throughout his career is to create such a character. Ethics is not primarily a matter of abstract principle and argument, but a practice that can be coherently or incoherently pursued, with integrity or hypocrisy. All the rest, as Nietzsche complained early in *his* career, is words.

I have said very little here (but a good deal elsewhere) about the nature of compassion, and the emotions, in general, but if compassion or any emotion were no more than a physiological disturbance or a rush of feeling – as many theorists and much of our vernacular conversation suggests – then ethics would seem like little more than an itch or a minor convulsion, something like the queasy feeling in the pit of one's stomach that some people identify as the source or symptom of their moral sensitivity.[18] But though this may occasionally serve as a sign that one's moral alarm system has been triggered, it hardly suffices as an analysis of or as a basis for ethics. But ethics is primarily, not secondarily or symptomatically, emotional. Ethics begins with caring, about ourselves and our place in the world, about those whom we love or feel akin to, about the way of the world and the fate of the sentient creatures in it. Without that, there can be no ethics. Why else would ethics matter to us? Ethics begins with our emotional engagement in the world, and Peter Singer, despite as well as because of his arguments, is an exemplar of ethics for our time.

Notes

Portions of this chapter have been adapted, repackaged, and patched together from a number of other writings, including my *Passion for Justice* (New York: Addison Wesley, 1990) and my essay "Beyond reason" (in Ogilvy, *Revisioning Philosophy* (Albany: State University of New York Press, 1991). This piece is dedicated (rather obviously) to Peter Singer, a first-rate friend and philosopher.

1 *Ethics and the Limits of Philosophy* (Cambridge, MA: Harvard University Press, 1985), p. 17.
2 In a parallel zoological note, Nietzsche famously writes, "That lambs dislike great birds of prey does not seem strange: only it gives no ground for reproaching these birds of prey for bearing off little lambs. And if the lambs say among themselves: 'these birds of prey are evil; and whoever is least like a bird of prey, but rather its opposite, a lamb – would he not be good?' there is no reason to find fault with this institution of an ideal, except perhaps that the birds of prey might view it a little ironically and say: '*we* don't dislike them at all, these good little lambs; we even love them: nothing is more tasty than a tender lamb" (Nietzsche, *Genealogy of Morals*, book I, para. 13).
3 For a good discussion of *needs*, see Gillian Brock, *Necessary Goods: the Importance of Meeting Needs* (Lanham, MD: Rowman and Little field, 1998).
4 It may actually be more suitable as a Jain allegory, but I do not want to get into the "who is more compassionate" religious competition.
5 Hume, *Treatise of Human Nature* (1738).
6 Peter Singer, *The Expanding Circle* (New York: Farrar Straus and Giroux, 1981).
7 Lecky, quoted in ibid., p. 1.
8 Jonathan Kozol, *Rachel and Her Children* (New York: Crown, 1988).

9 Virginia Held, *Feminist Morality* (Chicago: Chicago University Press, 1993), p. 223; and Michael Slote, "The justice of caring", in Ellen Paul, Fred D. Miller and Jeffrey Paul (eds), *Virtue and Vice* (Cambrideg: Cambridge University Press, 1998), pp. 171–95.

10 Lorraine Code, *Epistemic Responsibility* (Hanover, NH: University Press of New England, 1987).

11 Edmund L. Pincoffs, *Quandaries and Virtues: Against Reductionism in Ethics* (Lawrence, KS, University Press of Kansas, 1986).

12 Charles Murray and Richard Herrnstein, *The Bell Curve* (New York: Free Press, 1994).

13 Robert Nozick, *Anarchy, State, and Utopia* (New York: Basic Books, 1974).

14 *Mencius on the Mind*, trans. Lau (New York: Penguin, 1970).

15 "Sentiment and sentimentality in practical ethics," *APA Proceedings* (March 26, 1982), p. 19.

16 Ibid., p. 42.

17 For an insightful treatment of the diminishing role of arguments in philosophy, see Larry Wright, *Practical Reasoning* (Fort Worth, TX: Harcourt Brace, 1989).

18 For my arguments here, see, in particular, my books *A Passion for Justice* (New York: Doubleday, 1976), and *The Passions* (New York: Hackett, 1993).

5

Teachers in an Age of Transition: Peter Singer and J. S. Mill

ROGER CRISP

Peter Singer's *How Are We to Live?* is one of the most powerful books of the twentieth century (Singer, 1995a). With characteristic coolness, Singer subjects to historically informed criticism modern obsessions with material goods, consumption and the self, urging that unless a substantial number of us change our ways, and begin to live in the light of impartial reason, the future for the earth is bleak indeed.

I read Singer's book shortly after studying John Stuart Mill's *On Liberty* (Mill, 1859), and was struck by the similarities between the two works and their authors. Both Mill and Singer are well known and important philosophers, directing their attention to what they see as the central moral issues of their day. Both use sophisticated rational argument, embedded in skilful philosophical rhetoric. Most obviously, both are act utilitarians, who recognize that that theory places the requirement on its adherents to seek to remedy the defects of the world. In this essay I shall reflect further upon the similarities and differences between Singer and Mill, in the hope of understanding each a little better.

Welfare

Singer's act utilitarianism is tentative, in the sense that he is open to arguments for moving beyond utilitarianism (Singer, 1979a, p. 13). But there is no evidence that he has found any such argument persuasive. Mill is also an act utilitarian: 'actions are right in proportion as they tend to promote happiness, wrong as they tend to produce the reverse of happiness' (Mill, 1861, 2.2).[1] By 'happiness', Mill meant whatever it is that makes life worth living for the being living that life – what we might call, more neutrally, 'welfare'. Welfare is peculiarly central to act utilitarian theories, since not only is it the only value recognized by such theories, but the rightness of actions depends on the maximization overall of the balance of welfare over 'unhappiness', or harm.

Mill's account of welfare is hedonist: 'pleasure, and freedom from pain, are the only things desirable as ends' (2.2). Notoriously, Mill introduced into his hedonism a distinction between 'quality' and 'quantity' of pleasure (2.3–10). Previous utilitarians, such as Bentham, had claimed that the value of any pleasure depended solely on its intensity and duration. Mill suggested that the nature of the pleasure itself was also important, indeed so important that it could sometimes entirely outweigh intensity and duration. The pleasure of, for example, appreciating an outstanding opera could be more valuable than any amount of the enjoyment to be had from drinking lemonade. What, in the nature of the experience of listening to opera, makes it so much more valuable than drinking lemonade? Mill offers little in the way of elucidation here, but suggests, for example, that 'higher' pleasures appeal to our sense of dignity in a way that lower pleasures do not.

So Mill's theory of welfare represents a move away from subjective forms of hedonism according to which all human activities are equal, in the sense that their only value can lie in the amount of homogeneous pleasure they produce, and that individuals themselves are the sole arbitrators on the value of their experiences. We find the same sort of retreat from subjectivism in Singer. In some of his writings, Singer can be found apparently supporting hedonism, at least as an account of the welfare of non-persons (see, for example, Singer, 1979b, pp. 146, 152; 1993, p. 132).[2] But what emerges as his core position is not hedonistic. In *Practical Ethics*, a central text, Singer discusses hedonism and its implications, but claims that the kind of utilitarianism supported by his argument for the principle of the equal consideration of interests is a form of preference utilitarianism (Singer, 1979a, p. 80). According to this view, welfare consists in the satisfaction of preferences. Like Mill, Singer retreats from simple hedonism because of its unacceptable implications, in Singer's case the implication being that there is no weighty difference between killing a person and killing a non-person.

But the notion of preference-satisfaction does not do all the work in Singer's account of welfare. He speaks also of the possibility of a life's having a meaning (Singer, 1979a, pp. 217–18; cf. 1983, pp. 145–6). A meaningful life requires that one be concerned with long-term goals that involve the interests of others. Psychopathy, and indeed egoism, are not routes to meaningfulness. For this reason, Singer is unwilling to accept Richard Taylor's claim that the life of Sisyphus would be imbued with meaning were he to desire to roll stones up hills (Singer, 1995a, p. 196). Rather, meaning comes from 'getting out into the world and doing something worthwhile' (Singer, 1995a, 207; cf. p. 211). This will involve participation in 'transcendent causes' (ibid., p. 218), such as football clubs or corporations, or indeed advancing the interests of sentient life as a whole, that require the participant to look beyond their own personal concerns.

Because of their initial commitment to forms of subjectivism in welfare – straightforward hedonism in the case of Mill, hedonism and then the preference theory of welfare in the case of Singer – the move towards objectivity in each writer causes a tension which is not easily resolved. Mill believes that certain activities, such as listening to opera, or helping someone in need, are incommensurably more valuable to those who engage in them than certain other, less valuable, activities. He attempts to explain this value by appeal to qualities such as dignity or nobility (2.9). But these qualities cannot be genuine good-making properties, since the only good-making property for a hedonist can be pleasurableness. We are left with several questions. First, how can an experience's being dignified or noble affect how pleasurable it is? Second, is not any value these qualities have independent of pleasurableness? And, finally, why did Mill not give up hedonism altogether, and accept that the ultimate explanation of the value of worthwhile activities is independent of pleasure?

The tension between hedonism and the explanation of the value of higher pleasures is mirrored in Singer in the dissonance between the preference theory and Singer's notion of meaningfulness. Singer's description of the lives of the psychopath, the egoist, the consumerist housewife and others strongly suggests that he believes these people to have lives which are less good for them than lives dedicated to transcendent causes. Mere desires, in the case of Sisyphus, however strong, could not make his life worth living. What he must do is rise above his own personal perspective and consider the desires or preferences of all. But just as Mill's attempt to force the value of higher pleasures into a hedonist framework raises certain questions about his account of welfare, so we are left wondering about Singer's attempt to explain meaningfulness by reference to the intersubjective standpoint. Imagine that Sisyphus lives in a world of stone-rollers, each of whom has a preference for stone-rolling. If his satisfying his own meaningless preferences is insufficient for his life to be worthwhile, it is not clear why his dedicating himself to satisfying impartially as many stone-rolling preferences overall should make any difference. That Singer thinks that it would make a difference is suggested by his allowing that commitment to the Nazi party can make one's life meaningful (Singer, 1995a, p. 218).

Pleasurableness is, without doubt, a good-making property. Pleasure, that is, is one of the things that makes our lives better for us. But so is the importance or significance of what we achieve. Committing oneself to a worthless activity, such as promoting the Nazi party, cannot imbue one's life with meaning – quite the opposite. The same is true of preference-satisfaction itself, whether one's own or that of others. Mere satisfaction of a person's preferences adds, in itself, no value to his or her life, since all depends on whether what is preferred is worthwhile. Just as Mill should have recognized the limits of pleasure, so Singer should accept that his view of meaningfulness offers a much better prospect as an account of welfare than any preference theory.

Self-interest and the Proof of Utilitarianism

It is, of course, entirely obvious that neither Mill nor Singer is an egoist: that is, someone who believes that all of an agent's reasons for performing some action rest entirely on how far that action advances the agent's self-interest. But at various points both philosophers recognize the plausible base of egoism in the rationality of self-concern or self-interest, and this causes several problems.

At the end of book 6 of his *System of Logic* (Mill 1843, pp. 949–50), Mill outlines what he calls the 'Art of Life'. This represents Mill's mapping of the whole territory of practical rationality. The Art of Life has three 'departments': 'Morality', 'Prudence' or 'Policy' and 'Aesthetics'. This explains why Mill implies in *Utilitarianism* 4.3 and 4.9 that morality constitutes just one sphere of human conduct among others.

The department of Prudence seems to allow for the self-standing rationality of self-interest. That is, I can have reasons to advance my own good which are independent of morality or other considerations. Then, of course, the sixty-four thousand dollar question arises: what happens when self-interest and morality conflict? Could it not be that Mill's utilitarianism will ultimately be tempered by considerations of self-interest, that rational agents will balance their own self-interest against the demands of morality and make an overall judgement about what they should do from some point of view independent of each individual department of the Art of Life?

Mill is unwilling to offer such a task of arbitration to practical judgement, insisting right at the start of *Utilitarianism* that there must be a single principle to govern practical reason. He would have seen the kind of pluralistic position sketched in the previous paragraph as a failure. So what is the ultimate principle of practical reason? It is utilitarianism: 'the promotion of happiness is the ultimate principle of Teleology' (Mill, 1843, p. 951). The only difference between this principle and that which governs the department of Morality is in their wording: they both require the same actions of us. In other words, though he appears to recognize the reasonableness of at least some degree of self-interest, in the

end Mill swamps self-interest in morality.[3] Our ultimate reasons are
entirely impartial.

Singer too has some respect for the claim that there is a degree of
rationality in self-interest. He accepts the Harean position that a person's
moral judgements obtain their content from *that person's* own preferences
(e.g. Singer, 1988, p. 154). The 'ultimate choice' we must make, according
to *How Are We to Live?*, is between the life of self-interest and the ethical
– that is, the utilitarian – life (Singer, 1995a, p. 4). And if I choose the life
of self-interest, that choice is not irrational; it is merely not ethical (ibid.,
p. 174). Further, unlike Mill, Singer refuses to swamp self-interest in
morality. If I choose to attach greater weight to my own interests, or
those of my family or friends,

> I do not show that I am incapable of grasping the point of view of the
> universe, but only that this perspective does not motivate me as strongly as
> my more personal perspective. If to be irrational is to make a mistake, there
> is no mistake here . . . Sidgwick's old 'immoral paradox', the clash between
> self-interest and generalized benevolence, has been softened, but it has not
> been dissolved. (ibid., p. 233)

The upshot of this is that Singer's position on the relation of self-interest
and morality is in one respect better than Mill's, but in another respect
worse. It is better in that it does not begin by recognizing the – at least
partial – authority of self-interest, only in the end to ignore it. This leaves
Mill with purely impartial act utilitarianism, which has the consequence,
for example, that if you have the chance so to arrange things that some
severe suffering is experienced by you or someone else, the fact that it is
you who will be experiencing that suffering makes absolutely no ultimate
difference to your choice, and to think that it does is to make a mistake.

Mill does, however, at least place morality itself in a strongly author-
itative position. If I believe that my own interests matter more than those
of others, then I am making what amounts to a mathematical mistake in
the calculation of the value of happiness (5.36n). Singer, though leaving
room for self-interest, allows neither for the rationality of morality nor for
the rationality of self-interest. Rationality for Singer is what is now,
probably misleadingly, described as Humean: there can be no criticism
of ultimate desires, and it is these that ground reasons for action. The
problem here is related to the problem I raised for desire-based accounts
of welfare in the previous section.

Justifying or grounding reasons for action must be such as to give point
to action. Since merely satisfying a desire does not in itself advance
welfare, there is no welfare-based reason to do so. And if there is no
welfare-based reason to do so it is hard to see what kind of reason could

ever be based on mere desire-satisfaction. What Singer needs to be able to tell egoists, or persons who are giving local interests a skewed weighting in their practical reason, is that they are making a mistake. Without that, from the philosophical point of view, he is giving us no reason to change our lives. Once authority has been granted to reason, Singer could go on to claim that there are reasons not only of self-interest, but also of morality, and that in our lives at present we are giving far too much weight to the former.

A problem related to these arises in certain of both Mill's and Singer's arguments for utilitarianism, i.e. those which move outwards from the rationality of self-interest to utilitarian morality. Mill's famous proof of utilitarianism in the fourth chapter of *Utilitarianism* is not so much a proof of utilitarianism as one of hedonistic egoism: 'No reason can be given why the general happiness is desirable, except that each person, so far as he believes it to be attainable, desires his own happiness' (4.3). What really does the work in Mill's argument for utilitarianism is the intuition concerning the impartial value of happiness, which I discussed above.

Singer likewise moves in an argumentative direction from partiality to impartiality (see, for example, Singer, 1976, p. 3; 1979a, p. 9; 1983, p. 100; 1995a, pp. 174, 233). It is taken as read that I will believe I have a reason to promote my own interests. But then I shall, as a social being, wish to justify my conduct to others.[4] This will switch on the 'escalator of reason', and I shall find that the 'separateness of persons' (see Rawls, 1971, p. 27) must be ignored:

> From an ethical point of view the fact that it is I who benefit from, say, a more equal distribution of income and you, say, who lose by it, is irrelevant. Ethics requires us to go beyond 'I' and 'you' to the universal law, the universalizable judgement, the standpoint of the impartial spectator or ideal observer, or whatever we choose to call it. (Singer, 1979a, p. 11)

There is a question for Singer here, similar to that raised above, about what kind of 'requirement' ethics could be making on us if it is not a requirement of reasonableness or rationality. But in addition he faces another question that must also face Mill. If self-interest is such a plausible launching point for an argument for utilitarianism, how is it that the ladder can be entirely kicked away? The pure impartiality of act utilitarianism is in strong tension with the partiality implicit in appeals to self-interest. And even if one accepts (as I am willing to do) that there is a great deal of power in the utilitarian vision of morality, it might still seem that the rational agent will not ignore the separateness of persons in their reasoning, but give it its proper weight.

Giving the separateness of persons its due will have implications for the rationality of morality as well as that of self-interest.[5] At the moral level, both Mill and Singer, as act utilitarians, agree that equal interests matter equally. But many will feel that equality should be seen as a principle governing the weight to be attached not only to disembodied interests, but to individuals themselves. Movements towards equality which benefit no one we might agree are worthless. But this does not rule out what Derek Parfit (1993, p. 57) calls the 'priority view', according to which we have some reason to give priority to the worse off. Imagine that you can bring about only one of the following outcomes:

Equality		Inequality	
Group 1	Group 2	Group 1	Group 2
50	50	90	20

Assume that each group contains the same number of people (say, a thousand). The numbers are meant roughly to represent welfare. So all those in *equality* will have equally good lives, while those in *inequality* will have lives either much better or much worse than the lives in *equality*. The utilitarian is committed to the view that *inequality* is preferable, but this seems to ignore the fact that welfare is distributed equally between people in *equality*. Fairness, it seems, requires us to give some priority to those who would otherwise be worse off, and speaks in favour of choosing *equality*.

This has particularly important implications regarding our attitude to the poor and to non-human animals, two groups about which Singer is particularly concerned. The implication of the priority view is that our reasons for taking the interests of members of these groups seriously are even weightier than pure utilitarianism might suggest. The poor and non-human animals have lives which are less good than ours, through no fault of their own, and this grounds a reason for attending to their interests which is itself grounded on the separateness of persons (or, rather, the separateness of individual moral patients).

Self-interest and the Ethical Life

In the previous section, we examined arguments for utilitarianism in Mill and Singer which move outwards from self-interest. But in both writers we find arguments that stay with self-interest, and attempt to bring morality within its bounds. These arguments, to the conclusion that ethics is ultimately in the self-interest of moral agents, have their roots in ancient ethics. But in putting them to use to justify utilitarianism rather than the more modest virtue ethics of ancient times Mill and Singer run into difficulties.

Mill's self-interest argument, in chapter 3 of *Utilitarianism*, has received relatively little attention compared to the proof of chapter 4. Chapter 3 is primarily concerned with 'sanctions': that is, with motivation. What, Mill asks, might motivate somone to act in accordance with utilitarianism? He divides sanctions into two classes: external, such as the hope of favour from others, and internal, the conscience. There is no reason, he plausibly suggests, why both of these sanctions might not be attached to utilitarianism, if moral education were organized to that end.

But we are left asking why we should so arrange moral education to inculcate utilitarian dispositions. At this point, one might expect Mill to refer the reader straight to the proof in chapter 4. But in fact, in what I find the two most moving paragraphs in Mill's writings, he first provides a self-interest argument. He claims that human beings are naturally social creatures, who want to be in accord with one another. We have a strong desire that our interests be in harmony with those of others, and a natural dislike of discord. There is here a clear link with the higher pleasures, discussed above, one class of which Mill sees as moral. The conclusion Mill is driving at is that moral education will enable individuals to realize that, as they become progressively more impartial in their dealings with the world, so their lives will become better for them. Impartiality and partiality will coincide.

Singer's arguments are strongly reminiscent of Mill's. We are naturally social creatures, and ethics develops as a practice among us to regulate our lives and enable the achievement of ends we hold in common (Singer, 1979a, p. 209). When disputes arise, justifications will be demanded, and these justifications are what switch on the escalator of reason and take us into the ethical domain, all the way to impartiality (Singer, 1979a, p. 9; 1983, pp. 93, 114; 1995a, p. 173). And we find that our own preferences will change as the justification advances: 'In the case of ethical reasoning, we begin to reason impartially in order to justify our conduct to others, and then discover that we prefer to act in accordance with the conclusions of impartial reasoning' (Singer, 1983, p. 142). The escalator of reason will take us all the way from self-interest to morality, but because ethics can imbue our lives with meaning – as discussed above – it seems that in fact the tension between self-interest and morality is merely apparent, at least in the case of those whose preferences for rational consistency in their lives change as they think ethically. Commitment to some transcendent cause can begin to give our lives meaning, but reflection on such a commitment, if it is in the least partial, is likely to undermine it: 'The more we reflect on our commitment to a football club, a corporation, or any sectional interest, the less point we are likely to see in it. In contrast, no amount of reflection will show a commitment to an ethical life to be trivial or pointless. This is probably the most important claim in this book' (Singer, 1995a, p. 218).

There are two problems for attempts such as those by Mill and Singer to close the gap between self-interest and act utilitarian morality. The first is again related to that discussed in the previous section, that it is not clear how an argument which gives authority to self-interest can then deny that authority any independence from morality later in the argument. According to act utilitarianism, the separateness of persons is rationally irrelevant. So rather than provide agents with arguments for advancing their own self-interest by living ethically, it would seem more appropriate for act utilitarians to persuade agents that their own self-interest just does not provide them with any independent reasons. Self-interest arguments for morality provide hostages to fortune, since they allow from the start independent weight to the rationality of self-interest, and thus provide those whose conception of welfare differs from that of the proponent of the argument with a justification for deviation from the requirements of impartiality.

The second problem for act utilitarian self-interest arguments is their sheer implausibility as accounts of self-interest. Mill and Singer may be right that we have some desire to justify ourselves to others, and that we would be happiest were our interests to align with those of others. But of course the disvalue to us of a conflict between our interests and those of others may in fact be outweighed by other goods. We also like eating delicate foods, drinking fine wine, travelling to exotic locations on business or for our holidays, buying expensive presents for our friends and families, living in pleasant surroundings and so on. And in this world these desires are strongly at odds with the interests of others, as Singer brings out so powerfully (see, for example, Singer, 1979a, pp. 158–81). Act utilitarianism – for every individual – is extremely demanding, and I know of no one who has gone further than merely begin to live up to it. Fully living up to it would drastically impoverish the life of any person who did so, unless he or she were already very badly off.

There is one way in which Singer's argument could be bolstered, though it would not be sufficient to close the gap between self-interest and morality. This would be to develop an account of the meaningfulness of life which was consistent with the structure of utilitarian moral theory itself. Utilitarians deny, at the moral level, the distinction between acts and omissions. All that matters is the welfare value of the history of the world brought about by the way one acts or lives. But in their theories of welfare, they tend not to deny this doctrine. It is clear that both Mill and Singer believe that a valuable life lies in *doing* certain things; in particular, doing certain things for others. Many will agree with Singer that people who do a lot for, say, the poor or for non-human animals have added meaning to their lives, and they may well have achieved this at some cost to their material well-being. But consider the following case:

> *Poor Paul and Rich Richard.* Paul is not well off, but he dedicates his life to relieving the suffering of those worse off than himself. He enjoys few luxuries. Richard is vastly wealthy. He enjoys many luxuries, and does almost nothing for the poor, except that he makes a donation each year to Oxfam. This donation is much more effective than Paul's work in relieving the suffering of the poor.

It is hard to accept that, since Richard achieves more for 'the grandest cause of all' (Singer, 1995a, p. 218), his life is more meaningful than Paul's. But that is surely what a consistent utilitarian should accept.[6] This would have the advantage not only of attaining consistency between theories of morality and of welfare, but of providing a further rhetorical strategy for Singer: if the rich can be persuaded that it is really this easy for them to give meaning to their lives, then they may be tempted to begin to surrender some of their resources. That they will do so is surely more likely than that they will consider leaving their fulfilling jobs and large houses and going to work for a voluntary organization in India (Singer, 1995a, p. 235).

Empiricism, Naturalism and Normativity

Mill's ethical theory emerges directly out of the empiricist and associationist tradition he inherited from his father and Bentham, who themselves owed most to Locke and Hume. Mill saw himself as a member of 'the inductive school of ethics', which bases its views on 'observation and experience', and is opposed to the intuitive school, according to which 'the principles of morals are evident *a priori*, requiring nothing to command assent, except that the meaning of the terms be understood' (1.3).

Mill's empiricism is what explains his attempt to base the argument for utilitarianism in chapter 4 of *Utilitarianism* on an appeal to one of our 'faculties', that of desire. In the most discussed paragraph he ever wrote (beginning, 'The only proof capable of being given that an object is visible...'), Mill suggests that, just as I can prove to you that an object is visible only by showing you that you see it, so I can prove to you that happiness is desirable only by showing you that you desire it.

The classical utilitarians believed that there was something particularly salient in pleasure and pain, which are undeniable phenomena of the human mind and have clear importance to how well or badly our lives go. Thus morality will be more securely based if founded on these salient features rather than on appeals to a mysterious 'moral sense' or set of self-evident axioms. Singer is soundly within this empiricist tradition. His criticism of Kantian ethics is almost Benthamic in its stringency: notions such as the 'the intrinsic dignity of the human individual', 'the intrinsic worth of all men', 'ends in themselves' are 'waffle' (Singer, 1976, p. 267) – 'waffle on stilts', even? And Singer feels the same attraction towards grounding ethics on salient phenomena. In 1994, he was asked what it is about utilitarianism that attracts him more than any other philosophical system:

> Its concreteness. It takes things we can observe and makes them the basic data of ethics. It tells you that the good things are people leading happy lives or lives in which they get what they want. Bad things involve people suffering, being in pain, or having their needs and wants frustrated . . . Suffering and pain are concrete. We know them in our own experience, we can observe them in other humans and animals. Other philosophical positions base themselves on something more mysterious: the idea of a natural right, for instance. People put forward all sorts of things as natural rights or basic rights or human rights or animal rights, and then someone says, 'No, I don't think X is a right.' And at that point the argument stops. That's why I think utilitarianism is on much firmer ground than other views. (Singer, 1994, part II)

There is another, related tendency in both Mill and Singer: to 'instrumentalize' morality. An instrumentalist about morality is someone who sees morality merely as a social phenomenon, which is not a source of reasons, or normativity, in its own right. Instrumentalization is a consequence of naturalism, which is itself a consequence of empiricism. Morality, for the empiricist, should be entirely explicable in the unmysterious terms of natural science. Instrumentalism in Mill emerges most clearly in *Utilitarianism* 5.14, a paragraph in which Mill explains morality as a system of social coercion which has emerged as a means to the general good. Telling people that what they are doing is wrong – blaming them – is analogous to coercing them legally into more desirable ways of living.

Instrumentalization in Singer also involves the notion of moral judgement as social coercion. Ethics emerged in a process of biological evolution, as a way of guiding practice towards values held in common in society (Singer, 1983, p. 4; 1979a, pp. 2, 209). Moral praise and blame is an attempt to change a person's behaviour. Conscientiousness – acting out of the motive of duty – is a highly useful motive, and therefore worth praising, but we should not be misled into thinking that duty itself provides some reason for action. If we think that, then we shall see morality as 'no more rational an end than any other allegedly self-justifying practice, like etiquette or the kind of religious faith that comes only to those who first set aside all sceptical doubts' (Singer, 1979a, p. 211; cf. 1995a, pp. 183–6).

Singer's comparison of morality to religion is interesting, and one might characterize the instrumentalist view by employing a version of the Euthyphro dilemma usually found in the philosophy of religion. Morality says that we have a reason to relieve the suffering of others. Now do we have that reason because morality says we do? Or does morality say we do because we have a reason independently of morality? The former, non-instrumentalist option turns morality into a self-justifying practice like etiquette, and also seems to miss the fact that the real source of our reason to relieve suffering lies in the badness of the suffering itself. On the latter view, morality can be seen as a means of enabling, persuading or coercing people to do what there is reason to do.

Utilitarianism itself, of course, also lies behind instrumentalization in both Mill and Singer. No action is beyond the bounds of the utilitarian principle, and thus the actions of morally praising and blaming must be assessable by the utilitarian criterion. The utilitarian principle requires us to praise and to blame when this would maximize utility; there is no room for an independent, non-instrumentalist view, according to which praise should be directed at right action, blame at wrong action. And with no independent notions of moral praise and blame, it is hard to see how there could be independent notions of right and wrong.

Moral instrumentalism is a highly plausible view. It is a view held by others than empiricist utilitarians, Nietzscheans being the most obvious. But the fact that moral instrumentalism does not lead to the collapse of demanding utilitarian theories such as those of Mill and Singer shows that there is no direct route from moral instrumentalism to less stringent views such as egoism, or nihilism. For instrumentalizing morality is not to instrumentalize reasons. Thus Mill's 'ultimate principle of Teleology', which is to be stated in non-moral terms, can serve as a non-instrumentalized principle stating our ultimate reason for action: to promote the greatest balance of happiness over unhappiness. As Singer says, 'The language of obligation seems to assume a special view of morality. Utilitarians, for example, might prefer to talk solely in terms of doing whatever has the best consquences, without reference to "obligations" arising from past undertakings or relationships' (Singer, 1973, p. 5).

So the instrumentalization of morality is consistent with the view that we have strongest reason always to maximize welfare overall. The problem for Mill and Singer arises when this position is based on the rather slimmed down conception of empiricism they favour. Let us accept that pains, pleasures and desires are salient and undeniable features of our conscious experience. Nothing follows from this. It is not, after all, a position that most Kantians are likely to deny. To think that a utilitarianism based on slimmed down empiricism has any special claim to being unmysterious is just an error. In other words, there are only two options in normative ethics: intuitionism – the view that we have reasons to act which do not present themselves as salient features of our conscious experience – or nihilism about ethical reasons. 'Observation and experience' do not provide us with the utilitarian principle; rather, any version of utilitarianism – including those of Mill, Hare and Singer, as well as Sidgwick – must be based on some claim or set of claims which is found plausible in the light of rational reflection. And rational reflection just is all that need be understood by 'intuition'. In other words, the debate between utilitarians and Kantians must take place after agreement on intuitionism. My own view is that Singer is more likely to be on the winning side in this debate, but it cannot be avoided by denigrating Kantian principles as nonsense. For if they are nonsense, so is utilitarianism.

Levels of Moral Discourse

Mill and Singer are empiricists. But they are also, in a sense, rationalists, insofar as they claim to base their philosophical rhetoric on appeal to reason rather than to emotion. We cannot, Mill says, prove claims about ultimate ends (1.5). But here he is clearly speaking of deduction, since he continues, 'There is a larger meaning of the word proof, in which this question is as amenable to it as any other of the disputed questions of philosophy. The subject is within the cognizance of the rational faculty'. Singer, likewise, believes that the application of moral principles is 'demanded by reason, not emotion' (Singer, 1976, p. x). His argument for utilitarianism is that reason will lead us to see that the separateness of persons is irrelevant in deciding what to do. Its 'escalator' will lead us to the principle of equal consideration of interests, to what Sidgwick called 'the point of view of the universe' (Singer, 1979a, pp. 9–13; 1983, pp. 108–11; 1995a, pp. 225–33).

We have already faced the problem empiricist naturalists find with reasons to act. Whether reasons to believe are also to reasons to act, or whether they come in a separate category, the same difficulties concerning normativity apply here as well. Singer claims that in a dispute, such as an ethical dispute, a demand for a reason is a demand for a justification that can be accepted by the whole group, and that such justifications are what constitute ethics (Singer, 1979a, p. 9; 1983, p. 93; 1995a, p. 173). But what is the force of 'can' here? Naturalism deals only in the currency of things that exist from the naturalistic standpoint, and I am assuming, on the basis of Singer's scepticism about moral objectivity, that he can be understood as a naturalist (see, for example, Singer, 1988, p. 151). Now it is an undeniable fact that people do believe things, and do accept justifications. But what we need is the notion that they *should* accept a certain justification, because it is the best justification available. That kind of normativity is what I take it Singer believes the principle of equal consideration of interests possesses, and the question remains of how such normativity fits into his more general world view.

A related problem for rationalists such as Mill and Singer is the non-rational nature of the world in which they find themselves. If we were all what Hare has called 'archangels', there would be no such problem (Hare, 1981, p. 44). We could be told the correct moral theory, and put it into practice. But we are far from this ideal state. Note first of all that there is no implication in utilitarianism that we have any (practical) reason to believe it, because it is true, perhaps, or because the arguments for it are particularly powerful. All that matters is whether our believing it has the best outcome in utilitarian terms. There is, then, no requirement on utilitarian philosophers that they seek to persuade others of their views. Indeed, as Sidgwick believed, there may be good utilitarian reasons for not spreading the utilitarian creed to those who might misuse it (Sidgwick, 1907, pp. 489–90).

This suggests that the kind of justification Singer has in mind when he is characterizing ethics as a process of justification should be some kind of ideal or hypothetical justification. For one should engage in real justification, according to utilitarianism, only when it maximizes welfare so to do. In that sense, Singer's views may have more in common with Scanlon's version of contractualism than his critique of the Rawlsian variety might suggest (Singer, 1979a, pp. 68–71; Scanlon, 1982). A vital question for any act utilitarian, then, will be when to engage in philosophical argument for utilitarianism, and when to refrain. In particular, the utilitarian must consider whether to employ non-utilitarian, common-sense morality. According to Mill, common-sense or 'customary' morality has its origins in slavery and oppression (Mill, 1869, chapter 1). Although it is now at least partly founded on an unconscious appreciation of the utilitarian principle (1.4), there are also other sources: prejudice, superstition, envy, arrogance, self-interest (Mill, 1859, chapter 1). And it is an implication of Singer's own position on, for example, the place of the notion of the sanctity of life in customary morality that he would probably agree with Mill's generally critical view of that morality (Singer, 1995b).

Whether at a certain time to use customary morality is an extremely difficult question for a utilitarian, one's success or otherwise becoming clearer only in the aftermath. Mill was probably right to relegate utilitarianism to a mere mention in *On Liberty*, though it has had the effect that even critics of the stature of Isaiah Berlin have understood him as giving up on utilitarianism in that central work (Berlin, 1959). Sometimes, however, it could be argued that Mill got it wrong, and not only in his writings but in his life itself. As both Mill and Singer recognize, customary morality has its own 'sanctions': it motivates us, concerns us, keeps us awake at night, even if we think it rests on an error. That is because we are not archangels, perhaps, but it is a fact none the less. So utilitarians have to be particularly careful not to allow customary morality to govern their own actions if this is not sanctioned by the utilitarian position. Consider, for example, Mill's staunch support of a working-class parliamentary candidate, whom he knew to be widely disliked, in 1868. Although Mill had not been quite as effective as he had hoped during his first term in Parliament, he had managed to prevent a serious riot in Hyde Park, and had put women's emancipation squarely on the political agenda. The support he lent to his fellow candidate, however, led to Mill's defeat by a Tory, who we can safely assume did less for the general good than Mill would have done.

Singer also shifts discourses frequently. I began with a comparison of *On Liberty* to *How Are We To Live?*, and it is striking how that latter work makes no explicit mention of utilitarianism, though it is clear from, for example, Singer's discussion of Hare that his position remains unchanged (Singer, 1995, pp. 174–5). Like Mill, with his 'secondary principles' (2.24), Singer is ready to accept impartial justifications of common-sense prohibitions, such as that on killing (Singer, 1995b, p. 196), or of partial practices, such as love of one's own children (Singer, 1995a, pp. 229–30). He is also ready to use customary morality himself. In part I of the interview from which I quoted Singer's description of basic rights as 'mysterious', Singer was asked about the Great Ape Project. He describes the aim of the project as follows: 'We're asking that the community of equals, as we call it, the community of beings for whom we accept the same ultimate, basic rights, should cease to be the species homo sapiens and become the great apes as a whole' (Singer, 1994, Part I).

Singer has also, it could be suggested (and this is only a suggestion, to illustrate a general point), allowed customary morality to guide his own life at times when it is doubtful whether act utilitarianism would sanction it. Understandably enough, he has been outraged at the attacks on him and his writings in Germany (Singer, 1992). There is no doubt that the arguments of his opponents are mistaken, and that the position of these opponents rests largely on emotion.[7] But this emotional stance against applied ethics is part of a wider opposition to something much more serious in modern Germany: the rise of neo-Nazism (Glock, 1994, p. 223). It is unlikely that Singer's opponents will be converted to his form of rationalism, and it might even be that their opposition to neo-Nazism would become less strongly motivated were they to change. The opponents of neo-Nazism have certainly chosen the wrong target in Singer, but his readiness to confront them has perhaps led to his taking some of the flak which would have been better directed elsewhere in German society. But, as in the case of Mill's second election campaign, Singer's actions in Germany should not be permitted to distract us from the greatness of his achievements. Both Mill and Singer have made large contributions to philosophy, but they have also, as 'teachers in an age of transition', done an incalculable amount of good.[8]

Notes

1 References to Mill's *Utilitarianism* will be by chapter and paragraph.
2 The evidence of these passages is, however, inconclusive. It may be that the best interpretation of Singer's suggestion that happiness – the balance of pleasure over pain – is what matters to non-persons is that it is the satisfaction of the *preference* for happiness in these beings which constitutes welfare. Michael Lockwood interprets Singer's (1979b) view as dualist, but suggests that Singer may have held a preference or desire theory by the time of Lockwood's writing his paper (Lockwood, 1979, p. 158). It is anyway not surprising that Singer should demonstrate some attraction for hedonism. Hedonism attracts systematizers in ethics – consider the Socrates of the *Protagoras*, or Bentham. From early days Singer has been influenced by one of the most systematic moral philosophers of the past two centuries, R. M. Hare. Although Hare is not a hedonist, there may be a story to be told here in the history of ideas.
3 It may be argued that Mill can insulate self-interest from practical reason by seeing it as providing initial epistemic reasons for belief rather than action, initial evidence which is then denied on reflection. There are two problems here. First, the beliefs in question will concern practical reason. Second, it is not so easy to deny the practical authority of self-interest.
4 In the move from concern with self to concern with justification to others, there are hints of a move towards contractualism (with which, of course, utilitarianism is not inconsistent).
5 When, of course, the separateness of persons is combined with some degree of concern for other persons.
6 Unless the value of the relevant project is judged according to how close it comes to living up to the requirements of morality itself. Here, Paul achieves more than Richard. This strategy, however, seems to introduce a non-welfarist notion of moral worth which might seem out of place in a utilitarian framework. According to a utilitarian, the value of working for Oxfam arises from the relief of suffering, not from merely living up to the requirements of morality. Singer himself sees no value in acting from duty: see pp. 95–6.
7 The response is not merely to Singer's conclusions. Like Singer, the intellectuals who supported the Nazi 'euthanasia' programme offered redefinitions of

personhood and drew analogies between non-humans and some humans (see Burleigh, 1994, p. 298); Burleigh's discussion is a good example of how even a British academic may read Singer's work as dangerous political rhetoric rather than as sympathetic and humane philosophical argument (see especially Burleigh, 1994, p. 342, n. 30).

8   The phrase is from A. V. Dicey's description of Mill; (Harvie, 1976, p. 40; cited in Thomas, 1985, p. 126). For comments on a previous draft of this essay I am grateful to Brad Hooker, Dale Jamieson and the delegates at the Oxford-Copenhagen Ethics Summit held at St Anne's College, Oxford, in October 1997.

References

Berlin, I. (1959) 'John Stuart Mill and the ends of life'. Reprinted in J. Gray and G. W. Smith (eds), *On Liberty in Focus*. London: Routledge (1991).

Burleigh, M. (1994) *Death and Deliverance: 'Euthanasia' in Germany 1900–1945*, Cambridge: Cambridge University Press.

Glock, H. (1994) 'The euthanasia debate in Germany – what's the fuss?', *Journal of Applied Philosophy*, 11, 213–24.

Hare, R. M. (1981) *Moral Thinking*. Oxford: Clarendon Press.

Harvie, C. (1976) *The Lights of Liberalism: University Liberals and the Challenge of Democracy 1860–86*. London: Allen Lane.

Lockwood, M. (1979) 'Killing and the preference for life', *Inquiry*, 22, 157–70.

Mill, J. S. (1843/1973) *A System of Logic Ratiocinative and Inductive. Collected Works of John Stuart Mill, volumes 7 and 8*, ed. J. Robson. Toronto: Toronto University Press.

Mill, J. S. (1859/1977) *On Liberty. Collected Works of John Stuart Mill, volume 18*. Toronto: Toronto University Press.

Mill, J. S. (1861/1969) *Utilitarianism. Collected Works of John Stuart Mill, volume 10*. Toronto: Toronto University Press.

Mill, J. S. (1869/1984) *The Subjection of Women. Collected Works of John Stuart Mill, volume 21*. Toronto: Toronto University Press.

Parfit, D. (1993) 'Does equality matter?' In J. Radcliffe Richards (ed.), *Philosophical Problems of Equality: Offprints Collection*. Milton Keynes: The Open University.

Rawls, J. (1971) *A Theory of Justice*. Cambridge, MA: Harvard University Press.

Scanlon, T. M. (1982) 'Utilitarianism and contractualism'. In A. Sen and B. Williams (eds), *Utilitarianism and Beyond*. Cambridge: Cambridge University Press.

Sidgwick, H. (1907) *The Methods of Ethics*, 7th edn. London: Macmillan.

Singer, P. (1973) *Democracy and Disobedience*. Oxford: Oxford University Press.

Singer, P. (1976) *Animal Liberation*. London: Jonathan Cape.

Singer, P. (1979a) *Practical Ethics*. Cambridge: Cambridge University Press.

Singer, P. (1979b) 'Killing humans and killing animals', *Inquiry*, 22, 145–56.

Singer, P. (1983) *The Expanding Circle*. Oxford: Oxford University Press.

Singer, P. (1988) 'Reasoning towards utilitarianism'. In N. Fotion and D. Seanor (eds), *Hare and Critics*. Oxford: Clarendon Press.

Singer, P. (1992) 'A German attack on applied ethics: a statement by Peter Singer', *Journal of Applied Philosophy*, 9, 85–91.

Singer, P. (1993) *Practical Ethics*, 2nd edn. Cambridge: Cambridge University Press.

Singer, P. (1994) 'A conversation with Peter Singer', *The Animals' Agenda*, part I, March/April; part II, May/June; http://envirolink.org/arrs/aa/features/singer1.html, http://envirolink.org/arrs/aa/features/singer2.html.

Singer, P. (1995a) *How Are We to Live?* Amherst, NY: Prometheus Books.

Singer, P. (1995b) *Rethinking Life and Death*. Oxford: Oxford University Press.

Thomas, W. (1985) *Mill*. Oxford: Oxford University Press.

6

What, if Anything, Renders
All Humans Morally Equal?

RICHARD J. ARNESON

All humans have an equal basic moral status. They possess the same fundamental rights, and the comparable interests of each person should count the same in calculations that determine social policy. Neither supposed racial differences, nor skin color, sex, sexual orientation, ethnicity, intelligence, or any other differences among humans negate their fundamental equal worth and dignity. These platitudes are virtually universally affirmed. A white supremacist racist or an admirer of Adolf Hitler who denies them is rightly regarded as beyond the pale of civilized dialogue.[1] However, a very simple line of argument developed by Peter Singer challenges our understanding of these platitudes and forces us to rethink the basis and nature of the moral equality of all humans.[2]

One might try to explain the equal moral status of humans by appeal to our common humanity – all humans are all equally human, after all. But mere species membership is not a sufficient basis for picking out some beings as entitled to greater moral consideration than other beings. If we were to encounter alien beings from another planet, something that looks like green slime but engages in complex behaviors, we would not be justified in failing to extend respectful treatment to the aliens merely on the ground that they belong to another species. If they proved to be like humans in morally relevant respects, then they should be treated the same as humans. Very roughly speaking, if the aliens showed a capacity for rational, autonomous agency, we would be required to include them within the scope of our moral principles. This thought experiment suggests a justification for our current practice of according all and only human beings a special moral status and relegating all non-human animals to a lower moral status. There is some intellectual capacity or set of intellectual capacities, call it X, that entitles the possessor of X to treatment as an equal member of the class of persons, to whom special moral principles apply. It turns out to be the case that all of the persons that we have encountered are humans, but for all we know, there may somewhere be non-human persons, who are not less worthy just in virtue of being non-human.

Several years ago Singer pointed out two flaws in this rationalization of our current practice of singling out all and only humans for specially favored treatment. One difficulty is that on any plausible construal of the cognitive capacities that constitute X, the test for discriminating persons from lower-grade beings, some humans will be found to possess less of the X capacities than some non-human animals. Jeremy Bentham noted this early in the nineteenth century: "But a full-grown horse or dog is beyond comparison a more rational, as well as a more conversable animal, than an infant of a day or a week or even a month old."[3]

Bentham's claim might arouse skeptical resistance because we have no clear idea of what would qualify as fair cross-species intelligence tests, but this sort of skepticism will not support a convincing response to Singer: if the intellectual abilities of humans and other animals are incommensurable, then the intellectual abilities of humans can only be judged different, not superior, and the claim that the unique cognitive abilities of humans entitle them to a moral standing above all other known animals collapses. The claim then is that the rough and ready means of comparison that underwrite the idea that humans are smarter than chimps, apes, cats, dogs, lizards, tarantulas, etc. also support the idea that some individual non-human animals are smarter than some individual humans.

The second difficulty that Singer finds in the defense of special moral privileges for humans based on the superior cognitive abilities of humans is to my mind more troubling. The difficulty is simply that the appeal to the superior mental capacities of humans to justify according them superior moral status tends to undermine the case for the equal moral status of all humans, because the mental capacities that figure in this appeal vary by degree, and just as humans tend to be more capable than bonobos and chimps and gorillas, some humans tend to be more capable than other humans. The differing intellectual capacities argument that purports to justify the fundamental moral inequality of animal species also would justify the denial of the fundamental moral equality of all humans.

Singer's own response to this threat of elitism is to assert that "all animals are equal." By this is meant that that any interest of one animal comparable in quality and magnitude to the interest of any other animal should count the same in determining what actions and policies we should adopt. Only beings that have conscious experiences can have interests. A stone or a plant experiences nothing, so can have no interests: nothing is good or bad for it. One has an interest in something if attaining the something would be conducive to one's good or welfare, and only beings who have experiences can fare better or worse.

What I call the "Singer Problem" arises if one accepts that the morally significant cognitive capacities that are relevant to the determination of the fundamental moral status of a being vary from individual to individual by degree. The problem is to specify a moral principle determining fundamental moral status that assigns a superior status to humans compared to other animals on the basis of the superior cognitive capacities of humans but also assigns all human persons an equal fundamental moral status regardless of their differing cognitive capacities. More broadly posed, the problem is to specify moral principles that yield intuitively satisfactory implications for the treatment of human individuals and other individual animals given that cognitive capacities differ across species and individuals.

Singer's "all animals are equal" resolution implies that the pain of a toothache experienced by a rat that is the same intensity as a similar toothache that is experienced by a human should count the same in social policy calculation. The moral policy-maker in Singer's view would be austerely impartial in handling conflicts of interest of this sort between rats and people. If we must choose between imposing a painful toothache on a human child or a slightly greater toothache on a rat child, presumably social policy should tilt in favor of the rat. This result flies in the face of ordinary common sense, but Singer regards ordinary common sense as a poor guide. Singer's position does allow that humans generally have complex and rich interests that stem from their complex and rich mental life, and since non-human animals have no correspondingly complex and rich interests, the principle of equal consideration for equal interests as Singer interprets it allows for legitimate preference for humans when human and animal interests are in conflict.[4] If a human child has an interest in learning arithmetic, and nothing so fine can be attained by a rat, then the high quality of this interest renders its satisfaction more valuable than the satisfaction of non-arithmetical rat interests.

Once again one might raise a worry about incommensurability. If a dog is killed, its rich future of smells and chases is cut short, and these interests may be more complex and rich than comparable smell and chase interests of humans. Moreover, how does one compare the complexity of very different interests – a dog's complex interest in sniffing versus a child's complex interest in solving jigsaw puzzles?

Notice that this gambit by Singer might be regarded as reintroducing the elitism that he had seemed to want to disavow. For after all it is just as true that a creative genius has richer and more complex interests than those of an ordinary average Joe as it is true that a human has richer and more complex interests than a baboon. If the principle of equality is interpreted as equal treatment for equal interests, then the beings with fancier interests should get fancier treatment. Equal consideration for equal interests may not match what we had in mind by the slogan "equal consideration for all humans." The degree to which utilitarianism becomes egalitarian or elitist in practice depends on the theory of value that is conjoined to it. At one extreme, if one holds that pleasure is the good and that pleasures differ only in magnitude, the interests in getting pleasure of all creatures capable of experiencing pleasure will count the same. At the opposite end of the scale, if one holds a theory of value according to which the very highest intellectual accomplishments greatly outweigh any lesser satisfactions in contributing to the goodness of some-one's life, then the interests of some persons will have very little weight, compared to the interests of other persons, in determining what should be done. (Both one's capacity to have an interest of a given type and one's capacities that enable one to satisfy this type of interest will affect the utilitarian calculation that determines whether or not one should be helped to satisfy the interest.)

Notice that one could concoct a version of utilitarianism that would reject the norm of equal consideration for equal interests. One might hold that if a being possesses some threshold level of cognitive ability, that being has enhanced moral status, and the satisfaction of its interests counts for more than the satisfaction of the interests of lesser beings that are the same in quantity and quality. Call this view Threshold Utilitarian-ism. It would hold that other things equal, obtaining the pleasure of sucking a piece of candy for a small human child is morally more valuable, a matter of greater moral urgency, than obtaining an in all respects essentially similar pleasure for a monkey or rat. Threshold Utilitarianism does better than utilitarianism at fitting our common-sense moral judg-ments balancing the interests of humans against the interests of non-humans of lesser cognitive abilities, but runs against the Singer Problem.

What I am calling the Singer Problem applies to many different moral theories, though not to all. Singer makes the generality of the problem clear in his own writings on it. For example, a Kantian morality holds that all rational agents must always be treated not merely as means, but as ends in themselves. Possession of the capacity for rational agency confers an equal fundamental status on all persons as opposed to all other creatures, who lack rational agency. But if the capacity for rational agency is a capacity that varies continuously in magnitude, one wonders how one picks out some threshold level of the capacity such that varia-tions in rational agency capacity above the threshold do not generate corresponding differences in fundamental moral status. On the face of it, the Kantian account of rational agency is like an account of moral status that identifies height as the characteristic of living beings that determines their moral status, proclaims that tall is better than short, and identifies beings over six feet tall as the first-class citizens of the moral universe. The story so far is not incoherent, but one needs an answer to this worry: if being taller is better, and tallness determines moral status, why should not being taller than six feet confer a superior moral status over those who are just barely six feet tall?

A similar worry attaches to a Lockean view according to which morality commands respect for individual human rights that express the idea that each person should be left free to do as she chooses with whatever she legitimately owns as long as she does not thereby harm others in certain specified ways. The Lockean rights attach only to beings that possess certain traits. Robert Nozick identifies these as rationality, free will, moral agency, and "the ability to regulate and guide its life in accordance with some overall conception it chooses to accept."[5] By exercising this ability a being gives meaning to its life, and only beings with this ability can have meaningful life, Nozick adds. Again, the ability to pick a conception of value and guide one's life by it evidently admits of degrees, and no reason has been offered so far to suggest that the stringency of the protection afforded by rights should not vary with the degree to which one possesses the capacities on which rights are based.

An example of a moral doctrine that does not face the Singer Problem is egoistic contractarianism, as developed by David Gauthier.[6] According to egoistic contractarianism, moral constraints are constraints on unimpeded utility-maximizing behavior that it is rational to agree to, and to dispose oneself to conform to, because one's expected utility is thereby increased. This doctrine need not be encumbered by any principle of treating all humans or all persons according to the same principles which accord all a fundamentally equal moral status. The constraints it is rational for the egoistic contractarian to agree to will very likely differentiate among beings according to their individual capabilities, given their circumstances, of imposing costs and conferring benefits on others. Beings that have little or no capacity to make credible significant threats and offers will receive little or no consideration in a contractarian morality. Some may regard egoistic contractarianism's avoidance of the Singer Problem as a sleek advantage of this theory. Others may see this doctrine as jettisoning baggage that any adequate moral theory would have to carry successfully.

In this connection we might roughly distinguish earned and unearned worth. Moral theories that assert the fundamental moral equality of all human persons need not deny that in various ways some people act so as to be more deserving, more creditable, than others. For example, if all individuals have Lockean rights, individuals can forfeit their rights by bad conduct. Some human lives as actually lived are more worthy than others.

That individuals vary in their earned worth is compatible with asserting that all have equal unearned worth in virtue of their status as human persons. But since not all sentient beings have equal inherent unearned worth, the trick is to specify the characteristics that qualify a being for membership in the class of equally worthy persons.

An attractive response to Singer's puzzle would be to specify a threshold feature that determines moral status, in a way that does not vary significantly by degree, at least once the threshold is passed. The specified feature would have to be such that having more rather then less of it plausibly fixes a significant difference in moral status. The specified threshold of the feature would have to be non-arbitrary, and such that it is plausible to suppose that having more or less of the feature above this threshold should not affect one's basic moral status.

Another strategy of response would be to specify a moral feature that is normatively significant, separates the beings we want to think of as persons from non-persons, and does not vary by degree: either one has the feature or one does not. If we succeeded in locating such a feature, we would have dissolved the Singer Problem. If the basis for according beings the enhanced moral status of persons (rights-bearers) is X, and X does not vary by degree, then everyone who has X at all possesses it to the same extent, so there is no evident ground for denying an equal fundamental moral status to all X possessors.

A Range Property as the Basis of Equality

John Rawls pursues the first, threshold type of strategy in his *A Theory of Justice*.[7] He proposes that possessing moral personality above a threshold level renders one entitled to the equal basic moral rights of persons. The features constitutive of moral personality are a capacity for a conception of the good and for a sense of justice.

The features of moral personality that Rawls singles out are surely relevant to the moral status of personhood. One might quibble with their details, but they surely are on the right track, in the neighborhood of the solution. The difficulty with Rawls's proposal regarding the basis of equality is that no plausible reason is given for regarding the possession of more or less of the Rawls features once one is above the threshold as irrelevant to the determination of one's moral status. For simplicity, consider just the sense of justice. This is a steady disposition to conform one's conduct to what one takes to be basic norms of fairness, along with some ability reasonably to identify these fairness norms. But the disposition to be fair obviously admits of degrees; one can be more or less committed to behaving as one thinks fair. And the ability to deliberate about candidate norms of fairness and select the best of them also varies by degree. Offhand, the task of specifying some threshold level of these abilities such that further variations in the abilities above the thresholds should have no bearing on moral status looks hopeless. A further clue that something is amiss is that Rawls makes no attempt to specify the relevant threshold. Rawls stipulates that these features of moral personality are range properties. Once one is above the threshold, one is in the range, and no one, whatever his exact levels of the moral personality capacities, is in the range to a greater extent than anyone else with above-threshold levels. But it is not at all clear where one might nonarbitrarily place this threshold such that all beings above it are persons and all beings below are non-persons.

It might be thought problematic that according to a range view, it matters immensely whether one is just above or just below the threshold that marks the line separating persons and non-persons. This problem arises from conceiving of the threshold line as very thin, so a tiny difference in possession of a capacity makes a disproportionately huge difference to one's moral status. But one need not conceive the threshold line as very thin. The line separating persons and non-persons might be very thick, such that below the lower boundary of the line it is clear that beings in this range are not persons and above the upper boundary of the line it is clear that beings in this range do qualify as persons. Beings with rational capacities that fall in the gray area between the upper and lower boundaries are of indeterminate status. My worries then are that even if the line separating persons and non-persons is taken to be thick, it seems arbitrary where exactly the line is placed, and that above-threshold differences are stipulated not to affect fundamental moral status.

Second-order Volitions and Equality

Harry G. Frankfurt has proposed that the feature that distinguishes persons from other beings is that persons have second-order volitions. That is to say, persons have desires about their own actual or possible desires to act and be various ways, and some of these second-order desires are volitions: one desires that one's second-order desire become one's effective will and give rise to action proceeding from the associated first-order desire. Persons are distinguished from a lower grade of agents called "wantons." Frankfurt offers this definition: a wanton is an agent that has first-order desires and possibly second-order desires but lacks second-order volitions.

A being either has second-order volitions or not, and there does not seem to be an associated continuously varying property that underlies the presence or absence of second-order volition, which would threaten to fragment the uniform status of person into a hierarchy of many degrees corresponding to variations in this property. To this extent Frankfurt's proposal provides an attractive way of characterizing a uniform class of full moral agents possessing equal fundamental moral rights. This initial attraction fades on closer examination. The reason is that having or lacking second-order volitions does not seem to be a sufficiently morally significant matter to be a plausible basis for fixing moral status.

Frankfurt asserts that a being capable of second-order volitions must have sophisticated perceptual and reasoning capacities. He supposes that a being with second-order volitions is a being that reflects about the kind of being it wants to be and the kind of motivations it wants to have and to determine its actions. Such a being cares about the quality of its desires and motives. It has a certain psychological depth.

But it is not clear that the requirement that a being have some second-order volition really carries this load that Frankfurt associates with it. A creature might just have a desire about one of its desires, a bare desire that just occurs and does not emerge from any process of reasoning or evaluation. Perhaps when the animal is in heat, and feels sexual craving, it feels a wave of revulsion against its ordinary desires to graze and eat. This revulsion might issue in a passing momentary will that these ordinary desires should cease. This wrinkle of the agent's volition need not have any further consequences: it neither proceeds from reasoning, analysis, reflection, nor contemplation; nor does it give rise to any of these processes. Suppose there were two subspecies of deer that were essentially alike except that one type experiences, and the other lacks, the second-order volition just described. Call the former "Frankfurt deer." It would not be plausible to suppose that the difference between Frankfurt deer and its near relatives corresponds to a fundamental difference in moral status that would warrant conferring the honorific label "persons" on the beings on one side of the line.

A similar point holds in the other direction. We can imagine a race of creatures, perhaps beings evolved on some distant planet, who have complex perceptual and reasoning powers which they exercise to determine the good and the true, and who almost always act according to their conception of these best reasons that point to a preferred course of action. Since the cognitive and affective features of these agents tend to be in harmony, they aren't given to second-order reflection about their desires, and they altogether lack second-order volitions. Although we would want to be told more about such beings before we could confidently characterize them, as the story has gone so far, I would suppose that the agents' cognitive abilities and their ability to conform their actions to their considered idea as to what is best incline us to count them as full moral agents entitled to the full moral rights associated with personhood. Having second-order volitions does not then render one a person and lacking second-order volitions does not render one a non-person.

This last claim is open to challenge. One might hold that the ability to engage in moral reasoning as to whether it is appropriate to act on a given desire or just to engage in any reasoning concerning the quality of one's desires presupposes higher-order reflection and volition. Having second-order volitions would then be necessary though not sufficient for personhood. But this challenge, even if correct, still leaves the door closed on the possibility that the normative basis of the moral equality of persons could be their shared possession and exercise of the capacity for second-order volitions.

According to Frankfurt, what is crucial to personhood is having second-order volitions, not merely having the capacity for second-order volitions. Frankfurt's category of wantons would encompass both agents that are incapable of forming second-order volitions and agents that have this capacity and fail to exercise it. The wanton does not care what sort of desire motivates his actions; perhaps he cannot care. The question arises whether exercising a capacity that pertains to rational autonomy should be regarded as placing one in a significantly higher status than beings that have but do not exercise the capacity. If exercise does matter in this way, does more exercise of a capacity enhance one's status more than a lesser degree of exercise? The same questions arise if perceiving reasons and setting oneself to act as they dictate is thought to be the more pertinent capacity.

Notice that once the issue is raised, it is far from obvious that how one exercises a capacity should be deemed irrelevant to the determination of the fundamental moral status that is invoked when it is asserted that humans have a privileged place in the moral community. Suppose that biologists of the next century were to discover that a species of animal, a type of mouse, by some evolutionary accident was endowed with a dual nature. It has on one side of its brain unused rational abilities comparable to what humans have and on the other side a set of mouse-like cognitive capacities along with an iron disposition to desire only to exercise the capacities that issue in familiar rodent behavior. It is not clear that we should hold that the never used capacities would propel this creature to a moral status at the same level as humans enjoy.

Equality, Misfortune, and the Priority View

A recent essay by Jeff McMahan illustrates the difficulty of finding a stable resolution of the Singer Problem.[8] McMahan is considering the application to severely cognitively disabled individuals of moral principles that call for compensation for bad luck in the set of genetic traits that individuals inherit. An individual may find herself disadvantaged in life by unfortunate formative circumstances, which might include an unlucky genetic inheritance of traits that develop into talents and an unlucky formation by early childhood socialization experiences. This individual starts adult life with poor prospects for well-being that have befallen her through no fault of her own. Several types of principles of distributive justice will tend to favor redistribution of resources in these circumstances to offset the disadvantaged individual's initial unchosen circumstances. McMahan does not offer a characterization of the class of principles of justice that concerns him. He mentions the principle that Derek Parfit calls the Priority View, which holds that "benefiting people matters more the worse off these people are." According to the Priority View, the moral value of obtaining a small increase in well-being for a person is greater, the lower the person's well-being level prior to receipt of this benefit.

The Priority View implies that if we can give an ice cream cone to either of two persons who would enjoy it equally, and one of the persons is far worse off than the other, then we should give the benefit to this worse-off person. But the Priority View also would seem to imply that if someone is very severely cognitively impaired, and so is cut off from most sources of significant well-being, then even if we have already expended a lot of resources to alleviate the plight of this unfortunate person, he will remain at a very low level of well-being, far below what an ordinary person can expect, so the Priority View would seem to continue to attach a much higher moral value to achieving further gains in well-being to this severely cognitively impaired person than to achieving gains for the more fortunate. This implication McMahan wishes to resist.

McMahan argues that the appropriate baseline for determining whether a given person is unfortunate or not is the shortfall between the person's actual well-being and her maximum potential well-being, provided that the person is not on the way toward fulfilling her potential but is failing to realize it. Also, there is a double aspect to the idea of potential well-being. We distinguish a capacity for well-being that the person actually develops at some time in her life and potential capacity that the person has not developed yet, but might. I have a capacity to walk if I can walk now; I have a potential to walk if I could undertake a course of action or undergo an education that would develop a latent capacity I now have so that at some time in the future I could walk at that time if I chose to do so. The double aspect affects McMahan's proposal in this way: in measuring an individual's shortfall, we should give more weight to a loss of capacity than to a loss of mere potential.

According to McMahan, the scope of egalitarian theories of justice should be set so that they are limited to compensating for misfortune and whether people are suffering misfortune is not determined merely by whether or not their well-being level is low but by the extent of the shortfall between their actual well-being and their potential and capacity for well-being. This innovation yields the result, welcome to McMahan, that a person whose genetic inheritance renders him severely cognitively impaired, and who has only a small potential for well-being, is not suffering misfortune if he leads a life that is low in well-being but captures a high proportion of his potential. McMahan asks us to imagine that cognitively blessed Bertrand Russell, at the height of his powers, is suddenly brought low by accident or disease, can function only at the level of a severely retarded person, and from now on has correspondingly low prospects of well-being. Compare Russell's plight to the condition of (a) a congenitally severely retarded person and (b) a person who had normal mental powers at birth but suffered an incapacitating injury before his mental powers developed. Both the (a) and (b) individuals are able to function cognitively about as well as stricken Russell and have well-being prospects that are the same as Russell's current reduced pro-spects. McMahan aims to elicit agreement that Russell's condition con-stitutes a worse misfortune than the condition of either of the other two individuals, because he is so badly off now as compared to his potential and former capacity for well-being. For the same reason we are asked to judge that the (a) individual, impaired from conception, is in a less unfortunate condition than the (b) individual, who has lost so much of his potential.

McMahan supports the idea that whether one is unfortunate depends on the extent of the gaps between one's actual well-being and one's potential and capacity for well-being by noting that we would find it counterintuitive to suppose that egalitarian theories of justice would hold that an animal of very limited cognitive powers is unfortunate in virtue of the low prospect of well-being to which its genetic endowment consigns it. A rhinoceros lacks the potential to enjoy the opera, read the novels of Tolstoy, or fall in love in the way that humans do. These lacks do not render the rhinoceros unfortunate. Why not? McMahan's answer is that "Whether a being is well or badly off depends on how its level of well-being compares to the range of well-being made possible by the highest cognitive and emotional capacities that it has actually achieved or that it natively had the capacity to achieve. Call this the *Native Potential Account* of fortune." McMahan adds the further thought that the individuals whose treatment is regulated by principles of justice are persons, beings who have certain properties and capacities that are suffi-cient for moral agency. This restriction on the scope of principles of justice excludes non-human animals (except perhaps for the great apes) and also excludes humans whose severe cognitive impairments preclude even minimal agency.

We can see that McMahan is wrestling with the Singer Problem. He seeks a principled way to reconcile two different effects that differences in natural endowment may have on the treatment that an individual is owed under egalitarian principles of justice. On the one hand, other things being equal, the worse one's natural endowment, the more compensation one is owed according to principles that require that justice should to some extent redress the accidents of good and bad luck that give people vastly different prospects of well-being in ways that are beyond their power to control. On the other hand, the worse the potential for cognitive ability that one's natural endowment fixes, the less one possesses of the traits that are relevant to personhood and that determine whether one should be included within the scope of principles of justice at all. McMahan also wants to find a principled way to determine the moral status of individuals that does not rely merely on species membership but is instead responsive to traits of the very individual whose status we are considering.

The defects in McMahan's proposal provide testimony to the intractability of the Singer Problem. I have no quarrel with the idea that beings below a threshold of certain cognitive capacities and properties (leave aside for now just what these are) fall outside the scope of principles of justice that regulate relationships among full persons. But the Native Potential Account goes astray in holding that whether one is unfortunate and hence owed compensation according to egalitarian justice depends not merely on one's prospects for well-being but also on one's potential for well-being as established by one's native intellectual and emotional endowments. This proposal gives people a variable right to well-being depending on their native intelligence and charm. But the fundamental idea of the class of egalitarian theories of justice that McMahan claims to accept is that the inheritance of traits is like the social arrangements that determine inheritance of wealth and the distribution of favorable childhood socialization experiences. Both genetic and social inheritance distribute prospects for human well-being in ways that are arbitrary from the moral point of view. More specifically, the results of genetic and social inheritance cannot be rationalized by any notions of deservingness. One cannot take credit or claim to be praiseworthy for one's genes or for the quality of early childhood care one received from parents or guardians. Nor can one claim to deserve any enhanced prospects of well-being that these confer. So in principle there is no bar to redistribution engineered by society to offset the initial distribution of favorable prospects to render it more fair.

In the light of this beam of thought, consider again McMahan's Native Potential Account. Let's simplify by imagining that social inheritance just amounts to inheritance of initial bank account wealth, and genetic inheritance just amounts to one's capacity for intelligence and charm. Now consider three persons on the brink of adulthood in a society regulated by egalitarian justice as interpreted by McMahan. One is poor and has little capacity for intelligence or charm. One is poor, intelligent, and charming. A third is rich, and was initially blessed with extraordinary potential for intelligence and charm, which have blossomed to fruition in the course of very favorable childhood experiences. Unfortunately, person number three recently suffered a bad accident through no fault of her own, and now her potential charm and intelligence have been reduced to ordinary proportions. Person number one now has a low expectation of well-being, and persons two and three have identical high expectations of well-being. But three, though she can look forward to a good life, suffers by far the greatest shortfall between her current well-being expectation and the highest well-being that she could have achieved given the highest intellectual and emotional capacities that she achieved or natively had the potential to achieve. McMahan's principle for identifying society's truly disadvantaged persons, those whose misfortune is greatest, picks out person three as the most unfortunate member of society. Egalitarian justice will then call for redistribution to remedy misfortune, which in this three-person society will require taxing persons one and two to enhance the well-being prospects of person three. But this result is crazy, or at least highly counterintuitive. McMahan's proposal amounts to giving individuals rights to well-being that are greater, other things being equal, the greater the shortfall between the goodness of the life they could have lived given the potential of their genetic inheritance and the goodness of the life they can expect now given intervening vicissitudes that have curtailed or enhanced this potential. But then it becomes a requirement of justice that since my native potential for well-being was higher than yours, other things being equal, I should have more well-being than you, and if my expectation of well-being falls as low as yours in a way that was beyond anyone's power to control, then there is at least a prima facie justice case for compensating me to boost my well-being expectation.

McMahan's Native Potential Account is intended to apply just to human persons and to restrict the scope of Prioritarian justice: that is, to regulate the terms of cooperation among human persons. Ironically, the Native Potential Account is most satisfactory if we construe Prioritarianism as a more general fundamental principle that regulates relations among animals, humans included. The Native Potential Account applied generally would have it that the bonobo, born (let's assume) with lesser capacity for the good than a normal human, is not suffering misfortune, compared to the human, because the shortfall between capacity and expected benefit is not greater for the bonobo than for the human. There the account yields a plausible result. But applied on its home ground, to the issue of how to identify degree of misfortune among humans, the Native Potential Account yields weirdly elitist verdicts such as those I have criticized.

One issue that unsettles our responses to McMahan's cases is where to set the line that separates persons from non-persons. If we imagine Prioritarianism applied to extremely cognitively impaired humans, such as those in advanced stages of dementia or the equivalent, the idea that other things being equal, attaining a unit of benefit for such an extremely impaired human has far more moral value than attaining a comparable benefit for someone else looks far-fetched. But what may be tugging at our intuition here is that we are in fact imagining the impaired human as falling below the line separating persons and non-persons. If we confine attention to cases of conflict of interest among individuals all of whom are clearly above the line, the practical implications of Prioritarianism may not be so counterintuitive as McMahan supposes, and may not be counterintuitive at all. Notice that a cognitively impaired or mentally ill person often is a poor transformer of resources into well-being. A unit of some resource that might be applied to increase the well-being of an impaired or a nonimpaired persons often tends to produce more well-being if applied to the nonimpaired. On the other hand, insofar as there is overlap between the class of impaired persons and the class of persons who are very low in expected well-being over the course of their lives, Prioritarianism, favoring the worse off, will hold that it is morally more valuable, other things being equal, to gain a one-unit increase in well-being for a person, the lower the person's lifetime well-being prospects prior to the receipt of the benefit. Keeping in mind that the two effects that impairment can have (reducing one's capacity to benefit and increasing the moral value of the benefits one gets) may offset one another, and that both need to be considered independently, the supposed implausibility of the Prioritarian View if it is applied without qualification according to the Native Potential Account disappears. Suppose that a schizophrenic person or a mentally retarded person is able to benefit at a reasonable rate from some resource we might confer on her. She has low well-being prospects, but a vacation to Bermuda would significantly raise her well-being. I find it plausible to say that if we are choosing between gaining this benefit for a badly off person or for an already advantaged person, it is morally a matter of greater urgency to help the badly off person. The fact that the badly off person is impaired from birth by mental illness or retardation, hence her shortfall in expected benefits is not large, does not at all diminish the moral value of securing aid for that person.

Holding fast to the assumption that all human persons have the same fundamental moral status, so that having less cognitive capacity does not make my well-being increments morally less valuable than the comparable increments that accrue to others with greater cognitive capacity, I do not find McMahan's rejection of Prioritarianism to be plausible. For whatever it is worth, I also find plausible the implications of Prioritarianism applied to choices of whom to benefit when we are choosing among members of the same animal species. Other things being equal, it is morally more valuable to secure a one unit gain in well-being for a badly off bonobo than to secure an identical gain in well-being for a bonobo whose expected well-being over the course of her life is higher. Prioritarianism starts to yield implausible implications for conduct if we apply it across the divide separating persons and non-persons. If we can benefit either a normal person or a human who is so impaired as to fall below the threshold of personhood, the claim that it is morally a matter of greater urgency to benefit the being who is worse off rings false. The same point holds if the choice of whom to benefit includes persons and non-person animals whose well-being prospects are low because their capacity for well-being is low. But this is not a difficulty that the Native Potential Account as developed by McMahan is designed to solve. The underlying, perhaps intractable, puzzlement that motivates McMahan to embrace the Native Potential Account in fact leads straight to the Singer Problem and could only be resolved by a satisfactory resolution of it.

The difficulties that McMahan's position faces indicate an important respect in which the Prioritarian family of moral principles resembles Kantian and Lockean views and differs from utilitarianism. According to the Priority View, something matters other than the aggregate sum of utility: namely, how utility is distributed across persons. According to Singer's utilitarianism, one can in principle determine which of the available acts or policies is best to choose without knowing anything about the number or identities of the beings that are affected. One just needs to know the quality of each interest that is satisfied, hence the quality of the satisfaction, and the total sum of satisfactions. According to the Priority View, the moral value of a utility gain depends on the prior utility level of the person who gets it, with moral value increasing as the prior utility level of the person decreases. On this view, the distribution of utility matters, but the only feature of a person that affects the moral value of his gains and losses is his prior utility level. All persons are equal on this conception.

Utilitarianism can dispense with a theory of human equality; the Priority View cannot. In this respect it differs significantly from utilitarianism and is not, perhaps contrary to appearances, merely a slightly amended version of it.

Kant and Equality

Some readers of this essay will have become impatient by now, because they believe that the problem that perplexes me has been definitively solved by Immanuel Kant. It is certainly true that Kant held strong opinions on this matter. In an often-quoted passage, he reports a personal conversion from elitism:

> I am myself a researcher by inclination. I feel the whole thirst for knowledge and the eager unrest to move further on into it, also satisfaction with each acquisition. There was a time when I thought this alone could constitute the honor of humanity and I despised the know-nothing rabble. Rousseau set me straight. This delusory superiority vanishes, I learn to honor men, and I would find myself more useless than a common labourer if I did not believe this observation could give everyone a value which restores the rights of humanity.[9]

What Kant learned from Rousseau was the proposition that the basis of human equality is the dignity that each human person possesses in virtue of the capacity for autonomy (moral freedom). This moral freedom has two aspects, the capacity to set ends for oneself according to one's conception of what is good, and the capacity to regulate one's choice of ends and of actions to achieve one's ends by one's conception of what morality requires. According to Kant's psychology, brute animals are determined to act as instinct inclines them, but a rational being has the power to interrogate the inclinations it feels, to raise the question what it is reasonable to do in given circumstances, and to choose to do what reason suggests even against all inclinations.

The question arises whether Kant's psychology is correct, or remotely close to correct. Perhaps something like the conflict between conscience and inclination is experienced by social animals other than humans. Perhaps the freedom that Kant imputes to humans on metaphysical grounds can be shown to be either empirically non-existent or illusory. For our purposes we can set these questions aside and simply presume that the human psychological complexity envisaged by Kant does describe a capacity we possess, whether or not it is shared with other animals. My question is whether Kant's characterization, if it was correct, would have the normative implications he draws from it.

It might seem that the Kantian picture helps to show how moral freedom is a range concept, which does not significantly admit of degrees. If one has the capacity to set an end for oneself, one does not possess this freedom to a lesser extent just because one cannot set fancy ends, or because other persons can set fancier ends. If one has the power to regulate choice of ends by one's sense of what is morally right, one does not possess this freedom to a lesser extent because one cannot understand sophisticated moral considerations, or because other persons can understand more sophisticated moral considerations. Moreover, one might hold that it is having or lacking the freedom which is important, not having or lacking the capacity to exercise the freedom in fancy ways.[10]

But the old worries lurk just around the corner.

The Kantian view is that there are indeed capacities that are crucial for the ascription of fundamental moral status that do not vary in degree. One either has the capacity or one does not, and that's that. If the crucial capacities have this character, then the problem of how to draw a non-arbitrary line on a continuum and hold all beings on one side of the line full persons and all beings on the other side of the line lesser beings does not arise. The line separating persons and non-persons will be non-arbitrary, and there will be no basis for further differentiation of moral status. One is either a person or not, and all persons are equal. Consider the capacity to set an end, to choose a goal and decide on an action to achieve it. One might suppose that all humans have this capacity except for the permanently comatose and the anencephalic. So all humans are entitled to a fundamental equal moral status.

This view is strengthened by noting that there are other capacities that do admit of degrees that interact with the non-degree capacities. Individuals who equally have the capacity to set an end may well differ in the quality of their end-setting performances. Some are able to set ends more reasonably than others. But these differences in performance do not gainsay the fundamental equal capacity. It is just that having a high or low level of associated capacities enables or impedes successful performance. So the fact that individuals differ in their abilities to do arithmetic and more complex mathematical operations that affect their ability to make rational choices should have no tendency to obscure the more basic and morally status-conferring equality in the capacity of each person to make choices.

In response: first of all, if several of these non-degree capacities were relevant to moral status, one must possess all to be at the top status, and some individuals possess more and others fewer of the relevant capacities, a problem of hierarchy, though perhaps a manageable one, would emerge anew.

More important, I doubt there is a plausible non-degree capacity that can do the work this argument assigns to it. Take the capacity to set ends and make choices. Consider a being that has little brain power, but over the course of its life can set just a few ends and make just a few choices based on considering two or three simple alternatives. It sets one end (lunch, now) per decade three times over the course of its life. If there is a capacity to set ends, period, not admitting of degrees, this being possesses it. The point is that it is clearly not merely the capacity to set ends, but something more complex that renders a being a person in our eyes. What matters is whether or not one has the capacity to set sensible ends and to pick among alternative ends at a reasonable pace, sorting through complex considerations that bear on the choice of ends and responding in a rational way to these considerations. But this capacity, along with any similar or related capacity that might be urged as a substitute for it, definitely admits of degrees. The same point would hold if we pointed to free will or moral autonomy as the relevant person-determining capacity. It is not the ability to choose an end for moral considerations merely, but the ability to do this in a nuanced and fine-grained responsive way, that is plausibly deemed to entitle a being to personhood status. In general, we single out rationality, the ability to respond appropriately to reasons, as the capacity that is pertinent to personhood, by itself or in conjunction with related abilities, and rationality so understood admits of degrees.

Kant may well have held that the uses of reason that are required in order to have a well functioning conscience that can tell right from wrong are not very sophisticated and are well within the reach of all non-crazy, non-feebleminded humans. Ordinary intelligence suffices. His discussions of applying the categorical imperative test certainly convey this impression. But commentators tend to agree that there is no simple all-purpose moral test that easily answers all significant moral questions. Thus recent Kant scholars note that the categorical imperative test is not a "Geiger counter" for detecting the presence of moral duties. Barbara Herman observes that the application of the categorical imperative test to cases cannot be a mechanical procedure but relies on prior moral understanding by the agent and on the agent's capacity to make relevant moral discriminations and judgments and to characterize her own proposed maxims perspicuously.[11] These comments confirm what should be clear in any event: moral problems can be complex and difficult, and there is no discernible upper bound to the complexity of the reasoning required to master and perhaps solve them.

But suppose I do the best I can with my limited cognitive resources, I make a judgment as to what is morally right, however misguided, and I am conscientiously resolved to do what I take to be morally right. The capacity to do what is right can be factored into two components, the ability to decide what is right and the ability to dispose oneself to do what one thinks is right. One might hold the latter capacity to be the true locus of human dignity and worth. Resisting temptation and doing what one thinks is right is noble and admirable even if one's conscience is a broken thermometer.

However, one might doubt that being disposed to follow one's conscience is unambiguously good when one's conscience is seriously in error. For one thing, moral flaws such as a lazy indisposition to hard thinking and an obsequious deference toward established power and authority might play a large role in fixing the content of one's judgments of conscience. A conceited lack of healthy skepticism about one's cognitive powers might be a determinant of one's strong disposition to do whatever one thinks to be right. Even if Kant is correct that the good will, the will directed unfailingly at what is truly right, has an absolute and unconditional worth, it is doubtful that the would-be good will, a will directed toward what it takes to be right on whatever flimsy or solid grounds appeal to it, has such worth. Take an extreme case: suppose a particular person has a would-be good will that is always in error. This will could be strong or righteous, so that the agent always does what he thinks is right, or weak and corrupt, so that the agent never does what she thinks is right. If the will is always in error, the odds of doing the right thing are increased if the would-be good will is weak and corrupt. Some might value more highly on consequential grounds the weak and corrupt erroneous will, even though the strong and righteous invariably erroneous will always shines like a jewel in its own right. And some might hold that quite aside from the expected consequences, acting on a seriously erroneous judgment of right is inherently of lesser worth than acting on correct judgment of right.

Even if the disposition to do what one thinks morally right is unassailable, its purported value does not provide a sound basis for asserting the equal worth and dignity of human persons. The capacity to act conscientiously itself varies empirically across persons like any other valued capacity. A favorable genetic endowment and favorable early socialization experiences bestow more of this capacity on some persons and less on others.

If we think of an agent's will as disposed more or less strongly to do what she conscientiously believes to be right, different individuals with the same disposition will experience good and bad luck in facing temptations that exceed their resolve. Even if we assume that agents always have freedom of the will, it will be difficult to different degrees for different persons to exercise their free will as conscience dictates. Moreover, individuals will vary in their psychological capacities to dispose their will to do what conscience dictates. One might retreat further to the claim that all persons equally can try to dispose their will to do what is right, even if they will succeed in this enterprise to different degrees. But the ability to try is also a psychological capacity that we should expect would vary empirically across persons.

At times Kant seems to appeal to epistemic grounds in reasoning from the goodness of the good will to the equal worth and dignity of all human persons. We don't know what anyone's inner motivations are, even our own, so the judgment that anyone is firmly disposed to do what is right can never be confirmed. But surely the main issue is whether humans are so ordered that we ought to accord them a fundamental equal moral status, not whether, given our beliefs, it is reasonable for us to act as if they are so ordered.

The idea that there is a threshold of rational agency capacity such that any being with a capacity above the threshold is a person equal in fundamental moral status to all other persons prompts a worry about how to identify this threshold non-arbitrarily. It might seem that only the difference between nil capacity and some capacity would preclude the skeptical doubt that the line set at any positive level of capacity could just as well have been set higher or lower. Regarding the proposal to identify any above-zero capacity as qualifying one for personhood, we imagine a being with barely a glimmer of capacity to perceive the good and the right and to dispose its will toward their attainment. The difference between none and some might be infinitesimal, after all.

However, a threshold need not be razor-thin. Perhaps there is a line below which beings with rational capacities in this range are definitely not persons, and a higher level such that all beings with capacities above this level are definitely persons. Beings with rational capacities that fall in the middle range or gray area between these levels are near-persons. The levels can be set sufficiently far apart that the difference between scoring at the lower and the higher levels is undeniably of moral significance. But the difference between the rational capacities of the beings just above the higher line, call them marginal persons, and the beings at the upper end of the scale who have saintly genius capacities, is not thereby shown to be insignificant. At the lower end we might imagine persons like the villains depicted in the Dirty Harry Clint Eastwood movies. These unfortunates are not shown as having moral capacities which they are flouting, but rather as bad by nature, and perhaps not entitled to full human rights. No doubt this is a crass outlook, but the question remains whether the analysis we can offer of the basis for human equality generates a refutation of it. Suppose someone asserts that the difference between the rational agency capacities of the most perceptive saints and the most unreflective and animalistic villains defines a difference in fundamental moral status that is just as important for morality as the difference between the rational agency capacities of near-persons and marginal persons. What mistake does this claim embody?

Conclusion

My search for a resolution of the Singer Problem has led to disappointing results. In conclusion, I briefly consider further avenues that might be explored.

Speciesism

Perhaps we should reconsider the claims that belonging to the human species is *per se* morally relevant and that all humans, whatever their cognitive abilities, share an enhanced equal status above that of all non-human animals (at least, those that are non-persons). According to speciesism, even if my individual cognitive abilities are less than those of many chimpanzees, apes, and bonobos, I none the less retain the status of person with full human rights, the same rights as other humans possess, whereas the other animals do not share this status, because they are not members of the human species. No doubt current common-sense morality is speciesist, as can be seen by noting its solicitous attitude toward severely retarded and demented persons along with its tolerance of practices toward non-human animals including primates that would be seen as horrific if practiced on any humans.

Robert Nozick suggests the desirability of defending speciesism. He writes, "Even supposing a particular severely retarded individual turns out to be no more rational or autonomous and to have no richer an internal psychology than a normal member of another mammalian species, he nonetheless is a human being, albeit defective, and must be treated as one."[12] Nozick does not mention the problem of explaining why Arneson and Einstein should have the same basic moral rights despite their very unequal cognitive powers; one presumes he would invoke the fact that the two humans are both equally of the human species, hence entitled to the same basic rights. He cautions that we should infer "nothing much" from "our not presently having a theory of the moral importance of species membership that no one has spent much time trying to formulate because the issue hasn't seemed pressing."[13]

The warning is salutary, but cuts both ways. Nozick's words were written in 1983, and in the intervening fifteen years to my knowledge the theory of speciesism has made very little progress. Perhaps the issue still is not salient. I myself am skeptical about the prospects of such a theory. Consider two suggestions made by Nozick. He suggests that a moral requirement to favor members of the human species might apply only to members of the human species. This would be a form of morally allowable partiality; it might be thought to follow from a general principle that each species of persons may favor the members of its own species.[14] Species partiality might then be assimilated to partiality to one's family, clan, tribe, or nation. But besides inheriting all the doubts that attach to partialist moralities in general, the proposal that morality allows one to favor one's fellow species members is most plausibly construed as just that, a permission not a requirement. The version of species-partiality needed to resolve the Singer Problem, however, would have to take the form of a strict obligation to favor one's own species. What is needed, then, is a morally allowable partiality that takes the form of a strict requirement: all species members must favor their own species whether or not they wish to do so. The implausibility of this doctrine becomes evident if one imagines that it is being applied against humans: the Martian would prefer to save ten ordinary humans rather than one demented Martian, but recalling the dictates of "morality," he reconsiders, and favors his kind against his impartial sympathies.

Nozick also suggests that it might be a mistake to insist that there must be some simple bright-line morally significant differences between the human species and other animal species. Perhaps the morally relevant difference will consist in some complex pattern. In general, "it may be a mistake to expect there always can be a succinctly formulated distinction based on a manageably small set of properties. Sometimes the distinction between situations will lie in their differing places in a whole intricate tapestry (or in two separate tapestries whose extremities bear some resemblance)."[15] The trouble with this suggestion is that if it works at all, it works too effectively. Asked to justify favoring a demented human over a cognitively better endowed non-human, one responds that we see the human against a different tapestry of complex associations than we see the non-human animal. But by the same token, asked to justify discriminating in favor of Aryans and against Jews, the would-be discriminator can respond that there is no simple morally relevant distinction, but rather a difference so complex as to be effectively unstateable. We see the Jew placed in an intricate tapestry that is quite different from the Aryan tapestry. Of course Nozick is correct that there is no guarantee in advance that morality is uncomplex. An intricate web of principles may be needed to capture the judgments we wish to endorse after full reflection. But surely we should prefer simpler explanations other things being equal, and should insist that the differences between beings that we take to justify significantly different treatment of them should be capable of being characterized in plain language. What we initially intuitively believe to be a morally significant difference that proves resistant to explication may turn out to be a prejudice that should be discarded, if all attempts at explication fall short.

Deflating the issue

Another possible avenue to explore would involve querying the idea that any fundamental norm of human equality is needed for a humane and decent ethics. In place of an equality norm we substitute the idea that differences in the treatment of people should be based on morally relevant and sufficient reasons – reasons based either on differences among the persons or on other considerations. To this formal norm we might add a substantive presumption in favor of equal treatment: in the absence of reasons to treat people differently we should accord them equal consideration. The third ingredient in the pragmatic deflation of the issue would be to note that very often we are in a poor epistemic position to differentiate reliably among humans when significant benefits and burdens are being distributed. Assuming for the sake of the argument that discrimination among persons on the basis of the degree to which they possess and exercise capacities of rational autonomy would in principle be justifiable, one finds that in practice our attempts to sort people on this basis would be highly unreliable. The traits that are morally important and relevant for discrimination are complex and multidimensional and do not reveal themselves in behavior in ways that facilitate accurate measurement. The individual who scores high on one dimension might for all we know score badly on other dimensions, and a high or low score on one occasion might not be a true indicator of the individual's capacity even for that single dimension of rational autonomy being reviewed. Along with acknowledging our epistemic liabilities we should also acknowledge that we are often not able to be unbiased judges of other people's rational autonomy capacities but are swayed by myriad forms of prejudice and distorting emotion. These points apply with particular force to the realm of politics and governmental functioning, so they support ideals of equal citizenship and equal protection of the laws for all members of society as practical guidelines. Perhaps ideals of the fundamental equal moral status of humans are best seen as useful guides to the fulfillment of other more basic non-egalitarian moral principles rather than as morally foundational in their own right.

The pragmatic deflation strategy is worth further exploration. Its plausibility evidently hinges on the plausibility of the particular non-egalitarian principles that take the place of any substantive equality norm and their ability to match our considered judgments. I doubt, however, that most people's allegiance to a substantive ideal of human equality consists of nothing more than respect for a useful tool that is not valued for its own sake. Nor do epistemic liabilities entirely constitute our grounds for insisting on equality. In a Lockean framework, I will suppose my right to live as I choose as long as I do not harm others wrongfully should count for as much as any other person's similar right, even though it is undisputed that I am less intelligent and less disposed to be moral than many others. According to the Priority View, if I am badly off, getting benefits for me is morally a matter of greater urgency than securing extra benefits for those already well off, even if their intelligence and rational autonomy capacities far exceed mine. The current understanding of the constitutional equality norm of equal protection of the laws would have this norm fully applicable to severely retarded and demented individuals even though there is very little serious epistemic uncertainty concerning their reduced cognitive status. The pragmatic deflation strategy will end up revising our current common-sense understanding of the reach, scope, and importance of substantive equality norms and not merely altering our understanding of their rationale.

Reconsidering utilitarianism

The intractability of the Singer Problem within the framework of standard alternatives to utilitarianism provides indirect support for the normative adequacy of utilitarianism. Initially I regarded it as a black mark against utilitarianism that its doctrine of equal consideration for equal interests does not include a sufficiently robust substantive equality norm. If the non-utilitarian moralities with robust substantive equality ideals cannot be made coherent, utilitarianism's weakness in this regard becomes a strength. Utilitarianism supposes that if a being is capable of having an interest of a given quality and strength, the satisfaction of that interest counts the same as the satisfaction of any other interest of the same quantity and quality. On this view there is no need to distinguish among types of beings and discount the interests of some in favor of others. Nor does it become imperative to establish that all or virtually all humans fall into a single type whose interests should count the same. That utilitarianism avoids or resolves the Singer Problem is not a decisive defense of this doctrine, which has attracted many powerful and diverse objections. But to my mind utilitarianism's comparative success on this score is a non-trivial advantage.

Affection not cognition

This essay has assumed that the factors that morally distinguish human persons from other animals and which might distinguish some human persons from others concern cognitive powers. This might not be so. Perhaps we revere humanity partly for the capacities of humans to feel sympathy, solidarity, cheerfulness, friendliness, love, and so on. Have we perhaps gone astray by seeking the normative basis of human equality strictly in terms of cognitive capacities?

The relevance of affective capacities to moral status becomes evident if we consider popular culture science fiction stories of beings of incredible intelligence but entirely predatory and ruthless desires. Notice that in positing rational autonomy capacities as decisive for moral status, I have not entirely ruled out disposition to desire as irrelevant. The agent who is capable of being rationally autonomous is capable of being moved to action by her perception of good reasons for action, including moral reasons that attend to the interests of other beings. This in my view is an affective, not purely a cognitive, capacity. No doubt we might complicate the story of the basis of equality by widening the sorts of affective capacities that are to count as relevant to a being's fundamental moral status. However, I doubt that rendering the account more sophisticated in this way will in any way diminish the force of the Singer Problem. After all, if I am very cognitively deficient by comparison with the Einsteins of the world, I am also very affectively deficient by comparison with the planet's Mother Theresas.

Notes

For helpful comments on earlier versions of this essay I thank Steve Yalowitz, David Brink, and Dale Jamieson.

1 For a clear recent statement of the view that any plausible morality must include a commitment to some substantive ideal of human equality, see Amartya Sen, *Inequality Reexamined* (Cambridge, MA: Harvard University Press, 1992), preface and chapter 1.
2 Peter Singer, *Animal Liberation*, 2nd edn (New York: Random House, 1990). This basic argument originally appeared in a 1975 *New York Review of Books* essay with the same title.
3 Jeremy Bentham, *Introduction to the Principles of Morals and Legislation*, chapter 17. Note also Joel Feinberg's comment along the same line: "Human beings suffering extreme cases of mental illness, however, may be so disoriented or insensitive as to compare quite unfavorably with the brightest cats and dogs." See Joel Feinberg, "The rights of animals and unborn generations," in William T. Blackstone (ed.), *Philosophy and Environmental Crisis* (Atlanta: University of Georgia Press, 1974).
4 One might suggest that every interest of a cognitively more complex being is more complex and hence finer than the seemingly comparable interests of beings with simpler mental life. On this view rat pleasure from simple sensation is quite different from human pleasure taken in simple sensation because the

human will be aware of the simple pleasure as one in a complex array of goods among which it has a choice. I myself doubt that this point really shows that the pleasure I take in eating crunchy granola is really a finer thing than the pleasure a cat takes in eating kibble, but I am not sure how to argue the point. Notice the suggestion does not eliminate the problem of this essay, for the pleasure Einstein takes in eating his breakfast cereal will be a mentally more complex phenomenon than my comparable pleasure, just as mine is more complex than the cat's.

5 Robert Nozick, *Anarchy, State, and Utopia* (New York: Basic Books, 1974), p. 49.

6 David Gauthier, *Morals by Agreement* (Oxford: Oxford University Press, 1986).

7 John Rawls, *A Theory of Justice* (Cambridge, MA: Harvard University Press, 1971), pp. 504–12.

8 Jeff McMahan, "Cognitive disability, misfortune, and justice," *Philosophy and Public Affairs*, 25 (Winter 1996), pp. 3–35.

9 Kant's words cited in J. B. Schneewind, "Autonomy, obligation, and virtue: an overview of Kant's moral philosophy," in Paul Guyer (ed.), *The Cambridge Companion to Kant* (Cambridge: Cambridge University Press, 1992), p. 336.

10 For a clear short statement of this idea, see Christine Korsgaard, with G. A. Cohen. Raymond Geuss, Thomas Nagel, and Bernard Williams, and edited by Onora O'Neill, *The Sources of Normativity* (Cambridge: Cambridge University Press, 1996), pp. 92–3. She connects the capacity to set an end, as opposed to the capacity merely to respond to stimuli, with self-consciousness. The human animal alone is aware that it has desires, and to choose to act it must take some desire or another consideration it is aware of as a reason for selecting some course of action.

11 Barbara Herman, *The Practice of Moral Judgment* (Cambridge, MA: Harvard University Press, 1993), chapter 7. It should be noted that Herman herself wants to sustain the Kantian ideal that the reasons that determine how any agent should act must be transparent to that agent rather than assigned a secret or esoteric status by morality. See Herman, pp. 161–2, disavowing the strategy of "indirection."

12 Robert Nozick, "Do animals have rights?", reprinted in his *Socratic Puzzles* (Cambridge, MA: Harvard University Press, 1997), p. 307 (originally published as "About mammals and people," *New York Times Book Review*, November 27, 1983, p. 11).

13 Ibid., p. 308.

14 This suggestion is also made by Bonnie Steinbock, "Speciesism and the idea of equality," *Philosophy*, 53 (April 1978), pp. 247–56. It is unacceptable for the reason cited in the text.

15 Nozick, p. 308.

7

Must Utilitarians Be Impartial?

LORI GRUEN

A number of years ago, during the process of preparing the second edition of *Animal Liberation*, I asked Singer what he thought about the success of the first edition. In a characteristic way, he replied that he was surprised that the rational argument he presented for the ethical treatment of animals combined with the evidence of their mistreatment in Western societies did not lead to more significant changes in the attitudes and practices of those who read it. He thought that after he had carefully presented the case for vegetarianism as the morally appropriate response to intensive animal agriculture, no rational person could possibly continue to consume factory-farmed animal flesh. He seemed perplexed and dismayed that many people still did.[1] I remember being somewhat amused by his surprise: people are not always motivated to follow the conclusions of rational arguments. And this motivational lack is not necessarily a failure of their rational capacities, but rather stems from the existence of strong competing desires that pull them in different directions. Some extremely rational people really enjoy eating salami. They may recognize that they should not eat it, or perhaps that they should not desire to eat it, but they do have the desire to eat it and continue to eat it (perhaps less often) despite what reason tells them. At the time, I believed that Singer would have been caught less by surprise if he had recognized the complex ways in which emotion affects our moral thinking and behavior and suggested that he needed to allow more room for emotion in his theory.[2] I now believe that he cannot allow more room for emotion, if emotions are understood to be those particular, idiosyncratic, and personal affective states that cause us to think and act partially.[3]

In this chapter, I will argue that Singer's version of utilitarianism, unlike other versions of consequentialism, cannot coherently accommodate partial considerations. However, even if his theory could be modified so as to accommodate at least some partial considerations, Singer might find it undesirable to do so. Before I discuss the problem of partialism for utilitarianism and consequentialism generally, and for Singer specifically, it is necessary to discuss the different ways in which impartiality may operate within ethical thinking.

The Role of Impartiality

In *Practical Ethics*, while introducing his conception of ethics, Singer claims "that ethical conduct is acceptable from a point of view that is somehow universal." In writing about the "ethical point of view" as *somehow* universal, Singer is hinting at the historical variability in the meaning of the term "universal." He mentions a number of ideas associated with universality, e.g. the golden rule, universalizability in the Kantian sense, appealing to an ideal observer, and the veil of ignorance. He then notes that despite the disagreements between proponents of different characterizations of the ethical, all "agree that an ethical principle cannot be justified in relation to any partial or sectional group."[4] The ethical point of view is thought to be impartial, and universality is *somehow* meant to capture impartiality.

Singer's general discussion of the role of impartiality in ethical thinking conflates a number of different ways in which impartiality can operate. In order to get a clearer sense of what sort of impartiality Singer is committed to, it will be useful to disentangle the different roles impartiality can play in ethical thinking. One sense of impartiality captured by "universality" deals with the scope of moral thinking. A requirement of universality excludes those theories that, by their very formulation, privilege or favor a particular perspective or group of people. It is this sense of impartiality that has traditionally been a characteristic of all moral theories, not just consequentialism or Singer's particular version of it. Slave moralities, bourgeois moralities, and Nazi moralities, moral theories that apply to particular groups and not to others, are not impartial moralities, if they are moralities at all.

A moral theory with universal scope may or may not be impartial at the level of principle and at the level of judgment. For example, a theory with a universal scope, may nevertheless require that under condition C, short people are morally required to do X, where tall people are not so required, or are required to do Y. Such a theory may thus be partial in its principles. In addition, a theory that indudes both As and Bs in its scope, but that allows for some A to treat some B in a way that B is not permitted to treat A when both A and B are similarly situated, may be considered partial in its judgments.

Singer's utilitarianism is universal in its scope in that it requires the inclusion of all beings affected by the action in question. It is also impartial at the level of principle. Singer concurs with Sidgwick:

> It cannot be right for A to treat B in a manner in which it would be wrong for B to treat A, merely on the ground that they are two different individuals, and without there being any difference between the natures or circumstances of the two which can be stated as a reasonable ground for difference of treatment.[5]

If I desire to be treated well and believe that I ought to be treated well, and I accept that the process of rationally choosing ends is not specific to me, then it follows that insofar as it is rational for me to believe that I ought to be treated well it is rational for anyone similarly situated to believe that he or she ought to be treated well. Singer, agreeing with R. M. Hare, believes that moral principles must follow the logic of moral language, and adhering to moral principles commits the agent to applying the principle in all situations that are identical in their universal properties. Universal properties are "understood as including all the properties of the person in question himself, and excluding only his purely numerical identity as that individual."[6] Accordingly:

> Given two cases differing solely in that in one of them individuals A and B occupy certain roles, and in the other the roles are reversed, any universal principle must yield the same prescriptions about them both. In order to yield different prescriptions about the two cases, the principle would have to contain the names of the individuals, and would therefore not be universal.[7]

For Hare, universal properties are those properties that do not refer to specific individuals; they must not contain "proper names and definite descriptions."[8]

It is important to note that the type of impartiality that Singer advocates at the level of principle is a formal requirement; it does not provide any particular prescriptions for action. As Sidgwick rightly suggests "Such a principle manifestly does not give complete guidance – indeed its effect, strictly speaking, is merely to throw a definite *onus probandi* on the man who applies to another a treatment of which he would complain if applied to himself."[9]

Formal impartiality of this sort emerges from rational reflection on the properties of moral terms and on the requirement that our reflection be consistent and treat like cases alike. Thus, reason plays a central role in establishing the impartial nature of ethics. As Singer notes:

> Reason makes it possible...to see that I am just one among others, with
> interests and desires like others. I have a personal perspective on the
> world...but reason enables me to see that others have similarly subjective
> perspectives, and that from "the point of view of the universe" my perspect-
> ive is no more privileged than theirs. Thus my ability to reason shows me the
> possibility of detaching myself from my own perspective, and shows me
> what the universe might look like if I had no personal perspective.[10]

However, although the application of critical or rational reflection can
establish the way in which ethical principles must be impartial, reasoning
itself cannot always accomplish what impartiality is meant to accomplish,
namely the elimination of prejudice often associated with sectional or
partial perspectives. This is because it is not necessarily a failure of
rationality that creates and perpetuates such prejudice and an exercise
of reason will not necessarily remedy the outcomes of prejudicial perspectives. As Bernard Williams has pointed out, what makes racist or sexist
practices wrong is not that they are irrational or inconsistent (the only
conclusion that can be drawn, if it can, from formal impartiality) but that
they are unfair and unjust, harmful and cruel.

> It is wrong, because unjust, to treat blacks or women unfavorably by
> comparison to whites or men...It may be said that it is irrational because
> it is inconsistent. Reasons are not being applied equally, and that offends
> against a formal principle of universalizability. But this is rarely what is
> wrong, and if anything is irrational in these matters, this is rarely what it is.
> The formal and uncontentious principle of universalizability...says that if
> a certain consideration is truly a sufficient reason for a certain action in one
> case, it is so in another. But discrimination and prejudice can be run on that
> basis.[11]

For example, if a prospective employer determines that the general qualities of competence and intelligence are the basis upon which his hiring
decisions will be made, yet uses these criteria only in the case of men and
not when evaluating women, then he is failing to reason impartially. He is
being inconsistent in his application of a general principle that is meant to
apply universally. However, if he believes that competence, intelligence,
and gender are what his hiring decisions will be based on, then in hiring a
man over a woman, he is not acting inconsistently.

While Williams's worry is specifically directed at the inadequacy of
impartial ethical theories generally, it is one that has been made against
the adequacy of formal impartiality as determined through reason. Marilyn Friedman, for example, argues that "reasons can be couched in terms
which are universal...yet still advance special interests. Certain 'facts'
make this possible, for example, facts about the traits that correlate highly

with certain types of persons."[12] In the above case, particular reference to gender in hiring practices could be replaced by height, for example. Given that women tend to be shorter than men in general, chances are that the prejudice of the employer could be maintained without any seeming inconsistency, violation of rationality, or formal impartiality. Facts arising from historically prejudicial policies can also operate in this way. As Bernard Boxill has pointed out, the "grandfather clauses" in voting laws in many states in the south of the USA prevented blacks from voting without explicitly denying the vote to people of African descent.

> ...in Louisiana this clause stated that those who had had the right to vote before or on 1 January 1867, or their lineal descendants, did not have to meet the educational, property, or tax requirements for voting. Since no blacks had had the right to vote by that time, this law worked effectively to keep blacks from voting while at the same time allowing many impoverished and illiterate whites to vote – yet it made no mention of race.[13]

Clearly many instances of prejudice have been disguised in universal terms, so formal impartiality cannot do all the work of eliminating prejudice. To ensure that prejudice is not lurking in a moral theory, moral theory must require substantive impartiality, as well as formal impartiality. Substantive impartiality, unlike formal impartiality, will be theory specific: that is, what it will ultimately mean to engage in impartial thinking of the substantive sort will depend on the theory which is guiding such thinking. Unlike formal impartiality, which does not derive its meaning from the content of the theories to which it applies, the meaning of substantive notions, such as equality, justice, and fairness, may vary depending on the theory with which they are associated. These concepts require normative justification which is generated from the content of the specific moral theory in question.[14]

Substantive impartiality within consequentialist theories has generally been captured by what has been called the "impersonal" perspective or "the point of view of the universe." The determination of what is right, or what impartial morality requires in this sense, is to be made from a standpoint detached from any personal considerations or concerns. The pronoun "me" and possessive adjective "mine" have no place in moral thinking if it is to be substantively impartial. The most extreme expression of what I am calling substantive impartiality can be found in Godwin's now infamous example:

> ...the illustrious archbishop of Cambrai was of more worth than his chambermaid, and there are few of us that would hesitate to pronounce, if his palace were in flames and the life of only one of them could be preserved, which of the two ought to be preferred...Supposing the chambermaid had

been my wife, my mother or my benefactor. That would not alter the truth of the proposition. The life of Fenelon would still be more valuable than that of the chambermaid; and justice – pure, unadulterated justice – would still have preferred that which was most valuable. Justice would have taught me to save the life of Fenelon at the expense of the other. What magic is there, is the pronoun "my" to overturn the decisions of everlasting truth? My wife or my mother may be a fool or a prostitute, malicious, lying or dishonest. If they be, of what consequence is it that they are mine?[15]

Utilitarian theory is thought to be substantively impartial because it claims not only that the right action is that which promotes the greatest good for the greatest number of beings affected by the action, but that the effects of any action on individuals are to be weighed impersonally. No one individual's pain or pleasure is to count any more or less than any other individual's equal pain or pleasure. That the first person happens to be you or someone close to you does not figure in an impartial utilitarian calculation. This is because, for utilitarians, under all conditions, the right thing to do is that which brings about the best overall consequences from an impersonal perspective, which, of course, may result in a state of affairs in which the overall consequences for you or your nearest and dearest are not best.

   Singer's characterization of substantive impartiality is expressed by his principle of "equal consideration of interests."[16]

   The essence of the principle of equal consideration of interests is that we give equal weight in our moral deliberations to the like interests of all those affected by our actions. This means that if only X and Y would be affected by a possible act, and if X stands to lose more than Y stands to gain, it is better not to do the act. We cannot, if we accept the principle of equal consideration of interests, say that doing the act is better, despite the facts described, because we are more concerned about Y than we are about X.[17]

It is the substantive principle of equal consideration of interests that is specifically designed to remove morally loaded prejudice from ethical deliberations. As Singer discusses the principle, it prohibits granting any weight to particular features of a situation (i.e. whether the person affected by the action is friend or foe, one's partner or a stranger) or particular characteristics of an individual (i.e. his or her race, sex, mental or physical abilities). According to Singer, that some people have a different skin color, are from a different country, are of a different gender, or have different abilities than the person engaging in moral deliberation are not considerations that in themselves justify differential treatment. In most cases, such differences do not provide a rational basis for differences in our ethical considerations or treatment. For example, a theory which

justifies the distribution of goods under which men receive greater benefits and thus have more of their preferences satisfied than women do,
simply because they are men, is a theory that violates the principle of
equal consideration of interests. According to the principle, all that is to
be considered in deciding the morally correct course of action is the
strength of the interests or preferences and the degree to which the
interests and preferences of those affected will be thwarted or advanced.
Naturally, determining this and subsequently making an impartial judgment will require knowing quite a bit about the particular features of
the situation and may well require knowledge of the characteristics of the
individuals affected, but this information is only relevant as it shapes the
interests and preferences of the individuals. Singer has forcefully argued
that given that it is interests that matter ethically, and given that ethics is
universal in its scope, all beings with interests are the subjects of moral
consideration. The principle of equal consideration of interests then
applies not just to humans but to non-human interest holders as well.
To deny this is to succumb to

> a prejudice no better founded than the prejudice of the white slaveowners
> against taking the interests of their African slaves seriously ... the fact that
> some people are not members of our race does not entitle us to exploit them,
> and similarly the fact that some people are less intelligent than others does
> not mean that their interests may be disregarded. But the principle [of equal
> consideration] also implies that the fact that beings are not members of our
> species does not entitle us to exploit them, and similarly the fact that other
> animals are less intelligent than we are does not mean that their interests
> may be disregarded.[18]

Just as Singer's substantive impartiality condemns granting additional
consideration to the interests or preferences of one's racial or ethnic
group, so does it condemn granting additional consideration to the interests or preferences of humans over non-humans, simply because they are
humans.

Partialist Criticisms and Consequentialist Responses

Despite the non-prejudicial appeal of substantive conceptions of impartiality, it has none the less been the target of continuous criticism.[19]
Feminist theorists, for example, have mounted strong objections to
impartiality in ethics.[20] These theorists have objected to theories that
are impartial in the sense that they are impersonal by suggesting that
such theories are illusory at best and suspicious at worst. Critics of the
latter sort have argued that not only is there no impersonal perspective, or

"point of view of the universe," but that any claim that a theory is impartial merely obscures certain values or interests that it seeks to promote. This is the criticism made by some "feminist standpoint theorists"[21] who argue that advocates of impartiality wrongly assume that personal value commitments are escapable and thus theorists who appeal to impartiality are failing to recognize the personal and social values they do in fact bring to their moral and political deliberations. These theorists suggest that rather than being able to achieve impartiality, as all systems of thought are imbued with particular values, those who claim to be impartial simply obscure their own hegemonic interests in impartial language. Thus, rather than eliminating prejudice, this form of impartiality simply hides it.

Instead of pretending to achieve a false impartiality, these theorists suggest that we not only attempt to recognize the partiality we inevitably bring to moral thinking, but specifically and publicly address it as a way of eliminating prejudice. As Friedman suggests, "our conceptual reference points should be particular forms of partiality, that is, named biases whose distorted effects on moral thinking we recognize, and whose manifestations in moral attitudes and behavior can be specifically identified." She suggests that "the methods for eliminating recognizable biases from critical moral thinking" would emphasize "interpersonal and public dialogue."[22] It might also be suggested that some biased perspectives actually represent important information that can add to an understanding of what a non-prejudicial moral theory requires. For example, feminist standpoint theorists argue that because most women have personally experienced prejudice their personal points of view are crucial to an adequate moral theory.

In terms of the criticism that claims of impartiality really hide certain prejudices, utilitarians, perhaps unlike other theorists, can simply deny the charge. The values or interests of the utilitarian are hardly obscured, they are right on the surface – promoting the greatest possible good for all affected by the action where each individual affected has his or her like interests considered equally. Critics may object to such a theory of value, or may criticize the values contained in certain versions of utilitarianism, or may object to specific aspects of the theory itself (e.g. maximization, or interpersonal utility comparisons), but these would be different criticisms, not an objection to substantive impartiality.

The claim that particular perspectives may add important insights to considerations of what morality requires can surely be incorporated into an impartial utilitarian theory. Indeed, utilitarians must examine the subjective, personal interests of those who are affected by an action in order to determine how they are affected and thus to make an informed decision about what course of action to take. Unlike other moral theories, utilitarianism places great emphasis on the context in which a moral decision is made and an individual's pains and pleasure, desires and interests serve as the most important data in the moral calculus. What an impartial utilitarian theory cannot do is give greater weight to the interests of any individual because they are that individual's. Thus, a utilitarian would not give greater weight to the interests of a woman or a disabled person simply because she is a woman or disabled, but would weight those interests heavily if her suffering is greater than the suffering of others. As Singer has noted in the case of disabled individuals,

> Many disabled children are capable of benefiting from normal schooling, but are prevented from taking part because additional resources are required to cope with their special needs. Since such needs are often very central to the lives of disabled people, the principle of equal consideration of interests will give them much greater weight than more minor needs of others.[23]

It is not the characteristics or abilities in themselves that provide the justification for providing different treatment, but the equal consideration of the interests of those individuals as compared to the interests of others, that can provide the basis for differences in treatment. If one individual, given her circumstances, will suffer more than another by a particular action (all things considered), then impartial morality requires that the greater suffering be avoided and thus will on many occasions prescribe different treatment.

One way of knowing that the suffering of one person is greater than that of another is precisely by adopting an impersonal perspective. We can achieve this perspective by stepping into the position of another and this can be accomplished in at least two different ways. The first is to step into the position of another with one's own set of preferences, desires, interests, beliefs, etc. While this way of achieving an impersonal perspective assumes that everyone has the same or complementary psychological make-ups and thus does not truly provide us with a perspective of what it is like to be them, it can allow us some understanding of the general shape of the lives of others. There is also a second sense in which a person can imagine herself in the place of another, and that is to take on that individual's preferences, desires, motivations, etc. Thus, in addition to imagining what it would be like to be in a different position, one can also imagine what it is like to have feelings other than one's own.

Critics of impartiality deny that one can ever imagine oneself into the position of another, "especially positions that we ourselves could never be in,"[24] and thus believe that impartiality is impossible to achieve. They ask us to consider what would be required to think oneself into the perspective of another. Actual perspectives are the sort of things that are shaped and refined by many different events; they are cumulative and unique to an individual's life experiences. So, for example, to imagine oneself pregnant[25] is not just to imagine oneself thirty pounds larger, but to be able to imagine oneself a woman, with a particular view about mothering which in itself is shaped by a whole range of cultural, religious, and familial influences. It will also require knowledge about a particular individual's physiology and economic situation. Since pregnancies themselves vary in ease and discomfort, this too would have to come into the analysis. It is suggested that it is hard enough for one pregnant woman to imagine what it would be like to be another pregnant woman who happens to be in different circumstances, let alone for a man to imagine what it would be like to be pregnant.

Although it may be difficult to engage in such sophisticated imagining, it is surely possible. People can and do imagine themselves at some time in the future and justify making sacrifices in the present by reference to some greater future benefit. Often the person one becomes is strikingly different from the person one is now, but a recognition of this possibility does not prevent an individual from engaging in this sort of imagining and acting according to it. Similarly, in personal relationships we are often called upon to take the perspective of the other, to try to see things from the point of view of a family member or a lover. Indeed, it is in these sorts of personal relationships where most of us learn how to take on the perspective of another and thus the personal point of view is essential for the development of impartial ethical deliberation skills.[26] The difficulty of achieving a perspective other than one's current perspective should not be minimized, and though people may not always be successful at it, that is not enough reason to abandon the effort. Indeed, that many of us are not particularly skilled at adopting an impersonal perspective suggests the need to develop better means of achieving such a perspective, rather than reject impartiality.[27]

A more difficult criticism of impartiality for the utilitarian, one that has been made by feminists as well as others, is not that achieving impartiality is impossible but that it is undesirable. This was central in the concerns expressed nearly two hundred years ago by one of Godwin's critics, Dr Samuel Parr, who wrote:

> ... under the pretence of some obligation, which stern, inflexible justice lays upon us, to be extreme in marking what is done amiss, and to weigh every action of man, every motive to act, every consequence of action, in the balance which every individual may set up within his own bosom for adjusting in every case the direct and most efficacious means to promote the general good – what would become of society, which parental affection,

which friendship, which gratitude, which compassion, which patriotism do not uphold? how changed would be the scenes around us? how blunted our finer affections? how scanty the sum of our happiness? how multiplied and embittered the sources of our woe?[28]

More recently the criticism has taken form in what has been called "the alienation objection," first expressed, somewhat opaquely, by Williams.[29] The problem, according to partialist critics, is how an individual acting according to impartial utilitarian morality can have a meaningful life and meaningful relationships. The substantive utilitarian requirement of impartiality – that is, the requirement that an agent detach him or herself from his or her personal concern and see that concern as one among many equally significant concerns – raises doubts about the possibility of an individual being concerned about anything at all.

According to this objection, a utilitarian agent, when determining what to do in any given situation, would often be forced to act against the interests of a lover, friend, or family member if doing so would bring about greater good overall. If one was on her way to dinner with her partner, who was just fired for no apparent reason and was in desperate need of cheering up, and upon entering the restaurant found the place full of disgruntled and hungry people reacting very loudly to the sudden resignation of two cooks, the utilitarian thing to do may very well be to grab an apron and head for the kitchen, particularly if the person in question was a competent cook. Surely feeding a crowd of unhappy people would lead to greater overall utility than the utility lost by dis-appointing one's partner. Indeed, perhaps rather than taking one's part-ner to dinner in the first place, one should have used the money and/or time to help those whose needs were greater than the partner's need to be cheered up. There are countless cases like this and the impartial utilitarian answer in each appears to be the same – the personal connections one has cannot always, if ever, outweigh the morally required activity of promot-ing the greatest good.[30] Impartial utilitarian morality appears to require the sacrifice of relationships and any other personal interests or concerns if, when judged from an impartial perspective, the sacrifice contributes to more overall good.

There are now well rehearsed utilitarian responses to the criticisms expressed here. Godwin attempted to accommodate his critics by arguing that insofar as impartial considerations would lead to a society or state of affairs that was sub-optimal in terms of overall utility, then a consistent utilitarian must allow for some partiality to enter into moral deliberation so as to promote the greatest utility overall.[31] Contemporary utilitarians have followed suit, with varying degrees of sophistication.[32] While utili-tarians aim at promoting the best possible consequences given the actions open to them, how this is achieved will vary depending on the circumstances. It may well be that deliberately and directly acting to promote the greatest good will in fact lead to an overall state of affairs that is suboptimal. For example, acting impartially and thus failing to satisfy one's own interests or those of a loved one in order to promote the greatest good may, as partialist critics suggest, lead to serious breakdowns in our cultural, social, and personal expectations which in the long run may lead to bad consequences. So, some utilitarians have suggested that utilitarianism doesn't require substantive impartiality "in normal circumstances."[33]

In his recent work Singer, following Hare, has suggested as much, and appears to now advocate a two-level view in response to partialist criticisms. According to the two-level view, one need not apply impartial reasoning at every decision point as long as the decision procedure that is applied can be justified impartially. So, for example, if in the long run it is more conductive to promoting the overall good that parents look after the needs of their own children before the needs of the children of others, then such partialism is justified. On a two-level view, it is appropriate for parents to develop strong attachments to their own children and to pay particularly close attention to them in order to understand their needs and thus provide for them. Such attitudes and behaviors will intuitively lead to partial decisions when conflicts arise, say between providing one's own children with certain educational opportunities and providing financial assistance to sick children who lack proper medical services. If one adopted utilitarianism as a decision procedure in the immediate circumstances it seems likely that the best course of action is to help the sick children, but according to the two-level view, in the long run it may be more conducive to the greater good to allow for and even promote the partial relations that parents have for their children, and thus the critical level of morality will judge it morally acceptable to provide special opportunities to one's own children and to hope that the sick children will receive the care they need. Accordingly, impartial moral thinking can thus accommodate partial considerations at the level of everyday decisions.

Problems for Singer

In response to partialist critics, many consequentialists have adopted a strategy of indirection of the sort recently adopted by Singer. This strategy is meant to allow those who are committed to a moral theory aimed at promoting the most good to act in ways that do not immediately promote the best consequences as long as it is likely that the immediate sacrifice of good will lead to the promotion of the greater good in the long haul. Not all partialist critics find this response satisfactory, however. For example, Samuel Scheffler has argued that this concession to partiality does not recognize the "independence of the personal point of view." The utilitarian can allow for personal, hence partial, considerations only insofar as they are thought to lead to an overall promotion of utility, but, the partialist argues, there is value to these considerations over and above the instrumental value they have in a utilitarian calculation. Friendship, loyalty, familial ties, self-respect, etc. are important independently of their contribution to the best overall state of affairs.[34] Whether or not some indirect strategy or another can adequately answer partialist criticisms is a large and difficult question that I cannot fully address here. Rather, for the sake of argument, I will assume that in the main it is an acceptable (initial) response to critics and focus instead on whether or not such a response is fitting for Singer's particular version of utilitarianism.

The coherence of the partialist concession

The indirect strategy succeeds (insofar as it does) as a response to partialist critics because certain partial judgments and principles can be justified impartially. But the impartial justification is a formal one. For example, it is not morally justifiable to act according to a principle that states "I am morally entitled to help my mother commit suicide" because such a principle is not formally impartial. As Singer has recently written, however,

> while "being my mother" is not a universal property, because of its ineliminable reference to me, the speaker, "being the mother of the person helping one to commit suicide" is a universal property, since it does not contain a reference to any specific individual. It is this exclusion of references to oneself, or to any individuals in so far as they are specific individuals, that makes the requirement of universalizability a way of ensuring a kind of impartiality in moral judgments. But it is impartiality at a higher and more philosophical level of thought, and so is compatible with some forms of partiality at the level of everyday moral judgment. Thus the judgment "Parents ought to buy treats for their own children before buying them for other children" is one that encourages parents to be partial to their children, but it is itself universalizable and impartial. (Contrast it with the non-universalizable and less plausible judgment: "Parents ought to buy treats for my children before buying them for other children.")[35]

Many consequentialists can thus accommodate partialist critics without thereby sacrificing their consequentialism, because they are committed to formal impartiality but not necessarily committed to substantive impartiality. But this move does not appear to be open to Singer, as such a concession appears incompatible with the substantive impartiality that is central to Singer's version of utilitarianism.

As I noted earlier, substantive impartiality for Singer is captured in his principle of equal consideration of equal interests that maintains that it is not the characteristics or abilities in themselves that provide the justification for providing different treatment, but the equal consideration of the interests or preferences of those individuals as compared to the interests or preferences of others that can provide the basis for differences in treatment. If we are to accept the centrality of this principle for moral deliberation then it appears that we cannot focus on certain characteristics (i.e. being a child of X, being a parent of Y, being a friend of Z) as the basis of differential treatment, no matter how universal the principle containing such characteristics turns out to be. According to Singer's substantive impartiality, acting to promote the interests of Z over the interests of A is only morally justified if in favoring Z more interests are satisfied than dissatisfied overall, all things considered. That Z is one's friend doesn't allow one to give extra consideration or more weight to his or her interests.

It is hard to see, to return to the example used earlier, how providing one's own children with certain educational opportunities and hoping that the sick children will receive the care they need is consistent with Singer's utilitarianism. The satisfaction of the educational interests of one's own children, even when combined with one's interests in one's own children's success, surely cannot count for more overall interest satisfaction than providing the sick children of others with the care they need.[36] In this case, and many others like it in a world where disparities of wealth and access to basic goods are so great, the view that we are morally permitted to follow partial affections and discount the interests of those to whom we stand in no personal relation (or what amounts to the same thing, give extra weight or consideration to those to whom we do stand in such a relation) seems to contradict the principle of equal consideration of interests, when understood as a substantive view. The two-level strategy for accommodating personal relations works for certain consequentialist theories because the formal requirement of impartiality can be maintained at the critical or justificatory level and relaxed, when justified, at the level of everyday decision-making. It is unclear, however, how the two-level strategy can work for Singer's substantive impartiality requirement.

The desirability of the partialist concession

Even if it was possible for Singer to coherently accommodate partial concerns within his utilitarian theory while maintaining the centrality of the substantive principle of equal consideration of equal interests, such a concession may not be desirable for at least two reasons. First, one of the strengths of Singer's version of utilitarianism is its direct action guiding nature. A concession to partialists of the sort Singer has recently suggested would undermine this characteristic of his view and may lead to complacency.[37] Second, Singer's theory is one of the strongest anti-discriminatory contemporary moral theories, in that it expands the sphere of moral concern to all beings with interests. Concession to partialists will potentially compromise this position. Let's consider each of these reasons in more depth.

In "Famine, affluence, and morality" Singer set out a position that in many ways characterizes his overall moral position and one that many find hard to dispute, but none the less hope they might. He argues that "if it is in our power to prevent something very bad from happening, without thereby sacrificing anything of comparable moral significance, we ought to do it."[38] He has us consider coming upon a drowning child in a pond on our way to lecture. In order to save the child from drowning we only need wade into the pond and pull the child out. In the process we will get a bit wet and perhaps muddy and we will be late for our lecture, but the child's life will be saved. Singer suggests that consequentialists and non-consequentialists alike will agree that saving the child is the right thing to do. From this decent insight, Singer goes on to argue that our proximity to the drowning child is not morally relevant and thus we have a moral obligation to prevent like suffering in all similar situations. The logical implication of this argument is that those of us living in relative wealth are wrong not to give some of what is ours to others in need. While Singer does not provide a figure that will serve as the minimum amount that should be given, he suggests that one-tenth of the income of those who earn average salaries is a reasonable amount.[39]

Very few people who earn average salaries give even 1 percent of their income to others in need, and often their reasons are based on their partial interests. They have projects that they want to invest in, hobbies they want to pursue, children they want to save for, or trips with friends they want to take. Such personal considerations are, Singer argues, not of comparable moral significance. But maybe in some cases they are believed to be. Perhaps someone who earns $60,000 a year really believes that her life will be made much worse if she does not continue her piano lessons and buy the new piano she wants. Sending $6,000 to save the lives of thirty children that she does not know and will never come in contact with would mean that she can no longer afford her lessons and she will, as a result, become a less well rounded person, someone who is not as interesting or entertaining to be around. This in turn will have a negative impact on her sense of her self and completely alter her life plans. She may well believe that such a sacrifice will make her ideal for the good life impossible to obtain. Or to alter the case slightly to make a similar point, suppose it is not her own piano lessons she must sacrifice but the therapy sessions that she and her partner have been going to weekly. If she is willing to spend the money to save the lives of the children this must mean, her partner seriously believes, that their relationship is just not as important to her. The significance of personal interests and relationships, some argue, is morally comparable to lives and health of others and thus these individuals think themselves justified in not giving their money away.[40]

What is the right thing – sending the money to those who are in desperate need, or achieving one's ideal or preserving one's relationship? This is the question at the heart of the partialist/impartialist debate and it is an important and difficult one to answer. My point here is that the principle of equal consideration of interests gives us a clear and action guiding way of answering it. In life or death cases, the interest in saving a life (or many lives) is going to outweigh the interest in making one's own life better if the lives saved are lives worth living. While this direct and simple method for answering the question tells us what is right, Singer acknowledges that acting according to the answer is not going to be easy.

> What is the point of relating philosophy to public (and personal) affairs if we do not take the conclusions seriously? In this instance, taking our conclusion seriously means acting upon it. The philosopher will not find it any easier than anyone else to alter his attitudes and way of life to the extent that, if I am right, is involved in doing everything that we ought to be doing.[41]

Making personal sacrifices or altering the personal relationships we have so as to do the right thing is indeed hard. It may be so hard that some may try to justify not doing the right thing by adding extra weight to their own projects and relations. The principle of equal consideration of interests attempts to prevent this from happening. Concessions to partial interests allow for differential weighting and thus serve to weaken the force of the moral dictate and ultimately may serve to make the morally right answer more abstruse and condone a certain moral complacency.

In "Famine, affluence, and morality," Singer suggested that "what it is possible for a man to do and what he is likely to do are both, I think, very greatly influenced by what people around him are doing and expecting him to do."[42] An uncompromising moral theory – that is, one that recognizes the importance of personal relationships and projects but only as some of the important things among many – can serve to raise expectations. In a world in which so much suffering can be alleviated by relatively small, yet difficult, sacrifices, it seems that raising expectations is preferable to the complacency that allows us to retreat to the sanctuary of our personal and partial commitments and justifies not helping those in need.

A second reason why conceding to partialism may be undesirable for Singer is that personal interests and relations often conceal prejudices and a promotion of the personal may condone prejudicial actions. For example, no one would deny that friendship is one of the things that makes a life worth living and recognizing the importance of some friendships is important for any moral theory. Friends often provide each other with support and encouragement and can act as important models for each other. Indeed, many friendships provide the ground upon which moral behavior can flourish. But some friendships provide just the opposite. Consider friendships among Klansman or neo-Nazis. In these cases, friendships are often particularly strong and bonds of loyalty run quite deep. That friendship exists and that loyalty is strong in itself should not be reason to accept these personal claims as particularly weighty. Indeed, it is precisely such personal biases that impartial utilitarian theory is meant to overcome. The concession to partial concerns, such as those that arise in promoting friendships, may be undesirable. Even in less overtly prejudicial cases, friends are often made between individuals who share the same racial or socio-economic backgrounds and thus can serve not only to preserve certain prejudices, but in some cases to promote them.

Of particular concern for those who extend the sphere of moral consideration to non-human animals is the likely and frequent conflicts that arise between the demands of personal relationships and the requirement to take the equal interests of non-humans seriously. At the beginning of *Animal Liberation*, Singer expressed his worry that when he became a vegetarian he would offend his friends and family and disrupt dining experiences with them. Fortunately for him, Singer's friends and family were not offended, and like many others who know him or his work, many of his friends and family became vegetarians as well. This is not the case for many people, however. Often, skipping out on a family gathering because dead animals will be served or repeatedly refusing invitations to dine with non-vegetarian friends can cause serious strains on such relationships. These strains are often less serious than the ones that occur when one accepts the invitation and then discusses one's moral reasons for not eating animals with family members or friends who become extremely upset with the topic. Perhaps to maintain good relations and preserve family unity, one should simply remain quiet, or even eat what one is served. But Singer's utilitarianism suggests that this is not the right thing to do. Preserving harmonious personal relationships in a culture in which eating animals is the norm may require rejecting equal consideration of non-human animal interests. If this is what conceding to partialist critics requires, it seems clear that Singer would want to reject such a concession.

There are clearly hard questions about what, in the end, will bring about the greatest overall interest satisfaction, and giving weight to personal relationships and projects may increase the total level of interest satisfaction in some cases, but allowing prejudice to continue will certainly not promote the greatest good overall. Perhaps once the world is free of prejudice (against humans and non-humans alike) and the gap between the haves and have-nots is greatly minimized a utilitarian like Singer will be in a better position to make a case for considerations of the partial affections that attach to personal relationships, but until then, it looks as though Singer's utilitarian morality must maintain its commitment to impartiality in the strongest sense.

Notes

1 Singer's modesty is also revealed in this anecdote, as many people have changed their lives and gone on to help to change the lives of others as a direct result of Singer's work.

2 I suggest this in my essay "Animals," in P. Singer (ed.), *A Companion to Ethics*, (Oxford: Blackwell, 1991), pp. 343–53, and in my "Dismantling oppression: an analysis of the connection between women and animals," in G. Gaard (ed.), *Ecofeminism: Women, Animals, Nature* (Philadelphia: Temple University Press, 1993), pp. 60–90.

3 In using "emotion" in this way, I do not mean to suggest that is all emotions are, nor will I defend this understanding, as such a defense is not necessary for the argument of this paper. For present purposes, emotion can be understood simply as one of the influences that lead to partial reasoning.

4 *Practical Ethics*, 2nd edn (New York: Cambridge University Press, 1993), p. 11.

5 *Methods of Ethics*, 7th edn (Indianapolis: Hackett Publishing Company, 1981), p. 380.

6 *Moral Thinking* (Oxford: Clarendon Press, 1981), p. 8.

7 Ibid., p. 114.

8 Adrian Piper, "Moral theory and moral alienation," *Journal of Philosophy*, LXXXIV (February 1987), p. 102. By suggesting that impartiality requires generality in the sense that it not contain specific reference to individuals, Hare in particular is not maintaining that a universal theory or principle be general in every way. He writes: "generality is the opposite of specificity, whereas universality is compatible with specificity, and means merely the logical property of being governed by a universal quantifier and not containing individual constants" (*Moral Thinking*, p. 41).

9 *Methods of Ethics*, p. 380.

10 *How Are We to Live? Ethics in an Age of Self-interest* (Melbourne: The Text Publishing Company, 1993), p. 229.

11 *Ethics and the Limits of Philosophy* (Cambridge, MA: Harvard University Press, 1985), p. 115.

12 "The impracticality of impartiality," *Journal of Philosophy*, LXXXVI (November 1989), p. 654.

13 Bernard Boxill, "The color-blind principle," from *Blacks and Social Justice* (Totowa, NJ: Rowman and Littlefield, 1984), reprinted in L. May and S. Collins (eds), *Applied Ethics* (Englewood Cliffs, NJ: Prentice Hall, 1994), p. 321.

14 My distinction between formal and substantive differs slightly from R. M. Hare's, for example, in that he believes that the formal element of a moral theory is obtained from the logical properties of moral words, whereas what he calls the substantial comes from empirical examination of facts about the world. Which facts are important and how they are important is going to be theory dependent, and thus some examination of the theory will be necessary to understand the requirement of substantive impartiality. I believe that Hare's notion of the formal requirements actually contains a substantive component in my sense, which may be why he believes he can derive utilitarianism from the meaning of moral terms alone, but this is another matter.

15 William Godwin, *An Enquiry Concerning Political Justice and Its Influence on General Virtue and Happiness*, 1st edn (1793), pp. 41–2.

16 I thus disagree with Singer's belief that this principle is merely a restatement of the idea that ethics ought to be universal. As I have argued, there is an important distinction between the scope of morality, formal impartiality, and substantive impartiality within moral theories that I believe Singer has failed to make.

17 *Practical Ethics*, p. 21.

18 Ibid., pp. 55–6.

19 The criticisms are directed not only at utilitarian theories, or consequentialist theories more broadly, but at all impartial ethical theories. Indeed, utilitarian theory is often neglected in these criticisms, particularly when they are embedded in what has come to be known as the "justice/care" debate. For a discussion of the relation between the partiality/impartiality and the justice/care debate and the place that utilitarian theory fits in, see P. Singer, L. Cannold, H. Kuhse, and L. Gruen, "What is the justice/care debate really about?" *Midwest Studies in Philosophy* (1997).

20 While there are many feminist theorists that have mounted criticisms of both formal and substantive impartiality, none, I believe, would argue against the basic anti-prejudicial insight that impartiality is meant to capture. The criticisms are instead targeted at the impossibility of achieving impartiality, the way that important features of situations are ignored or overlooked in attempts to achieve impartiality, and false claims of impartiality that disguise bias or prejudice. I discuss some of these criticisms below.

21 Sandra Harding, Nancy Hartsock, and Elizabeth Fee, for example. For a discussion of feminist standpoint theory see Alison Jaggar, *Feminist Politics and Human Nature* (Totowa, NJ: Rowman and Allanheld, 1983), chapter 11.

22 Friedman, "The impracticability of impartiality," p. 655.

23 *Practical Ethics*, p. 53.

24 Susan Okin discusses this issue in reference to Rawls in her *Justice, Gender, and the Family* (New York: Basic Books, 1989), p. 102.

25 Okin uses the example of three male judges looking down at their pregnant bodies and saying, "Perhaps we'd better reconsider that decision" (ibid.).

26 Chris Cuomo and I expand on this idea in "Animals, intimacy, and moral distance," in Bat-Ami Bar On and Ann Ferguson (eds), *Daring to Be Good: Essays in Feminist Ethico-politics* (New York: Routledge, 1998).

27 On a generous reading, this seems to be one way of interpreting Marilyn Friedman's suggestion in "The impracticality of impartiality."

28 Samual Parr, "A Spital Sermone preached at Christ Church upon Easter Tuesday, April 15, 1800," pp. 9–10, as cited in P. Singer, L. Cannold and H. Kuhse, "William Godwin and the defence of impartialist ethics," *Utilitas*, 7 (May 1995).

29 Since first articulated by Williams in *Utilitarianism for and against*, and later in "Persons, character and morality" and *Ethics and the Limits of Philosophy*, the various forms of the "alienation objection" have received wide attention. See P. Railton, "Alienation, consequentialism, and the demands of morality," *Philosophy and Public Affairs*, 13 (1984), S. Scheffler, *The Rejection of Consequentialism* (Oxford: Clarendon Press, 1982), O. Flanagan, *Varieties of Moral Personality* (Cambridge, MA: Harvard University Press, 1991), S. Wolf, "Moral saints," *Journal of Philosophy*, 79 (1982), and M. Stocker, "The schizophrenia of modern ethical theories," *Journal of Philosophy*, 63 (1976). In these analyses, the alienation objection is made against moral theories generally, not just utilitarian theory, and alienation is represented as occurring in a number of forms, as alienation from oneself, one's projects, one's emotions, one's relationships, and morality itself. For present purposes, I will overlook much of the nuance of these rich discussions and focus primarily on the impact such an objection has for an impartial utilitarian theory.

30 These sorts of examples also raise problems for utilitarians in terms of the "demandingness" of the moral theory generally. When, if ever, can I as a utilitarian agent relax when there is more good to promote? An attempt to answer this question, though obviously related to the issue under discussion, would take us too far afield, and thus I will not discuss it. Lest this particular example seem absurdly trivial, note that in his criticism of impartiality in general and Singer in particular, John Cottingham uses the following one: "Bank holiday weekend comes round – a chance to relax. But my house needs painting – a job I detest. Nonetheless, I set to, because it is in my interest to 'keep up' the property. But wait: applying the impartiality thesis I am forced to admit that my interests cannot, just because they are mine, count for more than anyone else's. It follows that I have no moral reason for selecting my house for redecoration rather than my next door neighbour's. Indeed, in order

to be moral it seems that I must be quite neutral and impartial in deciding whether my weekend's labour is to be allocated to my own or my neighbour's projects... I [must] balance my own and my neighbour's interests just as if I were balancing the interest of my neighbour and some third party with whom I have no special connections; and if I find some relevant difference (perhaps my neighbour's house is more in need of painting than mine), then the moral decision would be to report for work next door" ("Ethics and impartiality," *Philosophical Studies*, 43 (1983), p. 86).

31 This seems to be Frank Jackson's strategy as well. See "Decision theoretic consequentialism and the nearest and dearest objection," *Ethics*, 101 (1991).

32 See, for example, Hare, *Moral Thinking*, Railton, "Alienation, consequentialism, and the demands of morality", and David Brink, "Utilitarian morality and the personal point of view," *Journal of Philosophy*, LXXXIII (August 1986), p. 424.

33 See Brink, ibid.

34 See *The Rejection of Consequentialism* (Oxford: Oxford University Press, 1982), chapter 3. See also Laurence Blum, *Moral Perception and Particularity* (Cambridge: Cambridge University Press, 1994), particularly part I.

35 Singer et al., "What is the justice/care debate really about?"

36 Especially considering that, "in 1995, it's true that, in each of the past 30 years, well over 10 million children died from readily preventable causes," and the cost of preventing such deaths is relatively low for most everyone reading this footnote. See Peter Unger's telling discussion in *Living High and Letting Die* (Oxford: Oxford University Press, 1996), pp. 3–8.

37 This is a point brought out in Dale Jamieson's "When utilitarians should be virtue theorists: the case of global environmental change," presented at the "Utilitarianism Reconsidered" Conference, New Orleans, March 22–23, 1997.

38 *Practical Ethics*, 2nd edn, p. 229.

39 Ibid., p. 246.

40 In the second edition of *Practical Ethics* and in *How Are We to Live?*, as a result of his concession to partialist critics, Singer allows that some personal relationships are of comparable moral significance and when they are one is not required to aid. Given that Singer leaves the concept of moral significance relatively unexamined it is hard to know what type of personal relationships and considerations he thinks would count. I think that he does not want to say that any personal commitment will serve to outweigh the requirement to aid.

41 "Famine, affluence, and morality," reprinted in George Sher (ed.), *Moral Philosophy*, 2nd edn (Fort Worth, TX: Harcourt Brace and Company, 1996), p. 704.

42 Ibid., p. 700.

8

Our Duties to Animals and the Poor

COLIN McGINN

There is, on any account, much preventable suffering in the world, both animal and human. There are also many deaths that occur before the biological forces of senescence have done their ineluctable work. Suffering is a bad thing, as is premature death. It would be good if there were less of these evils in the world. It would be good, perhaps, if they could be erased entirely, assuming this to be a feasible ideal.[1] As the world stands, things are very much worse than they ought to be. But what are our moral obligations in respect of all this suffering and death? Do we have a duty to relieve as much of it as is humanly possible? Do we, in particular, have the following two duties: (a) to relieve the suffering, and cease the killing, of the animals with which we have dealings; and (b) to relieve the suffering, and prevent the death, of the world's poor and starving and diseased? Peter Singer has argued memorably that we have both duties, and that both are morally stringent: not to fulfill either of these duties counts as a serious moral failing.[2] In this chapter I shall contend that he is right as to (a) but wrong as to (b). I thus invert what I take to be the standard liberal position on these issues, namely that our treatment of animals is not fundamentally immoral while our stinginess with respect to the Third World is morally disgraceful. There is more that is deeply wrong with our treatment of animals, I believe, than with our treatment of the world's poor. (This is not to say, of course, that animals are "more important" than humans.)

Consider the following two arguments:

Argument A

(1) It is morally wrong to cause the suffering and death of animals unnecessarily
(2) We do cause the suffering and death of animals unnecessarily

Therefore:

(3) What we do to animals is morally wrong

Argument B

(1) It is morally wrong to let people suffer and die unnecessarily
(2) We do let people suffer and die unnecessarily

Therefore:

(3) What we do in respect of suffering and dying people is morally wrong

Just to be a bit more concrete, we are considering, under argument *A*, eating meat, hunting, vivisection, fur coats, and the like; and, under argument *B*, not giving substantial amounts of money to charities that work to relieve the starvation, disease, and misery of the poorest people in the world. Our two arguments then purport to show that these kinds of acts and omissions are morally unacceptable. The arguments look very similar in form, and both concern the badness of suffering and death and our power to prevent them. My view, however, is that *A* is sound while *B* is unsound. Before I defend this view, let me clarify the force of "unnecessarily" as it occurs in both arguments. It does *not* mean "unless there is some reason to do so," for there *is* some reason to kill and eat animals and wear their skins and hunt them for sport – namely, that we derive some benefits from so doing. We enjoy the taste of their flesh, we keep warm and look attractive, we experience "the thrill of the chase." In just the same way, there is also some reason to do such things to other humans. These are not pointless actions; they are rationally motivated. But the force of "unnecessarily" is that these are not actions in which the ends really justify the means, since the benefit we derive is not commensurate with the harm that is inflicted. A large evil is caused for the sake of a small good. In order for the action to have been performed "necessarily" the end would have had to justify the means, everything considered, and not merely count as *a* reason to perform the action. It is not clear that there are any such cases, but they would have to amount to a situation in which the benefit we derive is at least equivalent to the harm we inflict – say, saving our own life by eating a chicken or a pig. Similarly, in the charity case, I do have *a* reason for not giving money to Oxfam, namely that I can spend it on a nice dinner at an expensive restaurant. It is just that this is hardly something I do "necessarily," i.e. for the sake of some value commensurate with the value of the life of the starving person I fail to save. So the force of "unnecessarily" is something like this: "unless there is some benefit to be derived that is at least equivalent to the cost inflicted." And the thought is that I should not be expected to do something whose cost to me outweighs the benefit I bring to someone else, animal or human. Then in the cases of interest to us here the two arguments enjoin us to refrain from actions that cannot be justified by appeal to parity in the costs and benefits of the action. And it is clear enough that the arguments do not violate this principle, since the costs of our not exploiting animals, or of sending substantial sums to charity, will not be at all large in comparison with the benefits that are brought about. The animal's life will be saved and we will have a somewhat less tasty meal (let's say), and the starving child's life will be saved while we forgo an amusing visit to the cinema. The force of both arguments derives from the fact that they draw attention to a massive disparity between the egoistic benefits we derive from certain actions and the harm to others such actions incur. The arguments depict us as caring far more for our trivial pleasures than for the very life of other sentient beings. We are ready to cause or tolerate untold misery in others as long as we derive some minuscule quantum of passing pleasure in the process. And that looks about as immoral as anything can be. The serious suffering of others is within our control but we choose to promote and permit it rather than give up our trivial pleasures.

I will not say much in defense of argument A, since it has been very well defended by Singer and others; I wish to make only two points about it.[3] The first is that it is not necessary to derive the argument from some general form of utilitarianism. We need not take the first premiss to depend upon some such general principle as that it is our duty to maximize pleasure and minimize pain. All the argument requires is that we should not *cause* the suffering and death of an animal unnecessarily; it does not entail that we have a duty to go out into the world and *prevent* as much animal suffering as possible. The argument of course assumes that animal suffering is a bad thing, but it does not commit us to the principle that we should do everything we can to prevent any animal suffering anywhere. Thus the argument is consistent with supposing that there exists animal suffering we have no obligation to prevent, or have a lesser obligation to prevent than that which obtains in respect of animal suffering of which we are the agent.

The second point is that we should not think of animal pain as intrinsically "ownerless."[4] Animal minds are not just bundles of subjectless sensations gathered around a single body. If we conceive of animal pain in this subjectless way, thus refusing to grant genuine selfhood to animals, then we will not see why it is morally significant, since pain matters only because it is pain *for someone*. Putatively ownerless pain sensations have no moral weight, since the alleged pain is not painful *to* a subject of awareness. In other words, animals need to be granted selves if their sensations are to matter morally. This may seem like a major provision, and one that threatens to exclude animal experience from the moral realm; but in fact it is simply a point about the very concept of experience. As Frege long ago noted (following Kant), the very notion of experience is the notion of experience *for* a subject: there is really no sense in the idea of ownerless experience.[5] An experience always comes with an owner built into it. It is not that you bundle some inherently ownerless experiences together and get a self, as Hume was (partially) inclined to suppose; rather, to speak of experiences at all is already to assume bearers for them – *subjects* of experience. (This is so whether or not the experiences are conceived to be embodied in an organism.) So, since animals have experiences, they necessarily have selves – by Frege's point. Thus it is wrong to cause them pain, because this will necessarily be pain *for* a subject of consciousness.

Let me also note, as a corollary, that this kind of argument cannot be deployed to contest the morality of abortion, since this is precisely a case in which the assumption of sentience is in question. *If* the fetus is sentient and hence, by Frege's principle, is a subject of awareness, *then* it is morally wrong to cause it to suffer and to kill it (unless there is some comparable benefit to be derived, such as saving the life of the mother). But nothing in the argument we have endorsed allows us to object to the termination of an *in*sentient fetus. So it is not, as I have heard it said, that we are irrationally and immorally preferring animals over babies!

Now let us turn to argument *B*. Our focus here must be on the first premiss, since the rest of it seems unquestionable. Is it true? It can sound plausible enough, but I think that is because we tend to hear it as if in a certain context, which the argument goes on in effect to switch. This is the context in which a person in front of us is suffering and dying and we can save her by some simple act of generosity – say, by giving her half our dinner. And I agree that omitting to do this would be morally monstrous. This shows that we cannot find an asymmetry between *A* and *B* by exploiting the act/omission distinction. It is quite true that *B* concerns the wrongness of certain omissions while *A* deals with positive acts, but I would not rest my rejection of *B* on that ground alone, since I think letting someone suffer and die can in certain circumstances be just as bad as killing her – or at least very very bad indeed. The asymmetry I see has far more to do with the context in which the suffering arises and the agent's relation to the sufferer. Let me explain.[6]

First let us turn to Singer's defense of the first premiss. He says: "if it is in our power to prevent something bad from happening, without thereby sacrificing something of comparable moral importance, we ought, morally, to do it" (p. 177);[7] and later "we ought to prevent as much suffering as we can without sacrificing something else of comparable moral importance" (p. 181). As an illustration of this principle, he gives the example of the shallow pond: we should clearly save a child from drowning even if doing so makes our clothes muddy, since the benefits so vastly outweigh the costs. He notes, however, that the "uncontroversial appearance of the principle just stated is deceptive" (p. 177), since it requires radical changes in our spending habits with respect to charities. For the principle is quite neutral as to the relative locations of the individuals involved, and Singer tells us that "we cannot discriminate against someone merely because he is far away from us" (p. 178). Just as we cannot discriminate on the basis of skin color or sex or species, so we cannot discriminate on the basis of geography – that would be to commit the sin of "spatialism" (to coin a term). Thus our duties with respect to the distant poor vastly exceed what we customarily assume.

How persuasive is this? By "comparable moral importance" Singer means something similar in type or weight to the suffering that would otherwise occur. We must make the kinds of sacrifices that are less in their costs to us than the benefits we bring to others. One way in which I could prevent a good deal of Third World suffering would be to disallow my child to attend college, thus condemning him to a life of underachievement; or I could decide never to see another ballet or play or film; or I could refrain altogether from eating in restaurants. I take it these are the kinds of sacrifices Singer thinks we should make, since if they are not his principle is toothless and morally conservative. He agrees that these things have intrinsic value but he thinks they are not "comparable" to the suffering that can be prevented by forgoing them. So he must think that the excusing kind of sacrifice would itself have to involve suffering – that, for example, you should not starve in order to relieve starvation.[8] The principle then is to the effect that we ought to relieve whatever suffering will not cause us (or others) to suffer comparably. We should certainly not read the principle as saying that we ought to prevent suffering as long as there is no reason to allow it – which is anodyne and virtually tautological. No, the principle enjoins each of us, in effect, to level the degree of suffering in the world. Thus stated the principle is extremely strong and to my ear lacks all appearance of self-evidence. *Why* exactly should I go around making myself suffer to the point that others suffer? Why, for example, should I give away all my money to New York City beggars, until there are none worse off than me? What about the idea that I *earned* that money and they did not? Why *should* we act so as to equalize the suffering in the world? Only some kind of impartial utilitarianism could sustain such an injunction: that we all have a duty to maximize the general well-being and minimize ill-being. I think this kind of view is generally indefensible – and certainly not self-evident – as consideration of future generations and other problems demonstrates.[9]

But let me just point out some of the more apposite consequences of adopting such a morality.

Suppose you are a beautiful woman sexually desired by many men. The men suffer from libidinal longings that you could easily fulfill. You can relieve these sufferings by having sex with them, say at the rate of ten a day. Let us suppose you could do this without suffering too much ("comparably") yourself.[10] So you could spread a lot of sexual happiness among the male population without sacrificing your own well-being to a comparable degree. (Of course, the same argument could be given for the case of a beautiful man.) Maybe some of your potential partners will become seriously depressed unless their sexual deprivation is relieved, suicidal even. Should you do it? Of course not: why should your life be made into a tool for the satisfaction of other people's desires? Or again, you may be such a witty conversationalist that you could bring cheer into the lives of many bored and depressed people: should you abandon your life and friends in order to minister to people's conversational needs? Obviously not, even though you will bring much more cheer to others than the misery you inflict on yourself. Or think of all the beneficial effects on other people's tennis game you could bring about if you abandoned your career as a top seeded player and devoted yourself to remedial tennis programs. Or consider a feckless gambler you know of who is rapidly sliding into bankruptcy but whom you can save by spending several hours a day with him in the local pub talking about horse racing and drinking beer. Unfortunately, this will involve neglect of your own family and you will not be able to finish the degree you are working toward in the evenings; still, this loss to yourself and your family is not so great as the loss that will result for him if he keeps up his reckless gambling (your pub-related suffering will not be anywhere near as great as his gambling-related suffering). Should you make the sacrifice? Clearly not, I say. The plain fact is that this gambler is not "your problem," though you could indeed help him overcome his (we can suppose that he isn't even a friend – just someone you have observed from afar). And note that there may be a long line of similar gamblers behind him all waiting for you to distract them from their habit while you live an impoverished and tedious life in awful pubs talking to these people. (The matter would be different, of course, if you were somehow responsible for their gambling habit.) Plainly, it is absurd to require people to make such sacrifices – that is, to calculate their duties according to the principle Singer recommends. These are all straight counterexamples to that principle. The principle has plausibility only as a *prima facie* principle of action: you should relieve suffering if you do not thereby comparably suffer, *unless there are reasons that override this* prima facie *obligation*. And the trouble is that there are many reasons that can override it. The issue then is precisely whether the case of the distant poor is one such reason; no simple recitation of the principle can secure the result that we have stringent duties of self-sacrifice in this regard.

Singer might reply that the suffering he is talking about is of the life-or-death variety, while my examples are not. That may be true, but why does it make a difference? Why is the principle valid for serious suffering but not for milder forms? Is he suggesting that we have no charitable duties toward those who are not in peril of their lives? What about the homeless in our own society, the mentally handicapped, the quadriplegic, the educationally deprived? If we think only "serious" suffering warrants our concern, then all these charities will go by the board. It is equally true in these cases that the relief I can bring about by my charity is far greater than the loss I incur, even though the suffering mitigated is not of the most extreme kind. I can see no reason to discriminate against the only "moderately" needy. And my point here is just that the existence of such a disparity is not *by itself* sufficient to warrant the kinds of remedial actions Singer is advocating – on pain of requiring such actions in the examples I cited. The utilitarian defense of Singer's unrestricted principle, which is the only one I can imagine, implies many other similar principles dealing with other degrees of happiness and unhappiness. But the simple fact is that it is not my moral duty to increase people's happiness until it coincides with mine, or reduce mine until no one is more unhappy than I am. If I should save the drowning child, or indeed the distant starving child, then it cannot be because of the correctness of such a principle, since it is not correct.

In fact, I think such a principle positively bad, morally speaking. It encourages a way of life in which many important values are sacrificed to generalized altruism. To take a particularly proximate one: I could not have become a philosopher if I had lived by such a principle, and neither could anyone else (including Singer), since doing so requires spending one's energies on things other than helping suffering people in distant lands. Every hour spent reading and writing and teaching is an hour that could be spent relieving the sufferings of the poor. But I don't want to live in a world in which people are morally required not to reach their intellectual potential. Just think of how much the human race would have lost if Newton and Darwin and Leonardo and Socrates had spent their time on charitable acts! It should be noted here that Singer's argument is that an individual's duties hold independently of what others decide to do, so that you have them whether or not anyone else does anything to fulfill their own. By this standard we could wipe out philosophy overnight: all philosophers have a duty to devote themselves to charity work, and they will not be saved by the willingness of others to pitch in. I think myself that the cessation of philosophy would be quite a bad thing. The only way to block this kind of consequence is to restrict the principle in ways that yield no startling revisions in moral policy. Suppose we say that we are obliged to reduce suffering as long as doing so does not interfere with anything such that if it were eliminated the world would be a worse place. Then we would still be allowed to support the ballet and other "frivolous" pursuits such as the arts and sciences, as well as eat good food and all the rest. In fact, anything of positive value will trump the altruistic principle, since anything of value is such that the world would be a worse place without it.

One should not use others as a mere means to one's ends: that is a sound moral maxim. But equally, one should not use oneself as a means to the ends of others. That is what I meant earlier when I wrote of becoming a tool for others' satisfaction. I should not regard my life purely as a means by which other people can have their well-being increased. Just such a conception lurks behind the principle Singer favors: that my duty is to live in such a way as to reduce the suffering of others by increasing my own suffering, or by lowering my level of well-being. That strikes me as a depressing and wrongheaded vision of human life. It involves seeing myself as a means toward the ends of others, and this is no more acceptable than my using them as a means to my ends – indeed, both are wrong for exactly the same reason. It is an abnegation of personal autonomy, of the right to live one's life as one's own, developing one's own talents and potential. Of course, one should not positively harm others – human or animal – as one lives one's own life, but there is no obligation to devote oneself to the relief of suffering one has had no part in producing. The case is really no different from that of the healthy person whose organs could save or prolong the lives of several individuals with diseased organs. Confronted by six people who could use my organs if I were to relinquish them and bid farewell to this life, should I hand them over? Absolutely not, I retort, even though, ranked according to "comparable moral importance," six lives count for more than one. And the reason is just that I should not regard myself as a means to their ends; my life is not yours to commandeer and control, still less to take. I could, similarly, choose to starve myself to death in order to prevent distant others from suffering the same fate, and I may well save more lives this way than in any other; but it is absurd to think that I now have a duty to starve myself to death, by sending all my money to Oxfam, including what I could get by selling food given to *me* by charities – even though my death is just one as against the ten I might save by such "heroism." The rule of equalizing well-being is simply a monstrosity if interpreted in this way. But I see nothing in Singer's discussion to block this kind of consequence. What underlies his position is precisely the kind of utilitarianism of which these cases are *reductions*. Nor is it possible to try to weaken and qualify the principle to weed such cases out, since then it will be robbed of its philosophical rationale. What is needed is a clean sweep: our attitudes toward charity should not be guided by any utilitarian principle that compares our well-being with that of potential beneficiaries and calculates our duties by the disparity between them. Any defense of charity that relies upon such principles will represent charitable giving, however small, as the first step on a slippery slope toward absurd levels of self-sacrifice, and hence will deter people from giving at all. It will look as if ethical consistency requires extreme levels of self-sacrifice, and then even minimal levels will be avoided in order to avoid intellectual inconsistency. Thus the kind of defense of charity Singer advocates is liable to prove counter-productive.[11]

So what do we owe to the poor of the world? By what principle should our charitable giving be guided? I think decent rational people feel quite unsure about this question; it is not that they know very well and decline to carry out their moral duty. And this seems to me to be the real state of things in this area: morality delivers no clear-cut answer to the question of how much we should deprive ourselves for the sake of distant others. Morality does tell us what to do about the child drowning in the shallow pond and similar cases, but it goes wobbly when it comes to remote sufferering. We naturally feel compassion for such suffering but its moral claim on our lives is unclear, perhaps even indeterminate.[12] The intuition here is that remote suffering is not "our problem" – it does not come within the cone of our moral responsibilities, strictly so-called. Yet we are also aware that we can do something to help the sufferers. The case is somewhat analogous to questions about military intervention in foreign lands: on the one hand, these are not our countries and hence are not "our business"; yet, on the other hand, we know that we could ameliorate the situation if we chose. We thus feel torn on the issue. These cases in turn are not unlike more domestic dilemmas, as when one's relatives are arguing about something and one does not know whether to intervene: the squabble is none of our concern, yet we may know that we could ease the situation by stepping in. I do not believe there is any simple way to resolve such conflicts. The right course of action is highly sensitive to the details of the case. If I were asked to propose a principle that makes the best of a problematic situation, then I could not do better than this: we should help out the distant poor when and only when their need is desperate and we will not sacrifice anything in our own life that makes it meaningful to us. This prescription is (intentionally) vague, and may appear hard-hearted, but as far as I can see it is the best compromise among the various considerations that complicate the issue. The prescription does not require me to cease being a philosopher, or indeed going to the ballet; it requires me only to give up pleasures that form no part of what makes my life significant to me. Nor is it a prescription I derive from some general theory of morality, such as utilitarianism; it is just an *ad hoc* rule of thumb that seems to strike the best balance between competing concerns and fits my real feelings about my obligations. There is nothing in it that requires me to live hypocritically or inconsistently. It is a mistake, I think, to suppose that we can get anything crisper and more glassily theoretical as a guide to action.

By "distant" here we do not mean, of course, merely spatially distant. My duties to my child do not fall off as he recedes from me in space – say by his going to Africa to do relief work. The relevant notion of distance is social or emotional or political or historical – the extent to which the community in question is bound up with my own by ties of these various sorts. When Singer says that mere distance should not matter he is parodying the relevant notion of distance: my family is close to me in the relevant sense even when I am thousands of miles away. Just as my duties to my family are greater than those I have to my neighbor's family (I should put my child through school, though not his), so my duties to people in Africa are less than my duties to those in my own neighborhood. Such social groupings are not only morally relevant but also morally central. Being especially kind to the stranger in our midst is one reflection of the way the notion of social grouping works: this is the notion of *hospitality*, a notion defined in terms of social group-ings. But none of this kind of moral complexity and subtlety shows up in Singer's simple principle. This is not the kind of irrational "spatialism" mentioned earlier; it is what we might call (this time borrowing a term) "socialism". In short: our duties to others are greater the closer they are to us socially.

Let me end with a thought experiment. Suppose Internet technology reaches the stage that we all have plugged into our brains a computer terminal that picks up news broadcasts from all over the world. One of the channels, the Charity Channel, which is compulsory viewing, reports disasters and starvation and disease from all points of the globe, so that we are constantly flooded with information about who is suffering what, with live pictures of the sufferers. Suppose too that we are all equipped with a banking facility that enables us to transer funds instantly to the scene of the suffering, where officials will administer the needed help. We might then see the effects of our charity minutes after we have acted charitably. What should we do in such circumstances? Is this a desirable state of affairs? It would certainly tax our natural compassion to an extraordinary extent, making it difficult to pursue any other interest, aside from keeping up our bank balance so that we can go on being charitable. I myself find this a dystopian prospect, in view of the tension it would set up in my system of allegiances; and I suspect that after a time

I would revert to my present policies, becoming hardened to things I should not have to become hardened to. Human compassion is not infinitely elastic, and it should not be burdened with more than it can handle. It should not, in particular, be dulled by demands that exceed our actual moral responsibilities. The danger of the "global village" is that it sets up an illusion of moral responsibility, in which our natural sympathies are excited in ways that go beyond our duties; and that will not be good for the health of our moral sense. There are, we know, tender souls who are so taken with the romantic sob stories of others that they neglect their real duties; this is not a moral strength, but a weakness. It is part of what we mean when we criticize people for "sentimentality." No doubt this is a better failing than callousness, but it is still a failing. Charities that exploit it are not to be commended for doing so. I am not saying that the charitable impulse is invariably, or even often, sentimental; my point is simply that sentimentality is not to be confused with moral obligation. I certainly feel keen sympathy for the starving people I sometimes see on TV, along with a sense of moral unease; but I do not believe that I have a moral obligation to reduce myself to something close to starvation in order to benefit them. To suppose so is to succumb to sentimentality, not to moral truth. This may seem a stern and flinty attitude, but I think it is the moral position we are really in – and a certain toughness is often the mark of true justice. It is an attitude that would come to the fore if we were continually flooded with broadcasts from the Charity Channel.

To sum up: argument *A* is a sound argument, turning upon the wrongness of causing harm to animals unnecessarily; it is not an argument that asks us to reduce our standard of living for the sake of animals that may be suffering quite independently of our actions. We have a strict duty not to cause animal suffering unnecessarily, whereas it is merely generous of us to relieve the sufferings of remote animals (as it might be polar bears in a bad winter). Argument *B* is unsound because we have no strict obligation to relieve any suffering the world may contain as long as this does not involve comparable suffering. That is just a bad utilitarian principle with no intrinsic plausibility and some highly disturbing consequences. By all means be generous to charities, but do not think of this as an exercise in hedonic redistribution. I am with Singer in believing that the richer nations of the world do far too little to aid the poorer nations, but I cannot accept the kind of utilitarian defence of extreme charity that he advocates. The great appeal of utilitarianism, especially to philosophers, is the promise it holds out of a simple and mechnical answer to moral questions; but moral life is far too complex and subtle for any such practical algorithm. The issue of charity is a textbook case for illustrating the limits and deformities of utilitarianism.

Notes

1 I say "perhaps" because it is not clear that a life totally free of suffering would be a good human life. Suffering builds character, as they say. Still, suffering should be eliminated to the extent that it has no positive side-effects.

2 See Peter Singer, *Animal Liberation* (London: Jonathan Cape, 1990), and Peter Singer, "Famine, affluence and morality," in J. E. White (ed.), *Contemporary Moral Problems* (St Paul, MN: West Publishing Company, 1985), originally published in *Philosophy and Public Affairs*, (Spring 1972).

3 For an appreciative review of Singer's *Animal Liberation* see Colin McGinn, "Eating animals is wrong," *London Review of Books*, January 24, 1991, reprinted in my *Minds and Bodies* (New York: Oxford University Press, 1997).

4 I elaborate on this point in "Animal minds, animal morality," *Social Research*, 62 (Fall 1995).

5 Gottlob Frege, "The thought," in P. F. Strawson (ed.), *Philosophical Logic* (Oxford: Oxford University Press, 1967).

6 There is more discussion of my objections to Singer's kind of position in my review of Peter Unger's *Living High and Letting Die* (New York: Oxford University Press, 1996), in *The New Republic*, October 14, 1996. The present chapter is a complement to that review, not just a restatement of it.

7 These quotations are all from Singer's "Famine, affluence and morality." Page references in the text are to the edition cited in note 2.

8 That is, unless you can save more people than you sacrifice: see below for more on this.

9 For more on this see my review of Unger, cited in note 6.

10 I hope it is clear that I am not supposing that doing this would in practice involve zero suffering for the woman. I am just stipulating that the suffering would be relatively minor in order to ask what consequences we should draw from this.

11 I think this is actually a very serious point that philosophers need to ponder carefully. It is always risky to gound one's firm moral intuitions upon contentious philosophical doctrines. The intuitions should not be made hostage to the vagaries of philosophical theory. And people should not be led to believe that their moral feelings require them to accept far-fetched philosophical constructions. Bad philosophical defenses of good causes can do more harm than good.

12 It is not just humans who evoke these feelings and generate these quandaries – there is also the question of distant suffering animals. Consider a colony of mice in Africa hard hit by food shortage. I could ease their suffering by donating the price of a ballet ticket. Should I do it? I would say that my strict duties do not extend this far, but there is still a case that could be made for me to be more generous toward these mice. But exactly how much I should give up for them seems to me entirely moot. What I would insist upon, however, is the point that this case is quite different from a case in which my *pet* mice are suffering a similar shortage. Social proximity is as potent here as in the human case.

9

Faminine Ethics: the Problem of Distance in Morality and Singer's Ethical Theory

F. M. KAMM

Peter Singer has famously been concerned with famine relief. In connection with this concern, he has denied the moral significance of distance. He says, "I do not think I need to say much in defense of the refusal to take proximity and distance into account. The fact that a person is physically near to us... does not show that we ought to help him rather than another who happens to be far away."[1] In this chapter, I ultimately wish to reconsider the question of the moral significance of distance. However, I will first consider the particular kind of consequentialism to which Peter Singer subscribes and his conception of the role of moral reasons. Based on what he says in various places in published works,[2] I shall first try to *reconstruct* and criticize his normative theory. I shall consider that topic generally, but will eventually give particular attention to his denial that the distinction between killing and letting die has moral relevance. I will argue that he does not prove that the distinction has no moral relevance. Only then shall I focus on the principles which he thinks generate our duty to give famine relief. The chapter ends with discussion of the role of distance in generating moral obligations. In that section, I also discuss the views of Peter Unger, who has been inspired by Singer.[3] (The discussion of distance can be read independently of the rest of the chapter.) I shall argue that the problem of distance in morality has not been correctly formulated, and that the claim that proximity is morally relevant is not, contrary to appearances, inconsistent with the claim that we can have equal obligations to aid near and distant people.

General Theory and Motivation

In *Practical Ethics* (PE), Singer commits himself to a two-level theory such as Richard Hare advocates.[4] The higher level is strictly impartial consequentialism. The lower level (which is implied by the higher level in conjunction with empirical facts) consists of rules or types of character traits. Apparently, on Singer's view, the rules are not merely rules of thumb which we may break on occasion, since he says it would be better from the point of view of maximizing good consequences that we not be able to think of breaking the rules, even if it would maximize good consequences on an occasion to do so. This is why I think he is committed to certain *character traits* or *patterns of thinking* (that make it impossible to think of breaking rules) that maximize good consequences overall, even if on occasion having them does not lead to maximizing the good.[5]

There is a second two-level theory to which Singer commits himself, but it does not tell us the content of a normative theory. Rather, he claims, it describes the *motivation to be moral*.[6] He does not think this motivation is derivable from a commitment to rationality *per se*. (He accepts Sidgwick's view on this.) Rather, he posits self-interest as the highest-level rationale for an individual's being moral.[7] Being moral is in one's self-interest because it is the best route to a *meaningful* life, he thinks. A meaningful life is a good, independent of happiness (understood as preference satisfaction). Happiness may be achieved by a sociopath as well as, or better than, a moral person, but not the meaningful life. Hence, Singer seems to believe that individuals have a stronger interest (in the sense that it is more in their interest) in having a meaningful life than in having a happy life.[8]

At the second, lower level in the motivational structure is moral conscientiousness. That is, while self-interest can reasonably motivate us to be moral, being moral involves acting for the sake of morality, not for the sake of self-interest.

Is Singer's account of the motivation to be moral plausible? He understands the content of morality at the highest level to involve strict impartiality, and (as we shall see below) its content at the second level is also very much concerned with producing the best state of affairs from an impartial point of view. Singer thinks that this is a quite secure basis for a meaningful life, and he contrasts it with purely personal aims that one is likely to grow out of.[9] But, in fact, many people find meaningful lives through work and personal relations and rarely grow out of attachment to those. (Indeed, in the chapter where Singer describes an environmentally sound lifestyle, he seems to describe just such a life based on engaging work and personal relations, without their meaningfulness being related to maximizing good from an impartial view.) If meaningful lives are frequently possible outside of a commitment to highly impartial morality, Singer's motivational argument will not succeed.

There may also be an inconsistency generated by the employment of *two* two-level models. The search for a meaningful life by a commitment to an impartial perspective suggests that one becomes conscientiously committed (at the second level in the motivational model) to the strictly impartial theory, which is at the first, higher level in the normative model. But his normative theory says that the morality one attaches to day-to-day life is at the second level, where one's traits may make it impossible to act on each occasion from a strictly impartial perspective. Indeed, one may be asked to forget about primacy of strict impartiality if one is to act in accordance with morality's dictates. Then, how could the meaningfulness of one's life derive from a conscious attachment to impartiality?

A general problem with the two-level model of normative theory is that it is most workable (even if not correct) if a few know the truth about the impartial consequentialist foundations of morality and the rest just know of commitment to rules or traits of character. But if we imagine one person knowing the real impartial consequentialist foundations of his morality, it is hard to see how *he* can treat the rules or traits as unbreakable and right in themselves, even though this may be necessary in order to maximize good consequences. It is possible that he should once *have* known the truth and then induced amnesia so that he now has forgotten the truth. If this is the only route to maximizing the good, he should follow it, according to consequentialism. One's life might then be meaningful because of its objective connection with impartiality, but one would know this only for a short period of time. Is a meaningful life, whose meaningfulness one does not know about, what Singer has in mind? It is also possible that someone can put out of his mind the true impartial theory in daily life and only be aware of it in reflective moments. But here, there is probably more danger of a spillover which will reduce commitment to rules. Still, if occasional reflection on impartiality did not conflict with overall good, one could occasionally (if Singer were right) provide oneself with a *sense* of meaning as well as with an objectively meaningful life.

The Moral Point of View and Normative Theory

Let us try to reconstruct in more detail the idea of the moral point of view and then the content of the two-level normative theory to which Singer subscribes. Singer believes that the strict impartiality of the highest level of the normative theory is suggested by, but not a necessary implication of, the very idea of the moral point of view. He thinks of the latter as justification of conduct in terms of the good of all. Impartiality involves (a) equal consideration of the relevant interests, where interests are to be understood as what each would rationally prefer for himself, and (b) maximizing the satisfaction of these interests in accord with the importance of the interests. Let us elaborate first on Singer's idea of the moral point of view.

The moral point of view and the weightiness of moral considerations

Singer's conception of the moral point of view militates against the idea that *at its basic level* the moral point of view permits agents to weigh things partially: that is, out of proportion to their weight from an impartial point of view. This understanding of the moral point of view contrasts with the one offered by Samuel Scheffler[10] and Thomas Nagel.[11] They think that morality at its most basic level itself endorses a prerogative to care and sometimes act from the personal point of view rather than the impartial point of view. In their views, impartiality is sometimes represented merely by universalization: that is, the prerogative to act from a personal point of view must be granted equally to everyone. Singer's conception permits acting on a partial point of view only at the second level, if it is a means to producing the best outcome impartially understood.

The alternative presented by a view like Scheffler's is that, at a *foundational* level in *morality*, it can sometimes be a determinative consideration that it would be a great personal sacrifice for someone to do what is approved by the impartial point of view; it would be *morally* wrong to *require* the large sacrifice. (Singer can only allow that, at a foundational level, the personal sacrifice is one factor, easily overridden by the losses to others, that an impartial point of view must consider.) Scheffler does not formulate a principled account of when the personal point of view can outweigh, *within the moral point of view*, impartial considerations, so that one would not have done anything morally wrong in following the personal point of view. This is because it is difficult to see how to do it. For example,[12] if each person were permitted to assign a single multiplicative factor to personal losses so that they had more weight, they could still be overridden in circumstances where, we might think, morally they should not be, and override in circumstances where, we might think, they should not. That is why some have attempted to distinguish different types of duties – for example, not harming from aiding – so that great personal losses might be required rather than harm people but not required to aid people. (This could not be represented by assigning a single multiplicative factor to my losses relative to those of others.)

There is a related matter with which Singer does not ever explicitly deal: Is the moral point of view, whether it requires impartiality of everyone or not, dominant over other points of view? How does the answer to this question relate to the question of whether explicitly moral considerations always dominate other considerations? Commonly, there are thought to be different types of factors that should be considered in deciding on a course of action: explicitly moral considerations (e.g. general concern for human welfare, respect for persons, fair treatment), aesthetic considerations, economic considerations, etc. Some, like Joseph Raz,[13] have claimed that when we decide what to do, we just consider the weight of different reasons, without being concerned about the category in which they fall (moral, aesthetic, etc.). Sometimes the moral considerations will be overridden by aesthetic or personal ones, he claims.

In considering this view that moral considerations may be overridden, I would note that there could be at least two senses of "overriding of the moral." One is that an explicitly moral consideration is overridden by, for example, an aesthetic one in a way that does *not* imply that one's behavior is immoral. That is, the conduct is consistent with the moral point of view. For example, if the presentation of a great work of performance art requires the telling of a small lie, then while a moral wrong occurs to the person who is lied to in the process of an aesthetic achievement, it is not morally wrong to pursue the aesthetic achievement. (This is similar to "overriding of the impartial" by personal considerations that Scheffler's view, as described above, allows for; it is supposed to be consistent with approval from the moral point of view.)

A second sense of "overriding the moral" would be that what is prohibited all things considered from the moral point of view can be overridden by what is demanded from the aesthetic point of view. So, if it is morally wrong to kill someone to produce a greater picture, perhaps it should be done anyway if producing the picture has superiority from the aesthetic point of view. Singer would clearly reject this sense of overriding of the moral, and some of those who support a big role for the personal point of view in determining what morality requires would no doubt agree with him in this.[14]

I wish to add that, even if we believe, as I do, that moral considerations can be overridden by non-moral ones in the first sense (i.e. a sense that is consistent with our still doing the morally right thing overall), we can believe that a consideration's being a moral one gives it extra weight relative to its being an economic or aesthetic one. That is, a very serious aesthetic consideration can override a very slight moral consideration (great art versus small impoliteness), and hence there is no lexical priority given to moral considerations. Still, a very serious moral consideration always weighs more than what is an equally serious consideration from the aesthetic perspective, or at least so I would claim. We might think of this in the following way. First, we weigh the seriousness of some behavior from each of various points of view – for example, moral, aesthetic, economic – and then we attach multiplicative factors for the categories. If the multiplicative factor for morality versus aesthetics is three, then if an act ranks at the highest level of seriousness in the moral category, it can get an overall score three times greater than an act that also ranks at the highest level of seriousness in the aesthetic category. The most serious offense from an aesthetic point of view can never override the most serious moral offense.

Another way I would make my point about the relative weight of moral and other considerations is to consider the following hypothetical case. Suppose different committees have been established to consider a policy, with each committee representing a different point of view, such as economic, aesthetic, etc. Now suppose we have time to listen to the report of only one committee. Which committee should we choose? One suggestion is that we should choose the committee which is such that if we run afoul of its advice, we will have gone wrong in the most serious way. This is a maximin policy: avoid the worst possible outcome. While an error in the aesthetic area could be more serious than an error in the moral area, the worst possible error can *only* occur in the moral area. (That is, the worst possible aesthetic error cannot be as serious as the worst possible moral error.) So maximin tells us to consider the moral committee's advice.[15]

That the moral category bears this relation to other categories can be seen after we make a choice about what to do, even if we are (as Raz claims) not conscious of weighing categories when we ordinarily decide what to do. That is, on reflection, we can consider how we judge the weightiness of factors in various cases. For example, we notice that a consideration that is slightly important from the aesthetic point of view is trumped by a factor that is even less important from the moral point of view. So, we learn that being a *moral* factor counts for something more. Therefore, while Raz may be correct to say that in deciding on conduct, we consider factors as reasons independently of their categories, it would be incorrect to conclude from this that there are no categories of reasons that vary in weightiness, and that reasons do not have extra weight simply because of the category to which they belong.[16] So those who disagree with Singer on the exclusion of partiality from the moral point of view can still claim that the moral point of view is non-overridable and that even narrow moral considerations that can be overridden by other considerations consistent with moral permissibility weigh more in virtue of their category than considerations coming from some other categories.

Component (a) in the higher level of normative theory

We identified component (a) as equal consideration of interests. What types of interests does Singer think should get equal consideration? The relevant interests need not include only the interest in pleasure and avoidance of pain. As noted above, Singer thinks we have an interest in having a meaningful life, even if we do not know that we do, or are too irrational to have a preference for it. (One complication with claiming that only interests (i.e. rational preferences for self) count in Singer's view is that he sometimes allows us to count not only people's rational preferences but *the effects* of their *irrational* ones. For example, in discussing immigration,[17] he allows that people's prejudice against newcomers may lead to social disruption, and then it becomes against the true interests of newcomers (and perhaps even those with prejudice who would be involved in disruption) to continue immigration.)

The "relevant" interests include those of any sentient being, and these interests are to be treated in a strictly non-speciesist way. While higher animals may have different interests than lower ones, a pain *per se* is equally bad in whichever species it occurs, and each species can have the same interest in not having pain. Presumably, he believes this is true of pleasure *per se* as well. So, if there were no additional morally significant reverberations (e.g. reflection on pain or pleasure) that give rise to new interests in one species rather than in another, one would have as much reason to produce considerable pleasure in a mouse as in a person. I wish to suggest, contrary to Singer, that there may be an asymmetry between pleasure and pain. Even if it is as bad a state of affairs if there is pain in a mouse as in a person (considering pain independent of its reverberations), I think it is morally more important that a good thing, such as pleasure (independent of reverberations) happen to a more important being (a person) than to a less important one.

On the other hand, Singer distinguishes between the beings in whose interest it is to go on living and those who have no such interest, based on the presence or absence of self-consciousness, respectively. The latter are replaceable beings (i.e. as long as one replaces the utility they would have experienced, there is no loss in painlessly killing them), because they have no sense of themselves as continuing entities (i.e. no self-consciousness) and hence cannot desire to go on living. I find this position puzzling as well. Something can continue over time even if it does not know it does. The absence of self-consciousness may not even mean that there is no psychological self in the sense of a unified locus of thought and psychological being. If the being's future time would be filled with good experiences, these good experiences would be *its* good experiences. Is it not in its interest to have these? Death would deprive it of this, and so it seems there is a reason not to kill it, even if it is not self-conscious and even if we replace it with another source of equal utility. There is also the opposite point for which one could argue on the basis of Parfit's work: even self-conscious beings who think of themselves as going on in time may not have a psychological self that in fact continues on in time.[18] If they do not, they will be no more closely related to their "future selves" than they are to other people, and hence they may be replaceable entities. So self-consciousness seems to be neither necessary nor sufficient for death being against one's interests.

Finally, it is significant to note that there are two ways in which Singer's placing *interests* at the foundation of morality might be challenged. First, Singer himself considers the proposal that non-sentient entities with no interests might have intrinsic moral significance: for example, trees or the planet. (He rejects this view, but wishes to argue that such entities should sometimes be protected against the current economic interests of sentient beings because their loss would affect the interests of future sentient beings.)

A second, more general objection to focusing only on the interests of sentient beings is that many of the things that make individual lives have worth (e.g. the quality of rational agency, the capacity for responsibility, commitment to truth and honor) should be attended to independently of their effect on the interests of sentient beings. This is the Kantian objection. It may be in the interests of sentient beings that these things are attended to, but they are not important merely because they are in the interests of sentient beings. For example, it may be right to punish people because they deserve it, even if it is in no one's interest that this be done. It may be right that the truth be told, even if it is no one's interest that this be done.

Component (b) in the higher level of normative theory

We identified component (b) as maximizing satisfaction of interests in accordance with their importance. In *Practical Ethics*, Singer is a maximizing consequentialist, but he does not seem a straightforward aggregationist. That is, he seems to believe that it is more important that the most important interests be satisfied first, even if we could produce greater overall satisfaction by satisfying many more less important interests.[21] But aggregation of the satisfaction of *equally* important interests is permitted. Furthermore, he eschews the "total view," for persons at least, as the basis for maximizing and favors the "prior existence view." That is, he thinks we should make already existing persons and persons who will exist in the future maximally well off rather than make (create) well-off persons.[20] Does this mean that he thinks we should not keep the human race going if we are tempted to stop reproducing? (If he rejects totalism for persons, why does he also claim that we may kill animals that are not self-conscious *only if* we replace them with new beings so as not to diminish *overall* good? For, if we do not have to create new persons to maximize good, why do we have to keep good constant by replacing non-persons?)

The fact that Singer endorses satisfying first the most significant interests does not, however, mean that he is a maximiner (i.e. seeks to make the worst-off best before improving those who are already better off). He explicitly rejects maximin on the basis of cases suggested by Derek Parfit,[21] in which we can do much less to help the person who will be worst off without our help than we can do for the person who would not be worst off. For example, if we can either help a blind man not lose a finger or help a fingerless person not go deaf, we should do the latter, even if it is worse to be blind and fingerless than to be deaf and fingerless. I believe this is correct.[22]

Like many other consequentialists, Singer insists on the moral irrelevance at the highest level of moral theory of the distinction between harming and not aiding *per se*, and so maximizing may proceed without a side constraint on harming some to help others. He also seems to accept this, and its implications, at the lower level of his normative theory, so I shall discuss it in the next section.

The lower level of the normative theory

The lower level of the two-level theory is concerned with the rules or traits of character that will further the impartial goals of morality, even if they are not in themselves impartialist. The only point I wish to make about Singer's subscription to rules that on occasion do not maximize good consequences is the role that "slippery slopes" play in their construction. Singer recommends a *very general* rule against eating non-self-conscious animals, though he believes it is strictly permissible to raise, kill, and eat them if this does not cause them pain. He does this because of the worry that we may slip into eating self-conscious animals, or cause the non-self-conscious but sentient ones pain in raising or in killing them. But, in the case of euthanasia, he recommends a *very fine-grained* rule which allows us to kill some people, rather than a general rule which excludes killing in cases where it is strictly permissible, for fear of a slippery slope to unjustified killings. What might account for the difference in willingness to tolerate untoward effects? While Singer does not say this, it is possible that what is crucial is how bad the effects on people will be if we have a more *general rule*: having an overly general rule, in the case of eating animals, deprives people mostly of gustatory pleasure; in the case of euthanasia, a more general rule would deprive people in great pain or misery from ending their lives. The cost of each of the general rules is very different.

Killing and letting die
Some of the rules and policies Singer recommends at the second level seem straightforwardly impartialist, with minimal alteration from what they would be at the first level. He denies the moral significance of the harming/not aiding distinction, and consistent with this, he accepts a strong doctrine of negative responsibility whereby we are responsible for harm we could have prevented as much as for that we cause, holding all other factors extrinsic to the harming/not aiding distinction (e.g. motive, effort required) constant. When he discusses this issue in detail,[23] he considers killing versus letting die, in particular. His claim is that we mistakenly think that killing is worse than letting die in itself because of factors extrinsic to killing and letting die, not intrinsic to them. That is, different and morally worse extrinsic factors commonly accompany killing than commonly accompany letting die. To show that it is factors extrinsic in killing and letting die which cause us to think killing and letting die differ morally in themselves, he first adopts the strategy of taking the factors which are common in killing cases – for example, bad motive – and putting them in letting die cases. This is a way of equalizing killing and letting die cases for all factors aside from killing and letting die. That we can take the factors common in killing cases and put them in letting die cases, he seems to think, *shows* that these factors are extrinsic to killing. But this is not true, because it is possible to export a property which is intrinsic to (i.e. necessarily true of) killing but not of letting die, and so *necessarily* common in killing cases, into a case of letting die; it is also possible to export a property which is intrinsic to letting die (but not to killing) into a case of killing. An example of the first is "causing death"; this is necessarily true of killing, I believe, but can be true of some letting die cases. For example, suppose A unplugs B from a life support machine that belongs to A and to which B has no right. If B dies of lack of life support, I think A lets B die, though he (in part) causes his death. An example of the second is "losing out on only what he would not have without my help"; this is necessarily true of the person whom I let die, but it can be true of the person I kill in some killing cases: for example, if I fatally stab someone to whom I am providing life support and who would not have lived without the support.[24]

Suppose we export a property intrinsic to killing into a letting die case and it makes the letting die case morally worse, but no property intrinsic to letting die makes a killing case worse when it is exported. Then this would be evidence that killing but not letting die has an intrinsic property which can make behavior worse. This, in turn, would be evidence for a moral difference between killing and letting die *per se*. If letting die has an intrinsic property which, when exported into a killing case, makes the case less bad, but killing has no property that has the same effect when exported into a letting die case, this would also be evidence for an intrinsic moral difference between killing and letting die. (Notice that this is true even though particular cases of killing and letting die do not differ morally, because they have had properties intrinsic to the other behavior exported to them.)[25]

In the cases I have described, it seems that the "causing" property of killing does not really make the letting die morally worse (e.g. when I unplug a life support system), but the intrinsic property of letting die does, I believe, sometimes make a killing easier to justify. (For example, when I fatally stab someone I am providing with life support the killing seems more acceptable than killing someone independent of me or even imposing on me but not receiving the life I take). If so, this is evidence for an intrinsic difference between killing and letting die. "Evidence" does not mean conclusive evidence, however, for that an intrinsic property has a significant moral effect when exported does not necessarily mean that it has the significant moral effect on its "home ground": that is, the behavior from which it is exported. This is due to what I call the Principle of Contextual Interaction: properties may interact differently within different contexts. It is only if the property has the same effect on its home ground to the one it has when exported that we have secure evidence for an intrinsic difference between killing and letting die. I see no reason to believe it does not have the same effect.

Singer, however, believes he has shown that it is only factors extrinsic to killing that make killing cases worse than letting die cases, because he thinks only that equalizing the killing and letting die cases for the extrinsic factors leads us to make the same judgments about letting die cases as we make about killing cases. He does not consider that some factor intrinsic to letting die can be shown to make it less bad *per se* than killing is *per se* in the manner I have described above. Given this, the second step in his strategy[26] is to consider whether factors that are typical in letting die cases but extrinsic to letting die – these factors are just the reverse of the extrinsic factors typical of killing cases – not only *explain our* reactions to typical killing and letting die cases, but *justify* them. Singer's claim is that these extrinsic factors do not justify them. To show this, he takes extrinsic factors commonly found in letting die cases and adds them to killing cases. He claims that aim is to show that they do *not* make the killing morally acceptable. But if there is no intrinsic difference between killing and letting die, they should not make letting die acceptable either. For example, that we are ignorant of who the victim of our not aiding will be – typical of many but not necessarily all letting die cases – should not help make letting die permissible if our *not* knowing who we will kill does not make killing *permissible*. But notice that this strategy also implies that we may show that there is an intrinsic moral difference between killing and letting die by showing that extrinsic factors which make letting die permissible do not make killing permissible.[27]

Singer himself gives us an example of this. When he discusses the extrinsic factor of great effort and how burdensome it typically would be to aid many people, we would, given his argumentation to that point, expect him to try to argue for the *im*permissibility of letting die by seeing whether the argument from burdensomeness would hold any water when killing is in question. Presumably, that we had to do a lot to avoid killing someone would *not* defeat the duty not to kill. For example, if I drive down road A, I would run over someone stuck in the road. I have a duty to take road B, even if it is very dangerous and will cause damage to my back. This would imply, if killing is not intrinsically morally different from letting die, that burdensomeness should *not* defeat a duty not to let die. But it is striking that Singer does *not* inquire into whether the argument from burdensomeness defeats a duty not to kill. Instead, he merely accepts that we cannot demand "moral heroism" from people when it comes to aiding.[28] But if we can demand someone to suffer a lot rather than kill an innocent bystander, this suggests there *is* a moral difference between killing and letting die *per se*.

An additional example commonly used to support the thesis that there is a *per se* difference between killing and letting die equalizes for all extrinsic factors:

(a) I must rush five dying people to the hospital to save them. To get there on time, I must speed over a road where I know one person is trapped, thereby killing him. This is impermissible.

(b) I must rush five dying people to the hospital to save them. To get there on time, I must speed past someone drowning in a pond. This is permissible.

Here a goal which makes letting die permissible does not make killing permissible.

Of course, that killing and letting die sometimes make a moral difference does not mean they always do. But to rebut the general thesis that there is no intrinsic difference between killing and letting die *per se*, we need present only *one* case where the moral difference between the two shows up. By contrast, to support the thesis, it is insufficient to present one case where the difference does not matter.[29]

Suppose cases support a moral distinction between killing and letting die. Why should this be so: that is, *why* do some essential properties of letting die have different moral significance than those of killing? One possibility is that persons are entitled to certain things which are related to their identity as separate persons and which they have independently of the help of others: for example, their bodies (when they are not dependent on life support of others). They are entitled to these things even if they do not, in any deep sense, deserve to have the body they have. If this were so, then if we harm them and thereby cause them to lose these things they have independently of our help, this is an encroachment on their entitlements. However, if we do not aid someone, he loses out on only what he would have had with our help (rather than what he would have had independently of us) and our help may be something to which he is not entitled if we are entitled to our body. (Another possible rationale for the harming/not aiding difference does not assert that people are entitled to certain things they have which are intimately related to their identity as separate persons. It only claims that other people are *not* entitled to these things. Using this rationale, we might also account for why someone is not entitled to certain types of aid, but it would not imply that there was always an injustice (i.e. a violation of an entitlement) if someone is harmed.)

I conclude that Singer's arguments to show that there is no intrinsic moral difference between killing and letting die do not succeed.

Principles governing aid

Independent of whether there is no *per se* moral difference between killing and letting die, Singer suggests two principles that might govern aiding behavior (which I summarize as follows):[30] (a) unless something of *comparable* moral significance is at stake, we should help to relieve suffering; and (b) unless something of moral significance is at stake, we should help to relieve suffering. The first principle is more stringent in favor of aiding than the second, and it is the one Singer favors. (Both these principles focus on reducing suffering rather than just promoting good.)

Sometimes Singer fails to distinguish the first principle from the second. For example, while defending the first, more stringent principle, he argues that it does not require one to give up family relations because most find these necessities for a flourishing life, and to give them up would be to sacrifice something of great moral significance. "Hence, no such sacrifice is required by the principle for which I am here arguing." But the principle for which he is arguing says we need not sacrifice anything of "*comparable* moral significance"[31] and something that is very significant in the life of a person is not necessarily of *comparable* significance to the loss of many lives which his sacrifice might prevent.

This leads us to examine the two principles in greater depth. They both are supposed to yield strict duties to aid, something it is wrong not to do, not supererogatory generosity. They apply independent of whether those who aid and those to be aided belong to different societies, regardless of the distance between them, and regardless of whether there are other people who should also be aiding but do not. This means that Singer denies that obligations can vary depending on distance. (I shall discuss the problem of distance at length below). He also denies that what one has a duty to do is what would be fair for one to be required to do if others also fulfilled their duty to aid. Presumably, he believes this, because he thinks that even if we are treated unfairly by other potential aiders who renege on their duties, thereby requiring us to do more than our fair share, the unfairness to us is less important than the bad consequences to others if we do not aid.

Notice, however, that even if we agree with this, it would still be possible to argue that before we do more than our fair share, we have a right to *force* those who would renege on their duties to aid as well. Furthermore, if we are treated unfairly *by those who need our help*, perhaps their unfairness to us does override their need for aid. This may be one reason – though not the one Singer gives – for denying aid to countries that do not use birth control or appropriate farming techniques and thereby bring on their problems of overpopulation and famine. However, while it might make denying aid to the parents permissible, this argument could not be used to deny aid to the children, who have not acted unfairly. But, given the importance of saving the children's lives, it would then seem we could *force* the unfair parents to change their behavior before imposing further on our own resources. Oddly, given his consequentialism and dismissal of the harming/not aiding distinction, Singer is at pains to argue (independent of considering consequences) that he would not *coerce* those needy people who are responsible for causing their own plight into improving it.[32] However, if they do not change their bad behavior, we are at liberty, he says, not to aid them because (and only because) our aid would do no good.

Now, how do the two principles differ? What the less stringent principle implies depends on what is of moral significance. If a promise is of moral significance, it seems to imply that we need not break a minor promise to relieve much suffering, and this is not true. Further, if consumerism is necessary to create wealth needed to save people from starvation, but consumerism itself has negative moral significance (as Singer suggests when he says "that consumer society has had a distorting effect on the goals and purposes of its members"[33]), then we should not create the maximal wealth needed to save people from starvation. This seems at least debatable.

Singer thinks that the more stringent principle implies that one must bring oneself and one's family down to a level which is such that if one did any more, one would be worse off than those one is trying to help.[34] But this does not seem to be the correct limit, for it is possible that making oneself and one's family *worse off* than those one is trying to help, *considered as individuals*, might still prevent more suffering when *we aggregate all* those whom our sacrifice helps. (This is especially likely to be true given the relative cost to feed people in different countries – the money that comes from my depriving myself of food can buy the meals for hundreds of people in Africa.) I think that the death of me and my family is not of comparable moral significance to the death of many hundreds that is avoided, considered impartially. Further, if Singer believes there is no *per se* moral difference between killing and letting die, or between intending and foreseeing death, one should be required to do what we foresee will kill a few in order to save many lives, and also to intentionally kill a few in order to save many lives.[35] If the more stringent principle requires all this, it would certainly require that someone sacrifice his arm to save lives, since an arm is not of comparable moral worth to lives. If I believe we are not morally required to make such a sacrifice, it is not because I believe that someone's arm not being lost is of comparable moral worth to eliminating much suffering or the continued survival of many people. (However, I may believe that someone's arm not being lost is of comparable worth to the creation of many *new* lives.) The evidence for this is that if a third party had to choose between saving my arm or saving other people's lives, I think it is perfectly understandable that he should save the lives rather than the arm. Does this mean that if I believe that we are not required to sacrifice our arm, it must be because I reject Singer's more stringent principle?

It seems that the only way for us to avoid this conclusion is to argue that people's having the *right to lead their own lives*, which gives them a certain *inviolable status* as not mere devices for reducing overall suffering and death, is of greater moral significance than saving a greater number of lives. If it were required of people to make large sacrifices to prevent all sorts of suffering and death, or permissible for them to be sacrificed by others to that end, their status as certain sorts of beings would be lost. It is the loss of this status, rather than the loss of an arm, that may have greater moral significance than saving many lives. This status is not lost if it is permissible to save many from dying rather than prevent the loss of your arm. It is not lost if it is impermissible for me to sacrifice your arm to prevent many other people's arms from being taken from them. This is because even if many lose their arms – this is what happens to them – their status as people who have a right not to have their arms taken is not lost unless it is *permissible* to take their arms. We do not (and morality does not) endorse the permissibility by allowing them to be abused; but we and morality would endorse the permissibility if it was said to be correct to take the arm of one person to save the arms of others. Furthermore, the status is lost if it is required of you to give your arm to save lives. Some may find this view about the importance of a certain sort of status attractive, but I do not think Singer would.[36]

A methodological note: I have argued against Singer's stronger principle by considering its implications for cases, such as whether I have a duty to give my arm in order to save people in Africa from famine. Our intuitive response to the case may be negative, but Singer seems to believe that even if this is so, and a positive response to the case is implied by the principle, this does not defeat the principle. He says, "the way people do in fact judge has nothing to do with the validity of my conclusion [that we must give away a great deal to famine relief]. My conclusion follows from the principle... and unless that principle is rejected, or the arguments shown to be unsound, I think the conclusion must stand, however strange it appears."[37] This, at least, suggests that Singer does not think a moral principle that seems plausible on its face (or follows from plausible higher-order principles) could be defeated by our intuitive judgments about cases. Hence, a conflict between intuitions and principles may just remain, and the intuitions will remain unjustified. Perhaps he thinks that an error theory can be provided to account for them.[38]

I disagree with Singer on methodology. He relies on some intuitions – those about general principles. I think our intuitions about general principles must be tested by our intuitions about the implication of general principles for cases. Notice that Singer himself relies on intuitions in cases in order to try to defeat the principle that there is a moral difference between killing and letting die, so his position does not seem consistent. Furthermore, I do not think our intuitions about cases are less reliable than those about principles. They can serve to build up a theory and reveal principles.[39]

In the section that follows on moral distance, I shall rely on intuitions about cases. However, I shall be mostly concerned with characterizing our intuitions rather than justifying them or justifying the use of them in searching for a correct theory. I shall try to show what our intuitions about cases are about. Only at the end of my discussion shall I consider whether our intuitions could possibly be correct: that is, revealing of moral truth.

The Problem of Distance in Morality

The problem of distance in morality (henceforth, PDM) in ethical theory is standardly described as the problem of whether the degree of physical *distance* per se *between ourselves and strangers who need help* should ever affect our obligation to help. So, the problem is about the role of distance in generating or eliminating obligations.

Those who think distance does matter do not think that it is the only factor that matters, of course. For example, if I can help more people at a distance and fewer who are near, this might be a reason to help the distant. Furthermore, to say that distance matters is not to say that we need do *nothing* to help distant strangers; nor is it to say we must do *everything* to help strangers who are near. To say distance matters is just to say, minimally, that, other things equal, we will have to do more for the near than for the distant. One measure of this difference could be whom we have a duty to save when we cannot save all; another measure could be differential upper limits on required costs to ourselves for saving – higher for the near and lower for the far.

One of my aims is to show that the standard description of the PDM is misleading. It is a useful antecedent to solving a problem that the problem be correctly stated, and it is one of my aims in this chapter to state it correctly.

A reason for saying that there is a PDM of any sort, even as standardly described, is that our so-called common-sense intuitions about cases suggest that we think that at least sometimes we have a stronger obligation to help those in need who are physically near us than those who are at a greater distance. The classic set of cases that has been used to discuss this point was presented by Peter Singer.[40] Here is a variant of it:

Pond: I am walking past a shallow pond and see a child drowning in it. If I wade in and pull the child out, my $500 suit will be ruined. I ought to wade in to save him.

Overseas: I know there is a child starving to death overseas. To save him, I must send $500. I am not obligated to do so.

If we are using cases to see whether distance *per se* matters, all other factors in the cases should be held constant. But these two cases have many differences between them besides distance. In Overseas, money is a means to saving someone. In Pond, money will be lost as a consequence of wading in, which is the means to saving someone. The person who is near me in Pond may well be a fellow citizen or member of my community, whereas the person overseas may not be. In Pond, I may be the only one who can help, but not so in Overseas. Nearness may increase success of aid, distance may decrease success. That a child is starving in Overseas may suggest that an issue of basic justice is at stake, rather than a life threatening accident, as in Pond. We might eliminate these differences (if not others) to better focus on the role of distance *per se* by revising the cases as follows:

Near alone case: I am walking past a pond in a foreign country that I am visiting, and I *alone* see a child drowning in it and I alone can save him. To save him, I must put the $500 I have in my pocket into a machine that will certainly scoop him out.

Far alone case: I *alone* learn that in a distant part of a foreign country that I am visiting, a child is drowning and I alone can save him. To save him, all I must do is commit the $500 I carry in my pocket to his cause so that rescue machinery can certainly save him.

Near many case: I am walking past a pond in a foreign country that I am visiting, and I and many others see a child drowning; any of us can save him, but the others will not. To save him, I must put $500 I have in my pocket into a machine that will then scoop him out.

Far many case: I and many others learn that in a distant part of a foreign country that we are visiting, a child is drowning; any of us could save him but the others will not. To save him, all I must do is commit the $500 I carry in my pocket to his cause so that rescue machinery can be successfully deployed.

Near/far case: I learn that in a distant part of a foreign country that I am visiting, a child is drowning and someone is near him. Either one of us could as successfully help by depositing $500 in a device that will trigger a machine that will scoop the child out. Who has a stronger obligation to help?

Do we still intuitively think there is a difference in our responsibility in these cases that at least may be based on distance? I suspect so. Of course, the difference may not be due to distance *per se*, as there may still be important differences between these cases besides distance.

The methodological point here is that if we are trying to find out whether a factor x matters *per se* in our intuitions, we must construct a set of comparable cases, one with factor x and one without it, and hold all other factors in the two cases constant. I call this "equalizing the cases." (The methodological issues here are the same as in the discussion of whether killing and letting die are intuitively thought to be morally different *per se*.[41])

What if we formed a set of equalized cases in which distance intuitively made *no* difference. Would this show that distance *per se* intuitively makes no difference? No, since the claim that distance *per se* matters intuitively is not the claim that it *always* matters intuitively. (It could be overridden by contextual factors.) It is the claim that at least sometimes it matters intuitively: that is, if there is even one case in which it *does* matter, this shows that it matters *per se* intuitively (assuming non-intensional contexts). If someone found that there was an intuitive difference between Near many and Far many but not between Near alone and Far alone, distance would still be of some significance *per se*, though it would be a less important factor than if it had import in a wider range of cases.

Similarly, if famine relief implicates issues of basic justice and distance is not relevant to the duty to promote basic justice, distance could still matter morally when other aid is at stake. (Notice that a duty to promote basic justice may obligate us only to support just institutions, not to aid directly. Even the strength of this obligation may vary, not with distance, but with social membership.) Suppose one found an intuitive moral difference only in Near/far, and so claimed that those who are near have first responsibility to aid, but if they cannot or simply will not, those who are far have as strong a responsibility to aid as those who are near. (This would be like arguing that one has a stronger obligation to one's own children than to one's sister's, but if one's sister's children are orphaned, one has as strong an obligation to them as to one's own.) This claim would be consistent with there being no intuitive difference between Near alone and Far alone or between Near many and Far many, yet it would still reveal that distance mattered *per se*.

It is plausible to assume that certain contextual factors should be altered equally in the near and far cases in the hopes of finding cases where distance intuitively matters. For example, as we vary the effort required to aid, we should look to see if we think we have an obligation to aid at large cost in the near case but not in the far. We could also vary probability of success of the aid equally in both cases to see, for example, if we intuitively think that we are obligated to aid in the near case but not in the far case when probability of success is low.[42] We could vary how great a harm or absence of benefit is at stake for the person not aided, and ask if we must help prevent a small harm that is near but not one that is far.

We must also be more precise about whether we are interested in the intuitive moral significance of any difference in distance or rather a certain type of difference in distance. There is a difference in distance when one child is near and another is in a distant part of the country. But a third child could fail to be near me yet be much closer to me than the one in a distant part of the country. Would there be any case in which our intuitive responses would tell us that our obligations to this third child were weaker than to the near one but stronger than to the more distant one? The claim that (1) all intervals of distance matter intuitively is different from the claim that (2) the distinction between the near and far matters (where the non-near is the far). The latter claim is compatible with there being no intuitive differences in our obligation to the second and third children. I suspect that it is really the second claim with which the PDM is concerned. Hence, we really want to know if *proximity* matters intuitively.

Some, like Singer, think that, on reflection, we would have a hard time justifying the different intuitions in various Near and Far cases if they did reflect the effect of proximity *per se* in our intuitions. So, the PDM as standardly described arises through an apparent conflict between

(a) intuitions that proximity matters, and (b) the possibility of theoretical justification of these intuitions.

One of my concerns is that the cases that have been used to gather intuitions to support the standard description of the problem – or the slightly revised problem of whether proximity *per se* between ourselves and strangers who need help should affect our obligation to aid – are incomplete. Hence, the description of the problem and the presentation of intuitions for which theoretical justification is needed have been inadequate. This means that we are not quite clear about what needs justification.

My outline for proceeding is, first, to distinguish the idea of proximity from the idea of salience (or vividness) and see which is expressed by our intuitions. So the first question is whether proximity matters intuitively. Here I begin what will be a continuing reference to, and examination of, some ideas on distance and aiding that Peter Unger puts forth in his *Living High and Letting Die*.[43] Second, I hope to get clearer about what our intuitions indicate about how we measure proximity. Third, I present certain crucial cases that I hope will make clearer the actual contours of our intuitions concerning the role of proximity: that is, *how* proximity matters. I hope to show two things by these cases: (a) (as I have already said) I hope to show that the standard description of the PDM is a misdescription; and (b) I hope to show that the actual contours of our intuitions express the belief that I can be strongly obligated to help those far from me even while they also express the belief that proximity matters morally. Fourth, I consider whether and why intuitions that proximity matters are correct: that is, might be revealing of what our obligations really are. Finally, I consider how we should decide what to do if proximity does matter in generating obligations.

Moral distance versus salience

Salience of need refers not only to the obviousness and inescapability of noticing need, but also to the continuing imposition of this knowledge on us. Peter Unger,[44] for example, says salience is not always present when something is clearly visible close up, since we may well be able to pass over what we notice. The salient event, according to him, is the one that attracts and holds our attention so that we cannot stop thinking about it; it presses itself upon us. So need that is near and obvious may not be salient if I can simply put the need out of my mind. This understanding of salience suggests that it is "subjective salience" with which Unger is concerned: whatever a person cannot get out of his mind is salient to him. But there is also a notion of "objective salience" which suggests something that is such that it would attract and hold the attention of a normal (or ideal) observer. When I want to distinguish varieties of salience, I shall speak of S_s and S_o.

Some need that is near may be S_s and S_o, even though it is not obvious or easily observed. For example, suppose I am informed by a detecting device that someone just outside my door is dying and I could help. Even though I cannot see or hear him (and he cannot see or hear me), his need can be salient to me in the sense that I cannot stop thinking about it and a normal individual would not stop thinking about it (Door case).

Need that is at a distance could be salient. Suppose I have very long-distance vision and can see great need at a distance; the need is then obvious. The need may also be salient in that I cannot get the scene out of my mind and a normal observer could not. In the Far case as described, we can assume I do not have long-distance vision. Let us assume this makes the need non-salient in both senses. In the Near case, the child's need is obvious and, let us assume, salient in both senses.

My claim is that if the Near and Far cases also differ in salience, it is nearness and not salience which gives rise to our intuition that we have a strong obligation to help in Near. That is, when we think we have a strong obligation to aid in Near and not in Far, it is the difference in distance represented by the cases rather than the difference in salience that is determinative of the sense of obligation. This is contrary to what Unger argues for. He thinks it is salience – I suspect S_s – and not nearness that our responses to cases track, *even though he does not think salience can be theoretically justified* as a morally relevant difference determining obligations.

Here is the key point in showing that it is not S that our intuitions about obligation track: The mere fact that we cannot take our mind off someone's need does not mean that we would think it impermissible to do what *would* take our mind off of it, if we could, though this interfered with our aiding. If we do not think there is some other reason besides salience why we have a duty to aid, I think we intuitively believe that we may eliminate salience, even if this interferes with our aiding. If we think it would be permissible to do what would take our mind off the need, though we then do not aid, this indicates that salience alone is not generating the intuition that we have an obligation to aid, for if we believed salience gave rise to an obligation, we would think it wrong to alter the salience if this reduced our tendency to help. Here is an example: suppose that when I directly see the suffering overseas with long-distance vision, I also cannot stop thinking about it. Is this likely to make me send money when I would not otherwise? I doubt it. But, if it is likely to lead me to send money to aid, I may sense this only as psychological pressure, which is not the same as a sense of duty. Indeed, I intuitively think this is one of many cases where it would be permissible to do what eliminates the salience of need, unless there is some other ground for a sense of duty. For example, I think it is permissible to turn off my long-distance vision if this will help me stop thinking about the long-distance need and make it less likely that I will aid. It is probably because I believe that I am not strongly responsible for helping distant people that I think it is permissible for me to eliminate the salience of their need, so the salience of their need does not imply that I think I have a duty.

This applies to S_o, too. Suppose the person I see with long-distance vision is truly striking, dressed in a clown suit and much more dramatically exhibiting his need. He stands out from the crowd of equally needy people – so that a normal observer would attend more to him. I do not intuitively believe that I have a greater obligation to this person than to the others at a distance, even if I feel under more psychological pressure to aid.[45] I may permissibly reduce a certain sort of S_o of this person by getting rid of my long-distance vision (since seeing him may be what makes it impossible for an ideal observer to forget him).

By contrast, suppose the person outside my door is in great need. As noted above, his need may be salient (S_s and S_o) even though it is not observed. May I take a pill to eliminate its salience? If I think that I am obligated to help someone who is near, I should not eliminate salient knowledge if it is necessary to help me fulfill my obligation. Another sign that I intuitively believe it is nearness that obligates me to help is that once I am near, I do not think I am permitted to move myself to a greater distance merely in order to avoid being near (though I may move if this is necessary to bring aid). Contrast this with my sense that I am permitted to change the salience of need if no other factor obligates. If I thought salience obligated, I would not be permitted to change it to avoid being obligated, as I believe I am not permitted to change nearness in order to avoid being obligated. Another sign that I believe I have obligations to those who are near because they are near is that if a free device is available that will help me detect need that is near to me, I think I have an obligation to get it, whereas I believe I have less obligation to get a free long-distance device in order to know what need exists at a distance.

It might be thought that I may eliminate my salient knowledge of the far need because it came to me via an *unusual* sense; long-distance vision is unusual for our species. By contrast, my knowledge of the person near me comes via my ordinary senses, and perhaps this is why I may not eliminate it if this interferes with my aiding. But in the Door case, I get the knowledge of the near person via an unusual machine. Similarly, we can imagine that I would not know of the person outside my door if I did not have an *unusual* capacity to detect heart beats through a wooden door. I do not believe that the fact that I am unusual in having the sense (or machine) – and I would not know of his plight without them – means that I have a right to ignore his plight once I find out about it or to move so I am far.

I have argued that we may not alter the characteristic (our nearness) that we intuitively think gives us the obligation once we have it in order to avoid the obligation. This does not, however, mean that we *have to acquire* the characteristic, that we may not avoid having it. For example, if I want to have a quiet vacation, intuitively I may permissibly avoid going to places where I am likely to have an obligation to aid those near me. By contrast, if I have an obligation to aid independent of distance, I may well have a duty to go where I can be useful.[46]

But here is a problem: since it is permissible to avoid acquiring the characteristic which gives one a duty, it may well be to the mutual advantage of an agent and the person who could be aided by him to compromise on the demands made of the agent in virtue of his nearness in order to induce him to be near. For example, if I want to avoid being imposed on and so stay in my own backyard, I may deprive myself of enjoyment I can have if I go to a hotel in a place where many accidents happen. I also deprive someone who needs my help of even such minimal assistance as calling for an ambulance when she is truly desperate. Could we imagine a hypothetical agreement that yields a Pareto optimal outcome? I get to be near someone and only have to do a small fraction of what would be required of me just in virtue of being near? I believe, intuitively, it is not morally acceptable to limit the duty in this way. If one is near, one cannot be relieved of the full responsibilities incumbent on someone who is near in this way. This is true, I believe, even if it implies fewer people will allow themselves to be near needy people.

Peter Unger argues against the intuitive significance of distance in the course of his discussion of variations on two cases, Sedan and Envelope.[47] In the first version of Sedan, we are driving by some stranger who is near us and who needs to be taken in our car to the hospital. In the first version of Envelope, we are asked to send money to needy strangers who are far away. (Their plight is not the result of an accident, and implicates basic justice.) Intuitively, we think we have a stronger duty to aid in Sedan than in Envelope. The question is what difference between the cases accounts for our intuitive responses (even if it does not justify them). Unger's strategy in answering the question is to consider various candidate differences by, for example, (a) removing a difference from Sedan to see if our intuitions change from the original Sedan, and (b) adding the difference to Envelope to see if this changes our intuitions from the original Envelope.[48]

He removes nearness from Sedan and claims that when we hear on our car radio that someone at a distance needs aid, our sense of obligation to drive him to the hospital is not reduced. By contrast, I believe our intuitive responses *do* change, and we sense a reduced obligation, once we take account of the fact that what is costlessly "near by car" may not be the same as what is near if I am not in a car. Next, he considers a version of Envelope to which nearness is added: On vacation, someone visits a poor country. Near his vacation house are people dying. He receives an envelope in the mail from a local charity asking for money.[49] Unger thinks that, at least intuitively, we believe the visitor does no wrong in not giving the money. One alternative analysis of this case is that the visitor need not give only if it is not clear that the money will go to the *very* people who are in need near his vacation house. If it is clear that the money goes to the people next door, he *is* under the more stringent obligation to give. A second alternative analysis explains why he does no wrong in not aiding directly by distinguishing issues of basic justice from accidents: if many people outside the vacation home are drowning the visitor should save the one he can.

In sum, not only are salience and distance different concepts, but far things can have salience and near things can lack salience. Salience alone does not intuitively ground an obligation (let alone truly ground an obligation in being theoretically justified). Evidence for this is that we think it is permissible to eliminate salience when there are no other grounds for the obligation to aid. Obligations do, at least intuitively, seem to vary with the near and non-near in some cases; near things should be salient if this aids us in meeting the obligation that nearness generates. The obligation can be avoided by staying far rather than being near, but not limited by reasoning based on mutual self-interest of agent and needy stranger. At least, I claim, this is the report of our intuitions.

If we intuitively think obligations can vary as a function of proximity, we can account for our responses to two puzzles Unger raises.[50] In the first one, someone who has already given a lot to Oxfam feels morally free to refuse to respond to another request for life-saving aid. The same person, however, does not feel that simply because he has already given a lot to Oxfam, he may refuse services to a person he meets on the road who needs life-saving help. Since Unger denies the significance of distance, he concludes that one cannot refuse the additional Oxfam request for aid to distant lands any more than one can refuse the person on the road.

But suppose we think we have a duty to help those who are near and not as strong a duty to help those who are far. Then, by our intuitive lights, giving a great deal to Oxfam will not have been a duty, or will have satisfied whatever duty of direct aid we have to the distant. Performing supererogatory acts or different duties at one time does not necessarily relieve one from doing a different type of dity at a later time: for example, to help the stranger one meets on the road.[51] But doing supererogatory conduct at one time or fulfilling one type of duty *can* relieve one from doing more of the same at a later time; hence the sense that one may permissibly decline the additional Oxfam request in good conscience.

What if one has already performed a duty – for example, saved some-one one came across on the highway – and then one receives a request from Oxfam? Having performed a strenuous duty can lead one, in good conscience, to refuse a strenuous supererogatory act – if it is such – without even being ungenerous. Can having performed a strenuous duty of one type relieve one of performing another of the same type: for example, saving the next person on the highway? Only if there is a limit to how much of a price one must pay to perform such duties.

Hence, it is not merely that one has aided in the past, but whether one's aid was seen as a supererogatory or a different type of dutiful act, that can affect one's sense of what one must do in the future.

Unger's second puzzle arises in connection with his views on what he calls futility thinking. This is the tendency to not help anyone if one cannot help a significant proportion of those who need help. (He claims that salience helps to overcome futility thinking.) The puzzle is, when do I *not* have a case in which I can only help a non-significant proportion of those who need help? Unger says that the case in which I can definitely save the only person near me who is drowning is *not* a case in which I can take care of "the whole problem," any more than I do when I save a few of those doomed by starvation in distant Africa.[52] This is because the one person who is drowning is just one of many people in the world who are drowning. But suppose we sometimes intuitively distinguish morally between cases of near and distant aid. Then it is understandable that when I take care of the only person near me who needs aid, I think I have completely dealt with a problem.

Measuring distance

What is the intuitive measure of proximity? Let us first try to answer this question for the standard type of case that has been considered in the literature, namely distance from *an agent to a needy stranger*. First, is the distance measured by finding where the agent stands and where the needy stranger stands? Suppose I stand in one part of India, but I have *very* long arms that reach all the way to the other end of India, allowing me to reach a child drowning in a pond at a distance (Reach case). Is this case treated as one where the child is near or far? Intuitively, I think it is treated as a case where the child is near. Suppose the child is so far away in India that I cannot reach there even with my long arms, but the child can reach toward me with *her* long arms so that she is within my reach. Again, I think this case is treated as one of a near victim. These cases might suggest that one intuitively relevant measurement of distance between strangers (whom I shall henceforth call agent and victim) is from the *extended* parts of agent's body to the extended parts of victim's

Figure 9.1   Far but non-continuous reach.

body. The question is, are these extended parts near or far from each other?

Notice that this does not necessarily mean that someone with long-distance reach is near everyone who is *within* the territory from his central location to the outer rim of his extended reach. For it is possible that his reach is not continuous, as illustrated in figure 9.1. He may reach to *a* and all the way back of *a* to his centered location, but his arm may fail to *extend and stop* within area *a* to *b*, so he has no reach there. It extends and stops again within *b* to *c*. Intuitively, there can be a point somewhere between *a* and *b* from which he is distant, even while he is near a physically *further point* between *b* and *c*. (I shall ignore such unusual cases in the following discussion.)

Suppose that while I can reach the child in the Reach case, no part of me that reaches her is *efficacious* in helping her. So, while I can reach her, I cannot lift her from the pond. Is the intuitively relevant measurement of the distance between agent and victim from the *efficacious extended* part of agent's body to the extended part of victim's body? *I think not.* Here is why. Suppose that I, who am in one part of India, can reach the victim in another distant part of India, but I must make use of my machine in Canada to save her. I cannot directly reach that machine in Canada (my arms do not go in that direction), nor can my victim reach anywhere near it. So, we are both far from *the means* of help. Still, my sense is that when even a non-efficacious extended part of me is near an extended part of victim, I am strongly obligated to help by the use of a means that is mine, even though it is far from both me and my victim but can be easily mobilized by remote control.[53]

But how can a measurement of near and far that focuses on distance from extended parts deal with cases where we think someone who is far by this measure nevertheless has a strong duty to aid? For example, if I alone know about the child drowning in distant India and a mere phone call from me can lead to her being saved, I certainly have a strong duty to make the call. This is not inconsistent with the claim that distance (as measured in the way I have described) tracks our intuitions. For the claim only implies that as the efforts involved in saving the distant person increase, the duty to make them is less than the duty to do this for the near person.

Now let us consider the fact that we can alter the proximity of people's extended parts by moving them nearer to each other. Above, we said that someone may be "near by car" but not by foot. This may mean that their extended parts can be brought near *within a short period of time*. So, for any given period of time, different vehicles may cover different distances; someone may be far by car but close by plane. Once we relativize near and far to a vehicle (x), I believe, we are dealing with a *set length of time* (not distance) that it takes to bring people to a certain distance from each other's extended parts. If within a certain length of time (yet to be determined) we can bring people to a certain distance from each other's extended parts by x, they are *near by x*.

Suppose we could settle on the relevant period of time. What if it is very expensive to bring people's extended parts near? Suppose A is near by car, whereas B is near without any alteration in his current location. If B would have to expend $500 to save someone, would A have to expend $500 on getting a car to get to the victim if there were then no further cost to speak of in saving him? In other words, does near-by-car give one the same obligation as near *tout court*? I do not think so. (Nor would he have to transmit the $500 to help the person instead of using it to be transported so as to have his extended parts be near the other's extended parts.)

I conclude that the non-relativized sense of near is primary for our intuitive sense of when we must do more. However, if there is small cost involved, one may have a duty to use a vehicle to make oneself near in the primary sense, even though one will then have to make a big effort to save someone.

We began this section by considering how we measure the intuitively relevant distance between agent and victim. We saw that in the standard near cases, like Near, victim and agent are near, as measured from where their centers are located. Yet we get intuitions that are like those for the standard near cases when only agent and victim's extended parts are near. But, in trying to answer the question of how we measure distance between strangers, we have had to broach the *problem of distance between things other than the agent and victim*, namely distance between agent and agent's means, and between victim and agent's means. This is because the part of agent that is near may not be efficacious, and so agent's means may not be where part of agent is. In the standard cases, not only the victim but the means are near the agent. Furthermore, the means also belong to the agent. (For example, he has his money or his body with him and they are efficacious.) But, in the non-standard case we examined, Reach, the means were distant. *Yet our intuitions in this case are like those in the standard near cases*. This shows that agent's and victim's distance from agent's means is *not* relevant to agent's obligation when victim and agent are near in the sense of near I have delineated. So the failure of previous discussions to notice that *distance of agent's means from agent or victim* is a factor that can be varied independently of distance of agent and victim to each other has not been disastrous.

But this is just the tip of the iceberg. The separability of this factor from others leads us to think about the separability of other factors usually present together in the standard cases, and possibly varying some while holding others constant could make a moral difference.

There are four separable factors on which I shall focus: agent, victim, threat, and means. Under means, I shall consider (for the most part) two categories: agent's means and victim's means. Cases I consider which involve one category of means will not (unless specifically noted) involve the other category of means. Distance (in the sense of near or not near) can vary between each of the four factors and the other three. Let us consider some select cases which raise important points immediately.[54]

Revising the problems of distance in morality

The general point of all the selected cases that I shall present in this section is that the intuition that nearness matters morally does not, contrary to the standard interpretation of the PDM, conflict with our having a strong obligation to help distant strangers.[55] The first case to be considered will show that the standard way of presenting the PDM is incorrect. As noted above, the problem starts because it is claimed that our intuitions can support a strong obligation to help those strangers who are near but not those who are not near. But suppose I am *near* (in the sense elucidated above) *to a threat* which will shortly travel *far* away and kill someone who is far from me (in the sense elucidated above). (Call this the Near threat case.) Must I help that faraway person? My sense is that, intuitively, my obligation to stop the threat to him, like my duty to help in the Near case, is strong. So, without leaving the level of intuitive responses, we see that *when the threat is near to the agent but the victim is far*, the agent still has a strong duty to help. Even if nearness is intuitively important, it does not imply that we have no strong obligation to distant people.

It is also appropriate at this point to note that when the victim is near to the agent but the threat to him is still far from both him and the agent, the agent's intuitively felt obligation can still be as strong as in the Near case, where the threat is near both victim and agent and victim and agent are near. (Call this the To-be victim case.) This is so, at least when the threat, which is now far, will eventually affect the victim while he is still near to the agent. (What if a victim near the agent needs help now to intercept a threat that is still far and that would intersect with the victim once he is away from the agent? Perhaps the strength of obligation is less here, though I doubt it.) So, our obligations, intuitively, are not limited to people we are near *who are already facing a threat* (as in the Near Case). (Though I shall still use the term "victim" to describe people who *will* face a threat if not helped.)

From these two cases, we can conclude that, intuitively, we think that we have greater obligations to take care of *what is in the area near us*, whether this is threats that will cause harm at a distance, or persons who are or will be victims. So the standard description of the PDM – that the distance between ourselves and needy strangers matters morally – is too narrow, since it is also the distance between ourselves and threats that seems to matter. Furthermore, contrary to the standard description of the PDM, our intuitions do not tell us that we always have weaker obligations to aid strangers who are far than those who are near, yet this is consistent with proximity making a moral difference. This is because it may be our *nearness to a threat* to distant people that is morally relevant.

Now, consider a third case in which the agent is far both from the victim and from the threat to the victim (which is either close to or far from the victim), but the agent's means are near to the victim and can be activated by the agent (by remote control). (Call this the Means near victim case.) (Intuitively, the nearness of the means to the victim is measured in the same way as the nearness of a person, from extended parts versus center of location.) I suggest that, intuitively, we think that the agent has a strong obligation to let his means be used because something efficacious that he owns is near to the victim, even if he is not.[56]

Similarly, suppose that the agent is far from both the victim and the threat (which is far from the victim), but the agent's means are close to the *threat* to the victim, though far from the victim. (Call this the Means near threat case.) Again, I suggest that, intuitively, we think that the agent has a strong obligation to let his means be used because something efficacious he owns is near to a threat which will eventually harm the victim.

If the agent is far from the victim and threat and his means are also far from the victim or threat, intuitively the agent would not be strongly obligated to aid, barring some other relevant consideration.

If this is so, does it open a truly vast potential obligation? Consider that one's money now seems to be locatable almost anywhere in virtue of banks and cash machines. Suppose there is a cash machine in a distant part of India, and with it I could access my money if I were there. If my money is there whenever I need it (or anyone who has my code needs it), why is it not simply *there*? I think there is still a difference that may have moral significance between (1) things of mine being transmitted to distant India rapidly or things that are not mine becoming mine rapidly (in virtue of exchanges in bank balance), and (2) what is mine being there, in distant India, already. Certainly, my money cannot now actually be wherever there is a cash machine that would give me money if I were there, since that would mean my assets were enormous, when actually they are very small.[57]

The Means near victim and Means near threat cases suggest that means – which are by definition *efficacious* for helping – that belong to the agent function like the presence of his extended part in obligating him. But recall that we said that the agent's *presence need not be efficacious* in order for him to be obligated, for example, to use his distant efficacious machine. However, what he owns must be efficacious in order for him, at a distance, to be obligated to help by triggering the means by remote control, intuitively. If something I own is near a victim or a threat but it is not an efficacious device, intuitively I am not obligated to trigger something else that I own which would be efficacious but is at a distance from the victim and threat. (I return to this point below.)

Once again, intuitions support the claim that I can be obligated to help those who are not near me, even while also confirming that, at an intuitive level, nearness seems to matter morally. This is contrary to the standard construal of the PDM, where the significance of nearness is taken to eliminate as strong an obligation to distant strangers. In our most recent cases, it is distance between the agent's efficacious device and either the threat or the victim that is morally relevant. Our most recent cases also show that describing the PDM so that it involves reference to the distance between *ourselves* and strangers or threats is misleading, since it may also pertain to distance between our *means* and strangers or threats.

It is now possible to see an important relation between the case in which my means are close to a victim (or threat) but I am distant and the cases in which an agent who is near a victim (or threat to a victim) makes use of means which belong to neither him nor the victim, but to someone else who is distant (Distant owner case).[58] For example, suppose a rich foreigner is in Chicago, but his boat is at Cape Cod where a victim is drowning. I am at Cape Cod, observing the victim, and the boat is near to me and the victim. One justification for my taking the boat to help the victim is that if the owner of the boat were near, he would have a duty to use his boat to help the victim. He is not near, but his means are, and so, according to what was said above, he is intuitively thought to be obligated. In taking his boat, I help him fulfill the duty he has even while he is in Chicago, in virtue of his means being near. (It may well be contentious that I am permitted to enforce someone else's duty, but certainly it is less contentious than that I am permitted to take something from him that he has no duty to give. It may also be less contentious that it is permissible to enforce people's duties to give if the alternative is that others, who are already doing what they are responsible for, will have to increase the amount they give in order to compensate for those who do not do their duty.)

Peter Unger discusses a case like Distant owner. In his Yacht case, an agent takes a boat that belongs to another to help someone near him. The rescue will result in a million dollars worth of damage to the boat for which he cannot compensate. Unger compares this with the Account case, in which a delivery boy to the office of a rich person can do a computer transfer of funds from his account to Unicef's. Unger claims that our intuitions are approving in Yacht and disapproving in Account, but there is no morally significant difference between them. One difference between these cases which might be suggested on the basis of my analysis is that the owner's yacht in Unger's case is near the victim, whether or not the owner of it is, but in Account, *both owner and his means* are far from the victim or the threat to him, at least as long as his money is located far from the victim. In Yacht, when I take the yacht to help someone, I am carrying out someone else's duty for him, based on either his nearness or the nearness of his property.[59] In Account, I cannot say I am enforcing an owner's obligation to a victim if nearness is a ground for obligation. It is also true in Account, but not in Yacht, that the *agent* is not near the victim. I shall return to this below.

If the nearness of the yacht but not the account were explanatory of different intuitions, what about the following revised version of Account? On his way in, the delivery boy sees someone in danger nearby. (An accident, rather than a social justice issue, like the Yachet case.) Only if he transfers funds out of the account will a machine that will help the endangered person be activated. Here we have made the account near the victim, so if we still think the delivery boy may not transfer funds, the factor to which I have pointed will be insufficient alone to explain the difference between Yacht and Unger's version of Account. Suppose the money that would be transferred in the revised Account case were from the yacht repair personal account of the owner: that is, money that was set aside for a luxury rather than for a business item. Furthermore, the transfer is intended to be temporary, since the money must go into the machine only for a short period of time. However, the boy foresees that some of the money (a million dollars) will get eaten up in transaction costs. I suggest that these changes, but only in combination with nearness, make the delivery boy's transfer more acceptable.

But if we have isolated nearness as a reason why we think it is *permissible* for the agent to take the boat in the Distant owner and Yacht cases, how can we explain our sense that he is *obligated* to do so? If I am *near*, I seem to have an obligation to take advantage of another's obligation in order to help a victim. If I am far away (in Alaska) but see the victim in Cape Cod via long-distance vision, do we think I am as strongly obligated to move (by remote control) the means at Cape Cod owned by someone who is in Chicago? Our intuitions say no, I believe. So, even if the person in Chicago is thought to have an obligation to use or let his means be used, it does not seem that I am as obligated to act on his obligation if I am distant from the victim (or threat).[60] However, we think it is still permissible for me to do so.

Now, suppose the Chicago person's boat is close to him but *at a distance* from the victim (it is on Lake Michigan). I am near the victim (or threat) on Cape Cod. Do we think I have a strong obligation to move the Chicago person's boat to help the victim? Is it even thought to be permissible for me to do so? These are, of course, two different questions. The first question also suggests two separate issues: what do we think my obligation is, and what do we think the obligation is of the owner of the boat? When the owner is distant from victim or threat,[61] and his means are as well, intuitively he has no strong obligation to aid. So, in this case, I cannot justify bringing his distant means to use at Cape Cod by saying I am the agent of his obligation, for he is not thought to have any. Does my felt obligation in virtue of my nearness give rise to a felt obligation on my part to use the means that another is thought to have no obligation to use and that belong to him? (This is what Unger seems to be considering when he imagines that I am near a drowning victim and I must forge a check on a billionaire's account in order to buy a yacht to save her.) Possibly, I have such an obligation, but I doubt it. More likely, I am thought to have a strong excuse rather than a justification for taking the other's means. But notice that this is still different from the case in which I am not near a victim or a threat, and I am tempted to use means that are not near the victim or threat and whose owner is not near the victim or threat. (Arguably that is what is true in Unger's Account case).[62] If the means that are distant from me are *unowned* and I have a strong obligation arising from my nearness to the victim, I do, intuitively, have a strong obligation to employ these distant means by remote control.

Classifying all these Distant owner cases as our fifth type, let us consider a sixth case. It is a version of the Near case in which I see a lifesaving machine that belongs to a victim floating in the pond near me. Unless I throw my $500 jacket in the pond, thereby ruining it, the machine will go down the drain. The point here is to construct a case in which *the means belong to the victim, the agent knows this, and these means are near the agent when the victim and threat are far from him.* (Call this the Victim's near means case.) In this case, intuitively, the agent has a strong obligation to save the machine that will help the distant victim. If the victim's machine were distant from the agent (and the victim and threat were also distant), there would not intuitively be such a strong obligation.[63] Once again, our intuitions tell us that the strong obligation to help a distant stranger is consistent with nearness having moral significance and, contrary to the standard description of the PDM, it is our nearness to the victim's means that is relevant.

One hypothesis for why being near a victim's means is significant is that what is owned by a victim stands in for him and we react as though he were near. This is on the model of the agent's means being close to victim or threat (discussed above). But this does not seem quite right, and indeed it is not an accurate extension of the model. For it is not enough that *just anything* belonging to the victim be near the agent; for example, if his TV set is floating in the pond, this does not obligate the agent to give money to help the distant stranger. It is only if the victim's means that can help him are near that the agent has a stronger obligation to rescue these means. As was noted above, in the model case of an agent's means being near a victim from whom the agent is distant, *efficaciousness of the agent's item, not mere ownership*, is necessary. Does this mean that what triggers an obligation when one person is near another, though neither is efficacious, is fundamentally different from what triggers an obligation when something that belongs to one person is near another?

But an agent, even when not efficacious (able to help directly), can help by triggering his efficacious distant device. In that sense, even if he is not directly efficacious, he can *relate usefully* to the victim. A device must be able to do this too to be analogous to the presence of an agent. Efficacious means are clearly like this, and the agent's TV is not. What about the agent's computer that is near the victim or threat and cannot help directly but can monitor the scene and trigger the use of the agent's means distant from the victim? Is the agent intuitively thought to be obligated to let the computer trigger a distant device? I suggest he is.

But what about *victim's non-efficacious property* that is close to the agent when the victim is distant? It is more puzzling that what belongs to the victim has to be efficacious or be able to relate usefully to his need than that what belongs to agent must do so. For the victim himself *is not efficacious, nor need he relate usefully to his own need.* The characteristic shared by cases in which the agent's means are near the victim or the victim's means are near the agent seems to be that *only what is pertinent to satisfying the need of the victim* (whether it is person or machine) is relevant to establishing an obligation. The victim is certainly *pertinent to* satisfying his need, even if he is not efficacious, unlike just anything he owns.

In the seventh case, my efficacious machine, which is distant from me, the threat, and the victim, *is near the victim's means*, which are distant from agent, threat, and victim. (Call this the Means–means case.) (It is a case in which the means of both agent and victim are present.) My means can rescue the victim's means, which can then help him. My sense, in this case, is that, intuitively, I have a stronger obligation to aid in virtue of some form of morally relevant nearness than if there were no nearness. Once again, I intuitively seem to have a duty to help someone far from me, yet this is because nearness is intuitively a matter of moral significance. This time, it is nearness of my means and the victim's means.

Notice that what we have said implies that our intuitions about the sources of an agent's obligation may be overdetermined. For example, an agent's sense that he is obligated may arise because he is near the victim, while the same agent may also believe he is obligated because his means are near to what will threaten the victim. Overdetermination does not necessarily increase the strength of the obligation.

My tentative conclusion is that the PDM should be understood as whether we can justify our intuition that we have a greater responsibility to take care of what is going on in the area near us or near our efficacious means, whether this involves needy victims, threats, or means belonging to victims.

But there is one final question to be dealt with in this section: given that all these factors are relevant in the issue of moral distance, is there still some greater weight given intuitively to some of these factors relative to others? If we have "threat near agent" (T_N), "victim near agent" (V_N), "victim's means near to agent but far from victim" (M_N^V), "agent's means near to victim but far from agent" (M_N^A), there are six possible combinations of these factors to consider in determining the weight of each factor relative to the others. Let us consider them on the supposition that I am visiting France and all the victims are somewhere in France.

1   T_N versus V_N. In one near pond, there is a threat to a faraway victim and, in another near pond, there is a different (unseen) victim. To which pond should the agent go if one life is at stake in either choice? Perhaps to the pond with the victim. If so, $V_N > T_N$. But what if T_N will kill two distant victims? Then, T_N may dominate V_N. If so, the dominance of $V_N > T_N$ *per se* is not very great.

2   T_N versus M_N^V In one near pond, there is a threat to one far victim, and in the other pond, a different far victim's means. Intuitively, there may be some sense that one should go to the pond with the threat. This may be because we do not wish to be associated with the *cause* of death more than we want to be associated with a rescue from death. (This is piggybacking on the harming/not aiding distinction, and perhaps the loss/no-gain distinction.)

3   T_N versus M_N^A. In a near pond, there is a threat to one distant victim and, at a distance, the agent's means are near another victim. Is there a sense that one should deal with the threat rather than trigger the means? If so, this may be because it is the *agent* rather than his means that are near. (On the other hand, one's means are near the victim.)

4   V_N versus M_N^V. One (unseen) victim is near an agent and also a distant victim's means are near. Intuitively, there is a sense that one should go to the near victim, but this may be overridden if more distant victims would be helped by the means.

5   V_N versus M_N^A. One victim is near an agent and the agent's means are near one distant victim. V_N intuitively takes precedence over activating

the distant means, but if more distant victims could be helped by M, this may override the weight of V_N.

6 M_N^V versus M_N^A. One victim's means are in a near pond but the agent's means are near a different distant victim. The pull to help each seems equal.

My tentative conclusion was that, intuitively, there is greater felt responsibility for a threat, victim, or victim's means when they are in the area near an agent or an agent's means than when they are far from these. Now we can add to this that, intuitively, the responsibility to the near person is stronger than that to other near factors, and nearness to an agent has greater significance than nearness to an agent's means. Responsibility to deal with a near threat may take precedence over dealing with a victim's near, or an agent's distant, means. In some sense, then, $V > T > M_V$, and $A > M_A$ when other things are equal. This internal difference may have further ramifications.

Temporally various cases

Our tentative conclusion has been based on consideration of near cases in which aid is to be rendered at the time the agent or means are near. But what if, for example, when the agent is near to the victim (or to-be-victim) he does not then know of his plight. Consider the following case, which I call a temporally various case:

> *Near-then-far*:   I am passing near by the child drowning in the pond, who I am able to help. But, through no fault of mine, I don't know I am near (i.e. I don't know I am near the person and I don't know he is in danger). When I am already far away, I first learn that I was near him when he was in trouble. I can still save him from that trouble by putting $500 in a device that will activate a machine to scoop him out.

I believe that, intuitively, the obligation to help is stronger than it would be if I had never been near. Hence, I can be obligated when I am far because I once was near the person in danger. The obligations I have at t_n to take care of the problems going on in the area near me is not limited to problems in the area near me at t_n.

We can imagine variations on this case. What if when I was near: (a) the person was not in danger but only endangered once I am far; (b) the person was a to-be-victim, the threat to whom I could have averted; (c) I would have been unable to help, but am now able; (d) I knew the person was in danger, but not that I was near; (e) I knew I was near the person, but not that he was in danger? Intuitively, I think it is only in (a) that our obligation is not stronger than in ordinary Far cases. So, the fact that I was near (or, I would also say, *will* be near) someone does not mean that I have a stronger obligation to help, if it is only when I am far that he is in danger or a to-be-victim.

Is it necessary that I ever come to have knowledge when I am far in order to be obligated? I said that an agent may use the boat of a distant person whose boat is near a victim, because the distant person is obligated and there was no reason to suppose he had knowledge of the fact that his means were near the victim. Hence, knowledge may not be necessary here either.

Now we should consider different temporally various cases. In these, I was near a *threat* to a distant person, or near a far victim's means when it could have been useful for rescue, but I did not know it; now I am far from these (as well as the victim) but am able to stop the threat or get the means which are still needed for the same purpose to the victim. My sense is that, in these cases, it is also true that now that I am far, I have a greater obligation to help because I once was near.

What if in these temporally various cases it is not I but my efficacious means that were near to the victim, threat, or victim's means, but my means were then not known to be near or useful? Now they are far but still can be useful. My sense is that intuitively the obligation to aid is greater than in other Far cases. A possible difference between *my* having been close and *my means* having been close is that it is only the means that were close that one may be obligated to use when far. But if I was near, it is not only what I could have used at the time to help that I may be required to use now that I am far.[64]

In another form of temporally various case, a problem is now going on in an area from which I and my means are now far but it will still be present when I or my means are near in the future. It is only now that I or my means can deal effectively with the victim (to-be-victim), threat, or victim's means. Intuitively, I do not intuitively think I am more obligated to deal with a problem that will be near but is far, though I am sometimes more obligated to deal with what has been near but is far. A past tie based on nearness seems not to be wiped out once it exists, but a future one does not obligate before it exists. If so, there is an asymmetry between past and future, because a failure – even due to inability of means at the time – to do something about a near problem in the past may have to be made up for.

So, we can revise our tentative conclusion: the PDM should be understood as whether we can justify our intuition that we have a greater responsibility to take care of needy victims, threats, or means belonging to the victim that are or were in the areas near us or our efficacious means. Call this the revised PDM.

Suggestions for why distance matters

I have dealt with whether and how intuitively we think distance matters. In this chapter, I shall not deal in great detail with the question of whether distance actually matters morally: that is, with whether the intuitions are correct. But I do want to deal with some suggestions for why it might matter. Furthermore, I hope to show that the pattern of our intuitions may help to eliminate certain hypotheses as to why distance could really matter.

One suggestion for justifying the patterns of our intuitions is that the relation that events have to our *bodies* and the fact that we are embodied persons have significance in the correct moral theory. This hypothesis is insufficient to account for the fact that an obligation to aid is intuitively generated when certain things are near our *means*, not near us. However, if the strength of the obligation is weaker when nearness is to our means, then nearness to us may have a special role. If our intuitions could be generated for creatures that were locatable but disembodied, this would reduce the significance of embodiedness and shift importance to mere *locatability*.

It may be suggested that proximity matters as a heuristic device that correlates with morally significant factors, though it itself is not morally significant. One of these factors might be the need to set limits to our duty to aid strangers; being responsible in accord with proximity is a way to set these limits. Another factor might be the need to help those with whom we potentially have cooperative relations, and given our nature, these are near rather than distant people. But I doubt that these factors explain the significance of distance. And, indeed, the revised description of the nature of the bias in favor of the near which I have suggested can be used to show that these hypotheses are not adequate.

First, being responsible only for those who are near, or, as I have alternatively described our intuitions, being responsible for what goes on in the area near us, or our efficacious means will not alone necessarily limit the strenuousness of our obligation, for we may be near many needy people. (If Asian Indians were responsible for helping those in East Hampton, New York, they would have less strenuous obligations.) Furthermore, if one had long-distance reach and a reach to each interval from one's central location to the outer rim of one's reach, one's responsibility would be very great if responsibility was a function of proximity. But this would be, admittedly, a different world from the present one, and the limit-theorist might say that if we had such long-distance reach, proximity would *not* be our method for drawing limits. I doubt that we can just legislate proximity in and out of relevance in this way. Indeed, I believe that the considerations favoring limits on requirements to aid are not reflected in the grounds for favoring responsibility in accord with distance. Rather, these limits would be needed to *override* the proximity-based reasons that favor responsibility in order to *limit* it.

In addition, there could have been other *geographic* delimitations on aid if the purpose of geographic zones were to limit requirement to aid. New Yorkers could have been responsible for helping only those in Santiago. If setting limits on aid were all that justified giving us greater obligations for what goes on in the area near us, there would be no more reason to choose the form of limitation than any other geographic way of limiting responsibility. But it seems more than an arbitrary choice whether we do it one way or another.

Notice also that if alternative geographic delimitations are to function the way delimitation by near versus far function, they must share the other characteristics of the delimitation by near versus far. It must be true that, for example, New Yorkers are responsible for dealing with *threats* arising in Santiago that will hurt people in Paris: they will also be responsible for rescuing people in Paris if the means of the Parisians are in Santiago. When we discover that nearness affects our relation not only to people but to threats and to means, it may be harder to suggest that some other geographic delimitation is substitutable for proximity.

What of the second hypothesis, that distance tracks potential cooperative relations? If I visit Switzerland, I have no reason to believe that there will be further relations between me and the Swiss victim, and yet I am obligated to help more strongly than if the same person is at a distance, subject to a threat distant from me and distant from my means while I am distant from his means. Furthermore, if he is distant from me, but I am near to his means or to the threat to him, or he, his means, or the threat is near my means, then I do have the stronger duty to aid. Yet, in these cases, there has been and is no potential for future cooperative relations. Finally, the near/far distinction may apply to creatures with whom we could not have cooperative relations. For example, if a dog is suffering near me, my obligation to aid is intuitively greater than my obligation if I am the only one who can help a distant dog.

Perhaps it will help to understand how proximity affects the duty to aid by considering how it does *not* affect the duty not to harm. That is, negative and positive duties and negative and positive rights behave very differently in response to proximity. We have at least as strong a duty not to harm someone who is far as not to harm someone who is near. I suggest that this is because in standard cases in which we would harm someone, we would deprive her of what she would have had independently of our aid. These things people have independently of us are protected by the negative right. This "protective coating" goes with the person wherever *she* is located – near or far. So, the strength of her negative right is something that has its source in her, not us, and is based on properties located where she is. Efforts we make not to harm her involve doing things in order not to impose first on that to which she has right.

This contrasts with someone who needs our help: if we do not aid, he will lose something that he would not retain without our aid, i.e. something he would not have independently of our aid. If we do things for him, he imposes first on us. The focus would then seem to be about what comes *from us* and adds to what the person would have independently of us. This may seem to explain why the focus is on us, and hence on where *we* are.

But this is much too quick for at least two reasons. (1) Even when someone is near us and he needs aid, he still loses only what he would not have had without our aid. If this factor explains why the focus is on the agent rather than the victim, it can seem to justify the absence of *any* duty to aid, even those who are near. (2) Suppose someone has a positive right to aid based on considerations *other* than his being near to us. His right to aid and our duty to aid him does not necessarily disappear just because he is not near.

All this suggests that (a) we have to show that we have a special responsibility to do something about what goes on in the area near us or our means (so nearness is a sufficient condition for some duties), and (b) we have to show that there is a duty to aid whose *origin* lies in nearness, so that when nearness stops, the duty stops (hence nearness is necessary for some duties). If we had a duty to aid a stranger – even though the fact that he needs our aid means he loses only what he could not retain without us and he imposes on us first – which stranger we must aid is connected with the fact that the focus in aiding is on the agent from whom aid comes and who is imposed on first, and that agent has a responsibility for the area around him or his means.[65]

Now, why might he actually have such responsibility for the area around him or his means? It is commonly thought that one has a moral prerogative to give greater weight to one's own interests rather than giving equal weight to oneself and to others.[66] This is a permissible option, not a duty. But possibly, if one takes advantage of the option of giving greater weight to oneself and what one cares about, there is an *associated duty, the flip side of the prerogative*, generated from the perspective on life which leads to the prerogative, to take care of what is associated with oneself: for example, the area near one. This would imply that the person who does not act on the self-focused prong of the prerogative, but treats himself impartially relative to others quite generally, would not have a greater duty to take care of those who are near than those who are far.

What must I do?

Suppose there really is a stronger duty to take care of the area near us or our means – for example, to rescue the near child in the pond – and not as strong a duty to take care of a comparable event far from us or our means. Does this imply that I must always fulfill my strongest duty to aid rather than perform a weaker one or engage in supererogatory aiding?

Peter Unger believes this implication holds, for he argues that to say we have a duty to aid the person near us but not a duty to aid distant people implies that we have a duty to save one person close to us rather than do what will save many at a distance.[67] In discussing whether distance *per se* affects our intuitions about obligation to aid, I have tried to keep constant the number of people and the loss they will suffer in the near and far cases. Theoretically, therefore, everything I have said is consistent with our having a duty to save two in the Far case rather than one in the Near case. But I now wish to assume that the intuitive bias in favor of the near is strong enough so that there is *no* strong duty (e.g. one for which one would have to sacrifice a significant amount) to rescue several in the Far case. The question is whether this implies that we have a duty to save one person close to us rather than do what will save many at a distance.

One ground for the implication would be the claim that in a choice between a duty and a supererogatory act, one always has to do the duty. But this claim is not true.[68] For example, suppose I have a duty to meet someone for lunch because I promised to do so. On my way, I see someone dying of kidney failure. I am willing to give him my kidney, a supererogatory act (let us assume). It is wrong to say that the supererogatory aiding may not take precedence over the duty. I believe this is so, even if the person to whom I am obligated would lose so much if I do not aid him that he would not be morally required to waive his right to my performance. For example, suppose I have promised to save one person's life if he is in danger, but as I am about to help him, I see a thousand people drowning nearby. Aiding them, but not him, would cost me my leg, so it is supererogatory of me to save them. Still, if I am willing, I think I may choose them over the one person to whom I am obligated.

What these cases show[69] is that the following intransitivity is true: a personal preference not to suffer a loss (P) can take precedence over some aiding behavior, which then becomes supererogatory (S); supererogatory aiding (S) may take precedence over some duties (D); but it is not true that personal preference not to suffer a loss (P), therefore, takes precedence over a duty, and hence one still has a duty. That is, P may take precedence over S, S may take precedence over D, but it is not the case that P may take precedence over D.

This suggests that even if it is wrong not to save a near person when there is nothing else to do and not wrong to fail to save a greater number who are far, if one had a choice between saving the near or a greater number of the far, one might permissibly do the latter. So, for example, this suggests that I may permissibly abandon the one drowning near me in France to rush off with a check to catch the last postal delivery to a distant area of India and thereby save hundreds from drowning there. Hence, it would be wrong to think that one may not do the supererogatory act, simply because one would be failing to do one's duty.[70] It may not matter morally which act one does, and this is compatible with its being a duty to help the near but not the far. One may not need to abstain from helping the far in order to help the near.

Notice, however, that in the specific context in which one fails to do one's duty in order to do what is supererogatory, it is not true that $P > S$. That is, one cannot fail to do one's duty, to do which one might have had to sacrifice P (e.g. personal goods), and then go on to fulfill those personal goals instead of running to deposit the needed check. Forsaking duty, one is then bound to do the supererogatory act. But still one may not have to do everything to do the supererogatory act that one would have had to do to accomplish one's duty.[71]

Unger himself would, presumably, wish to make use of the permissibility of doing a supererogatory rather than an obligatory act. This is because he argues that we have a duty to give our money to help the poor[72] (i.e. it would be wrong not to), but he also argues that it is permissible and morally worthwhile to steal from others to help the poor, though it may not be wrong not to.[73] This means it is supererogatory to steal. If he believed the duty took precedence over the supererogatory act, he would be committed to thinking that a person who had few resources would have a duty to give a small amount to the poor rather than steal a lot of money from a rich person to give to the poor if he could not do both, even when he was willing to steal. But, presumably, Unger would think it is permissible to do the supererogatory act instead of the dutiful one. This helps us deny his claim that if we have a duty to help the near but not the far, we have a duty to help the near instead of the far.

Notice, however, that there may be a moral difference between different types of supererogatory acts. In the case in which I must choose between my obligation to one person and saving a thousand near people, saving the thousand people would be at least one of my duties if it were not for the great cost to me. If it were costless to me, then this *duty* would conflict with my duty to keep my promise to save one person. Since we are free to absorb a cost if we want to, an account of why one kind of supererogatory act may compete with a duty is available. But it is not necessarily the great cost to me that makes aiding those far away not a duty; we intuitively think it has something to do with distance *per se*, so that a high cost that would be required in the Near case would not be required in the Far case. And, it might be suggested, we are *not* free to make the plight of those who are at a distance as important as that of those who are near – in the way we are free to absorb a cost – in order that the supererogatory act compete with a duty. (Similarly, it might be argued that what greatcost we will absorb is up to us, but it is not in our power to make helping members of other societies a competitor with helping those in our own society.) If it were not permitted to put *this particular* supererogatory act in competition with the duty, this would be a *second ground* for the view that we *must* aid a smaller number of near people rather than aid a greater number of those far away. I shall not pursue this issue further here. Suffice it to say that if we are to fill in the outlines of our intuitive conception of duty that varies with distance, we need to deal with this issue.

Finally, there could be motivational oddities in the person who does the supererogatory rather than the obligatory. For example, suppose that when faced with saving a near drowning child at the cost of $500, one instead decides to save 300 far children because that will only cost $100. Or, someone who has never thought of saving distant children thinks that given that she now has a duty to spend $500 on the near child, she might as well spend it in achieving the better consequence of saving more distant children. These cases differ from the one in which someone who is independently motivated to save the distant children wishes not to give up that act in order to do less good for someone who is near; here these motivational oddities, at least, do not arise.[74]

Notes

1 "Famine, affluence, and morality" (henceforth FAM), reprinted in W. Aiken and H. LaFollette (eds), *World Hunger and Moral Obligation* (Englewood Cliffs, NJ: Prentice Hall, 1977), pp. 22–36.
2 My discussion of these issues will be based on the views he expresses in FAM, and *Practical Ethics* (henceforth PE), 2nd edn (New York: Cambridge University Press, 1993).
3 Unger's views occur in his *Living High and Letting Die* (New York: Oxford University Press, 1996).
4 In *Moral Thinking* (New York: Oxford University Press, 1981).
5 Parfit describes this as rational irrationality when he endorses similar character traits. See *Reasons and Persons* (New York: Oxford University Press, 1984), part I.
6 Discussed in the final chapter of PE.
7 He does not discuss the claim that morality is a system that it is rational for each agent to want all agents to follow. He merely focuses on the question

"why should *I* be moral?", the question a free-rider on the moral behavior of others might ask.

8 See p. 328.

9 PE, p. 334.

10 In his *The Rejection of Consequentialism* (New York: Oxford University Press, 1982).

11 In his *The View from Nowhere* (New York: Oxford University Press, 1986).

12 As Susan Wolf points out in "Above and below the line of duty," *Philosophical Topics*, 14 (Fall 1986), pp. 131–48; and Liam Murphy in "The demands of beneficence," *Philosophy and Public Affairs*, 22 (Fall 1993), pp. 267–92.

13 For example, in "The central conflict: morality and self-interest," presented at the Colloquium in Law, Philosophy and Social Theory, New York University Law School, October 17, 1996, p. 9.

14 For example, Thomas Nagel takes this view in *The View from Nowhere*. Scheffler does not, however, commit himself to the dominance of the moral point of view. See his *Human Morality* (New York: Oxford University Press, 1993).

15 But is trying to avoid the worst state of affairs itself a policy that is biased in favor of morality? It is possible that the best state of affairs requires aesthetic greatness, even though it cannot exist without also avoiding great moral wrong. Is it rational to risk the worst (great moral wrong) for the sake of ensuring the *possibility* of the best?

16 Raz seems to want to make both claims, in "The central conflict."

17 In chapter 9 of PE, "Insiders and outsiders," pp. 261–2.

18 See his *Reasons and Persons* (New York: Oxford University Press, 1984).

19 I conclude this from his claim (PE, p. 22) that "True scales favour the side where the interest is stronger or where several interests combine to outweigh a smaller number of similar insterests." Also from his claim (PE, p. 23) that "Slavery prevents the slaves from satisfying their interests ... and the benefits it confers on the slaveowners are hardly comparable in importance to the harm it does the slaves." In FAM he does not commit himself to more than negative utilitarianism; preventing suffering has significance even if maximizing happiness does not. But in PE, he moves beyond mere negative utilitarianism. See especially PE, pp. 14 and 37.

20 An indication that he eschews the total view is his position on famine relief and overpopulation. He claims that we would do no good, and hence are not obligated to aid, if we save people now who will produce another generation who will then starve to death (FAM, postscript, p. 35). The total view would imply, by contrast, that we *would* do good, even though the same number of people died of starvation whatever we do. For if we help, we save one generation and make possible several years of life for a new generation before they die; the latter additional good would not exist if we did not save the first generation.

21 In "Innumerate ethics," *Philosophy and Public Affairs*, 7 (Summer 1978), pp. 285–301.

22 For my discussion of this issue, see *Morality, Mortality, volume 1* (New York: Oxford University Press, 1993).

23 His detailed discussion of this issue is in PE, beginning on p. 224. My detailed discussion of this issue is in *Morality, Mortality, volume 2* (New York: Oxford University Press, 1996), chapters 1–4.

24 Singer himself presents a case that involves exporting into a letting die case a property which is a cousin of one necessarily true of a killing: "Finally, it may well be that the doctor is personally responsible for the death of the infant she decides not to operate upon, since she may know that if she had not taken this case, other doctors in the hospital would have operated" (PE, p. 225). Here a doctor, in taking a case, interferes with someone else aiding. One form of killing involves interfering with aid another *is* providing; this is close to interfering with aid another would provide.

25 I first presented this analysis in "Killing and letting die: methodological and substantive issues," *Pacific Philosophical Quarterly*, 1983, and it is discussed in detail in *Morality, Mortality, volume 2*, chapters 1–3.

26 Starting in PE, p. 215.

27 I discuss this strategy in detail in *Morality, Mortality, volume 2*, chapter 4.

28 PE, p. 228.

29 Singer also argues that there is no moral distinction *per se* between intending and foreseeing harm. The use of cases against that claim could involve the following set. (a) A doctor leaves one patient to die, foreseeing his death, in order to save five others' lives. This is permissible. (b) A doctor leaves one patient to die, intending his death, because observing that death makes it possible for him to help five others to live. This is impermissible.

30 In FAM, p. 24. In PE, he only presents the first principle (pp. 230–1).

31 PE, p. 245.

32 FAM, p. 35.

33 FAM, p. 32.

34 PE, p. 26.

35 Singer does not draw these conclusions, but Peter Unger, who considers himself a follower of Singer, does in *Living High and Letting Die* (henceforth LHLD). I discuss Unger's views in detail in "Grouping and the imposition of harm," *Utilitas*, November 1998, and in "Rescue and harm: a discussion of Peter Unger's Living High and Letting Die," *Legal Theory*, forthcoming but allow myself to comment frequently on some of his views in this article, since he thinks of himself as a Singerian.

36 I argue for such a view of status in *Morality, Mortality, volume 2*, chapter 10, and in "Inviolability," in *Midwest Studies in Philosophy*, 1995.

37 FAM, p. 28.

38 Peter Unger thinks this (see LHLD).

39 I have argued against Peter Unger's attempt to show that intuitions about cases are inconsistent and undependable in "Grouping and the imposition of harm".

40 In FAM; and PE.

41 For detailed discussion of that issue, see my *Morality, Mortality, volume 2*, chapters 1–5.

42 These tests are modeled on ones suggested for killing and letting die. See *Morality, Mortality, volume 2*, chapter 4. It might also be suggested that we

could run a Choice test, i.e. if we could only save someone near or someone far, but not both, which should we choose? However, I do not think this test is very revealing, since we are often free to choose to do what we have no duty to do rather than our duty. I will explain this point below.

43 Peter Unger in LHLD, and Shelly Kagan in *The Limits of Morality* (New York: Oxford University Press, 1989) both discuss salience (or vividness).

44 LHLD, p. 28.

45 One way in which salience works is to help me to really understand someone's need. But when I understand what her need is really like, I now also understand what every other person who is as needy is going through. So, insofar as salience is revealing of need, one would expect that salience would lead me to help everyone – salient or not – who is so needy. It would not bias me in favor of helping just the person who is, in fact, salient.

46 Similarly, Singer believes not only that I have an obligation to give away money once I have it; he also believes I must go and earn money in order to have it to give away.

47 LHLD, pp. 24–36.

48 The first step, I believe, is a sounder way than the second of seeing whether a factor had an effect in the original Sedan. This is because if a factor is "exported" into the Envelope case, as in the second step, it may have no effect in its new context, but this will not show it had no effect on its home ground. (This is due to what I call the Principle of Contextual Interaction.) For discussion of these points, see *Morality, Mortality, volume 2*.

49 LHLD, p. 34.

50 In LHLD, pp. 60–1.

51 Exceptions can arise if doing the supererogatory act has the further effect of *raising* the costs one would have to make to perform one's duty. For example, suppose Albert Schweitzer has been serving the poor his whole life supererogatorily, and this results in his only having a few days left in his life to play the piano. The cost of giving up one's *last chance* to play the piano might relieve him of certain duties to others.

52 LHLD, p. 41.

53 But note the following: above, I said that if nearness gives us an obligation, we could still avoid being near to victims. Suppose our nearness to a victim implies, as I have said, that we should activate distant means to help. Aware of this source of obligation to use means, it might still be permissible to see to it that our far means cannot be activated by remote control. It is possible that only those distant means which an agent can make efficacious *while still retaining his initial nearness* to a victim are the ones he is obligated to use. But do not we often have to leave a near victim, making ourselves far, in order to get means that help him? What if the movement away in order to get means puts us near another victim. Are we then obligated to him? I think not, since we already have an obligation.

54 The seven selected cases we will examine in some detail can be generated, along with many others, from mechanically combining the four different factors (agent, victim, threat, means) and four categories of means (agent's means,

victim's means, third parties' means, unowned means). It is also possible to consider who "owns" the threat. In what follows, I shall ignore threat ownership and only occasionally consider the possibility that means belong to third parties. The problem is simply to consider what intuitions one has about obligation to intentionally suffer a loss to save an innocent stranger from death in cases involving all possible combinations of the factors.

55 If I had not introduced a revisionist sense of "near to" and "distant from" in the second section, we might have already concluded this on the basis of the Reach case. That is, in terms of centers of location, I am distant from the child in India yet I have a strong duty to help in that case.

56 If the means is the agent's employee, he does not, of course, own the employee. Nevertheless, I shall understand him to have a relation similar to ownership to his employee, for our purposes.

57 Liam Murphy suggests an alternative account: money is too abstract to be dealt with like concrete means. (If it were in a sack next to a child in distress, this might not be so, I suggest.)

58 As a matter of biography, it was through trying to explain what goes on in such a case that I stumbled upon the possibility of separating the location of agent and means.

59 Oddly, even though Unger thinks he has shown, in chapter 2 of LHLD, that the owner of the yacht has a duty to use it to rescue, he does not make use of the conclusion in deciding why I may take the owner's yacht to do a rescue.

60 And distant from victim's own means, though the significance of this point will not be clear until later.

61 And the victim's means, as we shall see below.

62 In that case, the agent is distant from the victim or threat, means are distant from the victim or threat, and the owner of the means is distant from the victim or threat.

63 However, it is possible that when a victim has the means to alleviate his condition but is far from them, there is still an impetus on those who are also distant from these means (and from the victim and threat) to help the victim get his means, greater than if his rescue depends totally on means belonging to others. This is not because there is reduced cost in saving him if we use his means (since there may be no reduction), but because there is a sense in which we conceive of him as *more self-sufficient*. This issue deserves further examination.

64 If my device was not useful at the time but is now that it is far, it was not an efficacious means at the time, and I do not think its past presence obligates me now.

65 This special responsibility is not to be identified with any property-like stake in the area around him, since this would imply that he not only had special responsibilities for, but also special privileges in, the area near him. But this need not be true.

66 See Samuel Scheffler, *The Rejection of Consequentialism*.

67 LHLD, p. 55.

68 I first tried to show this in "Supererogation and obligation," *Journal of Philosophy* (March 1985), reprinted in *The Philosopher's Annual 1985*, and in an expanded version in *Morality, Mortality, volume 2*, chapter 12.

69 As I pointed out in "Supererogation and obligation."

70 Above, I said that our having done a supererogatory act need not, in general, free one from doing one's duty. Hence, the fact that one can often do a supererogatory act rather than one's duty when the two conflict should be consistent with one still having to do one's duty, if one can, once one has done the supererogatory act.

71 For more on this, see *Morality, Mortality, volume 2*, chapter 12.

72 LHLD, chapter 3.

73 LHLD, chapter 3.

74 I thank Liam Murphy for suggesting that I examine the PMD. I am indebted to the students and faculty of my graduate classes in ethical theory at UCLA and NYU for their discussion of the ideas in this article. I am also grateful for comments from Sigrun Svavarsdottir, Derek Parfit, and the audiences at the Philosophy Department Colloquia, Graduate Center, City University of New York, and the Philosophy Department, University of Calgary. I owe Franklin Bruno, Tyler Burge, Wei Cui, Barbara Herman, James Hicks, Jerrold Katz, Dennis McKerlie, David Mellow, Seana Shiffren, Michael Stocker and Sigrun Svavarsdottir for numerous cases, points and suggestions.

10
Empathy and Animal Ethics

RICHARD HOLTON AND RAE LANGTON

In responding to the challenge that we cannot know that animals feel pain, Peter Singer says:

> We can never directly experience the pain of another being, whether that being is human or not. When I see my daughter fall and scrape her knee, I know that she feels pain because of the way she behaves – she cries, she tells me her knee hurts, she rubs the sore spot, and so on. I know that I myself behave in a somewhat similar – if more inhibited – way when I feel pain, and so I accept that my daughter feels something like what I feel when I scrape my knee. The basis of my belief that animals can feel pain is similar.[1]

Singer here suggests that the epistemological problem facing animal ethics is really the more general problem of other minds: the Cartesian problem of how to escape solipsism, how to cross the bridge from my own thoughts and feelings to the thoughts and feelings of any other being. The suggestion is that no one can seriously be in the thrall of this sceptical problem. The method for building the bridge to other minds is familiar to us all: we use it every day in our ascriptions of thoughts and feelings to people near and dear, and to those far away. And we use it every day in our ascriptions of thoughts and feelings to animals.

What is the method, exactly? Singer's suggestion can be interpreted in two different ways. One idea is this. When I am in pain, I display a certain sort of behaviour: I rub the sore spot; I complain; if it is bad enough, I cry. From this sample I develop a generalization: those who show this sort of behaviour are usually in pain. So, when my daughter cries and rubs her knee, I conclude that my daughter is probably in pain. On this interpretation, the bridge to other minds makes use of a general law stating that this sort of behaviour is normally correlated with pain. The inference works by bringing this instance under that general law. It delivers a conclusion whose form is propositional: it delivers the conclusion that my daughter is in pain. The method does not essentially make use of the imagination. Indeed, although the passage from Singer suggests that my evidence for this general law comes from first personal experience, this need not be so. There is nothing in the method of inferring a general law from a sample, and making inferences about further cases on the basis of that generalization, which restricts it to first-personal evidence.

There may, though, be a second and different idea behind Singer's suggestion, which goes like this. How my daughter is behaving is roughly how I would behave if in pain. So what it is like for my daughter is roughly what it is like for me, when in pain. On this second interpretation, the bridge to other minds does not essentially make use of a general law about people. It does essentially make use of a projective act of imagination. It does essentially make use of the first personal experience of the one making the inference. And it delivers an extra conclusion that is not obviously propositional in form: it delivers not only the conclusion *that my daughter is in pain*, but also a conclusion about *what it is like* for my daughter.[2] We need handy labels for these two different possible methods of building a bridge to other minds; for now, let us dub them the *theoretical* and the *imaginative*, respectively.

It seems more likely that it is the second, imaginative, method that Singer primarily has in mind. The first-personal references do not seem merely accidental; the references to the behaviour and feelings of 'I myself' seem central to the kind of inference Singer envisages. And it seems important that the conclusion delivers something about *what it feels like* for my daughter – and, by extension, what it feels like for animals. Thus understood, the bridge to knowledge of other minds is that of empathy, of 'putting oneself in others' shoes'. To put oneself in the shoes of another is not to imagine that I am identical with the other: to take the above example, it is not for Singer to imagine that Singer is identical with Singer's daughter. That thought is incoherent. Rather, it is to imagine what it would be like for oneself to have the experiences of the other: to take the above example, it is for Singer to imagine what it would be like if he were to have the experiences his daughter has. There is nothing logically incoherent about the method of empathy.[3]

We have two interpretations of Singer's inference to animal pain, the theoretical and the imaginative, and we have said that the imaginative interpretation seems the better one. Now there are interesting parallels here with work in disciplines apparently remote from the concerns of *Practical Ethics*. The two interpretations of Singer's inference to animal pain match two distinct approaches within contemporary philosophy of mind; although these approaches are not simply concerned with pain ascriptions, but with mental state ascriptions more generally. According to the first, we go about the business of ascribing mental states to others by making use of a 'folk theory' of the mind, whose general laws entitle us to infer certain mental states on the basis of observed behaviour, and to predict further behaviour on the basis of those inferred mental states. Proponents of this *theory theory* of mental state ascription say that we each ascribe mental states to others because we have each mastered a theory about the mental states of others: we have each mastered 'a set of causal laws which interrelate stimulus inputs, internal states, and behavioural outputs'.[4] But theory theory has a competitor which says: we do not *theorize*, we *simulate*.[5] According to proponents of *simulation theory*, I do not make use of a theory in ascribing mental states to another: instead, I imaginatively put myself into the shoes of the other, and infer that it is for her how it would be for me, if I were in her shoes. Or, putting the point in the jargon of cognitive science, I work out how things are for her by using my own cognitive mechanisms *off-line*.

Theory theory corresponds to the first interpretation we gave of the passage from Singer, which involves the theoretical method of inferring on the basis of a general law. Simulation theory corresponds to the second interpretation, which involves the imaginative method of projecting first personal experience, to achieve imaginative acquaintance with what it's like for the other. The following kind of example is sometimes used to illustrate the difference. Suppose you have a Lotus Esprit, and I am wondering how fast it can go. Suppose I cannot take it for a test drive. One way for me to find out, none the less, might be for me to have a good theory of the Lotus Esprit: detailed knowledge of the engine specifications, the aerodynamics, the weight and so on. My methodology would be that described by a theory theory of the Lotus Esprit. Another way for me to find out is to take my very own Lotus Esprit for a test drive, see how fast it goes and infer from that. My methodology would then be that described by the simulation alternative. These are two options when it comes to ascribing velocities to the cars of others: and the suggestion is that when it comes to ascribing mental properties to the minds of others, the situation is analogous. I cannot take your mind for a test drive. But I might find out what is happening with you by means of a theory of creatures like you; or I may find out what is happening with you by taking my own mind for a test drive, and inferring from that.

We said that simulation of the other involves special imaginative acquaintance with what it's like for the other, but the example suggests that this needs some qualification. The example suggests that the method of simulation is that of discovering properties of x – or explaining or predicting the behaviour of x – by considering properties of a known model of x. Put that way, the method seems objective, compatible with, perhaps part of, scientific method. Engineers commonly test how bridges or cars or aeroplanes will behave by testing out models. There is no ineluctable reference here to a 'subjective view', no talk of discovering a further fact concerning *what it is like* to have those properties. Yet the method envisaged by simulation theorists is often contrasted with a scientific methodology. Simulation theory is said to draw on the heritage of *verstehen* philosophy, which makes a sharp contrast between our non-scientific understanding of human subjects and our scientific understanding of physical objects.

We suggest that two different streams in the simulation story need to be distinguished: one concerns knowledge via modelling; the other concerns knowledge of special what-it-is-like-for-the-subject facts. Part of what is interesting about *mental* simulation is these two streams typically come together. By simulating someone's mental state you might be able to learn that he or she is in a certain state; and by the very same act of simulation you might come to know what it is like to be in that state. It is possible that even here the two ideas might come apart: that mental simulation might enable us to tell what it is like for someone else without knowing what state they are in, or vice versa.[6] But we trust that such possibilities are sufficiently recherché that we need not be concerned with them here. We shall take it that mental simulation – imaginatively projecting oneself into another's shoes – is claimed to give us both (a) knowledge, via modelling, *that* someone is in a certain state, and (b) knowledge of *what it is like* to be him or her, in that state.

Perhaps it is plausible to suppose that the attempt to identify imaginatively with others is an attempt to simulate others in the way that simulation theorists describe. We proceed on that assumption, and in what follows we shall use the notions of putting oneself in the shoes of another, imaginatively identifying with another, empathizing with another and simulating another, as roughly synonymous.[7] Now Singer's use of this imaginative thought experiment is evidently in the context not just of epistemology – our knowledge of animal minds – but of practical ethics – our moral behaviour towards animals. So one might wonder whether simulation theory can be brought to shed light on ethics – and indeed on practical ethics of the kind that concerns Singer. Alvin Goldman is prominent among simulation theory's recent proponents, and he answers this question in the affirmative. He says that ethics has much to learn from cognitive science. He says that cognitive science can offer 'benefits to philosophy' in the domain of moral theory.[8] He says that simulation theory offers a better understanding of what it is to put oneself in the shoes of others. He says that this understanding can supply just the epistemological and motivational resources which moral theory needs.[9] If Goldman is right, then perhaps Singer's argument can be bolstered and given whatever sort of respectability cognitive science can add to ordinary philosophy.

Before assessing these ambitious advertisements from simulation theory – before considering whether ethics does have something to learn from simulation theory's account of empathy – we need to get clearer on the role that empathy is supposed to play in ethics in the first place.

Moral Theory

What role does putting oneself into others' shoes play when we pass from the theory of knowledge to moral theory? Suppose we confine our attention to the kind of utilitarian moral theory for which Singer has argued. Suppose, to simplify, we confine our attention to moral theory which enjoins us to act so as to maximize preference satisfaction. Then we might expect the thought experiment to have three fairly uncontroversial functions.

First, the thought experiment might have a role to play in *discovering the preferences of others*. You cannot calculate which action best satisfies preferences unless you know what others' preferences are, and know how strongly they are held. Putting yourself in their shoes enables you to know what they want, and how badly they want it. This is simply the epistemological role again, brought into a moral context. Importantly, here we might get a basis for interpersonal utility comparisons; in imagining what things are like for you we might get some grip on the question of whether they are better or worse than they are for us, in our very different circumstances. Singer thinks that it has such a role: 'By imagining ourselves in the position of others, and taking on their tastes and preferences, we can often arrive at a reasonably confident verdict about which action will satisfy most preferences'.[10]

Second, the thought experiment might have a role to play in *discovering who has preferences*; and for a utilitarian, this will determine the domain of moral salience. This role is closely linked to the first, but it is in a way more fundamental. The thought experiment of putting oneself in the shoes of others might be used to find out not simply how to compare preferences, but whether there are any preferences there to compare. It can be used to answer not only the question 'How do I compare the interests of the morally relevant parties?' but also the more basic question: 'Which parties are the morally relevant ones?' Again, Singer endorses such a role:

> There is a genuine difficulty in understanding how chopping down a tree can matter *to the tree* if the tree can feel nothing. The same is true of quarrying a mountain. Certainly, imagining myself in the position of the tree or mountain will not help me to see why their destruction is wrong; for

such imagining yields a perfect blank. . . . there is a sense in which the limits
of sentience are not really limits at all, for applying the test of imagining
ourselves in the position of those affected by our action shows that in the
case of nonsentient things there is nothing at all to be taken into account.[11]

Here the thought experiment of putting oneself in the shoes of others is
described as a test, the application of which shows that the tree and the
mountain are outside the domain of moral salience: there is nothing to be
taken into account.

Third, the thought experiment might have a role to play in *motivating*
people to act in accordance with utilitarian moral theory. At least as a
matter of empirical psychology, knowing how it feels to be in the shoes
of others can bring you to want what they want. Singer does not
explicitly mention this role; but as we shall see, he appears to embrace
an argument that has the consequence that he should accept it. And this
argument turns it into more than a simple empirical claim about human
psychology.

These three roles concern the use of the thought experiment in an
application of utilitarian moral theory: on the assumption that we ought
to maximize preference satisfaction, imaginatively putting oneself in the
shoes of others might enable us to know which parties we should be
looking at, to know what their preferences are and to care enough to do
something about it. It is unlikely that anyone will think that it has a
monopoly on any of the roles. There are surely other ways of finding out
who has preferences and what they are (we might ask them, for instance,
or see what they do, or perhaps examine their brains); and not everyone
will need imaginative identification to persuade them to the path of virtue.
But a fourth and more ambitious role might be hoped for, one in which its
function is not merely ancillary but essential. Imaginative identification
might have a crucial role to play in *justifying* utilitarianism in the first
place, via a philosophical argument linking universalizability to preference utilitarianism. Hare famously attempts to make such a link, arran-
ging a marriage between Kantian moral theory and its traditional foe.
According to Hare, it is of the very nature of some moral concepts, most
centrally 'ought', that they are both prescriptive and universalizable.
Universalizability requires that we put ourselves in the place of others;
this in turn requires that we give weight to the preferences of others in just
the way that utilitarianism says.

The details of how this argument is supposed to work are controversial.
But a reasonable gloss is this:

1   To say that something ought to be done in particular circumstances is
    to prescribe it in all like circumstances.

2   To prescribe something in circumstances in which I actually find myself is to desire to do it; to prescribe it in circumstances in which I don't find myself is to desire that if I were in those circumstances I would do it.

3   If I were fully rational, then whenever I believed that someone in certain circumstances desired to do a certain thing, I would desire that if I were to find myself in those circumstances, I would do it.

Therefore:

C   If I were fully rational, what I would say ought to be done is that which best satisfies my desires across circumstances in which I do find myself and do not find myself; which is what best satisfies what I believe are the desires of those actually in those circumstances (including myself); which is what utilitarianism prescribes.[12]

All three premises of this argument are controversial. We shall not be concerned with (1) and (2), which together give expression to Hare's non-cognitivism and to his view of the universalizable nature of 'ought'. Rather, we shall concentrate on (3), since it is here that the role of imaginative identification comes in. (3) requires that we will form an actual desire about a possible state of affairs; adapting Hare's terminology, let us call this an actual-for-possible desire. Here is Hare's own formulation of the principle: 'I cannot know the extent and quality of others' sufferings and, in general, motivations and preferences without having equal motivations with regard to what should happen to me, were I in their places, with their motivations and preferences.'[13] Following Alan Gibbard, we can call this the *Principle of Conditional Reflection*.[14] What is its status? It could be thought of as simply a generalization about human psychology. But that is not the status that Hare gives it. He argues that the principle is conceptual:

> If we try to represent to ourselves what it is like to have a certain desire, we have not succeeded unless there is something in our *present* experience to correspond to what we are trying to represent; and this has to be a desire too. We can utter the words 'I shall be desiring not to be whipped'; but we shall not really be *thinking what it would be like* unless there is a desire of equal intensity in our present experience, namely the desire not to be being whipped if we are in that situation.[15]

Hare here suggests that putting oneself in the place of another requires becoming imaginatively acquainted with what that place is like. He suggests that when one does so one comes to form the actual-for-possible desires required by the Principle of Conditional Reflection (and, perhaps, that doing so provides the *only* reliable method for forming such desires – we return to this further point in a moment). This has been a persistent theme in Hare's writings. Here is how he put the point in *Freedom and Reason* in 1963:

> He [i.e. *B*] must be prepared to give weight to *A*'s inclinations as if they were his own. This is what turns selfish prudential reasoning into moral reasoning. It is much easier, psychologically, for *B* to do this if he is actually placed in a situation like *A*'s *vis-à-vis* somebody else; but this is not necessary provided that he has sufficient imagination to envisage what it is like to be *A*.[16]

By 1981 in *Moral Thinking* the point is made even more explicitly. 'What exactly is it that we have to know?' Hare asks. He answers, 'What it is like to be those people in that situation' – the situation produced by one's own potential decision. He insists that a certain kind of theoretical knowledge is bound to be inadequate:

> I have to know what it will be *like* for [the other person]... We shall have to keep carefully in mind the distinction between knowing that something is happening to someone, and knowing *what it is like for him*. It is the latter kind of knowledge which, I am proposing, we should treat as relevant, and as required for the full information which rationality in making moral judgements demands.[17]

So the rationality alluded to in the Principle of Conditional Reflection is that which comes from full imaginative identification. The principle should thus be spelt out like this:

3*   If I were fully to identify imaginatively with someone, then whenever I believed that he or she desired to do a certain thing in certain circumstances, I would desire that if I were to find myself in those circumstances, I would do it.

Now Hare does not seem to think that imaginative identification is just one method among many for forming the actual-for-possible desires required by the principle. He seems to think that it is the only reliable method for forming such desires, and hence for bringing moral arguments to a successful conclusion. 'In most normal cases a certain power of imagination and a readiness to use it is a...necessary ingredient in moral arguments'.[18] And again: 'The difficulty of fully representing to ourselves absent states of experience (our own or other people's) is one of the main obstacles to good moral thinking.'[19]

We can now see Hare's position on the function that imaginative identification has in the third role that we identified above: that of motivating us to embrace the desires of others. Hare denies that, as a matter of empirical psychology, it is sufficient on its own.[20] Moreover, he thinks that there is no rational requirement on the amoralist to be moved. But once we engage in the practice of moral argument, he thinks that the argument he gives will rationally compel us to be motivated to maximize the satisfaction of the preferences of others – it will rationally compel us to be utilitarians.

Why, in a chapter on Peter Singer, have we focused so much on Hare? The answer is that Singer seems to endorse Hare's position. He does not spend a great deal of time discussing the foundations of morality; his focus is, famously, on its practical applications. But in his contribution to *Hare and Critics*, Singer defends Hare's moral theory. As he summarizes his own position, 'I have been arguing that... universalizability does require that we put ourselves in the place of others and that this must then involve giving weight to their ideals in proportion to the strength with which they hold them.'[21] Likewise, in *The Expanding Circle* Singer argues that Hare's approach, or something like it, provides the only way of resolving ethical disputes.[22] And the quotation with which we began is surely directed towards just this kind of reasoning. When I put myself in the shoes of my daughter I learn not only the desires of my daughter and their strength; I learn also to give weight to those desires. When I put myself in the shoes of an animal, I learn not only the desires of the animal, and their strength; I learn also to give weight to those desires. These passages are enough to show that Singer is, at the very least, *tempted* to go in this direction. In what follows we suggest he would be wise to resist the temptation.

We shall not try to assess the validity of Hare's argument; many others have laboured on that task.[23] Let us concede its validity, for present purposes. Our interest is rather in the capacities we have to put ourselves in the shoes of others, and of the significance of this for Hare and for Singer. First, some brief remarks on terminology. We take the notion of putting oneself in others' shoes not to be a success notion; on this usage, I may put myself in your shoes, without successfully putting myself in your shoes – without getting it right. I may simulate you without accurately simulating you. On our usage, the idea of success is not built in to the idea of putting oneself in the shoes of others. So keeping this in mind, we are concerned with two questions.

(a) Can we in practice successfully put ourselves in the shoes of others?

This is a question about whether we reliably get it right when we try to put ourselves into the shoes of others. It is an important question. For if our simulation fails, it will not fulfil the first role identified above: it will not help us find out what the preferences of others are, nor will it enable us to compare them. And if our simulation fails, it will not fulfil the second role: it will not help us find out who has preferences, and hence who is within the domain of moral salience. And if our simulation fails, it will not fulfil the third role either: while it may well motivate us to act, it will not motivate us to achieve the utilitarian outcome. So its use in the first three roles – its use, that is, in *applying* utilitarianism – will depend on returning an affirmative answer to this first question.

What, though, of the fourth role: does the use of imaginative identification in *justifying* utilitarianism require that we in practice be successful? Recall that the Principle of Conditional Reflection is of subjunctive conditional form. It says that we would form the relevant actual-for-possible desires *if* we were successfully to identify imaginatively with others. If, as a matter of fact, we are bad at doing so, this would not refute the principle, nor the argument for utilitarianism that Hare bases upon it. It would make us bad utilitarian agents; but it would not show utilitarianism to be false. It is enough for Hare's argument that the conditional is true; he does not require the truth of the antecedent as well.

A problem would be raised, however, if it were outright *impossible* to get into the shoes of others – and this brings us to our second question:

(b)   Can we in principle successfully put ourselves in the shoes of others?

If the answer here is 'no' then the Principle of Conditional Reflection will go wrong, and Hare's argument for utilitarianism will break down. For the Principle is of subjunctive conditional form; and if the answer to our question is 'no', the Principle will have an impossible antecedent. Quite how we should treat subjunctive conditionals with impossible antecedents is a matter of some debate.[24] One approach is to think of them as false. If we take this route, then Hare's argument will be unsound. The rival approach is to think of subjunctive conditionals with impossible antecedents as vacuously true. On this approach the principle will, of course, be true, but so will every other counterfactual with the same antecedent, including 'If I were to imaginatively identify with others I would *not* form the relevant actual-for-possible desires.' Moreover, while on this view Hare's argument may be sound, its conclusion, which is a subjunctive conditional with the same impossible antecedent, will itself be trivial. Either way then, the argument for utilitarianism will be in trouble.

We turn now to consider simulation theory, to consider whether it sheds light on these questions about our actual and possible capacities for empathy. Depending on the different roles required of it by moral theory, empathy needs to be in fact a reliable source of knowledge, or in principle a reliable source of knowledge. Goldman's recent work on simulation provides us with a useful focus, since he discusses what is required for empathy to be a reliable source of knowledge, and he offers some optimistic conclusions for moral theory.

Simulation

Prior to the question of whether we gain knowledge of other minds, through empathy, is the question of whether we gain *beliefs* about other minds, through empathy. If we empathize by *simulating*, then this is a question about whether we gain beliefs about other minds through simulation, and this is Goldman's starting point. He says that the thought experiment of placing oneself in the shoes of others is central to our practice of making mental state attributions to others. He offers this not – yet – as a philosophical truth of epistemology, but as an empirical hypothesis in cognitive science. I have a set of mental mechanisms that take some mental states as inputs and generate others as outputs: that take beliefs and desires as inputs, and generate decisions about action as outputs, for example. And I can, so to speak, 'unhook' these mechanisms, and use them 'off-line', so that instead of generating outputs for me they generate imagined outputs for someone else. For example, instead of generating my decisions, given my beliefs and desires as inputs, the mental mechanism generates the decision of someone else, given his beliefs and desires as inputs – or rather, it generates what I *believe* to be his likely decision, given what I *believe* to be his beliefs and desires. This 'off-line' use of mental mechanisms in the attribution of mental states to others is thought to be just one function of simulation among many. There is, in addition, the practice of first personal hypothetical deliberation, where I imaginatively place myself in the shoes, not of another person, but of myself in different circumstances, and I generate my own imagined decisions from imagined beliefs and desires. And there is, in addition, our practice of entertaining fictional stories, where I imaginatively place myself in the shoes of a merely fictional person.

Goldman discusses empirical evidence for the conclusion that we attribute mental states to others via a method of simulation rather than theory. In a 1982 experiment by Kahneman and Tversky, subjects were told the following story.

> Mr Crane and Mr Tees were scheduled to leave the airport on different flights, at the same time. They travelled from town in the same limousine, were caught in a traffic jam, and arrived at the airport 30 minutes after the

scheduled departure time of their flights. Mr Crane is told that his flight left
on time. Mr Tees is told that his was delayed and just left five minutes ago.

The subjects were asked: which of the two is more upset? Nearly all
replied: Mr Tees. Why? The theory theory of mental state attribution
should say that they inferred their conclusion from lawlike generalizations
linking desires, different kinds of desire-frustration and different degrees
of upsetness. But, says Goldman, it seems unlikely that the subjects were
acquainted with any such lawlike generalizations. What seems more
plausible is that their conclusions were reached by the method of imaginative projection: each subject put herself into the shoes of each character,
and wondered how she would feel in those shoes.[25]

So far this is a matter of psychology. It is a hypothesis about how we do
in fact go about our business of grasping – and then comparing – the
mental states of others. So it is a hypothesis about how we do in fact go
about the business of making the judgements required by moral theory,
such as interpersonal utility judgements: 'In making hedonic comparisons
between two people other than yourself, you would simulate each of them
in turn and compare the resulting hedonic states.[26] Goldman says that
this is progress: simulation theory provides a 'helpful' account of our
practice of making these judgements.

However, the important question, both for epistemology and for ethics,
is not whether we do go about our business this way, but whether we are
justified in going about our business this way. Here we move from
psychology to epistemology. Do our simulation-based judgements about
other minds count as *knowledge* of those minds? As we have seen, the
different roles assigned by moral theory to the thought experiment of
putting oneself in the shoes of others all require it to be a source of
knowledge. Goldman answers this question in the affirmative. Simulation
may provide a reliable means of knowledge, provided – and here comes
the crunch – that I am *similar* to the person I am simulating. 'Interpersonal simulation can only succeed if there are certain psychological
homologies or similarities between simulators and simulatees.'[27] Neolo-
gisms aside, this is a basic, obvious and important point; and it is not
news. A test drive of my Lotus will tell me something about yours only if
yours is similar to mine. A test drive of Mr Tees's unhappy situation will
tell me something about Mr Tees only if Mr Tees is roughly similar to me.
Whatever else simulation theory may have to offer, to the extent that it is
a normative and not a merely descriptive account of our mental state
attributions – to the extent that it an account of knowledge, and not just
of belief formation – it is no answer to the problem of other minds. It
assumes not only that other minds exist, but also that they are basically
similar to my own.

An affirmative answer to the question of whether empathy yields knowledge of other minds depends, then, on a general similarity assumption. We can use simulation to gain reliable knowledge of other minds only when we are already similar to those other minds. What is the status of this similarity assumption?

Perhaps the general similarity assumption may be an *a posteriori* premise that is empirically verified. A first possibility here is that I imaginatively put myself into the shoes of another and infer, by this simulation, that lo and behold he is roughly similar to me. But that would hardly do! A simulation-based justification of simulation's background similarity assumption would be entirely circular. A second possibility for empirical support might be predictive success: if simulation-based predictions about the behaviour of others are successful, then that success provides evidence for the background assumption of similarity. A third possibility might be a more theoretical kind of *a posteriori* verification. Goldman cites a discussion by Roy Sorenson of the similarity requirement.

> Stepping into the other guy's shoes works best when you resemble the other guy psychologically. After all, the procedure is to use yourself as a model: in goes hypothetical beliefs and desires, out comes hypothetical actions and revised beliefs and desires. If you are structurally analogous to the empathee, then accurate inputs generate accurate outputs – just as with any other simulation. The greater the degree of isomorphism, the more dependable and precise the results.[28]

Sorenson argues that the similarity required for empathy to work will be selected for by evolution, and that evolution therefore delivers a certain kind of empirical support for an assumption of similarity. These are some candidate defences of an *a posteriori* similarity assumption – and we shall not pause to assess them here.

A different possibility is that the assumption has an *a priori* status. According to John Harsanyi, empathy-based interpersonal utility comparisons rest on a similarity postulate that is ultimately non-empirical: once allowances have been made for empirically notable differences in situation, education, tastes and the like, it is reasonable for me to assume that your mental states are similar to those I would have in your shoes.[29] The similarity assumption has, on this suggestion, the kind of status that postulates of simplicity and parsimony have as constraints on scientific theory choice. Again, we shall not pause to assess this – or other candidate possibilities – here. Let us instead return to our two questions, and consider the bearing of the above discussion upon them.

We asked whether putting ourselves in the shoes of others can in practice be a source of knowledge of others; and we asked whether putting ourselves in the shoes of others can in principle be a source of knowledge of others. The answer to both questions seems to be yes – *provided that* I am similar enough to the other into whose shoes I try to put myself. The method of empathy cannot stand on its own: it needs to be backed by an assumption of similarity that cannot, without circularity, be supported by the method of empathy itself. It can, perhaps, have the *a priori* status that Harsanyi assigns it, as a methodological norm of simplicity: 'in the absence of evidence to the contrary, assume that others are similar to yourself'. Thus stated, the principle supports a default assumption of similarity, while at the same time assigning a crucial role to empirical evidence in disconfirming the default assumption. It is not obvious whether, thus understood, the similarity assumption is good methodology or sheer arrogance. However, we need not make a judgement about this, since our concern lies with domains where the similarity assumption clearly fails – and hence where the method of empathy must break down.

Back to Moral Theory

If imaginative identification is to play the role it is supposed to play, then we must be similar enough to those to whom we should show moral consideration. But are we similar enough?

This is a difficult question even when restricted to the domain of our fellow human beings. Our fellows are, to be sure, physiologically similar to us. But that might not be enough. We can have little conception of what it is like to be mentally ill in certain ways. Singer himself suggests that there will be some people for whom we cannot in practice achieve successful imaginative identification – 'we cannot enter into the subjective states of psychopathic people, nor they into ours'.[30] We think that considerations like these place very real limitations on the usefulness of imaginative identification in applying utilitarianism across a human population. Indeed, the situation is more serious than this. Singer says that when we imagine ourselves into the position of psychopathic people, our imagining yields a perfect blank. He also says, as we have seen, that when we imagine ourselves into the position of a tree or a mountain, our imagining likewise yields a perfect blank. Yet this latter result is exactly what is supposed to tell us that in the case of a tree 'there is nothing at all to be taken into account' morally – and that destruction therefore cannot matter to the tree. This latter result is supposed to show us that the tree is outside the domain of moral salience.[31] Should the former result likewise tell us that in the case of the psychopathic person 'there is nothing at all to be taken into account' morally – that destruction therefore cannot matter to the psychopathic person? That the psychopath, like the tree, is outside the domain of moral salience? That would be an abhorrent outcome. We can leave the point as a hypothetical one: if there are human beings for whom the attempt at imaginative identification 'yields a perfect blank', then such human beings seem – by the test of imaginative identification – to be outside the domain of moral salience. Yet they ought not to be. This should make us have second thoughts about the role of the test in moral argument.

It might be thought, however, that in these cases we *could* achieve a successful identification, but that it would require a lot more effort than we are prepared to put in – that when Singer says we *cannot* imagine the subjective states of psychopaths, what he really means is that we *can*, but with great difficulty. This seems to be Hare's view:

> The difficulty of fully representing to ourselves absent states of experience (our own or other people's) is one of the main obstacles to good moral thinking – that is obvious . . . The remedy, for humans, lies in sharpening our sensitivity, and above all in cultivating considerate habits of thought for use at the intuitive level.[32]

The difficult cases might pose a problem for the potential of human beings to be good utilitarian agents towards other human beings; but it is not obvious that they pose a problem for Hare's attempt to provide a justification for utilitarianism as such. As we have seen, that argument requires only the *possibility* of successful imaginative identification.

However, that very possibility becomes doubtful when we turn to non-human animals. As Sorenson reminds us, 'stepping into the other guy's shoes works best when you resemble the other guy psychologically'. What happens when we step into the shoes of the other guy, and the other guy is neither guy nor girl, man nor woman? The very metaphor betrays a bias towards the shod. If the method of simulation barely gets us beyond the average guy, there seems little hope of its getting us as far as we need to get with the non-human animals. Indeed, if one were to take seriously Sorenson's evolutionary account of empathy, then the tendency of natural selection to push species into specialized niches should make us especially sceptical that there will be the necessary inter-species similarity.

Hare is remarkably sanguine. He thinks that we can think our way into the position of bears:

> Those who indulged in bear-baiting did not reason: 'If we were bears we should suffer horribly if treated thus; therefore we cannot say that it is all right to treat bears thus' . . . The bear-baiter does not really imagine what it is like to be a bear. If he did, he would think and act differently. Another way of putting this is to say that these people are not paying attention to the

relevant similarities between themselves and their victims... the bear-baiter is not thinking of the bear as his brother – or even cousin.[33]

More remarkably, he thinks that he can think his way into the position of a trout:

> In our village there is also a trout farm. The fish start their lives in moderately commodious ponds and have what I guess is a pleasant life for fish, with plenty to eat. In due course they are lifted out in buckets and put immediately into tanks in the farm buildings. Purchasers select their fish, which is then killed by being banged smartly on the head and handed to the customer. I am fairly certain that, if given the choice, I would prefer the life, all told, of such a fish to that of almost any fish in the wild, and to non-existence.[34]

More remarkably still, he seems to think that he can think himself into the position of inanimate objects:

> It is sometimes said that stoves, mountains, and trees are outside the scope of morality (we cannot have duties to them) because we cannot put ourselves in their positions. I think that this is badly expressed. We can put ourselves in their positions, but, since when we do this we have no sentience and therefore no concerns, it simply does not matter to us what happens if we turn into such things.[35]

We shall leave aside this last idea (what could it be to think oneself into the position of a stove?) and confine ourselves to the non-human animals. Hare's confidence that we can, in general, think our way into their positions is surely misplaced. Thomas Nagel has celebrated the difference between ourselves and bats. We have, he says, no idea what it would be like to perceive the world by bat sonar:

> If I try to imagine this I am restricted to the resources of my own mind, and those resources are inadequate to the task. I cannot perform it either by imagining additions to my present experience, or by imagining segments gradually subtracted from it, or by imagining some combination of additions, subtractions and modifications.[36]

To take another example: platypuses can detect, with their bills, electrical discharges from the muscles of other creatures around them. We have no idea what it is like to see the world this way either – and no amount of sharpening our sensitivities could ever help us to find out.

Moreover, the discovery that we don't know what it's like to be a bat or a platypus doesn't come from trying to think ourselves into their positions and failing. It comes because we have independent biological evidence that they are *not* like us in important respects. The method of imaginative identification has achieved nothing. To say this is not to be a sceptic about animal minds. The difficulty we are considering is not – contrary to Singer's suggestion in our opening quotation – simply the problem of other minds. We do not doubt that the bat, or the platypus, has a mind. But we do not know *what it is like* for them.

If a moral theory – whether that of Hare or Singer or the simulation theorists – demands that we place ourselves in the shoes of animals to discover what it is like for them, then that moral theory will be in trouble. For someone like Singer, who has devoted so much work to the inclusion of non-human animals in the moral domain, the problems are especially pressing. They emerge, we think, in both spheres: that of applying utilitarianism, and that of justifying it. Let us take them one at a time.

Problems of Application

We suggest that if you want to discover the preferences of a bat or a platypus, the last thing you should do is to try to imagine yourself into their place. Is it cruel to screech loudly at a bat? Is it cruel to pass a 12 volt shock through the water near a platypus? We don't know, and imagining ourselves in their place won't help. Imagination 'yields a perfect blank'. Doubtless there *are* methods of finding out: we could check their behaviour, measure their heart rates and endorphin and serotonin levels, test whether they continue to thrive under these circumstances. All such evidence would be relevant. But imaginative identification will get us nowhere. Even when we consider animals that are not so different from us in their perceptual systems, it is doubtful that the method will get us very far. An example from Singer will make the point. He remarks that keeping calves in narrow stalls is especially cruel, since it inhibits 'their innate desire to twist their heads around and groom themselves with their tongues'.[37] Human beings do not have an innate desire to twist our heads around and groom ourselves with our tongues. We won't discover that desire by imagining what it's like to be a calf. Nor will we discover, by imaginative identification, any other innate desires peculiar to non-human animals.

Second, it seems to us that imaginative identification is a bad method of discovering which animals have preferences, and hence of determining the domain of moral salience. Try it with a slug or a sea anemone. Try it with a locust that goes on eating while itself being eaten by a mantis. Here again, imagination 'yields a perfect blank'. The differences are too great for our imagination to get any useful purchase. Any serious effort to discover whether these animals have preferences will require, once again, the application of biology rather than of imaginative identification.

Third, it seems to us that reliance on imaginative identification as a source of motivation is extremely dangerous. Perhaps it works. But if it does, it will skew our concern to those for whom we find imaginative identification easy. It will invite precisely the kind of parochialism that an impartialist moral theory rejects. We are familiar with the problem that long-lashed large-eyed animals get a disproportionate share of our concern – that the killing of baby seals provokes more outrage than the killing of coypu. A motivation that is based on an ability to empathize is equally parochial.

Suppose, as Nagel says, that we cannot know what it is like to have the experiences of a bat. One might, in response, pursue the thought that this does not matter much: that the utilitarian who invokes imaginative identification need not be able to acquire what-it's-like knowledge of all of an animal's experiences. Perhaps the utilitarian may merely need to know what-it's-like facts about pain – Singer's original example – and know that what the bat experiences, when in pain, is something like what I experience when I am in pain, since pain experiences remain constant across diverse species. Perhaps I don't know what it's like to be a bat sonar-tracking a moth; but perhaps I do know what it's like to be a bat in pain.

One response to this suggestion is Nagel's. He says that even pain itself will have a different subjective feel for the bat: 'We believe that bats feel some version of pain, fear, hunger and lust, and that they have other, more familiar types of perception besides sonar. But we believe that these experiences also have in each case a specific subjective character, which it is also beyond our ability to conceive.'[38] This seems speculative. Pin pricks may feel alike to bats and human beings. The physiological evidence suggests that all vertebrates, at any rate, have similar neurological pain structures.[39] None the less, the resort to similarity of pain is beside the point, for two reasons. First, there is an *ad hominem* consideration. Hare and Singer are preference utilitarians. They are concerned with minimizing unsatisfied preferences, what Hare rather eccentrically terms 'suffering', and suffering, in this sense, is distinct from pain. As Hare writes: 'It is possible to have pain without suffering, and without having a motive for ending or avoiding the pain.'[40] That thought is familiar enough to the marathon runner, and, perhaps, to some women in labour. And it is familiar in a rather different guise in David Lewis's example of 'mad pain': we can – perhaps – have imaginative acquaintance with what it's like for a person in mad pain, but his or her pain is nevertheless not suffering in Hare's sense.[41] Once we turn to suffering, Nagel's contention that it will have a 'specific subjective character' is plausible, since suffering cannot be abstracted from the creature's other experiences. So imaginative identification will not, it seems, be able to supply us with the requisite knowledge.

Second, even if it is true that pain feels much the same for all vertebrates, this fact is altogether too parochial to do the work required of it. There might, for all we know, be creatures elsewhere in the universe that have a state functionally similar to our pain: a state that they typically hate, and try to avoid, and that indicates damage to their bodies. Lewis provides us with a philosophical example in the idea of 'Martian pain'.[42] This state might have a quite different physiology and give rise to a quite different experience. Such creatures may have pains as different from any of ours as a burn is different from a headache. We will not be able to imagine what their pain feels like. Yet to exclude them from our moral concern would be to commit precisely the kind of parochial mistake that Singer has campaigned so strenuously to avoid.

Problems of Justification

As we remarked earlier, Hare's argument justifying utilitarianism requires only the truth of a subjunctive conditional: If I were to identify imaginatively with other beings, I would form the relevant actual-for-possible desires. But the considerations we have raised call into doubt whether it is possible for us to identify imaginatively with such animals as bats and platypuses. Given how we are constructed, we cannot do it, no matter how hard we try. This means that the Principle of Reflection goes awry: it has an impossible antecedent.

To be fair to Hare, we need to attend to a character whom we have not so far considered: the Archangel. Aware of our limited abilities, Hare asks us to imagine 'a being with superhuman powers of thought, superhuman knowledge and no weaknesses'.[43] Perhaps the Principle of Reflection will not go awry if its antecedent can be fulfilled by the Archangel. Perhaps even if *we* cannot imagine what it is like to be a bat or a platypus, at least the archangel can.

Well, we doubt it. We doubt that any being could do what Hare requires of the Archangel. The point is made well by Zeno Vendler, in his response to Hare, 'Changing places?'[44] Vendler asks whether or not the Archangel is embodied. Suppose, as an angelic being, he has no body. Then he cannot have, and cannot imagine having, a toothache or a tickle. Then he cannot know that I have a toothache or tickle: or rather he cannot know *what it is like* for me to have a toothache or a tickle. So the Archangel, thus described, cannot after all put himself in my shoes. Suppose, then, the Archangel is nicely embodied. If he has a body, he is an organism of a particular kind. But then he can have experiences – and can imagine having experiences – only of the kind had by organisms of that particular kind. It will not make any difference how 'perfect' we allow the Archangel's body to be. As Vendler says, 'We are at a loss to imagine what it must be like to be a bat or a frog partly because our bodies are far more "perfect", i.e. developed and sensitive, than theirs.'[45]

What is Hare's reply to Vendler? It is to cite poetry. Blake wrote, of God, that

> He doth give His joy to all;
> He becomes an infant small;
> He becomes a man of woe;
> He doth feel the sorrow too.[46]

God can put himself into the shoes of each of his creatures. Hare's Archangel is Blake's God.

As philosophical tactics go, this one is dubious – unless we are to concede validity to the argument 'Blake wrote that possibly p, therefore possibly p'. We doubt there could be a being that could be acquainted with the experiences of all creatures in the necessary way. We could perhaps suppose there to be a Protean God who really did *become* an infant small, a man of woe – and every other creature besides; and could, as a result of this pan-Incarnation, imagine what it is like to be an infant small, a man of woe and every other creature besides. But if it is to underwrite the formation of the relevant actual-for-possible desires, such a being would need not only to *transform* itself into any creature, but also to *remember* what its experiences in its other incarnations are like, and then to *compare* such radically different experiences. We doubt that such a being is possible.

Conclusion

Many critics of utilitarianism have complained that it is too impartial, that it does not make room for the parochial concerns and biases we have and ought to have. Our complaint here has been just the opposite: the utilitarianism of Hare and Singer risks being not impartial enough. It is too parochial if it ties ethics to what we can in principle imagine. We do not deny that empathy can be useful for moral thinking, that it can *help* in the first three roles we identified. We do not deny that one of the most important failings in our dealings with animals is our habitual failure to empathize with them; or, more accurately, our habitual tendency to empathize selectively; our skewed empathy which is stony-eyed to the plight of orang-utans yet weeps for a dead budgie. But we object to the idea that moral thinking should confine itself to what empathy can – in practice, or in principle – provide. We object to the idea that empathy provides the basis for ethics. If, as Singer believes, we owe moral concern to the sentient, then we cannot restrict that concern to those whose shoes we can, in imagination, borrow. Sentience transcends imaginability. And these objections are at the same time objections to an over-ambitious simulation theory, which claims that our knowledge of other minds proceeds chiefly or exclusively by the method of putting oneself in the shoes of others. Instead of finding that simulation theory can help an empathy-based ethics in the way that was advertised, we find that both are flawed in the same way: both place the same unwarranted limits on what we can know and what we can care about. The bounds of our moral concern transcend the bounds of empathy; the bounds of our knowledge of other minds likewise transcend the bounds of empathy.

We intend this chapter less as a criticism of Singer than as a challenge. We have said that Singer is at the very least *tempted* to give imaginative identification the roles we have described here. But he is eclectic in his philosophical methodologies. Alongside arguments that our knowledge of animal minds proceeds by imaginative identification lie empirical arguments drawing on facts about animal neurology. Alongside the endorsements of Hare lie counsels on the dangers of sentimentality and anthropomorphism. If Hare's methodology is implicitly anthropomorphic, we would expect Singer to distance himself from it, and we invite him to do so. We sense too that there has been a shift in his position. In the first edition of *Practical Ethics* Singer suggests that the domain of moral salience is the domain of beings into whose shoes we can manage to place ourselves. Plants don't count because there our imagination must draw a complete blank.[47] In the second edition he seems more cautious. The negative conclusion about the plants has gone. He now seems to contemplate extending the bounds of the moral beyond the bounds of sentience itself. We have said that the bounds of sentience transcend the bounds of imaginability – but to go beyond the bounds of sentience, as Singer seems now to contemplate, would be to go even further beyond the bounds of imaginability. So perhaps Singer has begun to do as we have counselled him to do here: namely, to refuse to base morality on facts about what we can imagine. If we are right about this apparent shift of direction, then we end our chapter not on a note of complaint, but on a note of applause.

Notes

Thanks are due to the audiences at Monash and ANU who heard this chapter; and especially to Martin Davies, Dale Jamieson, Peter Singer and Michael Smith.

1 Peter Singer, *Practical Ethics*, 2nd edn (Cambridge: Cambridge University Press, 1993), p. 69.

2 We leave open the question of the nature of *what it is like* knowledge – whether it is *sui generis*, whether it is a form of *knowledge how*, or whether it is ultimately reducible to *knowledge that*. All we need is the idea that there is a distinction between the knowledge that a creature is in pain, and the knowledge of what that pain is like. For a discussion of the issues and options see Frank Jackson, 'Epiphenomenal qualia', and David Lewis, 'What experience teaches', both reprinted in W. Lycan (ed.), *Mind and Cognition* (Oxford: Blackwell, 1990).

3 For a discussion of this merely apparent problem, see R. M. Hare, *Moral Thinking* (Oxford: Clarendon Press, 1981), pp. 119–21; Zeno Vendler's article 'Changing places?', in D. Seanor and N. Fotion (eds), *Hare and Critics* (Oxford: Clarendon Press, 1988); and Hare's reply to Vendler in that volume.

4 This is from Alvin Goldman's description of theory theory, 'Empathy, mind and morals', in M. Davies and T. Stone (eds), *Mental Simulation* (Oxford: Blackwell, 1995), p. 186; reprinted from *Proceedings and Addresses of the American Philosophical Association*, 66 (1992), pp. 17–41.

5 Or, more accurately, we do not *merely* theorize; as we discuss below, simulation involves the use of some theory, in particular a theory about relevant similarities between the thing that is doing the simulation and the thing that is simulated.

6 Suppose, for instance, that you can work yourself into such a state as to know what another's anger is really like; then it might be that the very simulation of that anger clouds your judgement as to which state you, and hence the other, are in.

7 We shall avoid detailed examination of the debates within philosophy and cognitive science about exactly how the activity of simulation is supposed to work; in particular about whether it really does involve the 'off-line' use of our normal mechanisms.

8 Goldman, 'Empathy, mind and morals', p. 185. See also Robert Gordon, 'Sympathy, simulation and the impartial spectator', *Ethics*, 105 (1995), pp. 727–42.

9 Goldman, 'Empathy, mind and morals', pp. 199–203; 'Simulation and interpersonal utility', *Ethics*, 105 (1995), pp. 709–26.

10 Peter Singer, *The Expanding Circle* (Oxford: Clarendon Press, 1981), p. 101.

11 Ibid., pp. 123–4. A similar passage occurs on p. 92 of the first edition of *Practical Ethics*: 'Is there really any intrinsic value in the life of a weed? Suppose that we apply the test of imagining living the life of a weed I am about to pull out of my garden. I then have to imagine living a life with no conscious experiences at all. Such a life is a complete blank; I would not in the least regret the shortening of this subjectively barren form of existence. This test suggests, therefore, that the life of a being that has no conscious experiences is of no intrinsic value.'

12 For simplicity, we have formulated this characterization just in terms of the agent's preferences for what she might *do*; it should, more fully, make reference

to her preferences for the circumstances in which she might find herself, whether or not these result from her own doing. Our characterization is influenced by that given by Nagel in 'Foundations of impartiality', in *Hare and Critics*, p. 104. However, it is not identical to it. In particular, we have taken account of Hare's complaint, in his response to Nagel, that what is rationally desired in hypothetical cases 'does not depend *only* on what I want to happen to myself if I occupy the various positions, though it has to consistent with this'; see *Hare and Critics*, pp. 249, 250. We have therefore formulated (3) as a conditional, rather than an identity statement.

13 *Moral Thinking*, p. 99.
14 Allan Gibbard, 'Hare's analysis of "ought" and its implications', in *Hare and Critics*.
15 Hare, 'Comments', in *Hare and Critics*, pp. 216–17.
16 Hare, *Freedom and Reason* (Oxford: Clarendon Press, 1963), p. 94.
17 *Moral Thinking*, pp. 91–2.
18 *Freedom and Reason*, p. 94. 'Most' since in some cases one is actually acquainted with the relevant experience, and hence has no need for imagination.
19 *Hare and Critics*, p. 217.
20 *Moral Thinking*, p. 99.
21 Peter Singer, 'Reasoning towards utilitarianism', in *Hare and Critics*, p. 152. The ellipses conceal an important qualification: it is only 'as long as we reject the idea that there can be objectively true moral ideals' that utilitarianism follows from universalizability. And the talk here is of ideals rather than desires, since Singer has been arguing that ideals should be thought of as desires.
22 *The Expanding Circle*, pp. 101ff.
23 See, for example, the contributions of Gibbard, Nagel and Brandt to *Hare and Critics*.
24 See David Lewis, *Counterfactuals* (Oxford: Basil Blackwell, 1973), pp. 24–6 for a discussion of the merits of the two approaches.
25 D. Kahneman and A. Tversky, 'The simulation heuristic', in P. Slovic, D. Kahneman and A. Tversky (eds), *Judgement under Uncertainty: Heuristics and Biases* (Cambridge: Cambridge University Press, 1988); discussed in Goldman, 'Empathy, mind and morals', p. 187.
26 Goldman, 'Simulation and interpersonal utility', p. 720.
27 Ibid., p. 723.
28 Roy Sorenson, 'Self strengthening empathy: how evolution funnels us into a solution to the other minds problem', typescript, New York University, cited in Goldman, 'Simulation and interpersonal utility', p. 723. Since Sorenson's paper is not yet published, we do not address it here; but we are bewildered at the suggestion that it offers a solution to the other minds problem, and astonished at the suggestion that, when it comes to generation of human like-mindedness, evolution is supposed to be more relevant than culture.
29 John Harsanyi, 'Morality and the theory of rational behaviour', in A. Sen and B. Williams (eds), *Utilitarianism and Beyond* (Cambridge: Cambridge

University Press, 1982). This candidate possibility and most of the preceding ones are discussed by Goldman. He himself favours a comparison between the similarity assumption and our '*a priori*' knowledge of grammar, but his argument rests on mistakes about apriority.

30 *Practical Ethics*, 2nd edn, p. 329.

31 *The Expanding Circle*, p. 123.

32 *Hare and Critics*, p. 217.

33 *Freedom and Reason*, p. 224.

34 R. M. Hare, 'Why I am only a demi-vegetarian', in his *Essays on Bioethics* (Oxford: Clarendon Press, 1993), p. 228, and in this volume.

35 *Hare and Critics*, p. 283.

36 'What is it like to be a bat?', in *Mortal Questions* (Cambridge: Cambridge University Press, 1979), p. 169.

37 Peter Singer, *Animal Liberation* (New York: New York Review of Books, 1975), p. 124. See also the discussion there of the views of W. H. Thorpe, who argues compellingly that a humane treatment of domestic animals requires us to respect the innate behaviour patterns and needs that they have inherited from their wild ancestors; ibid., pp. 134–5.

38 'What is it like to be a bat?', pp. 169–70.

39 For a review of the evidence, see David DeGrazia, *Taking Animals Seriously* (Cambridge: Cambridge University Press, 1996), pp. 105–15.

40 *Moral Thinking*, p. 93.

41 See David Lewis, 'Mad pain and Martian pain', in Ned Block (ed.), *Readings in the Philosophy of Psychology, volume 1* (Cambridge, MA: Harvard University Press, 1980), pp. 216–22; reprinted with a postscript in Lewis, *Philosophical Papers, volume 1* (Oxford: Oxford University Press, 1983), pp. 122–32.

42 Lewis, 'Mad pain and Martian pain'.

43 *Moral Thinking*, p. 44.

44 *Hare and Critics*, pp. 171–83.

45 Vendler, 'Changing places?', p. 173.

46 *Hare and Critics*, p. 220.

47 *Practical Ethics*, 1st edn, p. 92; see note 11 above.

11

Why I Am only a Demi-vegetarian

R. M. HARE

1   The 'Why' in my title promises an explanation as well as a justification; so I can usefully begin with a little dietetic autobiography. I am speaking only from my experience, and not as an expert dietician. I had a normal British upbringing until I found myself in 1940 in the Indian Army. There I acquired a strong taste for curries, including the delicious *dāl* (lentil) curries that our Punjabi soldiers filled their *chapātīs* with. When in 1942 I found myself a prisoner of war after the fall of Singapore, we all knew that we were going to have a thin time, and most of us expected that we would suffer in health by eating little or no meat. But this turned out not to be the case. Our dietetic experiences can be divided into three periods. In the first, in Singapore, we had plenty of polished, or white, rice, a few musty rice polishings, and a very little meat, fish, and vegetables. There was not much ground to grow vegetables in; and a pig farm which the Japanese made us set up did not prosper. During this period we suffered a number of deficiency diseases owing to an unbalanced diet, there being too much carbohydrate in proportion to the other ingredients. But none of our troubles were attributed to lack of protein.

Then, when we were sent up for eight months to work as coolies on the Burma Railway, we got very little food altogether, and suffered from a lot of all kinds of diseases owing to our debilitated state and the numerous infections that were going around. Between 20 and 40 per cent of the groups I was in died (I do not know the exact figure, but there is relevant information in Dunlop 1987). When we got back to Singapore, we had for the first time larger vegetable gardens, and grew sweet potatoes, of which we ate mainly the leaves, Ceylon or Malabar spinach, kangkong (a kind of water convolvulus), tapioca (or cassava), and small quantities of other vegetables. At the same time our rice ration diminished to very little. The result was that we stopped suffering from deficiency diseases, because our diet, though insufficient in quantity, was now well balanced, and we got small quantities of legumes for protein. So insufficient was it that we were getting not much over 800 calories a day, and became very thin. I came out of prison in 1945 weighing about 30 pounds less than my pre-war weight of 150 pounds, and made it up in a month. I now, at age 73, weigh about 165 pounds, which is at the bottom of the ideal weight-range for my height. Since we did not appear to have suffered from lack of meat, I had become disposed to be a vegetarian, and had acquired a great love of growing vegetables, which had probably saved our lives.

When my wife and I married in 1947, we talked about our diet, and I wanted to eat only vegetables, not for the reasons usually advanced nowadays, but because rationing was still in force in Britain and it seemed sensible to leave the meat for those who thought they needed it. But my wife argued that when we had children they ought to be given meat to make them grow strong; and so, having no really convincing arguments to set against this, I gave in, and we resumed a normal British diet, growing as many of our own vegetables as we could, in continuation of the 'Dig for Victory' movement that had been popular during the War. At first we had little land and I had no time to travel to and from a rented vegetable patch. When we moved out into the country in 1966, we had a large and beautiful garden, but the vegetable garden attached to the property had been retained by the previous owner to expand his honey business. There are a few fruit trees, but it seemed a shame to dig up the flower beds and lawns; so in the end we got ourselves a vegetable patch five minutes' walk away and became almost self-supporting in vegetables. This made us feel good, and seemed to improve our health, and we have ended up eating very little meat at all. Very recently, when the swimming pool that we had inherited with the property perished from old age, we filled it with soil, gave up the other patch, and now grow most of the vegetables we need within the curtilage.

So we became demi-vegetarians largely by accident, and without having any of the moral reasons usually given (though, as I said, it did make us feel good to be growing such a large proportion of what we were eating). It was only relatively recently, under the influence of Peter Singer (1975) and other animal liberationists, that I have started to take seriously these usual moral reasons for not eating meat. I began then to contemplate becoming a full vegetarian, but was unable to convince myself that it was morally required. I did for a time give up eating fish (which in any case my wife intensely dislikes) on the ground that fish are nearly always killed cruelly; but I started eating them again after I had been persuaded (wrongly, I now believe) by a physiologist colleague that fish lack the part of the brain that mediates suffering.

2   So far I have not tried to give any philosophical arguments for my views. I have to repeat that, as a moral philosopher, I am pretty confident that the best ethical theory is a combination of Kantianism with utilitarianism (Hare 1993b: chapters 1.6, 11.4, 12.1, and Hare 1993a). Such a combination is thought by many philosophers to be impossible, because, misled by partisan expositors of Kant, they think that his theory is quite incompatible with any form of utilitarianism. This is, I am sure, wrong. Kant's theory of the Categorical Imperative is quite compatible with a form of utilitarianism such as I am able to defend on formal logical grounds; he was not a utilitarian, but only because his rigorist upbringing when young had imbued him with some very strait-laced moral opinions which he tried unsuccessfully to defend by his theory, but which very few moderns, whether they are utilitarians or anti-utilitarians, would accept – for example, that suicide is as wrong as murder, and that capital punishment of murderers is morally obligatory. He also thought that the only reason for considering the sufferings of non-human animals was that cruelty to them harmed the moral character of humans. On this point, however, he was put right by his follower Leonard Nelson (1956: 136), who argued on Kantian theoretical lines that all animals are equal in their right to consideration.

The ethical theory on which I would base moral arguments can thus be called both Kantian and utilitarian. It is also compatible with the doctrine of *agapē* which is the basis of Christian ethics (Hare 1993b: chapter 1.6 and refs; Hare 1992: chapter 3). What it requires is that we should treat the ends of others as of equal weight with our own ends (Kant himself says explicitly, in relation to humans, that his Categorical Imperative requires this – 1785: BA69 = 430). This is what it is to love them as ourselves, and to count everybody for one and nobody for more than one, as Jeremy Bentham bade us (Mill 1861: chapter 5, *s.f.*). So the argument about vegetarianism, if we accept such a theory, is going to boil down to an argument about how this would require us to treat non-human animals.

3   By this time I have become fairly confident in the Kantian utilitarian ethical theory that I have espoused, which is very similar to that of Singer. Neither he nor I talk much in terms of animal rights, as do some other vegetarians like Thomas Regan (1982). The reason is not that utilitarians cannot use the concept of rights – they can certainly find a use for it in their theories (see Hare 1993b: chapter 10.2 and refs) – but that what one needs to say about treatment of non-human animals can be put much more clearly in terms of duties to them than in terms of rights which they have.

Given this confidence, which I did not have before, it seemed to me that I ought to go into the moral question more fully and see whether the demi-vegetarianism that my wife and I were following ought, morally, to be abandoned in favour of full vegetarianism. I have come to the conclusion that there is insufficient reason for our taking this step, and I will now give my arguments for that view.

The arguments about meat-eating divide naturally into categories, of which I will deal with the less difficult first, in order to get them out of the way. There are first the dietetic arguments that I have already mentioned. I am quite convinced by my own experiences that one can live more healthily without meat, but not that one can live without protein. My wife now shares this view, and our children are grown up. That is not to say that meat is not a valuable source of protein, so that, if there are other reasons for producing some, they would be supported by dietetic considerations. Against this, it is now said that a diet containing a lot of animal products, especially fat, is bad for the cardio-vascular system, and I believe it. This, however, is a reason only for eating selected meat in small quantities, not for leaving it out of one's diet altogether. It is also a reason for avoiding other animal fats such as milk products, and also eggs; but I find it hard to believe that moderate consumption of these foods does one any harm. And the dieticians are now saying that we ought to eat fish. I have learnt recently that I have mild diabetes, like many people of my age, and I have to control it by diet; but I do not think this has altered the argument very much. The conclusion that I reach from these dietetic considerations is that it is right from the health point of view to eat very little meat, but not none at all. So far, then, my wife's and my present practice seems to pass muster.

4   Next, we have to consider the economic arguments, which tend to the same conclusion. There is a very good reason for saying that in conditions of food shortage it is more economical to grow food in the form of vegetables direct from the ground, than to grow fodder, feed it to animals, and then eat the animals. The reason is that enormously much more food is produced in the first way. From this point of view, it seems a scandal that so much land in America, Australia, and even Europe is given over to fodder crops. In theory, if it were devoted instead to growing human food, it would be much easier to feed the starving millions outside these regions.

To this, however, some important qualifications have to be made. It is often suggested that the present grain and other food surpluses in these regions should simply be distributed to countries where people are starving. The main objection to this is not financial, since the accumulation of food 'mountains' is a severe financial drain on the economies of countries that practise it. The trouble lies the other end; the effect of distributing food surpluses in this way, let alone producing even more human food by switching from animal husbandry, would be to ruin what remains of the agriculture of the recipient countries, and so put an end to any hope of their becoming self-supporting. There must be an answer to this problem, but I do not know what it is. If there is an answer, then economic considerations provide a reason for eating very little meat, but not, as we shall shortly see, for eating none.

The other qualification is that there are substantial, though not enormous, areas of the world which are suitable for pasture but unsuitable for crops. The reason is usually that the ground slopes too much, so that cultivation would result in soil erosion. Other areas are too arid and subject to wind erosion for crops, but will support some stock. When my daughter was working at an experimental farm in Jamaica, her Jamaican director, who had an impressive grasp of local problems, showed me with pride the two new breeds of cattle that they had achieved, suited to the Jamaican climate. The first was a Brahmin – Channel-Island cross called Jamaica Hope, bred for milk production. The second was called Jamaica Red Poll, also Brahmin-crossed, bred for beef production. I said to him, 'Why beef cattle in Jamaica, where people are short of food? Would it not be better to grow crops?' He replied that much of Jamaica is mountainous, and that one can pasture cattle on the slopes, provided that one does not overstock them; but that ploughing would be impossible or disastrous. So he thought that cattle could be an important source of protein for Jamaicans.

I also know a farm, to which I shall be recurring later, on the Cotswold escarpment in England, where the cattle graze the slopes which are too steep for it to be sensible to plough them. The owners, a brother and sister, Richard and Rosamund Young, are devoted organic farmers and claim that the stock is necessary to maintain the soil's fertility; this adds another reason for keeping animals. It is arguable that such land should be devoted to dairy cattle and the production of wool; but if economics favours meat production, there would be no argument here for not producing beef, bacon, or lamb, but only for confining such use to land that will not grow crops economically or even at all.

5   Our arguments so far favour demi-vegetarianism but not full vegetarianism. But of course they are not the most important arguments from the moral point of view. If there were moral arguments for full vegetarianism that I found convincing, based on our duty to respect the interests of other animals, I should think that I ought to give up eating meat altogether. Before addressing such arguments, it may be helpful to explain more exactly what I mean by 'demi-vegetarian'. I did not invent the term. I have been told by Onora O'Neill that it is used by the market researchers who serve the meat trade. It means someone who, while not being a full vegetarian, let alone vegan, eats little meat, and is careful what kinds of meat he (or she) eats. Usually the selection is on dietetic grounds (lean

meat rather than fat, fish rather than meat, etc.); but no doubt moral considerations come in too. She told me that the market researchers and the trade are much more worried about the growth of demi-vegetarianism than of vegetarianism proper. The reason is that demi-vegetarianism is catching on in Britain in a big way, whereas there are still relatively few full vegetarians. That the meat trade has something to fear from demi-vegetarianism was brought home to me when I found displayed in a vegetable shop a pamphlet headed 'WHAT DEMIVEG CAN DO FOR YOU', and singing the praises of the demi-vegetarian diet from a health and culinary point of view. So evidently what is bad for the butchers is good for the greengrocers. But more of this later.

My wife's and my own practice is to buy little or no meat or fish for ourselves to eat at home, to support ourselves so far as we can on our own vegetables (which is hard if one lives half the year in Florida and half in England, though we are gradually learning how to do it). When we have guests who we think will not like to eat no meat, we buy some; and we allow ourselves to eat meat in restaurants when there is no obvious alternative. When we eat in other people's homes, we tend to say that we are demi-vegetarians (it makes good conversation – and propaganda – explaining what this means), and ostentatiously ask for a half helping of meat and lots of vegetables. The result is that all told we eat extremely little meat by ordinary standards, since we do not eat out much except when travelling. So our practice is supported by the arguments so far.

6   The moral arguments from the duty to respect animals' interests fall into two sub-classes which it is important to distinguish. The first concerns the alleged wrongness of *killing* animals, regardless of whether this involves suffering or not. The second, and to me more persuasive, one concerns the wrongness of *causing suffering* to animals, whether or not one kills them. The first kind of argument tells against eating meat and fish of all kinds; but the second does not tell against eating meat and fish unless rearing or killing them involves their suffering; but it also tells against eating animal products such as milk and eggs, if those are produced in ways involving suffering. I will take first the arguments against killing as such.

For utilitarians like Singer and myself, doing wrong to animals must involve harming them. If there is no harm, there is no wrong. Further, it has to be harm overall; if a course of action involves some harms but greater benefits, and there is no alternative with a greater balance of good over harm, it will not be wrong. We have to ask, therefore, whether the entire process of raising animals and then killing them to eat causes them more harm overall than benefit. My answer is that, assuming, as we must assume if we are to keep the 'killing' argument distinct from the 'suffering' argument, that they are happy while they live, it does not. For it is better for an animal to have a happy life, even if it is a short one, than no life at all. This is an old argument, and there are well-canvassed objections to it (e.g. Singer 1975: 254f.); but I do not think they succeed. First, it is claimed that mere existence is in itself not a benefit. But this is irrelevant; I am not claiming that mere existence is a benefit in itself, but that it is a necessary condition for having the benefits that we can have only if we are alive. It is beneficial not in itself but as a means to these.

Secondly, it is claimed that, even if the benefit which existence makes possible is a real benefit, its absence is not a harm. For in order for it to be a harm, the state of not having it must be preferable to the state of having it. But in order for it to be preferable, we have to be able to *compare* one state with another. But, the objection goes on, we cannot compare the state of not existing with the state of existing, because non-existence is not a state accessible to us for comparison; we cannot imagine it, or say what it would be like; so the comparison cannot be made. To this we can answer that happy existing people are certainly glad that they exist, and so are presumably comparing their existence with a possible non-existence; so what the objection says is impossible actually happens.

This is a very complex question metaphysically speaking, and I shall not go into it here (see Hare 1993b: chapter 6.2f. and refs). I will cut the argument short by simply assuming that the combination of Kantianism and utilitarianism which I have said I hold is the right way to reason about moral questions. I shall assume further that the 'total' variety of utilitarianism is the most defensible one – that is, that which holds that what we have to do is to maximize the total amount of preference-satisfaction that is had in the world by beings capable of forming preferences, and distribute it impartially between these beings, giving to each, within the available resources, in accordance with the strength of its preferences, and not favouring any preference simply because it is ours or that of a group specified in terms of ourselves (e.g. our family, sex, race, or species). I have discussed total and average utilitarianism in Hare (1993b: chapter 5.1).

From the point of view of such a theory it would seem that the issue about *killing* animals, as distinct from causing them suffering, resolves itself into, not the question of whether it is all right to kill animals, but the question of how many live animals, of different species including the human, we ought to cause there to be. To be more accurate, I shall have to introduce the concept of a QALY, or quality-adjusted life year. The quality-adjusted life years that an animal enjoys are the number of years lived by that animal, multiplied by a factor corresponding to the average quality of life enjoyed during those years. This concept has been employed in assessing the merits of different medical treatments; for example, if a treatment will give n years of life of average quality q, it is assessed at nq QALYs; and if an alternative treatment will give m years of life of average quality r, it is assessed at mr QALYs; and the first is to be preferred if nq is greater than mr. Of course, the probability of these outcomes has also to be factored in, and the procedure involves judgements about quality of life (from the point of view of the person who has it) which are hard to make.

All the same, this does represent a good model of what we ought to be trying to do when we make clinical decisions. The fact that QALYs are not easy to quantify or measure numerically is not so important; after all, before weighing machines with numerical scales were invented, people could all the same pick up two sacks of corn and tell which was the heavier. They could not formulate the result in pounds and ounces, but they knew what they were doing. I think that the model does represent pretty well what I am trying to do when I am choosing *for myself* whether or not to have surgery for a particular condition.

If we can apply this concept to our problem about vegetarianism, what we ought to be doing is to maximize the amount of quality-adjusted life years or QALYs of sentient beings. And I do not believe that we should be doing this if we refrained from eating animals. The reason is that if we gave up eating animals the market for meat would vanish, and no more animals would be raised for meat-production. Such animals as there were would be either wild, or kept as pets, or kept for other economic purposes such as milk, egg, and wool production. And it is certain that there would be very many fewer domestic animals than at present live. This thought gives me pause when I walk in the fields around my home in England, and see a great many apparently happy animals, all destined to be eventually eaten. As it happens, they are mainly pigs, who would certainly not be kept except for the bacon market.

Let us, to make the position clearer, consider some more extreme, though not fictitious, cases. In our village there is also a trout farm. The fish start their lives in moderately commodious ponds and have what I guess is a pleasant life for fish, with plenty to eat. In due course they are lifted out in buckets and put immediately into tanks in the farm buildings. Purchasers select their fish, which is then killed by being banged smartly on the head and handed to the customer. I am fairly certain that, if given the choice, I would prefer the life, all told, of such a fish to that of almost any fish in the wild, and to non-existence.

Again, suppose that one were able to keep animals in ideal conditions under one's own supervision, as the Youngs whom I mentioned earlier do, and then kill them to eat without causing them suffering (at least more suffering than they would have from a 'natural' death); would I consider that one had done those animals a service by bringing them into existence to have that sort of life and death? The Youngs, I am sure, would answer

'Yes'; and they claim to have reconverted some converts to vegetarianism. They do not slaughter their animals themselves, but have made what they think are satisfactory arrangements with the local public abattoir, and always accompany their animals there to see that they suffer the minimum of fear. They claim that even their pigs never squeal – which is remarkable, because pigs, being highly intelligent animals, nearly always know when something nasty is in the offing. The Youngs' pigs, I must add, are the most well-looking pigs I have ever seen, and the same can be said of their sheep. If all farm animals were as well looked after as theirs, there would be no complaints about cruelty involved in animal husbandry.

7   To this question of cruelty, then, I now turn, as the second of the two headings under which moral questions about the treatment of animals have to be considered. I must at once admit that some animal husbandry practices are quite scandalous. The problem is, how best to get them improved, and in particular what effect on their improvement can be had by abstaining from eating meat. I find this a highly complex and difficult question, and to its complexities are due my remaining doubts about whether I ought to become a full vegetarian. On the face of it, the immediate effect of my not, on a particular occasion, buying meat is to reduce, very slightly, the demand for that kind of meat. It will not directly save the life of any animal, because the animal in question has been killed already. Any effect on the lives of the animals, including the quality of their lives, is bound to be indirect; and I find it extremely hard to assess it. I wish I were more of an economist, which is what one needs to be to determine the effects of one's actions in the market. However, I will try to make some guesses, under several headings.

First, there is the obvious effect, that a reduction in the market for meat lowers the price, and this, if many people do the same, may force out of production the least efficient marginal producers. We have therefore to ask whether these will also be the ones that treat their animals best, or worst, or a mixture. It might seem at first sight as if it would be the factory farms that would survive, because they are said to be the most efficient in the narrow commercial sense of that term. But I do not believe that this is the whole story, if only because the Youngs told me that they do quite well out of their farm in spite of treating their animals so admirably. The reason is that their meat and milk is so good that it earns a substantial premium. So, they say, does their wheat, grown by organic methods; but I am inclined to take all claims by organic farmers with a pinch of salt, and so am prepared to expect the financial collapse of farms like theirs if vegetarianism or even demi-vegetarianism spreads in a big way.

However, there are other equally important considerations. Demi-vegetarians have one very powerful advantage over full vegetarians when it comes to influencing the market. Since they eat little meat, but do eat some, they would be in a quite strong position to influence animal husbandry practices if they could get enough information to enable them to make use of their power. By selecting carefully the meat that they did buy, they might help to cause those practices to be abandoned which occasion most suffering to animals.

The obstacle to this is the extreme difficulty of finding out reliably where one's meat (and for that matter one's eggs and milk) come from. Even so-called free-range eggs are often nothing of the kind – or so it is said. Living in a country village, my wife and I are better placed than most people to find out the sources of what we eat. I think we usually know where the eggs we eat come from; and we are on good terms with the local butcher, who has an interest in philosophy, and once attended a discussion on vegetarianism with my students at one of the seminars I have given in our home. Almost the only thing we ever buy from him is an occasional turkey, which he assures us is free range; it certainly tastes like it, and I think with turkeys one can tell the difference. I am pretty certain that one of the most important reforms to agitate for, if one is the agitating sort, is a law requiring full disclosure of the sources of all foodstuffs. Even a non-governmental certification scheme, such as the Royal Society for the Prevention of Cruelty to Animals is said to be considering, would do a great deal of good.

Another way in which our eating habits can influence the treatment of animals is by their propaganda or publicity value. It might be urged in favour of full vegetarianism that to make a stand in this simple way against meat eating will bring home to people how awful some animal husbandry practices are, and so lead to public revulsion against them and thus possibly to legislation forbidding them. In my moral philosophy as a whole I do lay stress on the utility of having firm general principles of this sort, and not making complex cost – benefit calculations about particular cases; these calculations are bound to be unreliable and may even involve self-deception (Hare 1993b: chapter 2.3f.). But a steadfast full vegetarianism is not the only possible firm principle. One might even take against this position the line which its upholders could rightly take against veganism, if they were utilitarians. It is hard to be sure – indeed, it is on the face of it unlikely – that complete abstention from eggs and milk will do much for the welfare of animals (it is certainly likely to reduce their numbers). A firm abstention just from meat and fish is better. But is it not possible that a large reduction in one's consumption of them, coupled with as much selection of sources as is possible, would do even more?

On the question of the propaganda value of the rival policies, then, there can be different views. Here we have to ask what we are trying to achieve by our propaganda. It must be remembered that, if what I have said about the morality of killing animals is correct, our aim should be to bring it about, not that no animals are killed, but that the quantity multiplied by the quality of animal (including human) life is maximized. We therefore do not want everyone to be full vegetarians. Rather, we want there to be enough meat-eating in the world to sustain the number of animals that there ought to be, whatever that is. I shall come later to the even more difficult question of where this optimum lies. It is an open question whether it would be best and most quickly achieved by there coming to be a few full vegetarians, while the rest of us ate as much meat as most people in developed countries do now, or whether it would work better if there were much larger numbers of demi-vegetarians (with varying degrees of deminess).

I am inclined to think that these possibilities would work equally well, and that therefore the most material consideration is how easily each of them could be achieved. And I also think that we are more likely to persuade very large numbers of people to become demi-vegetarians (it is happening already) than to convert enough people to full vegetarianism to have the same effect on the market and on public opinion. But I am open to conviction on this.

8   But now we come to the most difficult question of all. How many animals ought there to be, and what proportions of these should be allotted to the various species? If one is not a specist (and I hope I am not) it is purely the quality multiplied by quantity of life that has to be considered, and not the fact that one of the competing species is our own. (I use the term 'specist', formed by analogy with 'racist', instead of the intolerably clumsy word 'speciesist' which seems to be becoming current.) I do think that humans are capable of a higher quality of life than *some* animals (earthworms, for example). I also think that some animals (oysters, for example) have no conscious experiences, so that we cannot sensibly ask what the quality of their lives is (they have none in the relevant sense). This presupposes an answer to the question of whether life can have quality, in the morally relevant sense, even if it is not conscious. There is also the further question, pressing for environmentalists, of whether plants and even non-living beings have a value that needs to be weighed in this balance. I have made a beginning of addressing both these questions, and shall leave them on one side now, although, once one has opened up the question of how many animals there should be of various species, this aspect of the matter has to be considered.

Ecological considerations will obviously be very important here. The ecology determines what combination of various species, and in what numbers, *can* coexist on this planet; and till we have settled that, there is no point in asking how many there *ought* to be. But, assuming some sort of answer to the equally difficult question of how we assess the quality of life of various species under various conditions, how do we determine the optimal numbers? Before going any further, it is important to distinguish between two entirely different ways in which humans can make use of other animals for food. I shall call them 'predation' and 'husbandry'. In predation the animals (fish are the most obvious example) live in their wild state and are hunted by man for food. In husbandry the animals are domesticated and kept more or less confined, and then slaughtered for food as required.

The effects of predation vary, but in general it can perhaps be said that, *provided* that there is not over-fishing or over-hunting (that is, provided that the stock of animals is not depleted), the hunting or fishing makes no difference to the numbers of animals (this is indeed a tautology). But we still have to ask what would happen if there were no predation by man. The answer must be that the populations would rise to the limit imposed by other predators, parasites, and diseases, and by the available space and food supply. My conclusion is that predation is all right within limits (which are frequently transgressed by fishermen, to their own ultimate ruin). However, the methods of predation need careful watching to avoid cruelty – though we have to bear in mind that, in the wild, animals often die miserable deaths from 'natural' causes, and that other predators, parasites, and diseases are even less merciful than man. Therefore, in spite of now disagreeing with the physiologist colleague I mentioned earlier, I feel inclined to eat fish in moderation when my wife lets me, but have misgivings about those caught with rod and line. I have misgivings about all kinds of predation, but they may be mistaken.

Before leaving the subject of predation, it is worth mentioning that it is urged by some people that in large tracts of Africa more economical use could be made of the land by having game preserves, with controlled predation by man, than by grazing cattle. I cannot judge of this; but it is claimed that more meat would thereby be produced more economically, with less soil erosion. If this is so, it would also solve some moral problems, if, as I have suggested, predation is morally less suspect than at any rate most kinds of husbandry.

Husbandry presents more difficult moral problems, some of which I have mentioned already. At the best, the fish farm, and the Youngs' farm on the Cotswolds that I described earlier, seem to me to be all right, and most forms of factory farming all wrong; but all kinds of farm in between need careful discussion in detail which I have no room to give them. If the most fundamental issue is one of numbers, then we might consider an extreme position (Derek Parfit's 'repugnant conclusion' applied to all animals and not just to humans – see Hare (1993b: 5.Iff.). This would require us to increase the population of both up to the limit at which the *total* (not the average) utility or preference-satisfaction was maximal. That is to say, we should increase numbers even at the cost of decreasing quality of life provided that the total utility or amount of QALYs resulting from the increased numbers at this lower level of quality was thereby increased. Obviously the argument is going to have to be even more complex in order to take in other animals.

At the other extreme we might argue that QALYs would be maximized if we adopted a much more primitive life-style, requiring the use of a lot of land per person and therefore a greatly reduced population of people (and probably of animals too, compared with what can be kept in intensive husbandry), and so had what some would try to persuade us is a much superior quality of life. I do not myself favour either of these extremes; but where, in between them, the optimum policy lies I could not decide without a great deal more information about the ecological possibilities than I, at any rate, have. I am very much in favour of experiments in living, and I think that what we achieved in our prison camps in Singapore was a quite successful one; but if, once set free, any one of us had been willing to go on with it just as it was, I should have been extremely surprised. However, I brought something away, especially my love of growing and eating vegetables. And I acquired some gastronomic arguments for at least demi-vegetarianism which I still think powerful.

9   I will try now to sum up my very tentative conclusions. First, there are good dietetic and economic arguments for demi-vegetarianism, but they do not support full vegetarianism. Secondly, the moral argument based on the wrongness of *killing* animals collapses completely in the face of the objection that by accepting it we should in practice *reduce* the number of animals, and thus the total amount of animal welfare. Thirdly, the *sufferings* of animals in most commonly practised forms of animal husbandry are scandalous; but the best way of improving matters is not easy to find. I am inclined to the view that, though homage must be paid to the courage of the full vegetarians who stand out completely against meat-eating, and though they undoubtedly do a lot to propagate better practices, more could perhaps be done if a much greater number of people could be converted to demi-vegetarianism, and if they had more easily available the information they need in order to select those animal products that are produced by methods which minimize suffering to animals. I think that there are some, and that controlled predation is one of them; but the factual questions involved here are so complex that I hesitate to discuss them, not being an expert in these matters.

Lastly, the question of how the numbers of various species should be apportioned within the available resources and ecological limits is an immensely difficult moral question, whose solution requires *both* an understanding of some rather deep philosophical issues which I have dealt with elsewhere, including the papers I have referred to, *and* a grasp of the enormously complicated ecological issues which affect the answer. Nobody that I know of has mastered both these groups of issues; few philosophers have even begun to master the ecology, and few ecologists and other environmentalists have even begun to understand the logic of the arguments, and the pitfalls which beset them. So there is everything to be said for the two disciplines getting together.

References

Dunlop, E. E. (1987) *The War Diaries of Weary Dunlop: Java and the Burma Thailand Railway*. Melbourne: Nelson.

Hare, R. M. (1992) *Essays on Religion and Education*. Oxford: Oxford University Press.

Hare, R. M. (1993a) 'Could Kant have been a utilitarian?' In R. M. Dancy (ed.), *Kant and Critique: New Essays in Honor of W. H. Werkmeister*. Dordrecht: Reidel.

Hare, R. M. (1993b) *Essays on Bioethics*. Oxford: Oxford University Press.

Mill, J. S. (1861) *Utilitarianism*.

Nelson, L. (1956) *A System of Ethics*. New Haven, CT: Yale University Press; Oxford: Oxford University Press (first published in German, 1932).

Regan, T. (1982) *And All that Dwell Therein: Animal Rights and Environmental Ethics*. Berkeley: University of California Press.

Singer, P. (1975) *Animal Liberation*. New York: Random House.

12

Respect for Life: Counting what Singer Finds of no Account

HOLMES ROLSTON III

There is nothing to be taken into account. (Peter Singer)[1]

Peter Singer is a remarkable philosopher, who has enlarged our vision of ethics, previously much too humanist, to include animals that formerly did not count. Few ethicists, indeed few persons responsible for the care and use of animals, are not more sensitive to animal welfare now than they were before the impact of Singer and his colleagues, voicing a concern about the pains that animals suffer on behalf of humans.

Equally remarkably, however, Singer has himself proved blind to the still larger effort in environmental ethics to value life at all its ranges and levels, indeed to care for a biospheric Earth. It is almost as though what it takes Singer to win his victory about the animals – his insistence that they do suffer and that, by parity of reasoning, we humans concerned about suffering in ourselves cannot logically and ought not morally to fail to count their suffering – leaves him at a loss about insentient life, all the plants, but also most of the animals, if we remember the mollusks, crustaceans, nematodes, beetles, and the like. His victory is mostly for vertebrates, who form only 4 percent of living things by species and only a tiny fraction of a percent by numbers of individuals. Really, it is mostly for the mammals, and declines with decreasing complexity in the central nervous system.

Also, Singer has yet to count the vital processes, such as speciation, natural selection, and ecosystemic communities in which these individual organisms live. Unless we can locate his mistake, his victory could prove pyrrhic in the fight for an environmental ethic. The question whether insentient animals and plants can be loci of value is our immediate concern. Once we open that question, however, the answer opens still further questions of species, ecosystems, and ultimately the whole Earth as the most comprehensive community of life. These latter questions we treat more briefly.

It is true, as Singer will say, that one can do much environmental conservation, operating out of a concern for humans and higher animals and their pleasures and pains. This is because humans and higher animals need a life support system; they live at the top of what ecologists call trophic pyramids, food chains. They can flourish only if the biotic community in which they reside is properly functioning, and that includes the plants, the fungi, the insects, the worms, and all those "lower" forms that Singer is otherwise unable to count. Singer can count them instrumentally to animal goods.

Consider such an argument moved a step further. Bryan G. Norton claims that an environmental ethic centered on human interests (an anthropocentric one) does not really differ in policy recommendations from an environmental ethic that considers directly animal interests, intrinsic values in plants, the flourishing of species and ecosystems (a biocentric or ecocentric ethic). But this is only provided that the anthropocentric ethic is sufficiently enlightened to become sensitive to the deeper values available to humans when they interact with nature, such as scenic beauty, or nature study and recreation, wilderness experiences, and so on. He calls this "the convergence hypothesis"; both the humanistic and the naturalistic ethical viewpoints converge.[2]

Singer would probably protest, as would I, that while an ethic that is anthropocentric may often coincide with one based on both animal and human welfare, they do not always so converge – not even for humans who are enlightened about deeper values to be enjoyed as humans enjoy wildlife, pet animals, and so on. If animal pleasures and pains do not count morally, not as intrinsically good and bad, then a great deal that we humans may wish to do with animals, using them for food, experiments, and so on, is permissible, which would not be permitted if they do count more directly.

But I wish to make the analogous point against Singer, now moved over further past the mammals and animals capable of similar psychological experience. Although an animal welfare ethic and an environmental ethic do often converge, they by no means always do so, and, in what follows, we will be giving numerous examples of when they do not. To put the point with some provocation, the people in the United States who join the Sierra Club do not always have the same agenda as the people who join the Humane Society.

Counting Insentient Life – in Principle

Singer considers an ethic of respect for life and rejects it. The question is, "Once we abandon the interests of sentient creatures as our source of value, where do we find value?"[3] In respect for life – that seems an obvious answer. But Singer finds problems. Albert Schweitzer claims that every living organism has a "will to live" and Paul Taylor claims that every living organism is "pursuing its own good in its own unique way." Singer dislikes the idea that plants have a "will" to live or that they "pursue" their good. Here is his reply:

> The problem with the defenses offered by both Schweitzer and Taylor for their ethical views is that they use language metaphorically and then argue as if what they had said was literally true. We may often talk about plants "seeking" water or light so that they can survive, and this way of thinking about plants makes it easier to accept talk of their "will to live," or of them "pursuing" their own good. But once we stop to reflect on the fact that plants are not conscious and cannot engage in any intentional behavior, it is clear that all this language is metaphorical; one might just as well say that a river is pursuing its own good and striving to reach the sea, or that the "good" of a guided missile is to blow itself up along with its target.... Plants experience none of these [emotions of will and desire]. Moreover, in the case of plants, rivers, and guided missiles, it is possible to give a purely physical explanation of what is happening; and in the absence of consciousness, there is no good reason why we should have greater respect for the physical processes that govern the growth and decay of living things than we have for those that govern non-living things.[4]

So, Singer concludes, the capacity to suffer or experience enjoyment or happiness "is the only defensible boundary of concern for the interests of others."[5]

The set that Singer groups together is revealing: plants, rivers, and guided missiles. He can see only what they have in common, or, more accurately, what they lack in common: sentience. Therefore, for ethical counting, they are all alike. But is this so? True, plants lack conscious will and intentional pursuit; Singer is right about that, and one has to be careful with metaphors. But are there no significant differences between plants, rivers, and guided missiles? No, claims Singer, because they are all purely physical processes. In Singer's dichotomy, there seem to be only two metaphysical levels: conscious experiencers and merely physical processes. He lingers in a Cartesian dualism. He is incapable of distinguishing between plants and rivers. Can we be more discriminating?

Consider plants. A plant is not an experiencing subject, but neither is it an inanimate object, like a stone. Nor is it a geomorphological process, like a river. Plants are quite alive. Plants, like all other organisms, are self-actualizing. Plants are unified entities of the botanical though not of the zoological kind: that is, they are not unitary organisms highly integrated with centered neural control, but they are modular organisms, with a meristem that can repeatedly and indefinitely produce new vegetative modules, additional stem nodes and leaves when there is available space and resources, as well as new reproductive modules, fruits and seeds.

Plants repair injuries and move water, nutrients, and photosynthate from cell to cell; they store sugars; they make tannin and other toxins and regulate their levels in defense against grazers; they make nectars and emit pheromones to influence the behavior of pollinating insects and the responses of other plants; they emit allelopathic agents to suppress invaders; they make thorns, trap insects, and so on. They can reject genetically incompatible grafts. This description of plant activities does not require the use of "will to live" or intentional "pursuit" of desires. It is hardly metaphorical; rather, it is a literal account of what is going on.

A plant, like any other organism, sentient or not, is a spontaneous, self-maintaining system, sustaining and reproducing itself, executing its program, making a way through the world, checking against performance by means of responsive capacities with which to measure success. Something more than merely physical causes, even when less than sentience, is operating within every organism. There is *information* superintending the causes; without it the organism would collapse into a sand heap. The information is used to preserve the plant identity.

In nature there are, if we consult physics and chemistry, two kinds of things, matter and energy; but if we consult biology there is a third thing: information. In the merely physical processes, such as those affecting rivers and stones, neither matter nor energy can be created or destroyed, though, at the more fundamental levels of atomic and astronomical physics, the one can be transformed into the other. Matter throughout natural history has been energetically structurally transformed. This happens in physics and chemistry with impressive results, as with the construction of the higher elements in the stars or the composition of crystals, rocks, mountains, rivers, and canyons on Earth.

The really spectacular constructions that are manifest in biology, making possible the diversity and complexity that environmentalists wish to value, do not appear without the simultaneous genesis of information about how to compose and maintain such structures and processes. This information is recorded in the genes, and such information, unlike matter and energy, can be created and destroyed. That is what worries environmentalists about extinction, for example. This genetic information separates rivers (and guided missiles) from organisms. In it lies the secret of life, and an environmental ethics will need a discriminating account of such life, and appropriate respect for it.

Such "information," Singer might protest, is metaphorical, since plants do not consciously know what they know. But that seems prejudiced in favor of only one kind of information, refusing to recognize that information can be genetic quite as much as it can be cognitive. The tree is doing what it is doing for its own sake. Perhaps Singer would reply that the tree does not have any "sake." Well, then the tree is doing what it is doing for its own life. He would hardly reply that the tree does not have any life, although he does not think rivers or guided missiles are alive. No, the tree has a life that it intrinsically defends as a value good in itself, and it does this on the basis of its genetic information.

Let's test Singer with another set of metaphors. Plants do not "will" or "desire"; set those metaphors aside. The plant information is carried by the DNA, which we can call a "linguistic" molecule. The DNA is a kind of "logical" set, not less than a biological set, informed as well as formed. Organisms use a sort of symbolic logic, use these base pair sequences and molecular shapes as symbols of life. The novel resourcefulness lies in the epistemic content conserved, developed, and thrown forward to make biological resources out of the physicochemical sources. This steering core is cybernetic: partly a special kind of cause and effect system, and partly something more; partly a historical information system making a way through the world.

The genetic set is really a "propositional" set – to choose an even more provocative term – recalling how the Latin *propositum* is an assertion, a set task, a theme, a plan, a proposal, a project, as well as a cognitive statement. These molecules are set to drive the movement from genotypic potential to phenotypic expression. Given a chance, these molecules "seek" organic self-expression. Perhaps we need to be cautious about a plant "pursuing" or "willing" anything; maybe even the word "seek" is metaphorical. But we do need some words to describe what is going on and metaphors can help us get at facts of the matter. An organism, unlike an inert rock, claims the environment as source and sink, from which to abstract energy and materials and into which to excrete them. It "takes advantage" of its environment. Life thus arises out of earthen sources (as do rocks and rivers), but life turns back on its sources to make resources out of them (unlike rocks and rivers).

Now let's turn to the source of value, about which Singer worries. Is nothing of any value to, or for, or in, a plant? We pass to value when we recognize that the genetic set is a "normative" set; it distinguishes between what *is* and what *ought to be*. The organism is not a moral system, for there are no moral agents in nature; but the organism is an axiological system. So the tree grows, reproduces, repairs its wounds, and resists death. The physical state that the organism defends is a valued state. A life is defended for what it is in itself, without necessary further contributory reference, although, given the structure of all ecosystems, such lives necessarily do have further contributory reference. Such organisms may have no will or desires, but they do have their own standards. Every organism has a *good-of-its-kind*; it defends its own kind as a *good kind*. In this sense, the genome is a set of conservation molecules. To say that the plant has a good of its own is not to be dismissed as mere metaphor. That rather seems the plain fact of the matter.

Now we can also see what is mistaken about grouping guided missiles with the plants. Singer is only half right that guided missiles are purely physical processes; they are machines, of course, but there are intentions further behind them. A guided missile has no good-of-its-kind; it is a good thing for people, who made this artifact to serve their purposes. A missile has no nature of its own; it does not exist by nature. Machines are not wild. Unlike wild rivers (which Singer also groups with the plants and missiles), a missile is a device produced by sentient organisms, namely humans, and can only be so understood, and valued. A missile is a means to human good (sometimes, a doubtful good). Missiles have no self-generating or even self-defending tendencies. Perhaps they have computers on board and various programs to lock onto their targets, or to dodge anti-missile rockets, but all these activities are programmed into them by their designing engineers, because their purpose – the mission of the missile, so to speak – is to defend humans and what they value.[6]

If humans were to abandon their missiles, perhaps realizing that missiles do not serve human desires for security as well as hoped, then, in those left-behind missiles, there is nothing to be taken into account. Missiles have only the value that humans gave to them in the first place. But none of this is true when a human walks away from a tree. The tree has a life defended before the logger walks up, and the logger destroys it.

The values that attach to machines are entirely instrumental, derivative from the persons who have created instruments. Machines have an end only mediately as the extrasomatic products of human systems. Wound-up machines wind down, sooner or later; the process is entropic. Informed organisms wind themselves up; they keep on winding themselves up; the process is negentropic. They too break and die somatically, but not before they reproduce themselves and pass on their up-winding information to a next generation. The values that attach to organisms result from their non-derivative, genuine self-organizing as spontaneous natural systems. The standards of performance, the norms of achievement, are in the organism itself. These are objective standards in that they are not generated by human subjective preferences. A machine is only a good kind because it is a good of my kind; an organism can have a good of its kind and be a good kind intrinsically. Machines are by us and for us; organisms live on their own.

The tree is valuable (able to value) itself. If we cannot say this, then we will have to ask, as an open question, "Well, the tree has a good of its own, but is there anything of value to it?" "This tree was injured when the elk rubbed its velvet off its antlers, and the tannin secreted there is killing the invading bacteria. But is this valuable to the tree?" Botanists say that the tree is irritable in the biological sense; it responds with the repair of injury. Such capacities can be "vital," a description with values built into it. These are observations of value in nature with just as much certainty as they are biological facts. That is what they are: facts about value relationships in nature. We are really quite certain that organisms use their resources, and one is overinstructed in philosophy who denies that such resources are of value to organisms instrumentally. But then, why is the tree not defending its own life just as much a fact of the matter as its use of nitrogen and photosynthesis to do so?

Singer will have to say that, even though plants have a good of their own and do these interesting things, plants are not able to value because they are not able to feel anything. There is no one there. Nothing matters to a plant. There is plant good, but not plant value. They do not have any interests. There is no valuer evaluating anything. Plants can do things that interest us, but the plants aren't interested in what they are doing. They don't have any options among which they are choosing. They have only their merely functional goods. This is so, Singer will reply, because nothing "matters" to a plant; a plant is without minimally sentient awareness.

But, though things do not matter *to* plants, a great deal matters *for* them. We ask, of a failing plant, what's the matter *with* that plant? If it is lacking sunshine and soil nutrients, and we arrange for these, we say, the tree is benefiting from them; and *benefit* is – everywhere else we encounter it – a value word. Biologists regularly speak of the "selective value" or "adaptive value" of genetic variations.[7] Plant activities have "survival value," such as the seeds they disperse or the thorns they make. Natural selection picks out whatever traits an organism has that are valuable to it, relative to its survival. When natural selection has been at work gathering these traits into an organism, that organism is able to value on the basis of those traits. It is a valuing organism, even if the organism is not a sentient valuer, much less a conscious evaluator. And those traits, though picked out by natural section, are innate in the organism: that is, stored in its genes. It is difficult to dissociate the idea of value from natural selection.

Any sentientist or humanist theory of value has got to argue away all such natural selection as not dealing with "real" value at all, but mere function. Those arguments are, in the end, more likely to be stipulations than real arguments. If you stipulate that valuing must be felt valuing, that there must be someone there, some subject of a life, then plants are not able to value, and that is so by your definition. But what we wish to examine is whether that definition, faced with the facts of biology, is plausible. Perhaps the sentientist definition covers correctly but narrowly certain kinds of higher animal valuing, namely that done by sentient animals, and omits all the rest.

Singer will protest: although philosophically unsophisticated biologists have used "value" regarding plants, careful philosophers will put that kind of "value" in scare quotes. This isn't really value at all, because there are no felt experiences, no pains or pleasures at stake. This so-called value is not a value, really, not one of interest to philosophers because it is not a value with interest in itself.

Why is the organism not valuing what it is making resources of? Not consciously, but we do not want to presume that there is only conscious value or valuing. That is what we are debating, not assuming. And what we are claiming is that life is organized vitality, which may or may not have an experiential psychology. A value-er is an entity able to feel value? Yes, and more. A value-er is an entity able to defend value. On the second meaning, plants too defend their lives. In an objective gestalt some value is already present in non-sentient organisms, normative evaluative systems, prior to the emergence of further dimensions of value with sentience. We agree with Singer that there is no feeling in such an organism, but it does not follow that humans cannot or ought not to develop "a feeling for the organism."[8]

Counting Insentient Life – in Practice

Our main concern so far has not been to address the question of how morally significant organisms are, nor what justifiable considerations may outweigh such value, only to establish in principle what sorts of things can command our moral attention. A frequent reply at this point is that, whatever the principle, plants and the lower animals have such insignificant value that this can make no difference in practice. Or, there is no way of calculating how much this value amounts to, in cases where we must trade off the interests of sentient creatures against these insentient lives. Singer complains: "Without conscious interests to guide us, we have no way of assessing the relative weights to be given to the flourishing of different forms of life."[9]

Certainly there is no calculus for such decisions; there is no calculus for how much sentient animals suffer either, such as the elk or the chickadees who must endure the winter's cold. But that does not mean nothing can be said about appropriate human behavior in the presence of insentient life. Consider some cases.

A favorite campground in the Rawah Range of the Rocky Mountains is adjacent to subalpine meadows of wildflowers, profuse displays of daisies, lupines, columbines, delphiniums, bluebells, paintbrushes, penstemons, shooting stars, and violets. The trailside signs for years were the standard ones: "Please leave the flowers for others to enjoy." One season I returned to the campground to find that the wasted wooden signs had been replaced by newly cut ones that read, "Let the flowers live!" The traditional signs imply that the only value in flowers is that they may be enjoyed by sentient humans. The new signs moved deeper, to a respect for life. According to this ethic, what the injunction "Let the flowers live!" means is: "Daisies, marsh-marigolds, geraniums, larkspurs are living organisms that express goods of their kind, and, in the absence of evidence to the contrary, are good kinds. There are trails here by which you may enjoy these flowers. Is there any reason why your human interests justify destroying good kinds?"

The old signs, "Leave the flowers for others to enjoy," were signs using Singer's ethic, where flowers count only for people. That ethic is, of course, reasonably effective in encouraging people to conserve wildflowers. But the new signs invite a change of reference frame, and this can mean changed behavior. Presumably, for instance, if one were in a remote area and further enjoyment of the flowers was unlikely, then no ethicist could object to my picking or even destroying them to suit whatever my whims, since, on their own, they do not count.

In the 1880s a tunnel was cut through a giant sequoia in what is now Yosemite National Park. Driving through the Wawona tree, formerly in horse and buggy and later by car, amused and impressed millions. The tree was perhaps the most photographed in the world. On holidays, there was a waiting line. The giant tree blew over in the snowstorms of 1968–9, weakened by the tunnel, although it had long stood despite it. Some have proposed that the Park Service cut more drive-through sequoias. But the rangers have refused, saying that one was enough, and that this is an indignity to a majestic sequoia. It is better to educate visitors about the enormous size and longevity of redwoods, their resistance to fire, diseases, insect pests, better to teach them to admire a durable, stalwart, marvelous tree, a sort of natural Ming classic. They will then wish to leave redwoods untouched.

Again, one could say that this is just leaving the redwood for others to enjoy. But if it turned out that tourists really got more pleasure driving through a sequoia, then the park rangers ought to cut another one. They ought to cut several, to avoid waiting lines. In fact, however, the rangers, as well as the park visitors, who largely approve of the new policy, seem to be valuing redwoods intrinsically. It is wrong, or at least inappropriate, to mutilate a sequoia to excite tourists. The question is not pleasing people, but respecting these especially majestic and ancient trees, among the largest and oldest living things on Earth.

People use trees all the time, for timber, fuel, paper pulp, and civilization is almost unthinkable without wood. There is no argument here that people ought not to use trees; only that they can, and sometimes do, consider the appropriate uses of trees, and that one constraint on such use is what the tree is in itself. For years, I went out each winter to cut a Christmas tree, seeking, if I could find one, a wild blue spruce. I cut them not far from where the signs read, "Let the flowers live!" Not infrequently, I would discover that others, seeking the ideal tree and unable to find a small one, would chop down a large blue spruce, to cut out just the top five or six feet, and leave the dead tree felled in the forest. That seemed a waste; I refused to do it.

One day, about to cut a small spruce, I asked myself. What's the difference? It's almost worse to cut down a young tree, which has perhaps hundreds of years of life ahead of it, than to cut down an older tree, of which the life is half over. In any case, I thought, I am going to sacrifice a tree, small or large, for only about ten days of my pleasure. Wouldn't it be better to leave the tree, allowing it to flourish for a century or more, and to use an artificial tree? At least I should use a farmed tree, which would not otherwise exist. So I refused to cut it, and I have not since cut a wild tree for my Christmas festivities.

That's a personal preference, one might reply, but one cannot urge any such ethic on others. Consider then the US national Christmas tree. Each year a giant tree is cut, carried across the country, and put up and decorated on the White House lawn. The lights are turned on with a ceremony; some photographs of it appear in newspapers; people go by to see it. After ten days, the tree is trashed. All this is well and good, on Singer's ethic. But what if such a tree were identified in place, and decorated for a few days, but left alive. There could still be the pictures in newspapers, serving Christmas festivities, with also some notice of the significance of forests, and a word about how the national tree was left uncut out of respect for the tree. There could be a trail to it, and people could hike year round, and for years afterward, to see the tree that was the national Christmas tree in 1996. Children born in that year could, a decade hence, go to see the Christmas tree in the year of their birth. With this tradition, eventually, a grandfather could take a grandchild to the tree of his year of birth. Why wouldn't this be a better national tradition, even though Singer has no grounds on which to recommend it?

One tree is a small item, and no one, myself included, would want to argue that the cutting of a single tree is an event of great moral significance. But tree-cutting can add up. It takes about a half a million trees each week to give two hundred million Americans the pleasure of their Sunday paper. Pleasure is all that counts on Singer's ethic; and we do need sustainable forestry so that future generations may have their Sunday papers too. But suppose conservationists were to recommend a recycling program, perhaps financed by some additional charge for the paper, that recycled half the papers, and thus saved a quarter of a million trees a week (which would also save considerable energy and greatly reduce air pollution). Singer can't count the trees; he would only have to look to see if the recycled newspapers maintained the pleasures of the Sunday paper and also permitted humans to use the saved energy for other purposes – perhaps to take a ride out in the mountains to enjoy the scenery in the saved forests.

The forests of North America were once one of the glories of the continent, and, while much of the continent remains forested, the old-growth forests are nearly gone. Only about 10 percent remains. Some environmentalists can feel quite strongly about saving what survives, to the point, for instance, of spiking such trees lest they be cut. These "tree huggers" certainly do not wish for lumbermen to be hurt, as they may be if they cut such trees and their saw blades strike the hidden spikes and shatter. So the spikers send anonymous letters to the US Forest Service, identifying spiked groves and warning loggers to leave them uncut. Probably they want such forests so that they and their children can visit them. But such environmentalists also hold that such trees have value, including value in themselves, that justifies putting loggers at such risk. That risks some human suffering on account of trees, which cannot suffer.

We have been considering plants because they have no neurons at all and the question of their sentience is easier to set aside. But in the fuller biological picture we must also realize that Singer cannot count most of the animals. Ninety-five percent of all the creatures in the world are smaller than a chicken's egg, yet often quite perceptive – sentient in the sense of variously responding to their environment (which plants also do). Typically, we do not know whether they are subjects of a life – sentient in the sense of psychic experience and feeling pain. Singer cuts things off somewhere between shrimp and oysters.

He may be choosing his examples because shrimp have eyes and oysters do not; that tends to register a conviction that there is "someone there" behind those eyes in shrimp and no one there inside the oyster. Beings with eyes can take an interest in what is going on. Shrimp, various species, are arthropods and crustaceans (phylum *Arthropoda*, class (or subphylum) *Crustacea*) with compound eyes. Insects (class *Insecta*) are arthropods as well as shrimp, and highly perceptive, but are they subjects of a life? Oysters, *Ostrea*, without eyes, are in class *Bivalvia* (or *Pelecypoda*) among the mollusks (phylum *Mollusca*). The scallop (*Pecten*) in that class and otherwise rather similar has eyes with cornea, lens, and retina, with which it takes some interest in, or at least processes some information about, the world around it.

Still other mollusks, such as squid and octopus (class *Cephalapoda*) have excellent eyes, which bear comparison with our own.[10] Such mollusks are quite intelligent, though we can only speculate about their consciousness. Perhaps insisting on knowledge about "conscious interests to guide us"[11] is not the way to evaluate what is at stake in the life and death of mollusks, arthropods, and other invertebrates. If that is his only criterion, what will Singer say about the 129 species of freshwater mussels (43 percent of the total number there) either already extinct or threatened with extinction in the Tennessee River Valley system, owing to human manipulation of the rivers?

Somewhere in there with the shrimps and the oysters are the crabs. Crabs have eyes. They also defend their lives in search of food. Fishermen in Atlantic coastal estuaries and bays toss beer bottles overboard, a convenient way to dispose of trash. On the bottom, small crabs, attracted by the residual beer, make their way inside the bottles and become trapped, unable to get enough foothold on the slick glass neck to work their way out. They starve slowly. Then one dead crab becomes bait for the next victim, an indefinitely resetting trap! Are those bottle traps of concern for those who respect life, after fisherman have been warned about this effect? Or is the whole thing out of sight, out of mind, with crabs too mindless to care about? Should not sensitive fisherman pack their bottle trash back to shore – whether or not crabs have much, or any, felt experience? One does not have to know whether or how much pain the crabs feel, or whether they have eyes and there is someone body there. If the discarded beer bottles were entrapping small oysters instead of crabs, ought one not to reach the same conclusion? One needs only to know that animals are dying as a result of one's action, and that a little care could prevent this. Evidence that the crabs were suffering might increase one's care, but it is not necessary for a respect for life.

Bryan Norton was walking along a beach and met an eight year old girl collecting sand dollars.[12] Some yards away, her mother and older sister were dredging sand dollars in large numbers from a colony of them not far under the surface. Upon inquiry, the girl explained that her mother used them to make things, first bleaching them in Chlorox, and then forming them into jewelry and souvenirs, and that any extras could be sold for five cents each. "You know, they're alive," Norton remarked, wishing that the sand dollars could be left in the lagoon.

Norton thought how sand dollars (phylum *Echinodermata*, class *Echinoidea*) propel themselves just under the surface of the sand by means of hundreds of tiny sucker feet, how they filter sand for minute bacteria and diatoms, using a remarkable siphon, ingeniously adapted to intake diatoms and algae, and expel waste. The functions of respiration, locomotion, and metabolism are distributed equally among the five sections of the pentagonal organism. There is a decentralized nervous system that emanates from a major nerve circling the mouth. All these organs are encased in the calcareous skeleton, and the sand dollars have, as a result, successfully colonized the sea floor. But Norton couldn't explain this to the child, and he was puzzled about what else to say. Norton's concern is real; he needed an ethic of "respect for life," admiring the "struggle to survive" even in the sand dollars, and was unable to articulate it.[13] Sand dollars must be several ranks down under the shrimps and oysters, so Singer doesn't have anything else to say either. Sand dollars don't count, so exploit them as you please for crafts, or amusement, or whatever.

Such respect for life will seem foolish, or even wrong, to those who think that nothing matters to, or for, or with trees or wildflowers, crabs or sand dollars. If they are to save such things, they will have to find sentient persons or higher animals with interests at stake. Trees and forests have value if and only if their well-being can be related to the well-being of these privileged higher animals and people. People will wish, of course, to keep a sustainable population of sand dollars for the pleasures of future humans. That means keeping also a biotic community such as a marine ecosystem, but everything must be evaluated for the pleasures it brings to present and future generations of people.

We may know little about the conscious experiences of marine invertebrates, but at least on the land, we can consider also the experiences of the higher animals, especially the mammals. We will conserve wilderness, as well as beaches and marine ecosystems, for our vacations. But we also need to consider how wilderness is a home for the higher animals, and is to be conserved for the welfare of the bears and elk. We have to "take into account" their lives, "experiencing their own distinctive pleasures and pains." "When a proposed dam would flood a valley and kill thousands, perhaps millions, of sentient creatures, these deaths should be given great importance in any assessment of the benefits and costs of building the dam." But the trees there, and most of the animals, who are insentient in Singer's pain-suffering sense, are "to be taken into account only in so far as they adversely affect sentient creatures."[14] That seems rather narrow minded for a comprehensive ethic of respect for life.

Counting Species, Ecosystems, and Earth

We have only begun enlarging our environmental ethic, when we move to valuing non-sentient organisms. The organism is a member of a species. Biology often focuses on organismic individuals, and we can interpret these as owners or loci of value, but biology always locates these individuals within species (populations) and ecosystems. How are we to count species? We can count species as valuable, of course, for humanistic reasons, or, if the species in question is a sentient one, as an aggregate of the various individual members who suffer their pains and pleasures. But if our ethic permits us to find value only where there is an experiencing valuer, and if plants and the lower invertebrates cannot value their environment, *a fortiori*, we cannot find value at the level of species.

Consider some cases that confront the welfare of animals with the value of plant species. Off the coast of California and isolated from the mainland, San Clemente Island has a number of endemic plant species. In the early 1800s, Spanish sailors introduced goats so that they could have a supply of fresh meat. The goats thrived, even after humans abandoned them. Over many decades there, they have probably already eradicated several never-known species. Following renewed interest in endangered species after the passage of the US Endangered Species Act, the Fish and Wildlife Service and the US Navy, which controls the island, sought to kill thousands of these goats to save three endangered plant species: *Malacothamnus clementinus, Castilleja grisea, Delphinium kinkiense* (as well as to protect ecosystem integrity). Often the goats were in inaccessible canyons, which required their being shot by helicopter. That would kill several goats for each known surviving plant.

The Fund for Animals filed suit to prevent this killing; and, although the court ordered all goats removed, after the shooting of 600 goats, the Fund by political pressures on the Department of Navy secured a moratorium on further shooting. Happily, the Fund rescued about half the goats with novel trapping techniques. About 15,000 were live-trapped and removed. But, unhappily, neither they nor others were able to live-trap them all. Unhappily also, the transplanted goats did poorly; they mostly died within six months. Eventually, the rest of the goats were shot, in all about 14,000 of them.[15]

The court judged, rightly, that protecting endangered species justifies the killing of the goats, which are not endangered and which are replaceable, as well as exotic to the island. If the tradeoff were merely one on one, a goat versus a plant, we might well judge that the welfare of the goats would override the plants. The goats, though feral, do merit some consideration. Goats are among the most nimble and sure-footed creatures on Earth, which is why they were so hard to eradicate. But the picture is more complex. The well-being of plants at the species level outweighs the welfare of the goats at the individual level.

Singer, however, could voice no protection for the plants, as long as the goats took pleasure in eating them. In fact, had the Spanish sailors not long ago introduced this exotic goat, Singer might well urge the Fish and Wildlife Service now to do so, since in result there could be thousands of happy goats on an island which they were unable to reach on their own.

Whether the animals on the island are native or introduced is irrelevant to a sentience-based ethic, unless perhaps the introduced animals are upsetting the life support system of other, native sentient animals.

Despite the Fund's objections, the Park Service did kill hundreds of rabbits on Santa Barbara Island to protect a few plants of *Dudleya traskiae*, once thought extinct and curiously called the Santa Barbara Live-Forever. This island endemic was once common. But European red rabbits were introduced after 1900 (brought from New Zealand where they had earlier been introduced), fed on these plants, and by 1970 no *Dudleya* could be found. With the discovery in 1975 of five plants, a decision was made to eradicate the rabbits. Here it seems that protecting endangered species justifies causing suffering and death in the rabbits.

An ethic based on animal rights will come to one answer. Singer will defend the rabbits; the plants don't count, much less their species. Perhaps he even will defend the introduced rabbits that so proliferated in Australia – unless a calculus shows that sentient native marsupials suffered in ways that outweighed the rabbit pleasures. The loss of any species there will be irrelevant. But a more broadly based environmental ethic will prefer plant species, especially species in their ecosystems on Santa Barbara or the Australian landscapes, over sentient animals that are exotic misfits.

This ethic for species will need a justification in principle, and we can suggest how that might work. The species is a bigger event than the individual, regardless of whether the member individual has interests or sentience. Much of what we have said about individual organisms as non-moral normative systems can be resaid, *mutatis mutandis*, of species. The species line is the *vital* living system, the whole, of which individual organisms are the essential parts. Processes of value that we earlier located in an organic individual reappear at the specific level: defending a particular form of life, pursuing a pathway through the world, resisting death (extinction), regeneration maintaining a normative identity over time, creative resilience discovering survival skills. The species has a good-of-its-kind.[16] Situations can be better or worse for the species.

The analysis we were giving, of life defended by an organism using the vital know-how in its genes, can be extended to the species level. Indeed, going to the genetic level turns out to be at the same time going to the species level. Properly understood, the story coded at the microscopic genetic level reflects the story of an ongoing species coping at the ecosystem level, with the individual a macroscopic mid-level between. The genome (genotype) is a kind of map coding the species; the individual (phenotype) is an instance incarnating it. The genetic set is as evidently the property of the dynamic species line as of the individual through which it passes. It is as logical to say that the individual is the species's way of propagating itself as to say that the embryo or egg is the individual's way of propagating itself. The value resides in the dynamic form; the individual inherits this, exemplifies it, and passes it on. If, then, at the specific level these processes are just as evident, or even more so, what prevents value existing at that level? The appropriate survival unit is the ongoing line of life, in which individuals play their part.

Reproduction is typically assumed to be a need of individuals, but since any particular individual can flourish somatically without reproducing at all, indeed may be put through duress and risk or spend much energy reproducing, by another logic we can interpret reproduction as the species keeping up its own kind by re-enacting itself again and again, individual after individual. It stays in place by its replacements. In this sense a female grizzly does not bear cubs to be healthy herself, any more than a woman needs children to be healthy. Rather, her cubs are *Ursus arctos* recreating itself by continuous performance. The lineage in which an individual exists is something dynamically passing through it, as much as something it has. The locus of the intrinsic value – the value that is really defended over generations – seems as much in the form of life, the species, as in the individuals, since the individuals are genetically impelled to sacrifice themselves in the interests of reproducing their kind.

We said earlier that natural selection picks out whatever traits an organism has that are valuable to it, relative to its survival. This makes for intrinsically valuable organisms. If we ask about the character of this value, it is not the somatic survival of the organismic individual; rather it is the ability to reproduce the species line, or at least those alleles in the species line which the individual possesses and can transmit. That locates value-ability innate or intrinsic within the organism, but it just as much locates the value-ability as the capacity to re-produce a next generation, and a next generation positioned to produce a next generation after that. The value-ability is an ability to continue the historical species line.

Singer insists that all this defense and reproduction of species lines of flora and fauna is of no value except as a few higher animals who can suffer pains and pleasures are affected. Animals can suffer, but in species "there is no such feeling. In this respect ... species are more like rocks than they are like sentient beings." Extinctions are "to be taken into account only in so far as they adversely affect sentient creatures."[17] But species are not very much like rocks at all; Singer's sentience-based ethic leaves him quite indiscriminating about vital differences. Things matter for species, like they do for trees. Things matter for sentient species, above and beyond the welfare of individuals.

The golden trout, state fish of California, evolved in three California creeks, the South Fork of the Kern River, Golden Trout Creek, and the Little Kern River, and is restricted to three drainages. It is an attractive, "flashy" fish, and anglers highly prize catching it, although it is now threatened and the catch is quite limited. The brown trout was introduced into California in the late 1800s and is widespread throughout the state. It encroached on the golden trout, coming to outnumber it a hundred to one in the golden's own range.

Over the centuries, the golden may well prove a better adapted fit in this kind of habitat, if one considers the infrequent extremes of climate found in California, very cold winters, hot summers, droughts, fluctuations in water level, and so on. But this species was selected for competence in such a challenging physical environment, not for competition biologically against other more aggressive fish. Especially in the golden's reduced numbers, due to overfishing by early Californians, it could not outcompete the introduced newcomer in the short run.

The California Department of Fish and Game decided to eliminate the brown trout in golden trout habitat and for eighteen years (1966–84) waged a campaign to accomplish this.[18] Three downstream barriers were built and upstream golden trout were rescued while brown trout were poisoned by the tens of thousands. After the poison was neutralized, the golden trout were returned to the streams. About $300,000 was spent on this effort. The justification of this was partly aesthetic, partly quality fishing, partly respect for a state fish. It was also in considerable respect for an endangered species, historically evolved to fit a particular ecosystem, even though the introduced species was outcompeting it in its native ecosystem. The argument was that the one species belonged there as an adapted fit; the other was there by human help, repeatedly introducing the browns, and by human excess, overfishing the goldens. Human pleasures in recreational fishing did not outweigh the loss of the evolutionary achievement in the golden trout.

There would have been many more brown trout than golden had the introduced browns remained. If we simply aggregated individual fish lives with their sentient pains and pleasures, oblivious to differences of species, the larger population would be preferred. But the Californians did not count individual lives; they counted species, because respect for species makes a difference. Assuming that fish suffer when killed, they even judged that the killing of brown trout in order that golden trout may live is justified on a differential basis of a hundred to one, because they were counting evolutionary achievement and ecological competence, an event of brilliance in fish speciation in a unique habitat, not just the number of fish that might live in these waters with human interruption and disturbance.

Once again, Singer's ethic can make no judgments of this kind. He would have to inquire, perhaps, whether the delight of anglers catching some of these restored golden trout might outweigh the suffering of all the poisoned brown trout. If he is counting only the lives of fish individuals, perhaps the California Department of Fish and Game should rather have modified the stream habitat (perhaps by check dams regulating the stream flow to make it less fluctuating) to hasten the extinction of the golden and to allow even more numbers of the introduced browns. On the sentience criterion alone, he is incapable of distinguishing between a monoculture of brown trout and the remarkable biodiversity of fish species in the US West. He cannot count species directly at all.

Species are what they are where they are, in ecosystems. An enlarging environmental ethic will need a principle for valuing ecosystems. "A thing is right," concluded Aldo Leopold, "when it tends to preserve the integrity, stability, and beauty of the biotic community. It is wrong when it tends otherwise.[19] Leopold wanted a "land ethic," one that embraced concern for individual plants, animals, and persons but also and fundamentally loved and respected biotic communities. But Singer cannot be so fundamental. "A thing is right," he will have to say, "when it tends to maximize the pleasures and minimize the pains of sentient animals, including humans, in the biotic community."

Or for that matter, the animals involved could be happy in zoos, if their life support was as well assured there as in ecosystems, and if they had rich enough zoo environments not to be frustrated. Also, if and where we can, we might remove the predators in the wild biotic communities, allowing for more herbivores, since the predators cause pain and suffering, and the herbivores do not. This will maximize the pleasures and minimize the pains there, though of course we will have to manage so that the herbivores do not overpopulate and suffer in result.

For most animals, Singer will reply, a biotic community, ordinarily an ecosystem, is the necessary habitat for their well-being, but an ecosystem itself has no feelings, and so cannot count in itself. "There is nothing that corresponds to what it feels like to be an ecosystem."[20] Concern for ecosystems is secondary, instrumental to a respect for human and other sentient life. The basic problem for Singer, again, is that ecosystems have no subjectivity, no felt experiences. They do not and cannot care, unlike the higher animals within them that can and do care. Ecosystems have no "interests" about which they or we can care.

But that is to make a category mistake, trying to apply criteria of value that are appropriate to sentient animals to ecosystems, where the criteria of value need to be something else. We should locate what is of value in ecosystems differently, which will involve their capacity to generate and support species – all the biodiversity environmentalists wish to conserve. These environmentalists are satisfying their preferences in such conservation, to be sure; but what they desire to preserve are the selective and life-supporting forces in ecosystems that once generated and still maintain the lives of individual plants and animals, what Leopold calls "the land," or the "biotic community."

Evolutionary ecosystems over geological time have increased the numbers of species on Earth from zero to five million or more. Extinction and respeciation have differentiated myriad natural kinds. Organisms defend only their own selves or kinds, but the system has spun a bigger story. Organisms defend their continuing survival; ecosystems promote new arrivals. Species increase their kinds, but ecosystems have increased kinds, and increased the integration of kinds. The system is a kind of field with characteristics as vital for life as any property contained within particular organisms.

The claim that value enters the world only in the conscious experiences of the subjective lives of higher organisms has too much subjective bias. It values a late product of the system, psychological life, and subordinates everything else to this. At this scale of vision, if we ask what is principally to be valued, the value of life arising as a creative process on Earth seems a better description and a more comprehensive category. One can always hang on to the claim that value, like a tickle or remorse, must be felt to be there. Its *esse* is *percipi*. Non-sensed value is nonsense. There is subjective experience; there is objective vitality; but it is only beings with "insides" to them that have value. "Someone" must be there to count. We nowhere wish to deny that such experiencers and their experiences are of value, but we deny that this is the whole account of value in a more holistic, systemic, ecological, global account. There can be value wherever there is positive creativity; and, while such creativity can be present in subjects with their interests and preferences, it can also be present objectively in living organisms with their lives defended. It is also present in species that defend an identity over time, in biological systems that are self-organizing and that project storied achievements.

"Where do we locate value, if not in sentience?" asks Singer. Consider a final level at which environmental ethics must provide an answer. We find ourselves located on a valuable planet. Earth is really the relevant unit to be valued, the fundamental survival unit. That, Singer swiftly replies, is going to extremes, and makes my point. Earth is not "Gaia," as though it were some conscious being.[21] Earth is, after all, just earth. The belief that dirt could have intrinsic value is really the *reductio ad absurdum* of any environmental philosophy that tries to maintain that insentient things can have value. Dirt is instrumentally valuable, but not, Singer will say, the sort of thing that has value by itself. Put like that, we agree. An isolated clod defends no intrinsic value and it is difficult to say that it has much value in itself.

But that is not the end of the matter, because a clod of dirt is integrated into an ecosystem; earth is a part, Earth the whole. Dirt is product and process in a planetary systemic nature. We should try to get the global picture, and switch from a lump of dirt to the Earth system in which it has been created. On an everyday scale, earth, dirt, seems to be passive, inert, an unsuitable object of moral concern. But on a global scale? The values inherent in earth depend on the scale, on the circumstances; and we on Earth live in some rather special circumstances.

Earth is, Singer could insist, a big rockpile like the moon, only one on which the rocks are watered and illuminated in such way that they support life, including some sentient life. Earth is no doubt precious as a means of life support, but it is not precious in itself. There is no one there in a planet. There is not even the objective vitality of an organism, or the genetic transmission of a species line. Earth is not even an ecosystem, strictly speaking; it is a loose collection of myriads of ecosystems. So we must be talking loosely, perhaps poetically, or romantically of valuing Earth. Earth is a mere thing, a big thing, a special thing for those who happen to live on it, but still a thing, and not appropriate as an object of intrinsic or systemic valuation. It is really the sentient life that we value and not the Earth, except as instrumental to life. We do not have duties to rocks, air, ocean, dirt, or Earth; we have duties to people, or sentient things. We must not confuse duties to the home with duties to the inhabitants.

The trouble, though, is that this is not a systemic view of what is going on on the valuable Earth we now experience, before we experienced it. We need an account of the generation of value and valuers, not just some value that now is located in the psychology of the experiencers. Finding that value will generate an Earth ethics, with a global sense of obligation to this whole inhabited planet. The evolution of rocks into dirt and dirt into fauna and flora is one of the great surprises of natural history, one of the rarest events in the astronomical universe. Earth is all dirt; we humans too come from the humus; and we find revealed what dirt can do when it is self-organizing under suitable conditions.

In this bigger picture, it is not just plants that are self-organizing, but plants and all living things, sentient ones included, are products of a more comprehensive process of self-organizing, or spontaneously organizing, that characterizes the planet. This generativity is the most fundamental meaning of the term "nature," "to give birth." This self-organizing has been called "autopoiesis," and there are excellent scientific analyses of this spontaneous generation of complex, living order.[22] The planet as a self-organizing biosphere is the most valuable entity of all, because it is the entity able to produce all the Earthbound values.

At this scale of vision, if we ask what is principally to be valued, the value of life arising as a creative process on Earth seems a better description and a more comprehensive category than the pains and pleasures of a fractional percentage of its inhabitants. Nothing matters to Earth, perhaps, but this creativity on Earth is the fact of the matter – the process and its products, speciation and species – and is greatly to be valued. Such an Earth is not just valuable because we humans and some other sentient animals value it. Rather, we are able to value it, and they are able to value their lives on it, because Earth is valuable, able to produce value. The production of value over the millennia of natural history is what we should most respect, not just the satisfaction of some preferences in sentient lives. Earth is the source of value, and therefore value-able, able to produce value itself. That is much more adequate as an environmental ethic than just to count everything else as a resource for a privileged few conscious valuers.

In that sense, a valuable Earth is not the *reductio ad absurdum* of valuing dirt. What is more nearly absurd is to claim that "trees, ecosystems, and species are more like rocks than they are like sentient beings"[23] and then to form a myopic environmental ethics insisting that "there is nothing to be taken into account" in all this display of vitality in insentient life.

Notes

1 Peter Singer, *Animal Liberation*, 2nd edn (New York: New York Review Books, 1990), p. 8.
2 Bryan G. Norton, *Toward Unity among Environmentalists* (New York: Oxford University Press, 1991).
3 Peter Singer, *Practical Ethics*, 2nd edn (Cambridge: Cambridge University Press, 1993), p. 277.
4 Ibid., p. 279.
5 Singer, *Animal Liberation*, p. 9.
6 There is a discussion about "artificial life," as, for instance, in the journal *Artificial Life* (MIT Press). Some even claim that it already exists, in certain computer viruses, though most deny this. Were humans to create life, they would need an ethic respecting it.
7 For example, Francisco J. Ayala, *Population and Evolutionary Genetics: a Primer* (Menlo Park, CA: Benjamin/Cummings Publishing Co., 1982), p. 88; Robert H. Tamarin, *Principles of Genetics*, 5th edn (Dubuque, IA: William C. Brown Publishers, 1996), p. 558.
8 Evelyn Fox Keller, *A Feeling for the Organism: the Life and Work of Barbara McClintock* (New York: W. W. Freeman, 1983).
9 Ibid., p. 277.
10 M. F. Land, "Optics and vision in invertebrates," in Hansjochem Autrum (ed.), *Handbook of Sensory Physiology*, volume III/6B (Berlin: Springer-Verlag, 1981), pp. 471–592.

11 Singer, *Practical Ethics*, p. 277.

12 Bryan G. Norton, "Sand dollar psychology," *The Washington Post Magazine* (June 1, 1986), pp. 10–14.

13 Ibid., pp. 11, 13.

14 Singer, *Practical Ethics*, pp. 275–7.

15 Details from Jan Larsen and Clark Winchell, Natural Resources Managers, Naval Air Station, North Island, San Diego, California. See also *Federal Register*, 47 (February 3, 1982), p. 5033.

16 This claim is pressed by Lawrence Johnson as the "interests" of a species (*A Morally Deep World*, Cambridge: Cambridge University Press, 1991), and Singer rejects species "interests" (*Practical Ethics*, pp. 282–3). "Interests" may well be a term that has too many psychological associations to extend well to species. But "good" is not.

17 Singer, *Practical Ethics*, pp. 283–4, 275–6.

18 Details from Edwin P. Pister, California Department of Fish and Game, Bishop, California.

19 Aldo Leopold, *A Sand County Almanac* (New York: Oxford University Press, 1949, 1967), pp. 224–5; cf. Singer, *Practical Ethics*, p. 280.

20 Singer, *Practical Ethics*, p. 283.

21 Ibid., p. 283.

22 Humberto R. Maturana and Francisco J. Varela, *Autopoiesis and Cognition: the Realization of the Living* (Dordrecht/Boston: D. Reidel Publishing Co., 1980); John Tyler Bonner, *The Evolution of Complexity by Means of Natural Selection* (Princeton, NJ: Princeton University Press, 1988); Stuart A. Kauffman, *The Origins of Order: Self-organization and Selection in Evolution* (New York: Oxford University Press, 1993).

23 Singer, *Practical Ethics*, pp. 283–4.

13

A Response

PETER SINGER

To be the subject of so much attention is both a flattering and an intimidating prospect. I am grateful to all of my critics, and I hope they will forgive me if, in order to avoid not only tedious repetition, but also the delicate task of expressing my gratitude in due proportion to the perceived merits of each essay, I thank them all now, collectively, for their generous remarks about my work, and for their stimulating contributions to this book. I have learnt much from their essays: about the holes in my thought that still need to be filled, the tensions between different ideas that I have espoused, and, more frustratingly, about the apparent impossibility of my ever learning to write with sufficient precision to make my meaning clear to every reader.

Some of my critics are friends, while others I have met only briefly. I hope that my friends will not take it amiss if, for the sake of the greater good of advancing our understanding, I have rebutted their errors with no less severity than I have rebutted errors made by mere acquaintances. That kind of treatment is, after all, what friends have to expect from utilitarians.

Jackson

Frank Jackson begins his essay by quoting me on the need to show that ethical reasoning is possible. He says that I am a non-cognitivist in ethics, and outlines a problem for non-cognitivists about the validity of inferences in ethical argument. He then offers a neat solution to this problem, but it has a sting in its tail. Once non-cognitivists accept the proffered solution, Jackson suggests, they have come so close to descriptivism that they may as well swallow it all and forget about being non-cognitivists.

While I do incline towards the view of ethics developed by R. M. Hare, according to which ethical judgments belong to the same broad family as imperatives,[1] I am less firm in my non-cognitivism than Jackson suggests. This is, in part, because I cannot deny the plausibility of Henry Sidgwick's claim that it is a self-evident truth that from 'the point of view of the Universe', the good of one individual is of no greater significance than the good of any other.[2] In *The Expanding Circle* and *How Are We to Live?* I have tried to argue that this, or something like it, is a common element in many developed ethical traditions, and that it is something that we come to understand through our capacity to reason. (I shall say more about this when I consider Solomon's essay.) Thus I have come very close to saying that there is at least one important ethical judgment that is true, or can be known. To that extent, I would not want to call myself a non-cognitivist.

I could, no doubt, accept Sidgwick's axiom but refuse to use the term 'true' of ethical judgments. Then I could be classed as an objectivist non-cognitivist, like those Jackson mentions (p. 19), who hold that 'X is good' is 'a prescription whose rationality is *a priori* derivable'. Sigwick's axiom would then become an *a priori* rational prescription. But at this point the distinction between non-cognitivism and cognitivism becomes so fine that it is scarcely worth insisting upon. The name 'ethical non-cognitivism' suggests a position that denies that ethics is concerned with anything that can be *known*, or as it is often put, a position that denies that ethical judgments can be true or false. But are not *a priori* rational derivations things that can be known, and are not claims about them true or false? Hume, who is an honoured ancestor of the non-cognitivist tradition, allowed that truth consists not only in matters of fact but also in 'relations of ideas', and *a priori* rational derivations are 'relations of ideas'. Even in terms of the cluster of ways of expressing non-cognitivism that Jackson lists in the second paragraph of his essay, it is not clear that the objectivist can be a non-cognitivist. Would objectivist non-cognitivists say, for example, that ethical judgments are expressions of attitudes *rather than* beliefs? Might they not say that ethical judgments are both expressions of attitudes and expressions of the belief that a certain way of acting is *a priori* rational?

The objectivist who remains committed to being a non-cognitivist could still say: 'We can know that one ethical judgment is rational and that another is not, but since ethical judgments are prescriptions, and truth and falsity do not apply to prescriptions, we cannot, strictly speaking, know anything about the truth or falsity of ethical judgments.' To which I would respond: 'Maybe so, but who cares? From the perspective of anyone interested in the prospects for reasoning in ethics, what your position has in common with objectivism in ethics – including objectivist forms of cognitivism – is much more significant than what it has in common with other forms of non-cognitivism.'[3]

Nevertheless, since Jackson has raised the problem of how ethical reasoning is possible on a non-cognitivist account, let me for the moment accept the mantle of a defender of non-cognitivism. Can the view that ethical judgments are a kind of imperative – to be more precise, universal prescriptions – give a satisfactory account of the issues Jackson raises? Consider:

Frank: What shall I make for dinner?

Morag: Make either chicken or Szechuan eggplant with garlic sauce.

Frank: Have you forgotten that Peter is coming, and he's a vegetarian?

Morag: So don't make chicken.

Frank: Shall I make the eggplant, then?

Morag (her voice rising):   Look, I told you to make either chicken or eggplant, and then when you reminded me that Peter is coming, I told you not to make the chicken. Can't you work out for yourself what I am telling you to make?

Frank (coolly):   I'm sorry, dear, but I really can't. You have uttered only imperatives. Since imperatives are not truth-apt, no inferences can validly be drawn from them.

If that is not a credible domestic scene *chez* Jackson, then even logicians must be able to make inferences from imperatives.

Here is another example:

Doctor: Here's the prescription. Get it filled at the pharmacy on the way out. But if you have to drive within four hours, don't take these tablets.

Patient: I have to go home in an hour, and I can't get home tonight without driving.

Doctor: Have the prescription filled and take the tablets immediately.

The perplexed patient would probably ask further questions, like:

Perhaps you didn't hear what I said – I have to drive to get home, and I can't wait four hours before going.

or possibly:

Are you saying that it is so important for me to get started on the tablets immediately that this overrides your general advice on not taking the tablets before driving?

Both questions presuppose the validity of the general form of the hypothetical syllogism as applied to imperatives. The first assumes that the doctor is not aware of the minor premise, that the patient must drive soon. The second asks the doctor if he has misstated his major premise – if perhaps he holds it only in a more restricted version, such as 'In circumstances other than when it is very important for you to get started with this medication, if you have to drive within four hours, do not take these tablets.'

Note that denying that validity applies to imperatives does nothing to solve the patient's problem. If the patient is a logician who knowingly says to herself, 'Well, there is no contradiction here, since imperatives are not truth-apt', she will be none the wiser about when to take the tablets.

I offer these conversations to show that the difficulty with which Jackson is concerned is a technical difficulty for philosophers, not a practical problem that hinders our ability to draw the right inferences from imperatives. The technical difficulty arises because logicians standardly define an argument as valid if the premises cannot all be true without the conclusion also being true. Since imperatives are not the kinds of statement that we regard as true or false, this definition does not apply to the examples above. But that is a problem for the standard definition of validity, not for our sense that the arguments are valid. No doubt logicians will eventually learn to broaden their definition so that it encompasses such obvious examples of valid reasoning.

Jackson has shown one way of broadening the definition of validity, but the notion of validity* that he introduces in his essay is limited to ethical sentences, ordinary truth-valued sentences and mixtures of the two. This leaves the problem of validity for non-ethical imperatives untouched. Since ethical sentences are imperatives, and we have a sound intuitive notion of validity for imperatives in general, not just for imperatives that are also ethical sentences, that seems to me an uncomfortably *ad hoc* way of dealing with the issue.

It ought to be possible to recognize that arguments consisting of imperatives can be valid, while preserving the difference between indicatives and imperatives. My guess is that the solution to this broader problem will provide us with an account of validity in ethical inference that can continue to support a distinctively non-cognitivist view of the nature of ethics. But finding such a solution is a task I shall leave for others. The issues we have been discussing are not what I had in mind when I wrote the remarks about reasoning in ethics with which Jackson begins his chapter. I just took it for granted that the standard rules of inference work for ethical judgments as they do for statements of fact. I was more interested in how one could get argument going between people who differ about the ethics of such questions as abortion, our obligation to assist famine victims in other countries or our right to use non-human animals as means to our ends. The reasoning needed to resolve these debates goes beyond the formal argument patterns with which Jackson's essay is concerned. Michael Smith's contribution to this volume provides an opportunity to discuss some of these other issues.

Smith

In a 1973 article, I argued that the debates then dominating moral philosophy, over the possibility of deducing an 'ought' from an 'is', and over the proper way to define 'moral', were merely terminological, and hence trivial. Instead of wasting time in such debates, I suggested, we could simply stipulate what we mean by the moral terms, and then move on to consider more important issues. Smith now argues that these debates are not trivial, because they are really about whether there can be reasons for action that are not dependent on the desires of the person to whom they are addressed. This, he says, is a crucial issue for moral philosophy. On the importance of this issue, Smith and I are in complete agreement – indeed, to put it at centre stage in ethics was the whole point of my article. In summarizing what I wanted to say then, I wrote:

> I hope that it is now clear that the issue that really matters, that is of practical significance, is how statements of fact are connected with reasons for acting, and not how statements of fact are connected with moral judgments. The latter question is encompassed by the former. To hold, as the neutralist [one who is neutral about the form and content of moral judgments] does, that action follows from moral judgments but moral judgments do not follow from facts, is to place morality close to the 'action' side of the 'fact–action' or 'reason–action' gap, while to hold, as the descriptivist [one who holds that moral judgments must have a specific content] does, that moral judgments follow from facts but action does not follow from moral judgments, is to place morality on the opposite side. The dispute between the neutralist and the descriptivist, therefore, is a dispute about where, within a limited framework, morality shall be placed. Since nothing of any practical significance hangs on the placing of this term within this framework – the prospects for going from facts to action are the same in either case – the dispute is merely terminological.[4]

Smith says that I misconstrued the debates by assuming, incorrectly, that both sides agree that reasons for action are dependent on desires. Having shown that the debate over the gap between 'is' and 'ought' is not trivial, he then offers his own way of crossing that gap. My response will address both of these aspects of Smith's essay. First, have I misconstrued the debates? Second, does Smith solve the 'is–ought' problem?

To substantiate his claim that I have misconstrued the debates about which I was writing, Smith would have had to provide an account of the writings of the protagonists in the debates before 1973 when my article appeared. He provides no such account – in fact his essay has no references to any pre-1973 contributions to the debates. Instead he writes:

> those who deny that there is an 'is–ought' gap say that there are norms which require us to acquire certain desires (this is the 'ought' that figures in the conclusion) simply when we have certain beliefs (this is the 'is' that is admitted on both sides to figure as a premise). They therefore deny the 'No desire out without a desire in' principle. Rather, as they see things, certain beliefs suffice all by themselves to cause and rationalize desires in us. (p. 42)

The key articles in the debates about which I was writing do not support Smith's characterization of it. To illustrate, I shall take three of the most discussed articles denying that there is an 'is-ought' gap: G. E. M. Anscombe's 'Modern moral philosophy', Philippa Foot's 'Moral beliefs' and John Searle's 'How to derive "ought" from "is"'.[5]

Anscombe argues against a gap between 'is' and 'ought' by asserting that if I order potatoes from my grocer, and the grocer has delivered them and sends a bill, then I owe the grocer a certain sum of money. My non-payment of the bill, she tells us, justifies the description 'I am a bilker', and she suggests some association between bilking and injustice, although without spelling out what it is.[6] She does not discuss whether I have a reason to pay the grocer the sum in question, although she does say that we lack the sound philosophy of psychology that we would need to explain why an unjust man is a bad man. She gestures towards an Aristotelian view of the virtues, in which it could be shown that we need certain virtues to flourish, but she does not develop this thought. It appears to be an implication of these comments that moral judgments such as 'I have acted unjustly' can be deduced from facts about grocery deliveries, bills and the absence of payment, but that it would take a lot more work in philosophy of psychology to show that the belief that I have acted unjustly provides me with a reason against doing what I have done, or gives rise to any kind of desire in me to act differently. (If I say this 'appears to be an implication' of what Anscombe writes, it is because so much in the article is left undeveloped. Re-reading it made me appreciate the extent to which the standard of argumentation required for publication in a leading philosophical journal has improved over the past forty years.)

Philippa Foot begins by discussing pride, and suggests that there are limits to what it is intelligible to take pride in. She then argues that there can be action-guiding force in such terms as 'injury', so that an injury is necessarily something bad. Finally she tells us that the crucial question is 'Can we give anyone, strong or weak, a reason why he should be just?' This seems closer to Smith's view of what people on this side of the debate are really arguing. Yet Foot also says: 'In general, anyone is given a reason for acting when he is shown the way to something he wants; but for some wants the question "Why do you want that?" will make sense, and for others it will not.'[7] And she concludes her article by denying Thrasymachus's assumption that injustice is more profitable than justice. This suggests that it may only be possible to give anyone a reason for being just if it can be shown that justice is likely to be profitable for that person – and to say that justice is profitable for a person is not far from saying that it will bring the person what she desires. Thus it is hard to find anything in Foot's article that challenges the Humean view that all reasons for action are desire-dependent.

Searle argues that if one person utters the words 'I hereby promise to pay you $5', then, other things being equal, that person ought to pay the other $5. Neither Searle nor his many subsequent critics discuss either desires, or reasons for action. Searle does not argue, and hence his critics do not deny, that uttering the words 'I hereby promise to pay you $5' provides a *reason* for me to pay you $5. In these exchanges the link between 'ought' and 'reasons for action' that Smith sees as so central is simply not discussed.

Smith might claim that, at least in the case of Searle's argument, we can assume that if the argument were successful, it would show that certain beliefs can cause certain desires in us. For the beliefs about what was said would have caused the belief 'I ought to pay you $5' and this means that I have a reason to pay you $5 – my reason being that I ought to do so. But this second step does not follow, or at least not for someone who takes Hume's view that reasons for action must start from desires. I might well agree that morality requires that, other things being equal, I keep my promises, and that therefore, having promised to pay you $5, it is true that, morally speaking, I ought to pay you $5. But, while agreeing with all this, I can also say that I don't give a damn about morality, it is all a social conspiracy for suppressing spontaneous free spirits like myself, and so the fact that I ought, morally, to pay you $5 does no more to provide me with a reason for paying you $5 than the fact that etiquette requires me to hold my fork in my left hand gives me a reason to switch my cutlery around. As I have said, this is not an issue that Searle addresses. His goal is more narrowly linguistic: to show that an 'ought' can be derived from an 'is'.

So I do not think that I misconstrued the debates about which I was writing. Why does Smith assume that I did? Through his own book, *The Moral Problem*,[8] he has made a notable contribution to a more recent – and much more substantive – debate about how moral judgments can necessarily be motivating, yet can express beliefs. Smith sees that at the heart of this debate is the issue of whether all reasons for action are dependent on desires. I suspect that because Smith sees this so clearly, he cannot imagine that this issue was not somehow at the centre of the earlier debates about the gap between 'is' and 'ought' or the definition of morality. Others who look back on the debate of the 1950s and 1960s with the perspective of the 1990s are likely to make the same assumption. It is easy to forget the extent to which philosophy in that period focused on questions of language, such as the definitions of key terms and whether other terms could be derived from them – and avoided the substantive issues. That, of course, is why I wrote my essay contending that these debates are trivial. My – admittedly incomplete – re-reading of the relevant evidence confirms it is a mistake to attempt to read into them the issues that concern us today, and which are anything but trivial. Those debates really were trivial.

Now I move to the second issue raised by Smith's essay: his solution to the 'is–ought' problem. Smith argues (p. 47) that it is rational to do what we would desire to do, if we had a maximally informed and coherent and unified desire set. Since 'what we would desire to do, if we had a maximally informed and coherent and unified desire set', is a matter of fact, this means that a fact can give rise to a reason for action. This, if correct, is an important conclusion, overcoming Hume's objection to the derivation of 'ought' from 'is'. But it is not enough to get us to a moral 'ought', as Smith seems to realize. For he also says that facts about rightness and wrongness are analytically equivalent, *not* to what we would desire to do if we had a maximally informed and coherent and unified desire set, *but to a subset* of what we would desire to do in these circumstances:

> Specifically, they are those facts about what we would desire, where the contents of the desires in question satisfy certain loose constrains on form and content: they are desires that in some way or other concern human flourishing, impartially conceived; or they are desires which in some way or other express conceptions of equal concern and respect; or they are desires that satisfy whatever other constraints on form and content get us into the ballpark of the moral, as opposed to the non-moral. (Here I echo the views of Singer's descriptivists.) (Smith, p. 56)

The precise nature of the constraints that define the subset is not crucial to Smith's argument, or to my response, so I will simply assume for the sake of this discussion that the constraint is the first one Smith mentions, namely being concerned with human flourishing, impartially conceived. (Why 'human' alone, I might ask – but we are dealing with an illustrative constraint only here, and I am sure that Smith himself would not want to limit the concern to human flourishing, so I shall leave that issue for my response to Arneson and others.) The important point is that on Smith's view, the rational thing for me to do, and the right thing for me to do, can – and presumably often will – come apart. For many people, at least, what they would desire to do if they had a maximally informed and coherent and unified desire set would be different from what they would desire to do under the constraint of being concerned with human flourishing, impartially conceived. This means that Smith's way of closing the gap between 'is' and 'ought' does not solve the problem of linking reason and moral action, with which I was concerned in my 1973 article. Someone could still say: 'Yes, I know that if I had a maximally informed and coherent and unified desire set, then what I would desire, under the constraint of being concerned with human flourishing, impartially conceived, would be to give whatever I can spare to famine relief; but without that constraint, my overriding desire would be to own a Porsche. So why is it rational for me to give whatever I can spare to famine relief?'

Smith may believe that if we all had a maximally informed and coherent and unified set of desires, we would all have a strong concern for human flourishing, impartially conceived, and hence would desire only what was compatible with this concern. This may be part of Smith's puzzling 'convergence thesis'. When Smith writes about 'what it makes sense to do *period*' I am not sure that I understand him. Does he mean 'what it makes sense to do irrespective of my desires'? That sounds like Kant's notion of duty for duty's sake, of action motivated by respect for the moral law *itself*, untouched by any desires generated by our empirical selves. Hegel rightly criticized this as empty formula, an imperative without content that can generate no action at all.[9] Smith's reason for wanting to disregard our actual desires is this:

> Given that our actual desires are caused in us by potentially arbitrary and idiosyncratic processes of enculturation and socialization – socio-economic factors, the media, advertising and the like – it follows that our actual desires too are potentially arbitrary and idiosyncratic in corresponding ways. Our actual desires, taken together as a whole, are thus not guaranteed to be desires to do things that it makes any sense to do whatsoever. (Smith, p. 58)

On purely factual grounds, this is wrong or at best seriously incomplete. Many of our actual desires are caused by our biological nature as evolved social mammals. This includes not only our desires for food, for shelter and for sex, but also our desires for the welfare of our offspring, for companionship and to rise higher in status within our group. (To say that these desires are part of our biological nature is not to say that everyone has them to an equal extent, and nor of course is it to deny that they are affected by the processes Smith mentions.) Would Smith see our biologically based desires as also 'arbitrary' and therefore 'not guaranteed to be desires that it makes any sense to do whatsoever'? If so, then the notion of what it 'makes sense to do' has become so detached from our human nature that Hegel's criticism of Kant really does apply to Smith. On the other hand, if Smith cannot exclude our biologically based desires as arbitrary and hence 'not guaranteed to be desires to do things that it makes any sense to do whatsoever', then his convergence thesis is in trouble. In one passage, Smith refers to 'our semi-independent ideas about what it makes sense for people to do, period'. He then refers to a defeasible assumption that 'it will always make sense for people to desire certain things like pleasure, achievement and the company of their fellows'. (Smith, p. 60). By his reference to things that it makes sense for *people* to do, and his inclusion on his list of a desire for 'the company of our fellows', Smith seems to wish to include some desires that arise from our nature as social mammals. But then, of course, one could ask what basis he has for excluding, from the desires that we would have if we had a maximally informed and coherent and unified desire set, other desires arising from our nature as social mammals that are essentially competitive, such as the desire for higher status. Once such desires are included, however, the reasons Smith offers for his convergence thesis no longer justify the assumption that our maximally informed and coherent and unified desire set would include a concern for human flourishing strong enough to override such self-directed desires.

Thus Smith's ambitious proposal for dealing with 'the moral problem' does not solve the problem of the definition of 'moral'. Nor does it solve the 'is–ought' problem – or not for the moral 'ought'. We can, if we wish, simply define the moral 'ought' so that we can derive a moral judgment from knowledge of what a person would desire, under the constraint of being impartially concerned with human flourishing, if he or she had a maximally informed and coherent and unified desire set. But then one can still ask the question of what reasons one has for doing what one ought to do. This is a particularly awkward problem for Smith, because when he tries to answer this question, he is liable to find that his objection against those who think that reasons are dependent on desires can now be turned against his own position. Recall that Smith argued that unless there are reasons for action that are independent of desire:

there is evidently a considerable problem involved in securing the motivation of those who have desires which would not be satisfied by doing what
morality requires of them. In order to secure moral motivation we would
have to cause them to have a desire for some relevant end...At a certain
level of abstraction, then, the task of getting people morally motivated
would be no different to the task of getting them to buy this or that product
as the result of a cleverly devised and manipulative advertising campaign.
(pp. 43, 44)

We can now see that insofar as Smith is right about this, it applies to his
own position as well. For even if we accept Smith's argument that we have
reason to do what we would desire to do if we had a maximally informed
and coherent and unified desire set, he has not given us adequate grounds
for thinking that we have reason to act only on the subset of this desire set
that is constrained by an impartial concern for human flourishing. There
are only two possibilities. Either everyone who has a maximally informed
and coherent and unified set of desires will have an overriding impartial
concern for human flourishing, or they will not. If everyone who has a
maximally informed and coherent and unified set of desires will have an
overriding impartial concern for human flourishing, then Smith's view
will indeed provide us with a basis for a rational argument for moral
motivation. But in that case, even if reasons for action are dependent on
desires, it would still be true that we could persuade people to act morally
by ensuring that they are better informed, and drawing their attention to
the conflicts between various desires that they already have. The arguments I use in *How Are We to Live?* to defend the view that an ethical life
is likely to be a more satisfying one than a life devoted to earning more
money and consuming more goods could be seen as an attempt to inform
people about the consequences of different ways of living, and thus to
help them to arrive at a maximally informed, coherent and unified set of
desires.[10] This is hardly like 'a manipulative advertising campaign'.
Manipulative advertising campaigns use misinformation or highly selective partial information, and attempt to play up desires which are often at
odds with other, more significant desires.

Now consider the other alternative. Suppose that even if everyone had
a maximally informed and coherent and unified set of desires, some of
them would not have an impartial concern for human flourishing. Perhaps then it is true that the only way to motivate these people to act
morally is to use techniques that are in some sense manipulative. But now
this is also true for those who accept Smith's view of reasons for action
that are independent of desire. For the only kind of reason for action that
Smith has suggested may be independent of desire – the claim that it is
rational to do what we would desire to do if we were maximally informed,

and our desires were coherent and unified – is now, by hypothesis, power-less to assist in bringing about moral motivation.

Solomon

Robert Solomon's discussion of my views in *The Expanding Circle* makes an intriguing counterpoint to Smith's discussion. Whereas Smith sees me as assuming too restricted a role for reason in action, Solomon, from an entirely different perspective, takes me to task for over-emphasizing the role of reason in building on our natural impulses and expanding the circle of altruism. To some extent, this is because I developed my views in the eight years between writing 'The triviality of the debate over "is–ought" and the definition of "Moral"', with which Smith is primarily concerned, and *The Expanding Circle*, on which Solomon focuses. But looking back at the various places in which I have discussed the role of reason in ethics, I find that – as I suggested in commenting on Jackson's firm statement that I am a non-cognitivist – I persist in having two thoughts that are not easy to reconcile.[11] One is that reasons for action are dependent on desires, and the other is that reason can take us to a broader perspective from which the good of one being is no more significant than the similar good of another. The dependence of reason on desire is simply the Humean view, which has always seemed to me the natural and obvious position about reasons for action. To explain the other thought I shall describe, very briefly, what I was trying to do in *The Expanding Circle*.

The book has as its subtitle *Ethics and Sociobiology*, and part of its aim is to consider what evolutionary theory may be able to tell us about the origins of ethics. As many others have done, I find the origins of ethics in altruism towards kin and towards those with whom one is in mutually beneficial relationships. This exists in other social mammals, and can readily be explained by the mechanisms of natural selection. So, perhaps, can a limited amount of group altruism. Altruism towards strangers, however, is much more difficult to reconcile with our best current under-standing of the process of evolution. Why would it not have been selected against, and hence disappeared from the gene pool? Some socio-biologists overcome the problem by denying the very existence of altruism towards strangers. But the evidence that it does exist is too strong, so it needs to be explained. Following a suggestion from Colin McGinn,[12] I seek to explain it by linking it to our capacity to reason. Our reasoning capacity, which confers obvious evolutionary advantages, also brought with it the capacity for what psychologists call 'cognitive dissonance' – a sense that something in our belief system does not quite fit.[13] I suggest that if, within our own tribe or society, we develop standards of impartial decision-making to resolve conflicts, and come to use such standards in order to justify our conduct to other members of our own group, then this process may develop a logic of its own. We may find it hard to avoid the conclusion that others outside our society are so similar to us, in relevant respects, that we should extend some form of ethical protection to them too. As reasoning beings we can *understand* that – for example – other human beings suffer as we do when they are without food or shelter. We can see that there is something odd about being concerned to give food and shelter to members of our own group and refusing them to others who suffer in the same way. This is especially likely to give rise to cognitive dissonance if our group is large enough to include members whom we do not know, or have had nothing to do with, while the outsiders are not in any way a threat to us. Thus we may be led by reason to extend to outsiders the altruism we already feel towards family and friends. Since this tendency could not be selected against without diminishing our highly advantageous capacity to reason, it has persisted.

Solomon would like me to place less emphasis on reason and more on feelings such as compassion. He doesn't like ethical theory much at all, and is even doubtful if I am, in practice a '*bona fide* utilitarian'. He seems to be saying that I am really a nicer person than you would think, if you believe what I write about ethical theory. Pleasing as it is to be thought a nice person, I don't think that being a *bona fide* utilitarian is at all incompatible with that description. Why does Solomon think that it is? Here is one passage that suggests the reason, and also allows us to see where Solomon has gone astray:

> The compassionate Peter Singer is often at odds with the utilitarian Peter Singer (which is not to say, however, that compassion and utilitarianism are incompatible). The utilitarian Peter Singer, following David Hume, observes that compassion (or what Hume called 'sympathy') quickly diminishes with 'distance' so that one should not expect to be moved by a stranger as one is moved by one's kin. (Nor will one be so moved by a warthog or a cow as he or she will be by another human being, a child, especially one's own child.) The utilitarian Peter Singer will not succumb to innocent mawkishness. He defends his 'humanitarian' vision, not in terms of compassion or sympathy but as 'altruism', that vacuous coinage of suspicious ethicists and sociobiologists referring to 'other-directed' behavior. We have a 'natural' response to our own kin, Singer allows, but that diminishes exponentially (inverse square) with genetic distance. What must take its place, if we are not to be purely selfish, is reason. But it is the compassionate Peter Singer who pushes us beyond this way of thinking. (Solomon, p. 67)

In this passage Solomon muddles my normative and descriptive views about ethics. It is not 'the utilitarian Peter Singer' who observes that compassion diminishes with distance, but the would-be social scientist Peter Singer. Utilitarianism is a normative position, and the statement that compassion diminishes with distance is a description of the human psyche, its truth or falsity equally accessible to utilitarians and Kantians. Similarly, my claims about altruism in *The Expanding Circle* are not part of anything as grand as my 'humanitarian vision'. They are my attempts to understand how ethics evolved. I use the term 'altruism' rather than 'compassion' or 'sympathy' to describe certain aspects of the behaviour of humans and other animals, because these are the terms used by those who apply evolutionary theory to the social behaviour of animals, including humans. In this context their meaning is clear enough.

In the last two sentences of the paragraph quoted above, Solomon's language switches to what appear to be normative claims: he writes about what (presumably, in my view) 'must' take the place of our 'natural' responses, and he refers to a Peter Singer who 'pushes us' onwards. But my suggestion that it is reason that has taken us beyond the 'natural' responses is a hypothesis about what has happened in the course of our evolutionary history. It says nothing about what should happen. If in seeking to understand the origins of ethics, I come to believe that reason has played a role in expanding the circle of our ethical concern, this is a distinct activity from what I am doing when I, as a compassionate person, or as a utilitarian, or as both, urge that we share our wealth with other humans who are genetically distant from us. I could hold that our capacity to reason has been the driving force in expanding the circle of our ethical concern, but take no stance on whether this circle should continue to expand. Or I could urge that we should do more to share our wealth, while having no thoughts about the role of reason in expanding the circle of ethics to its present point. (The latter was my position when I wrote 'Famine, affluence and morality'.)

Solomon disagrees with my view that reason has played a role in expanding the circle of our ethical concern. But his failure to keep apart the descriptive and normative aspects of my views means that some of his objections fail to meet their mark. For example, he says that he wants to be 'very cautious about joining Peter Singer in the invocation of reason as the means of building on our natural impulses', and gives as his reason the danger that reason may instead undermine those impulses. But an explanatory hypothesis should be judged by whether it gives the best explanation of the phenomena it seeks to explain, not by whether there are dangers lurking if we accept it. (A physicist who in the 1920s rejected Einstein's formula $E = MC^2$ because of the danger that it could lead to development of nuclear weapons would have been far-sighted about these dangers, but a poor physicist none the less.)

The most convincing ground for rejecting an explanatory hypothesis is to offer a better explanation of the phenomenon in question. I have already indicated that the suggestion that altruism towards strangers is tied to our capacity to reason makes it possible to explain why it has not been selected against. If Solomon prefers the view that our general sense of compassion, or sympathy, lies behind our capacity to make sacrifices for strangers, he needs to explain why this broad compassion or sympathy has not been selected against. This he has not done.

If we switch from the explanatory question of how ethics developed, to the normative question of what kind of ethics we should seek to encourage, then Solomon's concerns about the dangers of reliance on reason do become relevant. He is concerned about the abuse of utilitarianism. So am I. Terrible crimes have been committed in the name of the happiness of future generations. But I do not think that reliance on feelings or emotion is the way to overcome it. There can be abuse of that too. The Nazi leader Hermann Goering said: 'I think with my blood.' Feelings of racial hostility run particularly deep. Sometimes they can be overcome by compassion or sympathy, and sometimes they can be overcome by reason telling us that a difference in race does not justify giving people less consideration. At other times, tragically, neither of these will be of any use.

Solomon refers to my *Animal Liberation*, and suggests that the emotional impact of the photographs included in that book had more impact than the 'ethereally controversial utilitarian attack on "speciesism" that accompanied them'. But the text of *Animal Liberation* is not utilitarian. It was specifically intended to appeal to readers who were concerned about equality, or justice, or fairness, irrespective of the precise nature of their commitment. (Nor, for that matter, do I think there is anything in the least ethereal about it.) Significantly, the book succeeded in persuading thousands of people to change their diet and become involved in the animal movement. Earlier publications by animal campaigners, with photographs at least as disturbing as those in *Animal Liberation*, but texts that were lacking in philosophical argument and in any understanding of the nature of speciesism, did not. In fact, the crucial role that philosophers – not only myself, but also Tom Regan, Bernie Rollin, Stephen Clark, Steve Sapontzis, Evelyn Pluhar, George Cave, James Rachels, Mary Midgley, and many others – played in the rise of the modern animal movement is a telling counter-example to Solomon's thesis that it is emotional appeal, rather than reasoning or ethical theory, that brings good results. Of course, our emotions are important, and it is true in the animal movement as elsewhere that nothing great would have been achieved without passion. But our emotions must be channelled by careful thinking so that they run in the right direction. (In the anti-vivisection movement, it is relatively easy to arouse people to outrage about experiments on dogs and cats. Far more painful and more trivial experiments on pigs or rats evoke much less opposition.)

Before ending my discussion of Solomon's essay, I need to return to the question I raised earlier. Can I continue to hold, with Hume, that reasons for action always depend on desires, and at the same time suggest that reason has played a role in expanding the circle of ethics, or, more specifically, that the recognition that another being suffers as we do constitutes a reason for taking into account the suffering of that being – and even, perhaps, for giving it equal consideration with the like suffering of any other being?

Here is a possible answer. Cognitive dissonance is a feeling that is itself based on our capacity to reason. In evolutionary terms such a feeling would normally bring us advantages, as that capacity itself does. It would motivate us to sort out inconsistencies in our belief system and so save us from acting on the basis of false beliefs. How might this work in ethics? Suppose that I am a member of an ethnic group we will call Betas. Betas are a minority within my country, and it is the custom that at harvest time the dominant Alphas come and take half of our crop. Although we Betas don't like this, we are powerless to stop it. But in our village there is an even smaller minority, the Gammas, and at harvest time we Betas take half of their crop. They don't like this, but they are powerless to stop it.

We could all just accept this situation as showing that we are living in a 'dog eats dog' world. Then there would be no cognitive dissonance. But suppose that our society has rules of law, and develops principles of fairness and justice. We might then use these principles of fairness and justice to argue that the Alphas should not take half of our crop. We could argue that although the custom is an old one, that does not justify it. We might say that we have no more land than the Alphas do and we have to work just as hard as them to grow our crops and feed ourselves. Assume that eventually the Alphas accept our argument, and the custom comes to an end.

Now the Gammas come to us, and make the same arguments. We like having half of the Gammas' harvest, and we don't care for the interests of Gammas. Are we being inconsistent or irrational, if we reject the Gammas' case? Not necessarily. We might be acting on the principle: 'Do whatever is best for Betas'. Call this the Beta principle. That principle would lead us to do whatever would persuade the Alphas to stop taking half our harvest, and if appealing to universal principles of justice is the way to do that, then the Beta principle would direct us to do that. It would also lead us to reject the Gamma claim. Even in so blatant a case, then, there need be no inconsistency or irrationality. But there must be, at least, dishonesty. The Alphas, after all, would not have been persuaded by an open espousal of the Beta principle, since it has no greater merits than a corresponding Alpha principle, which would have led them to reject our arguments against a custom that served Alphas well. So in arguing against the custom to the Alphas, we had to pretend to hold more universal principles, which we now reject when dealing with the Gammas. It is plausible to suppose that we would feel the force of the principles of universal justice that we argued to the Alphas, and experience at least some discomfort in the knowledge that we are denying. Hence the likelihood of cognitive dissonance.[14]

This conclusion supports the claim made by Leon Festinger, who did much to develop the theory of cognitive dissonance:

> In short, I am proposing that dissonance, that is, the existence of nonfitting relations among cognitions, is a motivating factor in its own right... Cognitive dissonance can be seen as an antecedent condition which leads to activity oriented toward dissonance reduction just as hunger leads to activity oriented toward hunger reduction.[15]

Dissonance is therefore a feeling that is generated by our capacity to reason – neatly reversing Hume's insistence that reason is always 'the slave of the passions'. To my embarrassment, I find myself not far from what I have long thought to be one of Kant's most baffling ideas: that pure reason, in the form of the moral law, gives rise to a necessary feeling of respect or reverence. To Kantians struggling to understand just how we can have *a priori* knowledge of the existence of feelings, I offer the concept of cognitive dissonance. It may not be quite what Kant had in mind when he wrote 'respect for the law is thus by virtue of its intellectual cause a positive feeling that can be known *a priori*',[16] but at least it makes sense.

The acceptance of cognitive dissonance as a motivating force opens a door through which reason can make further inroads into ethics. The Sidgwickian axiom I mentioned earlier – the idea that from the point of view of the universe, my own good is of no greater significance than the like good of any other being – is also something that as a rational being I can come to understand. While it remains true, as Sidgwick himself said, that it is also rational for me to be concerned about the quality of my own existence in a way that I am not concerned about the quality of the existence of other individuals,[17] this very concern may set up another situation for dissonance. I may care much more for my own comfort than I care for the very survival of a person in Rwanda, yet I am aware that in doing so I am going against a broader point of view that I would want others to adopt, if they were able to save my life by sacrificing some slight comfort of their own. This too may lead to dissonance. Again, this seems close to something that Kant says when he describes the man for whom things are going well, who refuses to help others in need, but who, Kant claims, cannot will that this should be a universal law of nature, because that would rob him of all hope of assistance if he were himself to be in need.[18] There are echoes, too, of Hare's concept of universalizability, with the difference that since universalizability is a requirement of moral judgments, I can avoid violating it by refusing to make any moral judgments. Cognitive dissonance, on the other hand, is a property of my thoughts or beliefs, taken as a whole, and there are some thoughts or beliefs that I may not be able to help having. Finally, Smith's maximally informed, coherent and unified set of desires gains part of its attraction as an ideally rational way to be, because it avoids cognitive dissonance. Cognitive dissonance does not bring with it, however, any notion of 'what it makes sense to do, period'.

Unfortunately, as Festinger points out, there are many ways of reducing cognitive dissonance, not all of them equally satisfactory from a moral point of view. Turning one's attention away from the area in which the dissonance occurs is one; inventing implausible beliefs to overcome the dissonance is another. The Betas, for example, might believe that the Creator gave them dominion over all the other peoples, which entitles them to exploit and deceive them in order to reclaim their rightful inheritance. Even when cognitive dissonance persists, it may be relatively weak, and we may prefer to live with a certain amount of dissonance, rather than suffer other losses. But to accept the existence of even a weak motivating force that is based on reason rather than feeling is significant. It means that we have to reject the pure Humean line on reasons for action; and it opens up the prospect of an objectivist ethic. Nevertheless I put all this forward very tentatively. As a critic of numerous other arguments for providing ethics with a rational basis, I know how easy it is to deceive oneself into believing that one has found the holy grail of ethics – even if, in this case, the holy grail turns out to be a battered and leaky mug.

Crisp

It would have been immodest of me to compare myself with so fine a philosopher, writer and campaigner for progressive causes as John Stuart Mill; but since Crisp has generously done it for me, I have noticed further parallels. Mill and I have both written books demanding equality for an oppressed group: Mill's *The Subjection of Women* and my *Animal Liberation*. Both of our books have had some success in inspiring popular movements seeking to put our philosophical arguments into practical effect. Mill's goals in respect of the status of women have come much closer to being achieved than mine regarding animals, but I can only hope that when 130 years have elapsed since the publication of *Animal Libera-tion*, the status of animals will have made similar advances. Another parallel between us is that we have both tried to take our ideas directly into our country's legislatures: like Mill, I have stood for election to Parliament. (For the Australian Greens, in the 1996 Australian federal election.) This, however, is another instance in which my achievements fall short of Mill's; I was not elected.

I turn now to the points that Crisp makes about my views, leaving his insights about Mill for others to discuss.

An objective or subjective view of welfare?

Crisp finds a dissonance between my preference-based theory of value, which I defend most fully in *Practical Ethics*, and what I have written in *How Are We to Live?* about giving life a meaning by working for a cause broader than one's own happiness. But a cause broader than one's own happiness does not have to be based on values that are independent of the preferences of sentient beings. It can be found in enabling others to satisfy more of their preferences: for example, in avoiding suffering.

Crisp anticipates this response, and questions whether taking an inter-subjective standpoint can be enough to explain meaningfulness. If it would be meaningless for Sisyphus to roll a stone endlessly up a hill, even if that was what Sisyphus preferred to do, then how, Crisp asks, could Sisyphus find meaning in dedicating himself to satisfying impar-tially the preferences of other stone-rollers? The answer is, roughly, that Sisyphus's ultimate preferences are his own choice. At the end of his days, he must look back and reflect on why he dedicated himself to rolling a stone endlessly up a hill, only to see it go rolling down to the bottom again. In the Greek myth he had no other options, but Crisp has departed from the original story, so that answer will not do. Nor can Sisyphus simply say that he dedicated his life to rolling a stone endlessly up a hill 'to satisfy my preference for doing so'. To answer in that way would be to treat himself as the victim of an impulse over which he had no control. We have to assume that he had a choice, since otherwise there is no point in discussing whether to roll the stone up the hill or leave the stone at the bottom and do something else. On the other hand, the preferences of others are to some degree a given, an objective aspect of the world that Sisyphus cannot alter. This answer assumes, of course, that Sisyphus cannot persuade the other stone-rollers to adopt a different set of prefer-ences that they can fulfil without his help, or that would have more useful outcomes.

It is because the preference for rolling a stone up a hill (knowing that just before it reaches the top it will roll all the way down again) is so odd that it seems absurd to say that anyone could find meaning in helping people to fulfil this preference. It is much easier to imagine finding meaning in helping people to meet strong preferences that we know they cannot avoid having – like the preferences for enough to eat, for shelter from the elements, for health care and so on. But if we imagine that people do have this preference, and find the inability to fulfil it as frustrating as we would find, say, being constantly hungry, then it is not too hard to see why we could find meaning in helping people to satisfy their preferences for rolling stones up hills.

A clue to the nature of the disagreement between Crisp and myself on this point can be found in his rejection of what I say about the possibility of finding meaning and fulfilment in commitment to an evil cause. I listed a wide variety of causes 'larger than the self' which can make one's life meaningful: working against injustice and exploitation, supporting a football club, working for a corporation, belonging to a religious cult, or to a Mafia 'family', or to the Nazi Party. Then I wrote: 'No doubt a commitment to each of these causes can be, for some people, a way of finding meaning and fulfilment.'[19] Crisp denies that committing oneself to a worthless activity, like the Nazi Party, can make one's life meaningful. But my remark was not intended to be a value judgment. I was simply reporting what seemed to me to be a fact about human psychology – what it is that makes people *feel* that their lives are meaningful. Earlier in *How Are We to Live?* I had referred to Leni Riefenstahl's film of the 1934 Nuremberg Nazi Party rally. Anyone who has seen that film will remember the shining eyes of the rank-and-file Nazi faithful as, amidst stirring music and flying flags, they shout out their commitment to the German *Volk* and its *Führer*. I find it impossible to doubt that for the people taking part on that day, membership of the Nazi Party was bringing meaning and fulfilment to their lives. Later they may have been regretted their devotion to the party – I certainly hope so, anyway. But in those triumphal days for Nazism, many could surely have said, truthfully, that their membership of the Nazi Party had given meaning and fulfilment to their lives. And for those who died in 1935, or 1938, or perhaps even 1941, there may have been no disillusionment.

Crisp's comment shows that he has taken my discussion of what gives meaning to a life as something other than a discussion of human psychology. Understanding the limits of my comments about the meaning of life should help to dispel the idea that there is any dissonance between my theory of value and my comments about how people can find meaning in their lives. It also means, of course, that there is no prospect of my taking up Crisp's suggestion that I develop an account of welfare in terms of meaningfulness rather than preference satisfaction.

Self-interest, reason, utilitarianism and the ethical life

What happens when self-interest and morality conflict? Crisp thinks that my desire-based account of reason is in trouble, because 'Singer needs to be able to tell egoists... that they are making a mistake. Without that, from the philosophical point of view, he is giving us no reason to change our lives' (p. 90). But here I part company with Mill, and agree with Sidgwick's observation, quoted above, that it is rational for me to be concerned about the quality of my own existence in a way that I am not concerned about the quality of the existence of other individuals. Ethics may demand something different. To say this is not to say that ethics is *ir*rational, because there can be more than one rational course of conduct open to us. But for the reasons I have already indicated in my replies to Smith and Solomon, I deny that the egoist who rejects ethics must be making a mistake. Or if he is making a mistake, it may only be that he has misconceived his own interests, taking too narrow a view of what is involved in living a fulfilling life – a topic on which I shall say a little more shortly.

At this point Crisp raises the separateness of persons, which Rawls famously accused utilitarians of overlooking. Let me say, in passing, that Rawls's objection is misconceived, because utilitarians do not overlook the separateness of persons. Instead they wish to maximize the total sum of happiness, or welfare, or preference satisfaction, spread across all the separate persons affected by our choices, and they reject the idea that the separateness of persons should prevent us maximizing utility by harming one person in order to benefit others. (They reject this idea, I should add, at the ultimate level of ethical theory; for well known practical reasons, at the level of political constitutions, they may well support declarations of rights or other constraints on harming one to benefit others.)

I am digressing, however, and should return to Crisp's introduction of the separateness of persons. The debate over the separateness of persons is a debate within ethics, and I sense some confusion in its introduction into the topic of the choice between self-interest and utilitarianism, which as I conceive it is a choice about whether to embrace ethics at all. Nevertheless, since Crisp puts the frequently made suggestion that pure utilitarianism ought to be modified by some principle of fairness that requires us to give more weight to the interests of those who would otherwise be worse off, I shall say that in my view no such extra weighting is necessary. Utilitarianism is fair because it gives the same weight to the same interests, no matter whose interests they may be. If I had to choose the fundamental ethical principles to govern a society, without knowing what position I would occupy in that society, I would choose the principle of utility, because that would maximize my expected welfare. In making this choice, I would know that when it comes to justice in distribution, utilitarianism will in practice lead to a strongly egalitarian outcome because of the principle of marginal utility. This is not a separate moral principle, but an important psychological generalization, which states that the more one has, the less utility one gets by being given even more. In other words, giving $1000 to a millionaire does less to increase her utility than giving the same amount to someone living in poverty. In general, we can do more good by paying attention to the needs of those who are worst off than we can by trying to make contented people even happier.

If egoists are not making a mistake in preferring the life of self-interest to the ethical life, is it possible that a better understanding of their own interests would lead them in that direction? In the last chapter of *Practical Ethics* I briefly asked whether self-interest can provide a motivation for acting ethically, and this question is a central theme of *How Are We to Live?* As mentioned above, my answer relies on the idea that we seek meaning in our lives, and claims that this cannot be found by focusing only on self-centred concerns. Crisp finds two problems in answers of this kind. He does not think that utilitarians should allow independent weight to the rationality of self-interest, since this will give non-utilitarians a justification for deviating from the requirements of impartiality. But here a confusion is again evident between debates within ethics, and debates about ethics. Utilitarians agree that in making an ethical judgment, one's own interests count for no more than the interests of others; but they hold a wide variety of views about the rationality of acting ethically as compared to acting self-interestedly, or in any other way. Their views on this topic do not affect their commitment to utilitarianism as an ethical theory.

Crisp's second problem is summed up in his comment that while the arguments that Mill and I put about ethics ultimately being in accord with enlightened self-interest have their roots in ancient ethics, it is much more difficult to use them to justify an extremely demanding ethic such as act utilitarianism than to justify 'the more modest virtue ethics of ancient times'. This is true, and ultimately I have no fully adequate answer to it. Crisp suggests developing an account of the meaningfulness of a life that makes it proportionate to the amount of good done, thus making it easier for Rich Richard to live a meaningful life than it is for Poor Paul. Again, though, this suggestion assumes that I am putting forward a normative account of what makes a life meaningful. Since I see this as a factual matter, it is not up to me to declare Rich Richard's life more meaningful than Poor Paul's. Psychologically, as Crisp himself suggests, this is 'hard to accept', because Richard's donation to Oxfam, large as it may be, is such a small part of his life, compared to Paul's dedicated work for those worse off than himself. So Richard still has to ask himself whether he has used his life as a whole, and his vast wealth, for a purpose that he finds meaningful. If he spent his time and money touring the casinos of the world, lying on the beaches of exclusive tropical island resorts, or adding to his fleet of Rolls-Royces, he may eventually decide that he has not used his life meaningfully.

I will postpone discussion of what kind of answer I can give to this problem until my response to Kamm, who raises the same issue.

Ethics without mystery

Crisp is right to see me as 'soundly within' the empiricist tradition of which Mill is a leading member. But in his remarks about our tendency to 'instrumentalize' morality he has, like Solomon, failed to keep distinct passages in which we describe and seek to explain morality as a social practice, and passages in which we justify ethical views. Morality just *is* a social practice, and it is interesting to ask how it has evolved, what social purposes it serves and how these purposes have influenced the form it takes. This is an investigation in anthropology or evolutionary theory, not a normative inquiry, and hence it cannot lead to any conclusions about what we ought to do. An ethical naturalist might think that it could, but as we have already seen (and despite what Crisp suggests on p. 97–8), I am not a naturalist.[20]

In what sense, then, can I defend the claim I made in the 1994 interview from which Crisp quotes, that utilitarianism is based on something more concrete, and less mysterious, than many of its rival theories in ethics? Crisp objects: 'Let us accept that pains, pleasures and desires are salient and undeniable features of our conscious experiences. Nothing follows from this.' (p. 96). Nothing does follow from it, in the sense of deducing utilitarianism or any other moral judgments from this fact about the world. Nevertheless, a point that I made in the first chapter of *Practical Ethics* still seems right to me. We are all concerned about our own pains, pleasures and desires. When we begin to think ethically, we must universalize, and this means taking into consideration the pains, pleasures and desires of others affected by our decision. Suppose that Helen is a doctor, and one of her patients, who is terminally ill, has repeatedly asked her to end his life. After taking into account all the 'pains, pleasures and desires' of her patient and everyone else affected by her decision, she concludes that she ought to do as her patient asks. She mentions this to some non-utilitarian colleagues. One says: 'No, you mustn't do that. You're forgetting that all human beings have a natural and inalienable right to life.' Another says: 'I don't think you ought to help your friend

SINGER

either, because my moral intuition tells me that it is always wrong to kill an innocent human being.' A third tells her that to do as her patient asks would be a violation of the intrinsic dignity that all human beings possess, and a fourth pronounces it contrary to God's will. In sharp contrast to the utilitarian approach to this problem, these non-utilitarian responses refer to ideas of natural rights, intuitively known absolute rules, intrinsic dignity, and the will of a divine being, all of which are anything but 'salient and undeniable features of our conscious experience'. There is need for argument to establish the existence of each of them. While I do not rule out the possibility of such arguments being successful, the difficulties that they face are sufficient justification of my claim that utilitarianism takes a more concrete and less mysterious approach to ethics than its rivals.[21]

Levels of moral discourse

I agree with Sidgwick, and with Crisp, that there may be good utilitarian reasons – chiefly the danger of misuse – for not advocating utilitarianism in particular times and places. But this has generally not been the reason why I have, on several occasions, chosen not to argue from an explicitly utilitarian base. *How Are We to Live?* makes no explicit mention of utilitarianism because its focus is on a question about ethics in general, rather than about utilitarianism in particular. In *Animal Liberation* and 'Famine, affluence, and morality', I wanted to appeal to the widest possible audience, and so I sought to construct arguments based on considerations that most people would accept. In *The Great Ape Project*, Paola Cavalieri and I wrote 'A declaration on great apes' in the language of rights, because we were launching a political project that consciously seeks to parallel movements for the rights of various groups of human beings. The language of rights is part of modern political rhetoric to such an extent that it would have been strange to state our goals in any other language. There is, in any case, as already mentioned, no difficulty in providing a utilitarian justification for a doctrine of rights in the political arena.

Crisp concludes his essay with a comment on the opposition I have encountered in Germany to my views on euthanasia and related issues in bioethics. He seems to think that my 'readiness to confront' this opposition may not have been justified, in utilitarian terms, because it has led anti-Nazis misguidedly to direct their attacks against me, instead of against the growing German neo-Nazi movement. While Crisp makes it clear that he mentions this only as a suggestion to illustrate a more general point, his illustration does not support the point he wants to make. In Germany over the past nine years I have probably spoken publicly, or attempted to speak publicly, on a total of no more than ten days – hardly a major distraction for Germans keen to oppose the neo-Nazis who are active in their own country all year round. In any case, there are better ways of showing one's opposition to fascism than shouting down someone who is trying to give a talk. I like to think that the author of *On Liberty* would have supported my refusal to allow an easy victory to those who seek to suppress freedom of thought and expression.

Arneson

Those who have prevented me speaking in Germany have generally denounced me by presenting a travesty of my views, based sometimes on quotations taken out of context, and at other times on false citations that I have never said at all. To the extent that the attacks focus on anything at all that is really to be found in my writings, however, it is to be found in the line of argument that Arneson discusses. As he remarks in his opening paragraph, that argument forces us to rethink the basis and nature of the moral equality of all humans. In most of the world, this seems a reasonable philosophical enterprise. In Germany, however, there are some for whom any questioning of the equal moral status of all human beings can only be an attempt to go down a path that their country has trodden once before: the path to regarding some humans as *Untermenschen* and therefore available to be exploited or killed. In the light of Germany's past, the desire to keep the gate to this path firmly shut is obviously laudable, and hypersensitivity to anything that looks even a little like an attempt to re-open it is understandable. So would it not be more prudent to avoid raising these questions? Perhaps Crisp would have been on firmer ground if he had selected, as his example of my failure to act as a utilitarian should, my readiness, not just in Germany, but anywhere at all, to raise questions that have any probability at all – even an extremely low one – of leading to a repetition of so immense a human tragedy as the Holocaust.

The problem with keeping silent on such issues is that doing so will not cause the questions to go away. Every day, in hospitals throughout the world, doctors and parents must decide whether a severely disabled newborn infant is to live or die. The decisions they make show that they do not regard the human being whose fate they are deciding as having the same moral status as other human beings. Similar decisions are made at the other end of life, when people with advanced Alzheimer's disease have left no instructions about whether they want life-prolonging medical treatment. These decisions have always been part of medicine, but they have become far more acute as the rise of high-tech medicine has made it possible for us to keep the most severely damaged human beings alive almost indefinitely. Highly publicised legal battles, like the American cases of Karen Ann Quinlan and Nancy Cruzan, or the British case of Tony Bland, draw attention to human beings who spend years, sometimes even decades, in a persistent vegetative state. Hearing of these cases, people wonder whether there is any point in maintaining such an existence. In deciding Tony Bland's fate, the highest court in Britain went so far as to say that since Bland had 'no cognitive capacity whatever, and no prospect of ever recovering such capacity', there was no requirement to keep him alive, and indeed no point in doing so.[22]

Since we are forced to make decisions that reflect our varying judgments about the value of prolonging the lives of human beings with intellectual and emotional capacities ranging from nil to normal, our choice is between discussing these issues openly or keeping a taboo on any public repudiation of the myth that we value all human lives equally. In an open and democratic society, with relatively free news media, taboos are difficult to maintain unless they have near-universal support. This one does not. Moreover, in terms of the practical decisions which will become increasingly common as our medical techniques continue to advance, there are good grounds for believing that we will do better if we can discuss these issues openly than if they are suppressed. If a sound ethic cannot be discussed in public because it will lead to genocide or the murder of people with disabilities, we are in dire straits indeed. I am not so pessimistic. As compared with placing a taboo on discussions of the basis of human equality, an open discussion seems to me much more likely to lead people to a compassionate ethic that is at the opposite end of the spectrum to Nazi attitudes to racial minorities or to those with disabilities.

So much by way of preamble to Arneson's essay. As for the substance of my response, it can be brief because there is so little with which I disagree. The only point at which Arneson's lucid exposition of my views goes slightly wrong is his account of how I would apply the principle that 'all animals are equal' if it came to choices between rats and human children (p. 105). Here he presents me as both more and less egalitarian than I am. I am less egalitarian in that if (implausibly) we had to formulate a social policy about allocating a painful toothache to a human child or a slightly more painful toothache to a rat, it may not follow from my adherence to the principle of equal consideration of interests that we ought to come down in favour of the rat. For we should take into account other interests beyond the interest in not experiencing the pain of a toothache: the child's interest in being able to attend school, or the interests of the parents in not seeing their child in pain. These other interests will sometimes, but not always, tilt the balance in a different direction from where it would lie if we were to consider only the severity of the physical pain. On the other hand, I am more egalitarian than Arneson suggests when he writes: 'If a human child has an interest in learning arithmetic, and nothing so fine can be attained by a rat, then the high quality of this interest renders its satisfaction more valuable than the satisfaction of non-arithmetical rat interests.' If the last part of this sentence is read as 'more valuable than the satisfaction of *some* non-arithmetical rat interests', I have no problem with it; but if it is read as 'more valuable than the satisfaction of *any* rat interests', it does not reflect my view.

Arneson says that 'one could concoct a version of utilitarianism that would reject the norm of equal consideration for equal interests' (p. 106). He calls this view 'Threshold Utilitarianism' because it gives more weight to the interests of a being who possesses some threshold level of cognitive ability. One could, I suppose, concoct such a view, but it would be a version of utilitarianism only in the sense that it combined the essential utilitarian idea with another principle restricting the application of that idea. The principle of equal consideration (of pleasure or happiness rather than interests) was central to the views of utilitarianism's founding fathers, Bentham, Mill and Sidgwick. I question whether any moral theory that rejects it deserves the name 'utilitarianism'.

I am, of course, delighted that Arneson's search for a resolution of 'the Singer Problem' fails to achieve its goal. But this result is 'disappointing' only if we are committed to defending the status quo, or our ordinary moral convictions about all humans having equal moral status (and a moral status superior to that of any non-human animals). On the error in supposing that moral theory should aim to defend our common moral convictions, I shall say more in my response to Kamm. Here I will limit myself to the comment that from my perspective Arneson's search has yielded valuable results, in the form of new insights into the weaknesses of other attempts to justify the status quo. I shall highlight three of these results, not necessarily the most important, but perhaps the most novel.

First, it is useful to be reminded of Nozick's remark that we should infer 'nothing much' from 'our not presently having a theory of the moral importance of species membership that no one has spent much time trying to formulate because the issue hasn't seemed pressing.' Arneson points out that fifteen years have now passed since these words were written yet we still do not have a tenable theory of the moral importance of species membership. He comments that 'Perhaps the issue still is not salient', before going on to give reasons for his scepticism that we will ever find such a theory. His scepticism is well founded, but I can complement it by the factual observation that the search for a defence of speciesism was, contrary to Nozick's remark, already well under way by 1983, and has not abated since. Charles Magel's *Keyguide to Information Sources in Animal Rights*, which focuses on philosophical writings, and includes both sides of the debate, begins with Ovid but lists only 94 works over more than two millennia up to 1970, as compared with 117 between 1970 and 1983, and another 123 between 1983 and May 1988, when the last entry appears.[23] I have no doubt that the rate of publication on this topic since 1988 has at least equalled, and probably considerably surpassed, that of the preceding five years. The time has come to reverse Nozick's remark: there is, by now, a good deal to be inferred from the failure of all this philosophical activity to find a sound defence of speciesism.

Second, although I have myself often been confronted with claims that it is morally acceptable to show a preference for members of one's own species, simply because it is one's own, it had never before occurred to me that those who make this claim are arguing for something much weaker than is required to defend the standard view about the status of humans and animals.[24] Arneson is surely right to say that the problem I have raised is not solved by showing that it is *permissible* to favour one's own species. This claim is usually defended by arguing that we may be partial towards those who are in some way close to us. The standard example is partiality towards our own children. The usual view of partiality towards one's children, however, is that it is acceptable, within limits, to favour the interests of one's own child over the greater interests of other children, but not that it is *wrong* to be impartial between the interests of one's own child and those of other children. A similar partiality towards humans over animals would be insufficient to defend the standard view of the difference in moral status between humans and animals. Suppose, for example, that you are in a leaky lifeboat with a dog and an intellectually disabled human being without family or friends. You must throw one of them overboard or the lifeboat will sink. Even if the dog has a higher level of cognitive awareness than the intellectually disabled human being, the standard view of the status of humans and animals would say not merely that you *may* show partiality towards the member of your species, but that you *ought* to do so and are acting wrongly if you do save the dog. A defence of the permissibility of species partiality based on the analogy with partiality towards our own children gives no support for such a judgment.

The third point I shall highlight is Arneson's observation that utilitarianism has a 'non-trivial advantage' over other moral theories with commitments to substantive equality, because these theories have great difficulty in giving a coherent account of why one class of beings is entitled to equality and others are not. Utilitarianism is on firmer ground here because it has no need to draw this distinction. Someone might object that utilitarianism must draw a similar distinction between sentient and non-sentient beings, but that objection misconceives the nature of the problem. Utilitarianism does not so much exclude the non-sentient from equal consideration of interests, as find that they have no interests to consider. (I shall elaborate on this point in replying to Holton and Langton.)

Gruen

The problem that Lori Gruen finds with my approach to ethics stems from the fact that I defend an impartialist form of utilitarianism, and use it to reject racism, sexism and speciesism. There is a well known objection to impartialism in ethics, broadly along the lines that an impartialist would make a poor friend, lover or parent, because the very idea of such personal relationships is that one must be partial towards the other person with whom one is in the relationship. This means giving more consideration to the interests of your friend, lover or child than you give to strangers, and from the standpoint of an impartial utilitarianism, this seems wrong. I shall refer to this as the 'lousy lover' objection, since Chin Liew Ten, my friend and colleague at Monash University, used to give a guest lecture in my ethics course in which he argued that consistent utilitarians must make lousy lovers.

To these objections there are well known responses modifying utilitarianism in a direction that leads to less conflict with how we feel people should behave in their personal relationships. As Gruen notes, my own response to the lousy lover objection is based on Hare's two-level version of utilitarianism. At the critical level, the utilitarian must consider everyone's interests impartially. This critical level is used to decide which character traits one should seek to develop, and on which principles one should act, in order to live so as to bring about the best consequences in one's everyday life. This is not meant to preclude reference to the critical level in order to judge what is the right individual act, but in everyday life it will often be too difficult to work out the consequences of every decision we make, and if we were to try to do so, we risk getting it wrong because of our personal involvement, and the pressures of the situation. Moreover – as the lousy lover objection itself shows – unless we develop certain character traits, such as those required for being a good friend, lover or parent, we will be unable to share in or contribute to some of the richest sources of human well-being. This two-level view will therefore allow us – or even require us – to be partial, to some degree, in our everyday practices.

While Gruen's discussion of the two-level view presents my position accurately, I am less sure of the use she makes of the distinction between formal and substantive impartiality. She is right to say that it is substantive, rather than formal, impartiality with which I am concerned. But the two are connected. Universalizability is a formal constraint on the judgments we make, if they are to count as moral judgments; but if we apply universalizability properly, it must lead to outcomes that are, at one level, substantively impartial. For universalizability is not just a matter of formulating our principles so that they do not contain proper names, definite articles or personal pronouns. To be able to prescribe an action universally we must first put ourselves in the position of all those affected by our action, taking on their preferences; and then we can only prescribe the action if, taking all these preferences into account as if they were our own, we prefer it to any alternative action. If we can do that, we will be doing so on the basis of having given equal consideration to the preferences of all those affected by the action, because we will have put ourself in their shoes, one after another, with no discounting because of their race, sex, species or other characteristics, except insofar as those characteristics are relevant to the preferences they have or the way in which they will be affected by the action.

It is clear that the Louisiana legislation that Gruen cites as an example of formal but not substantive impartiality (p. 133) would not pass the test of universalizability – or to put it more precisely, no one who universalized properly would be able to prescribe that such legislation should be passed, or if passed, should remain in force. The fact that you are not a descendent of a person who had the right to vote before 1 January 1867 does not mean that it is less in your interests to have the right to vote. The white legislators who passed this legislation, and later kept it in force, were not putting themselves in the positions of the black citizens of Louisiana, and taking on their preferences without discounting them. Therefore they were not genuinely universalizing, even if the legislation seems to be impartial in a purely formal sense.

Gruen thinks that I am caught in a dilemma. She suggests that while other utilitarians may be able to meet the lousy lover objection by making concessions to partialism, I cannot do so without giving up much that is distinctive in my position. This includes my arguments for overseas aid and against our exploitation of animals.

To illustrate this dilemma, Gruen uses the example of a choice between spending money to ensure that one's own children have 'certain educational opportunities', or 'providing financial assistance to sick children who lack proper medical services' (p. 140). When she first raises this example, she suggests that at the critical level we will have impartial grounds for encouraging parents 'to develop strong attachments to their own children, and to pay particularly close attention to them in order to understand their needs'. These attitudes will then lead at the intuitive level, she continues, to partial behaviour that favours choosing to provide educational opportunities for one's own children rather than helping other children who are in greater need. When Gruen returns to the same example later, however, she views it differently: 'The satisfaction of the educational interests of one's own children, even when combined with one's interests in one's own children's success, surely cannot count for more overall interest satisfaction than providing the sick children of others with the care they need.' Indeed, it is true that it cannot. But in making this second judgment, Gruen is forgetting about the factors to which she gave weight when she had earlier reached the opposite judgment. The discrepancy in the two judgments has nothing to do with any distinction between formal and substantive impartiality, nor with any way in which at the critical level we supposedly focus on formal impartiality and at the intuitive level we focus on substantive impartiality. The judgments we make at the critical level should be impartial, in both a formal and a substantive sense; in other words, they should be based on the principle of equal consideration of interests. *Possibly* these critical level judgments will allow people to have character traits that lead them to act partially towards their friends, lovers and children. Whether we think that this is in fact the case will depend on our views about the benefits and costs of allowing or suppressing such character traits. In the example Gruen uses, the benefits of doing so are, as she suggests on p. 140, that children will generally have loving parents, attentive to their needs. The costs will be, as she suggests on p. 142, that these parents spend their money in ways that produce less overall satisfaction of interests than they could have produced, had they not been so attached to our own children. But if that were never going to be the case, then there would have been no need for a two-level view at all. Everyone could simply decide what to do in each specific situation by asking what act would produce the greatest overall satisfaction of interests. It is the recognition that this may cut us off from bringing about important goods that has led consequentialists to advocate a two-level view. Accepting a two-level view means accepting that people will have character traits, or will come intuitively to accept rules, such that they will sometimes do things that produce less overall satisfaction than they might have done, had they not developed these character traits or followed these rules.

Understanding this basic structure of the two-level view still leaves two questions open. The first is: what are the character traits or rules that we should develop? For example, in the case Gruen uses, should we encourage character traits or rules that lead us to provide educational opportunities for our own children when sick children cannot afford basic care? Strictly, as this example indicates, it is not always a matter of *encouraging* character traits, but sometimes of *allowing* them: that is, of not taking steps to suppress them. This is relevant to the costs and benefits of the options we face. The love of parents for their children, and the desire of parents to give preference to their children over the children of strangers, are as the experience of utopian social experiments has repeatedly shown, extremely difficult to eradicate.[25] Presumably they have their roots in our nature as social mammals. Unless we engage in an all-out campaign of intense moral pressure to suppress parental bias, we are bound to find that most parents constantly favour their children in ways that cannot be directly justified on the basis of equal consideration of interests. If we do engage in such a campaign, we will cause guilt and anxiety in parents who want to do things for their children that we have taught them to think of as wrong. (Mothers in the Israeli *kibbutzim*, barred from showing particular love and affection for their own children, used to sneak into the communal nursery at night to kiss and hold their sleeping children.) Guilt caused by the moral pressure against partiality will itself be a source of much unhappiness. Impartiality also seems not to be best for the children. The care of loving parents is likely to be better than the care of paid employees, no matter how benevolent they may be. In making decisions at the critical level about when we should praise people for being loving and caring parents, and when we should blame them for being excessively partial towards their children, we must take these costs into account. To be too harsh on parental partiality will not be for the best.

So to return to Gruen's example, my guess – and in this area we can only guess – is that if the educational opportunities in question are the only chance our children have of receiving the minimum amount of education needed to equip them for a decent life in the society in which we live, then we should not expect caring parents to forgo such opportunities in order to benefit the children of strangers, and we should not strive to create a moral system that demands this of parents. Hence we can argue, on the basis of equal consideration of interests, that we should not attempt to suppress the natural love that parents have for their children to such an extent that they will put the interests of the sick children of strangers ahead of these important interests of their own children. It is different, however, if the educational opportunities we are talking about are to go to elite private schools or colleges when there are free or much cheaper public facilities that still provide a good education. That goes beyond the degree of partiality that we need or should wish to encourage in parents, and we can, without pushing too hard against the flow of natural affection, reasonably ask parents to balance their love towards their own children with a degree of concern for the children of others.

The second question that is left open by an understanding of the structure of the two-level view arises when we consider an implication of having a two-level approach. As we have just seen, at the critical level it may be best to accept highly partial behaviour in certain situations. Yet when we actually find ourselves in these situations, we may know that we can bring about more good, impartially considered, by going against the standard of partiality that the critical level accepts. Gruen's parents again serve as an example. Assume that they can bring about more overall satisfaction of interests by helping sick children, but only if they sacrifice quite important educational opportunities for their own children. They would then be deciding against the interests of their own children in circumstances where the morality promoted at the critical level would allow them to decide in favour of their own children. We can assume that they are able to consider the consequences of their choice carefully, and they can be sure that acting impartially on this occasion will not have any further ramifications that could produce undesirable consequences. What ought they to do? Ought they to act partially, as the intuitive level of morality suggests they may? Or ought they to bring about the best consequences?

This apparent dilemma can be eased by distinguishing between a private, first person perspective and a public, third person perspective. If we ask the question from a private, first person perspective – what ought I to do? – then I ought to help the sick strangers, rather than my own children. But if we ask it from a public, third person perspective, then since we will in effect be propagating a public moral standard, we should take account of the reasons why critical morality accepts partiality, and we should accept it too. As such cases show, the distinction that Sidgwick drew between what 'it may be right to do and privately recommend' and 'what it would not be right to advocate openly' is a real one, much as some moral philosophers may dislike it.[26] We could do away with it simply by specifying that morality is something public; but that would not help at all with the practical dilemmas we may face when we can bring about good consequences by doing something privately, even though to advocate such practices would have bad consequences. Keeping this point in mind helps us to understand – though it may not resolve – the discomfort to which consequentialist reasoning often gives rise.

Gruen's own conclusion is an interesting one, considering that she has written extensively in and about feminist frameworks, and feminist philosophers have been among the strongest critics of impartiality. Gruen concludes, however, that, at least until the world is a much better place than it is today, I 'must maintain [my] commitment to impartiality in the strongest sense.' As we have seen, it is possible to do so, and still to hold a two-level view of morality.

McGinn

The critical part of McGinn's essay is concerned with my argument that not to relieve the suffering of the world's poor, when we can do so at little cost to ourselves, is a serious moral failing.

In considering the implications of my view that 'if it is in our power to prevent something bad from happening, without thereby sacrificing something of comparable moral importance, we ought, morally, to do it', McGinn lists three kinds of sacrifices that I might make:

> One way in which I could prevent a good deal of Third World suffering would be to disallow my child to attend college, thus condemning him to a life of underachievement; or I could decide never to see another ballet or play or film; or I could refrain altogether from eating in restaurants. I take it these are the kinds of sacrifices Singer thinks we should make, since if they are not his principle is toothless and morally conservative. (p. 154)

The first of these three examples of sacrifices raises the same questions as the example I have just discussed in the context of Gruen's essay. It is arguably different from the others examples McGinn gives, in two ways. First, as we have seen, at the level of critical morality there are strong arguments against trying to build into a society's morality a requirement that parents make such serious sacrifices of their children's interests, in order to help strangers. Hence we may not want to propagate the idea that not to make such a sacrifice would be a serious moral failing. (This does not preclude making the sacrifice being the right thing to do, when one thinks about it as a first person question.) The second difference relates to the consequences of our decision. If it is true that not allowing my child to attend college will condemn him to a life of underachievement, then not only will this harm him, it may also lead to less good being achieved for others. I may hope that my child will live an ethical life. But as a lifetime underachiever, she may be less effective at relieving suffering than she would have been, if she had been to college.

For these reasons the first sacrifice is not one that *clearly* falls within my category of not being of comparable moral importance to the prevention of suffering and death. The other two sacrifices McGinn mentions do fall within this category. But when McGinn goes on to interpret the principle as being 'to the effect that we ought to relieve whatever suffering will not cause us (or others) to suffer comparably', he goes beyond what I intended to argue in 'Famine, affluence and morality'. The argument of that article is presented so as to be persuasive to people with a wide range of ethical positions. I didn't want to limit the force of the argument to utilitarians – that would have been preaching to the converted.[27] I there-fore used the phrase 'comparable moral importance' rather than 'compar-able suffering', in order to allow readers to judge for themselves what is of comparable moral importance. Some, for example, may think that to cheat or steal to get money that could save the lives of people in the Third World would be to sacrifice something of comparable moral importance, namely the breach of the moral rules that prohibit such actions. For others the same would be true, to come to some of McGinn's other examples, of having sexual intercourse with people for whom one cares not at all, of neglecting one's family or of not being able to pursue a life as a philosopher, inquiring into some of the deepest questions about the nature of our world and the direction of our lives. The range of things that might be argued to be of comparable moral importance is wide – and it becomes much wider still if, like McGinn, we go on to consider cases where the bad thing that I am preventing is not death from starvation, but mediocrity at tennis! Thus McGinn's alleged counter-examples to my principle are not counter-examples at all, but claims that certain kinds of behaviour do not fall under it, because they would involve the sacrifice of something of comparable moral value. Some of these claims are highly plausible; for others, I would like to see a more detailed defence. But none of them touches the central argument of 'Famine, affluence and morality'. This central argument retains considerable force, despite everything McGinn says, because for each of us there will be many things on which we spend money that we do not truly believe to be of comparable moral importance to death by starvation (or by malnutrition, or by easily treatable illnesses), and since we can give up those things and prevent death by these causes, the principle is certainly neither toothless nor conservative.

After suggesting that my argument has a utilitarian basis, McGinn then offers another argument against it: it is 'liable to prove counter-productive' (p. 158). But this objection was refuted already in the very first work of the English utilitarian tradition: '"The principle of utility, (I have heard it said) is a dangerous principle: it is dangerous on certain occasions to consult it." This is as much as to say, what? that it is not consonant to utility, to consult utility: in short, that it is *not* consulting it, to consult it.'[28] In *Practical Ethics* I raised this objection to my views about famine relief, and replied to it along the lines Bentham suggests: 'The third version of the objection asks: might it not be counter-productive to demand that people give up so much? Might not people say: "As I can't do what is morally required anyway, I won't bother to give at all"' (PE 245). In response, I referred to the distinction already noted above, between first person decision-making and public advocacy, and said:

Is it true that the standard set by our argument is so high as to be counter-productive? There is not much evidence to go by, but discussions of the argument with students and others have led me to think it might be. Yet the conventionally accepted standard – a few coins in a collection tin when one is waved under your nose – is obviously far too low. What level should we advocate? Any figure will be arbitrary, but there may be something to be said for a round percentage of one's income like, say, 10 per cent – more than a token donation, yet not so high as to be beyond all but saints... No figure should be advocated as a rigid minimum or maximum; but it seems safe to advocate that those earning average or above average incomes in affluent societies, unless they have an unusually large number of dependents or other special needs, ought to give a tenth of their income to reducing absolute poverty. By any reasonable ethical standards, this is the minimum we ought to do, and we do wrong if we do less. (PE 246)

I disagree with McGinn's view that 'decent rational people feel quite unsure [about what they owe the poor]; it is not that they know very well and decline to carry out their moral duty'. Admittedly, the attitudes of people to this question may vary from country to country. Nevertheless, my sense, after many years of discussions with all kinds of people, mostly in Australia but also in the United States, England and other European countries, is that many people *do* think that they owe a lot more to the poor than they are actually giving, and have some residual guilt about not giving more. Some of them relieve this guilt, or excuse their failure to give, by convincing themselves that the money given to overseas aid agencies never gets to those who need it. (They do not make the enquiries that might threaten this convenient belief.)

I disagree, too, with the conclusion McGinn draws from his imaginary world in which a Charity Channel, plugged into our brain and therefore compulsory viewing, floods us with information about people in urgent need of our aid, which we have the means to provide effectively. McGinn says that he finds this a dystopian prospect. No doubt he is thinking of himself as a potential donor rather than as a person in urgent need of aid. From that perspective, the thought of being bombarded with images of people suffering is indeed dystopian. But if I imagine myself as a victim of a natural disaster, and think of my life and the lives of my family as being saved by the existence of the Charity Channel, I have a very different view. McGinn thinks that human compassion is not infinitely elastic, and we would become hardened to all the suffering that was forced on to our attention. Perhaps we would: that is a question of human psychology about which we can only speculate. If the Charity Channel did not lead to a substantial increase in the amount of aid that is received by people who need it, it would indeed be dystopian. But if human compassion – while no doubt not *infinitely* elastic – can be stretched to a significant extent by the provision of accurate information and effective means of giving assistance, then to view the world of the Charity Channel as worse than the present world seems to reflect the biased perspective of someone secure in the comforts of affluence.

In the end, after extensively criticising what he takes to be a utilitarian principle, McGinn has nothing to offer in its place except 'just an *ad hoc* rule of thumb that seems to strike the best balance between competing concerns and fits my real feelings about my obligations' (p. 159). I find this unsatisfactory because I don't think we should be constructing our moral theory in order to fit our 'real feelings', whatever they might be. But that raises issues of method in moral philosophy, to which I shall come in the following response to Frances Kamm.

Kamm

Kamm deals with many different issues. To take them in order.

The motivation for living an ethical life

Kamm begins her critique with some comments on my views about the motivation to be moral, directed against what I say on this issue in the final chapter of *Practical Ethics*. (As readers will know from Crisp's essay, a fuller account can be found in *How Are We to Live?*) Some errors in Kamm's account of my views need to be corrected. First, she says that I seem to think that it is more in people's interest to live a meaningful life than to live a happy life. She comes to this conclusion as a result of misunderstanding my observation in *Practical Ethics* that few of us could deliberately choose a way of life that we regard as meaningless, and that most of us would not choose to live a psychopathic life, no matter how enjoyable it might be.[29] Probably many of those who could not deliberately choose a way of life they regarded as meaningless could not see themselves as being happy under those conditions. And if few of us would choose to live a psychopathic life, no matter how happy it might be, that tells us something about the values most people have. But I make no general claim about whether a meaningful life or a happy life is more in people's interest. Since a person's interests are, in my view, related to her preferences, that would vary from person to person.

Next, Kamm says that I posit self-interest as the highest-level rationale for an individual's being moral. But what I say is: 'If, agreeing with Sidgwick rather than Hume, we hold that it is rational to act in our long-term interests irrespective of what we happen to want at the present moment, we could show that it is rational to act morally by showing that it is in our long-term interests to do so' (PE 322). The structure of the sentence is hypothetical. I am not sure that I do agree with Sidgwick rather than Hume. But even if I do, in the end, side with Sidgwick, he himself would not agree that self-interest is the 'highest-level rationale' for being moral. He acknowledges that some people may simply see it as rational to act morally, perhaps because they see that their own good matters no more, 'from the point of view of the universe', than the good of any other. These people need no further rationale for acting morally, and it would be absurd to say that unless they *also* believe that to act morally is in accordance with their long-term interests, they do not have as high a rationale for acting morally as someone who does so only because she believes that it is in her long-term interests to do so. So instead of saying that self-interest is for me a 'higher' rationale for acting morally, it would be better to say that it is a 'fall-back rationale' or a 'rationale of last resort', to be used when a person does not accept any other rationale as sufficient for acting morally. (This makes the two-level view I take of moral motivation quite different to the two-level view I take in normative ethics, where the critical level is indeed 'higher' in the sense that the principles accepted at the intuitive level must be justified at the critical level.)

There is also a difference at the second or lower level. Kamm says that for me, 'while self-interest can reasonably motivate us to be moral, being moral involves acting for the sake of morality, not for the sake of self-interest'. But Kamm is mistaking my *explanation* of a common moral view for a *justification* of it. Here is the key passage:

> This emphasis on motives and on the moral worth of doing right for its own sake is now embedded in our notion of ethics. To the extent that it is so embedded, we will feel that to provide considerations of self-interest for doing what is right is to empty the action of its moral worth.
>
> My suggestion is that our notion of ethics has become misleading to the extent that moral worth is attributed only to action done because it is right, without any ulterior motive. It is understandable, and from the point of view of society perhaps even desirable, that this view should prevail; nevertheless, those who accept this view of ethics, and are led by it to do what is right, without asking for any further reason, are falling victim to a kind of confidence trick – though not, of course, a consciously perpetrated one. (PE 324–5)

If Kamm takes my phrase 'and from the point of view of society perhaps even desirable' to be an endorsement of the idea that we should attribute moral worth only to an action done without any ulterior motive, then I did not make myself sufficiently clear. I put the matter more plainly in *How Are We to Live?*

Sceptics deride morality as something that society foists upon us for its own sake. If by 'morality' we mean the view that moral worth is to be found only in actions done for the sake of duty, they seem to be right. To put it bluntly: on this view, morality is a fraud. Unchallenged, it may be socially useful, but the gains are achieved at a high risk, for once questioned, this conception of morality has no means of resisting the sceptical challenge. Thus the sceptics score an undeservedly easy triumph.[30]

My two-level theory of moral motivation suggests that some people may choose to live an ethical life because they understand that this may help to make their lives more meaningful; and they may then come to act ethically, without always thinking of why they have chosen an ethical life. But if this thought often did come to their minds when they are faced with ethical choices, I certainly would not see it – as Kant would have – as emptying their actions of moral worth.

Kamm's main criticism of my position on this issue is that if people can find meaning in their lives through work, or personal relationships, in ways that cannot be seen as part of a more impartial morality, then my motivational argument will not succeed. This may be true. I did warn my readers of the speculative nature of my comments (e.g. PE 332) and my overall conclusion in the final chapter of *Practical Ethics* is that '"Why act morally?" cannot be given an answer that will provide everyone with overwhelming reasons for acting morally' (PE 335). All I can say is that I do not know of any other answers to the question that will do better.

Kamm also thinks that my two-level view of motivation may be inconsistent with my use of a two-level model in my normative theory. The alleged inconsistency is to be found in the fact that my model of moral motivation is based on the idea that we may find meaning in becoming committed to the idea of living from an impartial perspective, whereas in my model of normative theory, in our everyday life we should act on the basis of character traits or guiding rules that are not strictly impartial – for example, the rule that says parents may give preference to the interests of their own children over the interests of the children of strangers.

Is there really an inconsistency here? There would be, if I held a two-level normative theory suggesting that in acting at the intuitive level, we must blind ourselves to the ultimate, impartially based, justification of our actions, at the critical level. But I do not favour so sharp a distinction between the levels. Those who are in the mood to reflect on such questions as 'Why act morally?' can also reflect on the nature of ethics, and why it is that, in personal relationships and many other aspects of everyday life, we will not necessarily always do best to be thinking about what is justifiable from an impartial perspective.

'But what if', some may ask, 'there was evidence that people brought about better consequences when they did forget about the impartial basis of ethics, and acted only on the basis of rules and character traits that fall well short of impartiality?' Then, clearly, one should not motivate people to act morally by appealing to the idea of impartiality. If we really believed, as Ayn Rand did and some forms of ethical egoism suggest, that everything would work out better if we all acted in an entirely selfish way, then the motivation to act morally would be very different indeed. Much depends on what the intuitive level ethical life is like. But my guess is that ethical life at the intuitive level will not be purely egoistic. It will still seek to take people out of themselves, beyond their own selfish concerns, and give them some awareness of the importance of wider standards. If this guess is right, then much of what I say about the motivation to be moral would still be applicable. For example, I could still say, as I say in *How Are We to Live?*:

> If we are to find meaning in our lives by working for a cause, that cause must be...a 'transcendent cause', that is, a cause that extends beyond the boundaries of our self...The more we reflect on our commitment to a football club, a corporation, or any sectional interest, the less point we are likely to see in it. In contrast, no amount of reflection will show a commitment to an ethical life to be trivial or pointless.[31]

Impartiality again

Kamm correctly states that, in contrast to the views held by Samuel Scheffler and Thomas Nagel, my conception of the moral point of view does not, at the critical level, allow us to weigh things partially. Since I have already discussed impartiality, I shall make only two brief comments. First, as Kamm acknowledges, those who take the opposite view seem to have found no principled way to do it. That seems to be a major reason for not doing it. Second, the debates between me and others about partiality, and the related debates about, for example, allowing aesthetic considerations to outweigh moral ones, should be seen within the context of the issues I raised in 'The triviality of the debate over "is–ought" and the definition of "moral"' and have already discussed in responding to Michael Smith. At least part of the differences between me and my critics can be traced to different understandings of what morality is and how it relates to reasons for action. I recall a conversation I had with Nagel when I was living in New York, in 1973 or 1974. We were discussing 'Famine, affluence and morality', and Nagel was unable to accept that morality could be so demanding. But eventually it emerged that he was assuming that if morality did demand that we give so much to famine relief, then there must be overriding reason to do so. I was making no such assumption. On my view, I could recognize that if I were totally committed to doing what I ought to do, I would give away my wealth up to the point indicated in my article; but at the same time I may, without any irrationality, choose to be less than totally committed to doing what I ought to do. My own interests, or those of my family, may counteract the demands of morality to some degree, and I may think it reasonable to give in to them, while recognizing that it is morally wrong for me to do so. Once Nagel and I realized that we held these distinct understandings of morality, the practical difference between Nagel and myself over the demandingness of morality became less acute.

The same may be said for allowing aesthetic considerations to override morality, although the question is a little more tricky here, since aesthetic considerations are impartial in nature, and may therefore be brought within the scope of morality. Thus whereas there may be a clear conflict between morality and self-interest ('I know I shouldn't order the veal, because it comes from miserable calves, confined in stalls and deliberately kept anaemic – but it is my favourite dish'), the conflict between morality and aesthetics is less clear. The writer who steals from a pensioner in order to buy paint to complete her painting may argue that the creation of great art outweighs the petty concerns of ordinary people. For this reason it is rare to find people saying that they think aesthetic reasons outweigh morality – they are much more likely to say that aesthetic considerations outweigh the other, more conventional, moral reasons, and therefore it is morally right to follow aesthetics in these circumstances.

Finally, my account of these issues explains why Scheffler and others have not been able to find a principled way of allowing the personal point of view to outweigh impartial considerations. If what we are talking about is a clash of different kinds of reasons for action, independently of morality, then the weight that the different kinds of reasons have for any individual will vary with their long-term preferences, and it would be a mistake to expect there to be any general standard for balancing impartial and partial concerns.

What interests should get equal consideration?

As long as a being can feel pain and pleasure, it has an interest in not feeling pain and in feeling pleasure, and the concept of universalizability requires us to give those interests the same weight as the similar interests of any other being.[32] I have no idea why Kamm thinks that it is 'morally more important' that a good thing like pleasure should happen to a more important being, like a person, than to a less important one. If we really are considering the pleasure 'independent of reverberations' I can only regret that Kamm says nothing more to justify it.

Next Kamm questions the distinction I draw between beings who have a sense of themselves as a continuing entity, with a past and a (possible) future, and beings who lack sufficient self-awareness for this. The distinction is not relevant to the wrongness of inflicting pain or diminishing pleasure, but I think it is relevant to the wrongness of ending life, because those who understand that they exist over time can have preferences relating to the future, and those that cannot understand that they exist over time cannot. Thus the former have more to lose than the latter, and so, other things being equal, it is worse to end its life.

Against this Kamm says that something can continue over time even if it does not know it does, which is true, but so what? More to the point is her claim that if a being's future time would be filled with good experiences, it is in its interest to have these experiences, and this gives rise to a reason not to kill it. But that is also a claim that I accept. It is covered by the 'other things being equal' clause, and it is the reason why, in *Practical Ethics*, I accepted the controversial idea of replaceability.[33] That idea was not my invention – it was used in the nineteenth century by Leslie Stephen to argue that there is no moral obligation to be a vegetarian. The argument is that the loss of good experiences of the pig we kill to eat is made up for by the good experiences of the next pig we breed for the same purpose. If we did not eat pigs, there would be no such good experiences. In the first edition of *Animal Liberation* I rejected this argument,[34] but I later came to think that it did have some merit when restricted to beings who are incapable of seeing themselves as existing over time. (Pigs are highly intelligent and may well be sufficiently self-aware to see themselves as existing over time, but perhaps fish are not.) So the loss of a being's future good experiences is, if it is not aware of itself as existing over time, balanced by the gain of good experiences for another being, when the second being can only come into existence if the first one is killed. (I will say more about this when I discuss Hare's essay.) It is different if the being is capable of seeing itself as existing over time; then there is a personal loss that is not balanced by the creation of another being. Finally on this issue, note that, contrary to what Kamm says on p. 169, I do not think that we may kill animals who are not self-conscious *only* if we replace them with new beings. There may be other ways in which killing them will lead to greater overall utility – perhaps by saving the lives of existing beings with a greater interest in continued life. But there must be *some* justification for an act that will cause the loss of good experiences of the being killed.

Kamm's exposition of my views goes astray elsewhere too. She is wrong to say (p. 169) that I believe that it is more important to satisfy the most important interests first, even if we could produce greater overall utility by satisfying many more less important interests. On consequences, I am a straightforward aggregationist.[35] Similarly it is not true that I am at pains to argue 'independent of considering consequences' that we should not coerce needy people who are responsible for causing their own plight into improving it (Kamm, p. 175). All that I argue in the passage Kamm cites in support of that interpretation is that withholding aid from countries that do nothing to slow the growth of their population would not be coercion. I do not even go into the question of whether coercion would be wrong, let alone the question of whether it would be wrong independently of its consequences.

The slippery slope argument

Kamm raises a difficulty about my use of slippery slope arguments, pointing out that I appeal to a slippery slope argument against eating animals that are not self-conscious, but I reject slippery slope arguments against euthanasia. I shall discuss this when I come to my case against eating animals, in my response to Hare.

Killing and letting die

To avoid the need to write an essay as long as Kamm's just in order to reply adequately to all the points that she makes in her lengthy attempt to refute my views about killing and letting die, I shall focus on three key points.

What was I trying to show in my discussion of killing and letting die in Practical Ethics?
Kamm believes that in attempting to show that there is no intrinsic difference between killing and letting die, I have failed to consider that: 'it is possible to export a property which is intrinsic to (i.e. necessarily true of) killing but not of letting die, and so *necessarily* common in killing cases, into a case of letting die; it is also possible to export a property which is intrinsic to letting die (but not to killing) into a case of killing' (p. 171, italics in original). But we are at cross-purposes here, because Kamm and I do not mean the same thing when we write of intrinsic or extrinsic differences. In *Practical Ethics*, after considering some differences between killing and letting die, I explained what I meant by this as follows: 'These differences need not shake our previous conclusion that there is no intrinsic difference between killing and allowing to die. They are extrinsic differences, that is, differences normally but not necessarily associated with the distinction between killing and allowing to die.'

If there is a difference between killing and allowing to die that is necessarily true of killing, and sometimes true of letting die, then it is 'normally but not necessarily associated with the distinction between killing and allowing to die', and so it is not an intrinsic difference between the two, as I am using the term 'intrinsic difference'. I am not sure if my usage here is orthodox or not, but that is not crucial to the moral issue which is the whole reason for going into this question in the first place. That moral issue is how we should judge various acts that have as their consequences the loss of an innocent human life. Some of these acts are killings, and some of them are cases in which people are let die. Conventional morality relies on this distinction alone in order to judge that some of these acts (those that are killings) are seriously wrong, and others (those that are lettings die) are not seriously wrong or at worst less seriously wrong. My claim is that this is a mistake. That claim will not be undermined by Kamm showing that there are properties intrinsic to killing that are not intrinsic to letting die, but sometimes are present in cases of letting die. Even if these properties are morally significant, we will still be unable to use the simple distinction between killing and letting die to judge which acts are seriously wrong and which are not. We will have to look at each case in order to see whether the morally significant factors are or are not present.

Does 'losing out on only what he would not have without my help' distinguish killing from letting die?

The property that Kamm (both here and in part 1 of *Morality, Mortality, volume 2*) does think marks an important moral difference between killing and letting die is precisely one of those properties that is rarely associated with killing, but in special circumstances may be. This is the property of 'losing out on only what he would not have without my help'. As Kamm notes, the case in which I kill someone who is on life-support, and can only remain alive with my help, shows that this property can be true of killing. So it doesn't distinguish killing and letting die in all cases. Kamm thinks it still can show an intrinsic difference (in her sense of the term) between killing and letting die, because it is only contingently true of killing, but is 'necessarily true of the person whom I let die'. I doubt even this. In a footnote Kamm mentions a case I described, in which this property, or 'a cousin' of it, is *not* true of letting die. This is the case in which I am a doctor in a hospital who is more ready than my colleagues to let severely disabled infants die, without undertaking life-preserving operations. Then, when I decide not to operate, thus letting an infant die, it is not true that the baby 'loses out only on what he would not have without my help', since without my help he would have had the help of another doctor, who would have kept him alive. I am not sure what

Kamm wants to say about this case. If she wants to preserve the claim that this property is necessarily true of letting die, she would have to say that the doctor *kills* the baby. One sentence in her footnote suggests, though inconclusively, that this *is* what she would say. That is stretching language to breaking point in order to preserve the idea of an intrinsic difference between killing and letting die. And for what purpose? We will still end up judging the wrongness of actions, not by whether they are killings or lettings die, but by whether they cause someone to lose out only on what he would not have had without the help of the person who kills him or lets him die.

Explaining and justifying

Kamm correctly reports that the second step in my strategy is to consider whether the extrinsic factors which I have suggested can *explain* why we often think that killing is worse than letting die can also *justify* this attitude. She then claims that this strategy is reversible, and she tries to run it in reverse – that is, to show that extrinsic factors which make letting die permissible do not make killing permissible.

The factor she discusses is that of burdensomeness. I had said that one factor that does justify a difference in attitudes to killing and letting die is that to avoid killing people is normally not difficult, whereas to save all one possibly could save is heroic. Therefore we can demand, as a minimum standard of acceptable conduct, that people not kill; whereas we cannot similarly demand that they not let die. Kamm then describes a hypothetical case in which it is burdensome not to kill, and says that the burden would not defeat the duty not to kill. This suggests, she says, that there is a moral difference between killing and letting die *per se*. But I think all it suggests is that our moral intuitions are formed on the basis of everyday situations, and not bizarre hypothetical cases.

Kamm then sets out another pair of examples. In each case, my goal is to get five dying people to hospital in order to save their lives. In one case, to do so I must let someone drown when I could save her. This Kamm says is permissible, and I of course agree, since there is a net saving of four lives. In the other case, I must drive over, and thereby kill, a trapped person. About this Kamm says flatly: 'This is impermissible'. But it is not clear if Kamm is here reporting what most people's intuitions would be, or expressing her own views. Whichever it is, her claim seems dubious. If she is reporting what she takes to be most people's intuitions, it would be good to have some evidence that she is right. I would be prepared to bet that a jury would acquit a driver who had no other way of saving five lives than driving over a trapped person; and I think that whatever the law or 'official' morality says, most people would think the driver had done the right thing. Moreover that would be my view as well.

In summary, in the passage from *Practical Ethics* about killing and letting die, I sought to show that the moral differences found by conventional moral views between killing and letting die depend on factors other than the mere fact that one case is a killing, and the other is a letting die. Kamm has not shown that these arguments are unsuccessful. But although a deflation of the distinction between killing and letting die puts in a dramatically different light the fact that we allow people in Third World countries to die when we could easily save the lives of many of them, in the end my views on our obligation to aid these people do not depend on a denial of the distinction between killing and letting die.

Famine, ethics and moral methodology

I have already defended my views about overseas aid in my reply to McGinn. The most important additional issue Kamm raises is that of moral methodology.

Some people think that doing applied ethics is like doing physics. We have some data, and we have to find a theory that will match them. There can be some pushing and pulling between a plausible theory and the data, because if the data include some isolated findings that do not fit the theory, the data could be erroneous; but in the end, it is the data that are the proving ground of the theory. If a theory is in irreconcilable conflict with the observed facts, it can't be the right theory. In physics the data are the results of experiments. The data in ethics are our intuitive moral judgments about particular cases.

I first came across an explicit statement of this view of ethics in John Rawls's *A Theory of Justice*, where it is termed 'reflective equilibrium'. It immediately struck me as mistaken. Why should our intuitive judgments be seen as the touchstone of a sound ethical theory? A more inherently conservative way of approaching the subject would be difficult to conceive. But if I was surprised to see Rawls defending such a view, I was astonished to read his ascription of it to my philosophical hero, the far-seeing and by no means fundamentally conservative Henry Sidgwick. When *The Monist* announced a special issue honouring the centenary of *The Methods of Ethics*, I submitted an essay rescuing Sidgwick from the charge of doing moral philosophy in a way that makes it essentially a conservative enterprise. Instead, I showed that Sidgwick based his theory on careful argument for the self-evidence of fundamental axioms. While judgments of self-evidence may be regarded as appeals to intuition, they are intuitions about fundamental principles – like the principle I have already mentioned, that the good of one individual is of no more significance than the like good of any other – and not moral intuitions about what ought to be done in specific situations. In particular, he does not regard our ordinary moral judgments as the test of a moral theory, but rather as a safeguard against 'the errors of individual minds'. Our ordinary moral judgments may, in the end, be wrong.[36]

While in many ordinary situations our intuitions may be sound, in others they may not be a reliable guide to what we ought to do. Here I agree with Mill, who, as Crisp points out, thought that common-sense morality is influenced by prejudice, superstition, envy, arrogance and self-interest (Crisp, p. 98). To this list of influences I would add obsolete religious, metaphysical or factual views. On such topics as the moral status of non-human animals, and the sanctity of life, for example, the intuitions of the majority of people in Western societies have been formed under the influence of discredited Judeo-Christian beliefs about the way in which humans and animals came into existence.[37]

There is a special problem with appealing to our ordinary moral intuitions when we are considering bizarre imaginary examples. Our intuitions are formed to deal with situations that we face in the real world. They may therefore be said, somewhat charitably, to represent the accumulated experience of human beings about what to do in those situations, or similar ones. But can we really expect this accumulated experience to be of much use if I should find myself with arms so long that they reach from one end of India to another (but too weak to lift a child drowning in a pond in a remote part of that country), while I happen to possess a machine in Canada that can rescue another potential victim of drowning there?[38]

Kamm suggests that my position on the use of intuitions seems inconsistent, because I rely on intuitions about hypothetical cases in order to try to defeat the principle that there is a moral difference between killing and letting die. It is true that I have appealed to intuitive judgments about hypothetical cases, and sometimes also about imaginary ones, at various places in my writings. But it is one thing to generate intuitions about particular cases in order to show that a distinction widely believed to be morally significant is not really doing the work we ordinarily think it does in grounding our judgments of right and wrong, and another thing altogether to give these intuitions probative status. For me an appeal to intuitions is always an *ad hominem* argument. If you put forward a general principle, P, and I say that in a situation S a particular judgment, J, follows from that principle, you have three choices: you can deny that J follows from P in S; you can abandon P; or you can accept J. The strength of an argument that uses a counter-example to generate an uncongenial moral intuition is proportional to our unwillingness to accept the intuition.

The statement that Kamm quotes (p. 177) – 'the way people do in fact judge has nothing to do with the validity of my conclusion' – is therefore entirely consistent with my use of counter-examples. That use will succeed only if I am right in thinking that the proponents of the position I am arguing against will be very reluctant to accept the intuitive judgment that follows from their position. If not, the counter-example collapses. I would be inconsistent if I had argued that because 'people do in fact judge' in a certain way, any position that leads to a contrary judgment must be rejected. But that is not an argument that I have used.

Even though it has always seemed to me so evidently erroneous, the view that we must test our normative theories against our intuitions has continued to have many adherents, and Kamm is clearly one of them. But now it faces its most serious challenge yet, in the form of Peter Unger's *Living High and Letting Die*. On one level this book is an attempt to tighten the argument I advanced in 'Famine, affluence and morality'. Unger argues that we do wrong when we fail to send money to overseas aid organizations that will use it to save many lives. But he does much more than that. He makes his argument by presenting a wide variety of examples and telling us about the intuitive responses that he had found most people – especially his students – have to them. The responses are very difficult to reconcile with each other. Unger then offers explanations for them. His explanations are devastating for the view that we should take our intuitive responses to particular cases as the test of a sound theory, because the explanations show that our intuitive judgments are based on things that are obviously of no moral significance at all. Here is an example. Unger uses some variants on the 'trolley problem', much discussed by philosophers during the past thirty years.[39] The problem is posed by a runaway trolley rolling down the railway track, on course to kill several innocent people further down the line. In one version of the problem you can throw a switch that will divert the trolley down another track, where it will kill just one innocent person. In another version, there is no switch, but you could push a very heavy person off a bridge in front of the trolley. The heavy person will be killed, but the trolley will be stopped and the six people will be saved. Most people think that you should throw the switch, thus causing one to die, rather than six; but they think it would be wrong to push the heavy person off the bridge into the path of the trolley. To a consequentialist this difference is puzzling. In both cases you sacrifice one to save six. What does it matter how you achieve this outcome? A Kantian, however, can claim that the responses show that our intuitions are in line with the Kantian idea that it is wrong to use someone as a means, even if by doing so there is a net saving of innocent human life. According to the reflective equilibrium model of moral philosophy, this ability to offer an underlying theory that can account for our responses to such cases is the mark of a successful normative theory.

In most versions of the trolley problem, the agent has only two options: to pull the switch or not pull the switch, to push the heavy person off the bridge or not to push. In one the agent is active, changing what would happen if he or she were not there, while in the other option, the agent does nothing. Unger introduces intermediate options, and shows that this affects the way people judge the extreme options. In other words, when presented with a choice between A and E (where A, for example, is doing nothing, and E is pushing the heavy person into the path of the trolley) people will say that E is the worse option. When presented with a choice between A, B, C, D and E (where B, C, D and E progressively save more lives by increasingly active forms of intervention) people will say that E is the best option. The reason for this surprising result is that people see that B is better than A, C is better than B, D is better than C and E is better than D.

Why should adding or deleting intermediate options affect our intuitive judgments of pre-existing options? A defender of our intuitions might argue that Unger's intermediate options are a means of corrupting sound moral intuitions, but we would need to know why that should be so. When we look more closely at the options that people are inclined to reject, the picture looks quite different. The intuitive reactions are, Unger argues, based on factors much odder than not using a person as a means:

> First, when serious loss will result, it's harder to justify moving a person to, or into, an object than it is to move the object to, or into, the person. Second, when serious loss will result, it's harder to justify changing the speed of a moving object, or changing its *rate* of motion, than changing the object's *direction* of motion. Third, when there'll be big loss, it's harder to justify speeding up an object than slowing down an object. Fourth, it's a lot harder to justify taking an object at rest and setting it in motion than to justify taking an object in motion and increasing its speed...[Fifth] it's harder to justify imposing a substantial force on an object than it is to justify allowing a force already present (just about) everywhere, like gravitation, to work on the object.[40]

It's easy to agree with Unger's characterization of these ideas as 'silly'; but after reading Unger's exposition, it's not so easy to deny that they play a role in many people's intuitive reactions to the trolley problem and its variants. Clearly, if Unger is right, the method of doing moral philosophy that relies on our intuitive judgments of particular cases is in tatters. These factors just *cannot* be morally significant. If our intuitions really are based on them, then our intuitions are systematically unreliable. Perhaps these intuitions have been developed in situations where the factors Unger mentions frequently are pointers to something else of genuine moral significance, but in other situations we intuitively follow the pointers when they are no longer appropriate.

Admittedly, informal surveys of one's students do not prove anything. Unger is now exploring with a psychologist ways of more systematically testing his hypotheses, and I hope this will lead to more reliable data. Nevertheless, Unger has put the onus of disproving his hypotheses on to those who take intuitive moral judgments as the touchstone of a normative moral view. It is therefore regrettable that Kamm, who writes at length about Unger's specific cases, should spend the majority of her very lengthy paper exploring our intuitions about a wide variety of cases, without (apart from footnotes referring to unpublished papers) ever addressing Unger's damaging critique of the reliability of those intuitions. She says that her concern is with characterizing our intuitions rather than justifying the use of them in searching for a correct theory (p. 177) – but the pages that follow this comment are of limited interest unless one thinks that our intuitions are likely to be, in Kamm's words, 'revealing of moral truth'. I don't think that they are.

Holton and Langton

Richard Holton and Rae Langton launch their discussion of simulation theory from a brief passage in *Practical Ethics* in which I suggest that the difficulty of knowing that animals feel pain is not much greater than the difficulty of knowing that my daughter feels pain. They ask whether this suggestion is to be interpreted as bringing particular instances under some general law, or as a kind of imaginative entering into the mind of another. Drawing on this and other passages, and on my general support for Hare's moral theory, they conclude that I was probably thinking of the imaginative, rather than the theoretical, method of knowing that another being is in pain. They then argue convincingly that this method has serious problems when applied to non-human animals, and warn me not to make imaginative identification the basis of my ethics.

The warning is well taken, although the risk of my falling into the pitfall they portray may be less than it appears. As Holton and Langton note near the end of their essay (p. 229), I am eclectic in my philosophical methodologies, drawing on facts about animal neurology as well as on imaginative identification. Indeed, I cast the net wider than that. In the first chapter of *Animal Liberation* I refer to behaviour, anatomy, physiology and evolutionary theory in order to strengthen the case that animals can feel pain. When I consider specific issues such as (in chapter 3) the situation of animals confined in typical factory farm conditions, I do not try to identify imaginatively with the animal. Holton and Langton themselves note this in commenting on what I say about veal calves (p. 225); but there are many other examples. In looking at the lives of battery hens, for instance, I describe the signs of stress evident in the birds' behaviour when they are in cages. I show that they have many instincts – to flap their wings, to lay eggs in a sheltered, private nest, to dustbathe – which they cannot fulfil in cages, but which remain present throughout their caged lives, and which they will fulfil if released from the cages. I describe research in which hens have been able to choose between different environments. And I refer to morality rates.[41] Such facts might be relevant to an attempt to imagine oneself in the situation of a hen crowded with three other birds into a small wire cage, but they can also be read as direct evidence of the birds' suffering, and I am happy to leave it to my readers to decide how to use the evidence I provide.

Over the years I have, if anything, moved further away from imaginative identification as a basis for the belief that animals can suffer. Recently, for example, I began an essay on 'The significance of animal suffering' as follows: 'Nonhuman animals can suffer. To deny this, one must now refute not just the common sense of dog owners but the increasing body of empirical evidence, both physiological and behavioral (Dawkins 1980; Rollins 1989)'[42] If there is little danger of my relying on imaginative identification to learn what animals are feeling, what of my support for Hare's methodology, and in particular, my (qualified) support for his argument that universalizability leads to utilitarianism? Is this methodology 'implicitly anthropomorphic' and should I therefore distance myself from it?

How essential is imaginative identification to Hare's moral theory? I shall begin with Hare's key idea that moral judgments must be universalizable. In responding to Lori Gruen's essay, above, I described the requirement of universalizability in these terms: 'To be able to prescribe universally an action we must first put ourselves in the position of all those affected by our action, taking on their preferences.' And I went on to say that the Louisiana legislators who passed laws making it virtually impossible for blacks to vote had not been putting themselves in the place of black people, taking on their preferences. This sounds as if I think that universalizability relies on imaginative identification. But in the opening chapter of *Practical Ethics* I described the same idea as follows: 'I now have to take into account the interests of all those affected by my decision. This requires me to weigh up all these interests and adopt the course of action most likely to maximise the interests of those affected' (PE 13). I did not change my mind between writing *Practical Ethics* and my response to Gruen. Neither passage really implies the use of imaginative identification as the method by which I discover what it is like to be someone else in a specific situation. We could learn this by any means available to us, ranging from getting to know someone very well, to science-fiction brain scanners that can read off data which, when relayed to a computer, enable us to estimate the impact of various future situations on their preferences.

To say this is not to deny the problem of interpersonal comparisons of utility. That problem must face any ethical theory that gives any consideration at all to the impact of our actions on the welfare of others. It is simply to say that the idea of universalizability is neutral on the choice between the use of a theory-based or an imagination based approach to our knowledge of what it is like to be another person affected by our decision. Once we have that knowledge, we must take it into account in deciding what we are able to prescribe universally. Taking it into account means giving it as much weight as we give to our own preferences. Talk of 'putting yourself in the other person's shoes' is a helpful way of expressing that idea, but is not essential to it.

That point needs to be stressed, because at times Holton and Langton write as if Hare, and perhaps I also, think that the ability to imagine ourselves in the position of another is so essential to ethics that where we cannot empathize, we also cannot universalize – and that even if we could somehow know of the existence of another mind, if we could not empathize with it, then it would be beyond 'the bounds of our moral concern' (p. 229). But this is certainly not my view, and I doubt very much that it is Hare's either. Reading his 'Why I am only a demi-vegetarian', in this volume, shows that alongside the passage Holton and Langton quote, in which Hare imagines himself to be a trout, there are many others in which he refers to other kinds of evidence about the experiences of animals, including physiological evidence (Hare, p. 234). His reference to maximizing 'the amount of quality-adjusted life years or QALYs of sentient beings' (Hare, p. 240) is also not at all suggestive of the use of imaginative identification as a method of establishing levels of well-being. I am confident that Hare and I would agree that if we were, for some reason, utterly unable to identify imaginatively with another being but nevertheless had good evidence that that being had preferences of a certain kind, we could not ignore those preferences in making a universalizable judgment.

Thus if I accept Holton and Langton's plausible view that we cannot imagine ourselves in the position of bats, slugs or locusts, the consequence would not be that I no longer apply the principle of universalizability to these animals, but that in doing so, I avoid attempting to make use of imaginative identification. If, as they suggest, 'the application of biology' is likely to be more helpful in understanding the preferences of bats, or slugs, or locusts (p. 225) than imaginative identification, then that is what we should use. Of course, we should also be ready to admit that our understanding of biology is still far too limited to give us clear answers about whether creatures with nervous systems and behaviour very different from our own are capable of having preferences, and if so, what they are like. This puts a large element of uncertainty into much of our decision-making, but no plausible ethical theory can avoid the need to make decisions under conditions of uncertainty.

Holton and Langton might grant that the concept of universalizability can be stated and applied without making essential use of imaginative identification; but they would contend that even if this is so, Hare needs imaginative identification for his argument for deriving a form of utilitarianism from the idea that moral judgments are universalizable prescriptions. Before I comment on this, I must make two minor corrections to what Holton and Langton say. First, they say that in my contribution to *Hare and Critics* I 'defend Hare's moral theory' (p. 217). It would be more accurate to say that I defend some aspects of Hare's moral theory. Again, contrary to what they say a few lines further on, in the quotation Holton and Langton use at the beginning of their article, I was arguing simply for the reasonableness of our belief that animals can feel pain. I made no claim that in coming to believe that my daughter is in pain, I learn also to give weight to her desire to avoid pain. That would be a quite different, and highly questionable claim, which I do not make. I doubt that Hare would make it either – it would be inconsistent with his acceptance of the existence of amoralists who know that others feel pain, but do not care about it.

It is not *knowing* that another is in pain but making moral judgments that compels us to give weight to the desires of others, in proportion to how much they matter to those whose desires they are. This is because, according to Hare, moral judgments are not universalizable statements, they are universalizable *prescriptions*. If we make a moral judgment we must be prepared to prescribe it for all relevantly similar cases. This includes hypothetical cases in which I am in the position of one of the others affected by my action. Hare uses such hypothetical cases as a weapon against, for example, the Nazi who thinks Jews should be killed. If Nazis were to put themselves in the situation of the Jews they are killing, Hare argues, they would not have been able to prescribe that Jews should be killed.[43] The essence of Holton and Langton's argument is that while we may be able to make sense of Nazis putting themselves in the position of Jews, this will not work for normal humans putting themselves in the place of bats or chickens or humans with severe intellectual disabilities. But since Holton, Langton, Hare and myself all agree that we must extend our moral concern to – at least – all beings who can feel pain, Holton and Langton take this to show that moral concern cannot be limited to those beings into whose position we can sensibly imagine ourselves.

As Holton and Langton show, Hare sometimes writes as if making universalizable prescriptions involves imaginatively identifying with others, and this what makes it impossible for us to prescribe something universally unless it maximizes the interests of all those affected by it. I am not sure how strongly Hare would wish to defend our ability to identify imaginatively with all sentient beings.[44] If, for the sake of the argument, we grant that there are some sentient beings with whom we cannot imaginatively identify, the key issue then becomes whether imaginative identification is more than a useful device for portraying what it is to give equal weight to the desires of others. This is not the place to attempt to reconstruct Hare's argument for utilitarianism without making use of imaginative identification, but I can see no insuperable obstacle to that task.

Hare

I welcome the editor's decision to include 'Why I am only a demi-vegetarian' in this volume. As I have already made clear, I accept much of Hare's approach to moral issues, and it is pleasing that he agrees that this precludes discounting the interests of beings simply because they are not members of our species. (This is the attitude I call 'speciesism'. Hare's plea for the more euphonious 'specism' has probably come too late, for 'speciesism' now has the imprimatur of the *Oxford English Dictionary*.) Hare and I are also in agreement that, at least for some of the animals commonly eaten, the question of suffering is much more important than the fact that the animals are killed. (On my view, this is true of animals that lack sufficient self-awareness to see themselves as existing over time.) Precisely because there is so much common ground between Hare and myself, Hare's defence of a limited amount of meat-eating forces me to think along lines different from those I have already covered in replying to more familiar objections to vegetarianism from those who are speciesists, openly or in veiled form.[45]

Like Hare, I was brought up in a culture in which meat was the centrepiece of almost every dinner. I ate meat without questioning the morality of doing so until as a graduate student at Oxford a chance meeting with another student who was already a vegetarian led me to question the way in which animals are treated and – importantly – to inquire into the way in which animals live in modern factory farms. Reading about factory farming in Ruth Harrison's pioneering book *Animal Machines*, I was particularly struck by one phrase describing the way in which the modern agribusiness industry treats animals: 'Cruelty is acknowledged only where profitability ceases.'[46] This was no mere assertion – her book documented its truth over and over again. At that time, 1971, government 'codes of practice' were toothless and brushed aside by the power of the market. As far as the big agribusiness companies were concerned, everything that could be done to produce meat, eggs or milk more cheaply would be done. This included confining veal calves in crates so narrow that they could not turn around, and feeding them on a diet deliberately deficient in iron to keep their flesh pale; keeping four laying hens in cages that were not even wide enough for one hen to stretch her wings; debeaking chickens and turkeys with a hot knife so that the stress caused by their conditions would not lead them to kill each other; and locking pregnant sows into stalls where, for months at a time, they could not turn around or walk a single step.

My wife and I (again, as with Hare and his wife, this was a mutual decision) initially decided to boycott factory farm produce. This meant not buying veal, pork, chicken, turkey or battery eggs. Free range eggs were available from local farms that we could check for ourselves, and beef and dairy products still came overwhelmingly from unconfined animals, but free range veal, pork, chicken or turkey was either non-existent or beyond our limited budget. So we became, without knowing the term, demi-vegetarians, and began to explore cuisines that are not heavily meat based, especially those of India and the Mediterranean. Within a few weeks, however, we ceased to eat meat altogether. For a time we ate fish when we found ourselves at restaurants that did not cater for vegetarians, and then for some years we still occasionally ate molluscs like oysters and mussels before we eventually became full vegetarians.

Why did we move from demi-vegetarianism to ceasing to eat meat or fish at all? As our knowledge of farming grew, we learnt that not only in factory farming, but also in such routine events as the separation of mother and young, castration, transport, slaughter and many other aspects of their lives, animals are treated merely as things. We stopped eating fish because they die slowly and in distress. (Hare says that he has misgivings about eating fish caught with a rod and line (p. 244) but fish caught by commercial trawlers die either from suffocation, when hauled out of the water, or from decompression, if brought up from the deep. Neither form of death is likely to be quick or painless.) We continued to eat oysters and mussels because we thought that their nervous systems were too rudimentary for them to feel pain. While I still think that this is probably the case, since I have no need at all to eat them, I now prefer to give them the benefit of the doubt.

Reasons of health played no role in our decision. We knew that vegetarians are at least as healthy as meat-eaters, and we did not need to know more than that. We were more impressed by the greater efficiency of feeding people on a plant-based diet, with its implications that a switch from a diet heavy in animal products would make it easier to solve the world food problem, and would have environmental benefits. This bolstered our prior decision to stop eating meat, but did not bring that decision about. Our overriding motive was to stop the exploitation of animals, and the obvious first step was to cease buying the products of that exploitation. As long as people pay for these products, we reasoned, others will continue to exploit animals in order to produce meat cheaply.

For me, becoming a vegetarian was part of other activities that included campaigning and writing aimed at bringing about a fundamental change in our attitude to animals. I wanted people to cease to think of them as things, and instead to give their interests the same consideration as we give to the similar interests of human beings. Perhaps one reason why I rapidly embraced full vegetarianism was that I wanted to take a clear, uncomplicated stance that people could readily understand and associate with a radically different attitude to animals. Looking at that decision now, with the benefit of hindsight, I think it was the right one. I believe that becoming a vegetarian has helped me to be effective in persuading people to reconsider their accepted views about the status of animals. I am frequently asked what I eat, both privately and by the media, and people seem to understand and respect the commitment shown by being a vegetarian. They would, I believe, have been less convinced if I had had to go into a long explanation about which farms it is all right to buy meat from, and which it is not all right to buy meat from.

Admittedly, short of a vegan lifestyle – avoiding all animal products in food and clothing – no line is really clearcut. Even vegans have difficult decisions to make. Should they avoid buying car tyres because they contain minute amounts of animal products? I have subsequently moved to a near-vegan diet, but I am not strict about it, and do not advocate veganism to others, or at least not to those who are not already in the animal movement, because at the present stage of development of our society's concern for animals, this seems to be asking more than most people are prepared to give. In other words, to advocate veganism may be counterproductive, in much the way that, as we saw above, asking people to give more than, say, 10 per cent of their income to famine relief may be counterproductive.

Hare might point out that my reasons for not being a strict vegan parallel his reasons for being a demi-vegetarian rather than a full vegetarian. Just as I think that veganism is too demanding to gain widespread support, so he argues that demi-vegetarianism is a greater threat to the meat industry than vegetarianism, because of the much larger number of people attracted to it. In terms of impact on sales, Hare is right. The total volume of meat sold has dropped much more because of people cutting down on the amount of meat they eat than it has because of people giving up meat altogether. Most of these people have not been influenced by ethical concerns about animals at all. They are cutting down on animal products to lower their risk of heart disease and cancer. As a result they can expect to live longer, healthier lives, and the costs of public health services will grow less rapidly than they otherwise would have. All this is excellent, but it would be better still if these demi-vegetarians could be persuaded to adopt Hare's form of demi-vegetarianism, rather than (as many of them do at present) dropping beef from their diet and retaining chicken, the overwhelming majority of which comes from factory farms.

Hare suggests agitating for a law requiring full disclosure of the sources of all foodstuffs. He mentions a proposal for certification of humanely produced food that, at the time of writing, was under consideration by the Royal Society for the Prevention of Cruelty to Animals. This scheme has now come into practice in the United Kingdom, under the name 'Freedom Foods'. It has proved popular with consumers, but some animal advocates have objected that its requirements are too weak. They allow chicken producers, for example, to cut back the beaks of their chickens, although not as severely as the standard practice in the industry. While such compromises are understandable, they carry with them the danger that when a respected organization like the RSPCA labels food as humane, people are reassured that all is well, and it becomes much harder to bring about further improvements.

As Hare says, it is an open question whether the goals which he and I share will be more quickly achieved by a campaign aimed at encouraging people to become vegetarians, or one that promotes demi-vegetarianism. But we do not need to choose one or the other. It is probably a good thing if different people and organizations promote each of these goals. They will appeal to different people, and together, will move the entire spectrum of dietary habits towards the vegetarian end of the scale. The existence of a minority of active vegetarians makes demi-vegetarianism more of a mainstream position, and so may encourage some meat-eaters to become demi-vegetarians. On that basis, I would accept Hare's defence of demi-vegetarianism to this extent: it can be justifiable for some people to follow a demi-vegetarian diet of the kind Hare describes, and actively to encourage others to adopt this diet. At the same time, it can be justifiable for others to follow a fully vegetarian diet, and actively to encourage others to adopt this diet.

What, though, of Hare's argument that demi-vegetarianism is not merely a sound tactic for reducing the suffering of animals in factory farms, but also the right position to adopt because a world in which we were all demi-vegetarians would have a greater total amount of preference-satisfaction? When I became a vegetarian I rejected Leslie Stephens's argument that animals are replaceable – which relies on the total view – but as I said above in responding to Kamm, I later came to accept that in the case of beings who are not aware of themselves as existing over time, the loss of satisfaction we cause to one animal when we kill it can be made up by bringing another equally happy animal into existence. I embraced this view with no great enthusiasm, only because all alternatives to it face seemingly insuperable difficulties. Ask yourself, for example, if it would be wrong to bring a child into existence, knowing that the child suffered from a genetic defect that would make her life both brief and utterly miserable for every moment of her existence? If you answer yes, it would be wrong to bring a child into existence under those conditions, then you think that we can harm a being by bringing it into existence. Now consider bringing into existence a being who will lead a thoroughly satisfying life. Is that a good thing to do, other things being equal? If you answer this in the negative, you need to explain why it is wrong to harm a child by bringing a miserable being into existence, but not good to benefit a child by bringing a happy or fulfilled being into existence. Sound explanations for this are extraordinarily difficult to find.[47]

In the second edition of *Animal Liberation* I replaced the passage in which I had rejected the replaceability argument with another passage in which I said that while the idea that the creation of one sentient being can compensate for the killing of another still seemed peculiar, I could not say that it was wrong. I added that this argument could justify eating free range animals, incapable of forming desires for the future, as long as they have a pleasant existence and are then killed painlessly. Hare's argument is in keeping with this conclusion, except for two points. First, he seems not to give weight to the distinction I draw between animals who are capable of forming desires for the future and those who are not, and second, he urges that it may be not merely acceptable, but positively desirable, that we eat animals raised in this way. I have already defended the first point, in replying to Kamm, and I think it is a distinction that Hare ought to recognize, since it is based on the existence of preferences. Regarding the second claim, in arguing that it may be positively desirable for us to eat animals so that they can be brought into existence, Hare seems to assume that unless there are cattle grazing on the steep slopes of the Cotswold escarpment, there will be no sentient beings living from this land. Whether this is so is an empirical question, but in general, nature abhors a vacuum, and does not leave ecological niches unfilled for long. It may well be best, from the point of view of maximizing pleasant sentient existence, to allow forest to regrow on slopes that have been cleared for cattle. Perhaps the squirrels, voles and whatever else that might live there will experience more pleasure than the cattle they replace. (Allowing forest to regrow may have other benefits as well: for example, slowing the greenhouse effect.) So the argument for the positive desirability of eating well raised animals is, at best, unproven.

In the second editions of *Animal Liberation* and *Practical Ethics*, after acknowledging that the replaceability argument could justify eating some animals, I then added a practical consideration that counts against this conclusion. I argued that killing animals for food, except when necessary for our survival, makes us think of them as objects that we can use lightly for our own ends, and that as long as we continue to think of animals in this way, we will not succeed in changing the attitudes that lead to so much mistreatment of animals. Therefore, I suggested, it may be best to make it a simple general principle to avoid killing animals for food except when it is necessary for survival.[48]

This is the slippery slope argument that Kamm has said seems inconsistent with my rejection of such arguments in respect of euthanasia. Generously, Kamm helps me out of this difficulty by suggesting that I may be basing the distinction on how bad the effects of having a more general rule would be. Erring on the side of not eating animals is not going to do much harm, since at most it will deprive people of gustatory pleasure; erring on the side of prohibiting euthanasia will mean that people die in needless pain and misery. That is certainly one reason for the distinction. Another is that the likelihood of sliding down a slippery slope will depend on the attitudes that a society holds. Since our society has a strong and long-standing commitment to the protection of human life, there is little danger of sliding down a slippery slope from voluntary euthanasia to killing people who want to go on living. On the other hand, since our society has a deeply ingrained tradition of thinking of non-human animals as mere means to our ends, we need to take a firm stance to change this way of thinking.

As I have already said, for me becoming a vegetarian was part of an awakening to the neglected moral issue of speciesism. No more finely grained dietary stance could have been as effective a symbol of my rejection of our conventional attitudes and practices towards animals. I continue to advocate a vegetarian diet in order to encourage others to dissociate themselves, in a clear and public manner, from those attitudes and practices. To do so is not to deny that, for other people in different circumstances, a diet including a small amount of carefully selected meat could be an ethical choice.

Rolston

As the leitmotif for his essay, Holmes Rolston takes a quotation from me: 'There is nothing to take into account.' The implication is that this dismissive utterance encapsulates my attitude to all of non-sentient nature. But let me put this quotation in context:

> If a being suffers there can be no moral justification for refusing to take that suffering into consideration. No matter what the nature of the being, the principle of equality requires that its suffering be counted equally with the like suffering – in so far as rough comparisons can be made – of any other being. If a being is not capable of suffering, or of experiencing enjoyment or happiness, there is nothing to be taken into account. So the limit of sentience (using the term as a convenient if not strictly accurate shorthand for the capacity to suffer and/or experience enjoyment) is the only defensible boundary of concern for the interests of others. (AL 2nd edn, pp. 8–9)

The passage asserts that if a being is not sentient, it has no interests that we can consider. This is not a claim that Rolston denies. The passage does *not* say that if a being is not sentient, it doesn't matter at all what we do to it.

Regrettably, this is not the only instance of Rolston quoting me out of context. At the very end of his essay, for example, he quotes me as saying that 'trees, ecosystems, and species are more like rocks than they are like sentient beings', and describes this as 'absurd'. So it is, but it would not have been absurd if he had quoted the entire sentence, which begins with the words 'In this respect' – a reference to a preceding discussion of whether an entity can have experiences.

Since labels do affect the way we think, I must also demur at some of the terms Rolston uses. Consider the following passage in which he attempts to show that one cannot defend a sound environmental ethic without finding intrinsic value beyond sentient beings: 'Although an animal welfare ethic and an environmental ethic do often converge, they by no means always do so . . . To put the point with some provocation, the people in the United States who join the Sierra Club do not always have the same agenda as the people who join the Humane Society.' Rolston here refers to the kind of ethic I advocate as 'an animal welfare ethic', and suggests that it is 'the people who join the Humane Society' who are likely to share this ethic. But a genuinely non-speciesist ethic goes far beyond 'animal welfare', and most members of Humane Societies stop well short of what I would prefer to call a non-speciesist ethic. Few of them are vegetarians (or even the kind of conscientious demi-vegetarian that Hare defends). So Rolston's portrayal of my position is not so much provocative as inaccurate. His reference to the agenda of people who join the Sierra Club is misleading for a different reason. On environmental grounds alone, there is an overwhelming case for avoiding animal products produced by modern agribusiness, and fish caught from unsustainable fishing practices. But not all members of the Sierra Club avoid such products. If they did, the convergence between their practices and those of genuine non-speciesists would be much greater.

Nevertheless, in the end it is true that a non-speciesists ethic will not always converge with an ethic that seeks to give intrinsic value to things other than sentient beings. The real issue is what the basis of the alternative ethic is. For most of his chapter, Rolston defends an ethic of respect for life. To support this, he claims that living things are not merely physical objects: 'Something more than merely physical causes... is operating within every organism' (p. 250). This 'more than merely physical' something turns out to be information. Yet below Rolston tells us that plant information 'is carried by the DNA, which we call a "linguistic" molecule'. A molecule is a physical thing, so this appears to contradict Rolston's claim that living things operate by non-physical causes. (Just to make my own position clear, it is no part of my argument that sentient beings operate by non-physical causes, either. It is Rolston who appears to find it significant whether something has non-physical causes operating within it.)

Next Rolston claims that plants defend themselves against damage, and they *value* the state that they defend: that is, the state in which they are undamaged. Or that, at least, seems the only way to interpret his claim that this state 'is a valued state'. For if it is not valued by the plant itself, then in what other sense could it be valued? Rolston acknowledges that plants may have no will or desires, but says that every organism has a '*good-of-its-kind*'. This is, he insists, no metaphor but 'the plain fact of the matter'. Is it? Surely the plain fact of the matter is that over millions of years, those plants that evolved defence mechanisms that significantly improved their chances of passing on their genes had more offspring than those plants that did not, and over time tended to supplant them. There is no need here for talk of 'good' or 'standards', let alone of values or of what 'ought to be'. An evolutionary explanation suffices.

When Rolston tries to distinguish guided missiles from plants, he gives the game away. In *Practical Ethics* I introduced guided missiles into the discussion of Schweitzer's ethic of reverence for life in order to show that apparently purposive behaviour was not sufficient grounds for concluding that something has a 'will to live'. Rolston claims that a guided missile differs from a plant in that it has no 'good-of-its-kind', but only a good for the people who made it to serve their own purposes. If it dodges anti-missile rockets, it does so only because its designers programmed these activities into it. In contrast, when it comes to natural organisms, Rolston writes:

Natural selection picks out whatever traits an organism has that are valuable to it, relative to its survival. When natural selection has been at work gathering these traits into an organism, that organism is able to value on the basis of those traits. It is a valuing organism, even if the organism is not a sentient valuer, much less a conscious evaluator. And those traits, though picked out by natural selection, are innate in the organism: that is, stored in its genes. It is difficult to dissociate the idea of value from natural selection. (p. 253)

If human designers, no matter how clever their computer programs, cannot give a 'good-of-its-own' to a guided missile, why should we think that the blind process of natural selection can make a plant able to value?

Rolston struggles to defend his view. He asks what he hopes is a rhetorical question: 'Why is the organism not valuing what it is making resources of?' But we could just as well ask why the missile is not valuing its fuel, since it has devices on board that minimize fuel consumption. Does the difference lie in the fact that the plant's means of conserving water are encoded in its genes, whereas the missile's means of conserving fuel are encoded in its computer programs? Why would that make one a valuer and the other not? Like every defence I have yet seen of an ethic that goes beyond sentient life, the foundations of this ethical view remain a mystery.

Later, Rolston introduces yet another reason for extending value beyond sentient beings: 'The claim that value enters the world only in the conscious experiences of the subjective lives of higher organisms has too much subjective bias. It values a late product of the system, psychological life, and subordinates everything else to this' (p. 265). Rolston does not tell us why we should not believe that value entered into the world rather late in its development. In terms of the time that has elapsed since the big bang, the Earth itself is 'a late product of the system. So to avoid 'subjective bias', Rolston should believe that there was value even in the lifeless clouds of gases that drifted around the universe for untold aeons before our solar system was formed. This, however, must be a different kind of value from that which, as he has been arguing for most of his essay, is to be found in organisms, species and biological systems that defend themselves against threats.

The many mysteries of Rolston's environmental ethic are not cleared up by his discussion of practical environmental issues. Concerning the goats of San Clemente Island, he asserts that 'the well-being of plants at the species level outweighs the welfare of the goats at the individual level', and on Santa Barbara Island, protecting the endangered *Dudleya traskiae* 'justifies causing suffering and death in the rabbits'. He appears to defend the poisoning of entire stream systems, including tens of thousands of brown trout, in order to protect the native golden trout. These choices are the right ones, apparently, because a species, like an individual organism, has a 'good-of-its-kind' and when it comes to a clash between the survival of a species or of an individual organism, the species 'is a bigger event than the individual, regardless of whether the member individual has interests or sentience' (pp. 260–1). If that is the justification, why stop at rabbits or goats? If human beings are a threat to a plant species, as they often are, shouldn't they, too, be 'live-trapped and removed'? Or if that leads to them 'doing poorly', maybe they should be shot or poisoned? If Rolston thinks that this would be wrong, he should tell us why the distinction between human beings and other sentient animals is important enough to outweigh concerns about species preservation, but the distinction between sentient beings and non-sentient beings is not. (In view of my earlier discussion of arguments based on our common moral convictions, I should add that if Rolston's position does imply that we would be justified in killing humans in order to save endangered plants, this would not refute it. But it would be interesting to know how far he is prepared to go in defending the species over the individual.)

Rolston speculates that I will defend introduced rabbits in Australia, unless a calculus shows that their presence means that sentient native marsupials suffer in ways that outweigh the pleasures of rabbits. There is no doubt that the introduction of the rabbit has been a disaster for the Australian environment. It has contributed to the extinction of some native animals, as well as many plants, and to soil erosion and desertification. Rabbits also cause economic losses to farmers. To reduce this loss, they use a variety of methods to kill rabbits, many of which inflict a lingering, painful death. None have provided effective long-term control of rabbit numbers.

In this situation, what action is consistent with equal consideration for the interest of all sentient beings, now and in generations to come? The interests of native marsupials and the introduced rabbits must be taken into account, along with the interests of farmers, and of consumers of food made more expensive by damage inflicted by rabbits. It is also important to consider the impact of rabbits on the sustainability of the Australian ecosystem. If they will cause deserts to expand, thus rendering large parts of the country uninhabitable by any sentient beings, that is an important reason for not allowing this situation to continue. We should also take into account the value that we place on the preservation of Australia's unique original flora and fauna. In a world in which wilderness is increasingly rare, the preservation of diverse ecosystems is of great value to us, and we can expect future generations to value them too. On aesthetic grounds alone, to allow them to be destroyed is like letting Venice sink into its lagoon – a loss that would be regretted by generations to come.

There are many conflicting interests here. If we could eliminate rabbits, or significantly reduce their numbers, without inflicting great suffering on them, that would be an ideal solution. Research into methods of making rabbits infertile by means of a virus offers some hope that this may be achievable, although it is not yet feasible. In the interim, if it is reasonable to assume that rabbits do not have the capacity to see themselves as existing over time, quick-acting lethal methods of rabbit control will be the next best option. On the other hand, to spread a disease like myxomatosis, which leaves rabbits semi-paralysed and blind before they die, cannot be justified.[49]

As this example shows, it is quite misleading to summarize my view by saying that I insist 'that "there is nothing to be taken into account" in all this display of vitality in insentient life' (Rolston, p. 267). Such statements ignore – strangely, for an environmentalist – the aesthetic, scientific and recreational values of preserving natural ecosystems. For the same reasons, I do not have to agree that 'all is well and good' when a giant tree is cut down each year to serve as a national Christmas tree on the White House lawn. Rolston is just plain wrong when he says that I have 'no grounds on which to recommend' his idea of leaving a tree in place, decorating it and telling people why it was left uncut. I would recommend that this be done to symbolize the importance of preserving our beautiful and ancient forests, which provide homes and food for many wild animals and help to keep the climate of our planet stable. I would also use the opportunity to tell people about the waste of resources involved in the old practice of felling and transporting a large tree across the country. Instead of seeing nature as something for us to exploit and destroy to satisfy quite trivial desires of our own, I would say, we should see it as a precious heritage that we should preserve in order to pass on to our children and grandchildren.

Notes

1 R. M. Hare, *The Language of Morals* (Oxford: Clarendon Press, 1952); *Freedom and Reason* (Oxford: Clarendon Press, 1963); *Moral Thinking* (Oxford: Clarendon Press, 1981).

2 Henry Sidgwick, *The Methods of Ethics*, 7th edn (London: Macmillan, 1907), p. 382.

3 Hare makes the same point in his most recent work: 'The terms "cognitivist" and "non-cognitivist" are misleading... The important question is whether one can *think rationally* about moral questions. In other words, are there ways of doing our moral reasoning well or badly? This important question is

concealed by those who speak of cognitivism and non-cognitivism, and of knowing that moral statements are true.' *Sorting Out Ethics* (Oxford: Clarendon Press, 1997), p. 56.

4 'Triviality . . .', p. 54.

5 G. E. M. Anscombe, 'Modern moral philosophy', first published in *Philosophy*, 33 (1958); Philippa Foot, 'Moral beliefs', first published in *Proceedings of the Aristotelian Society*, 59 (1958); John Searle, 'How to derive "ought" from "is"', first published in *The Philosophical review*, 73 (1964). All three essays are reprinted in W. D. Hudson, *The Is/Ought Question* (London: Macmillan, 1969), along with several other essays discussing these articles, especially Searle's.

6 Anscombe, 'Modern moral philosophy'.

7 Hudson, *The Is/Ought Question*, p. 211.

8 Oxford: Blackwell, 1994.

9 See my discussion in *Hegel* (Oxford: Oxford University Press, 1983), pp. 32–3.

10 See especially chapters 10 and 11.

11 My principal earlier discussions are: 'Why should I be moral?' (Unpublished MA thesis, University of Melbourne, 1969); 'The triviality . . .'; *Practical Ethics*, 1st edn chapters 1 and 10, 2nd edn chapters 1 and 12; *The Expanding Circle*, pp. 140ff; and *How Are We to Live?*, UK edn pp. 268ff, Australian/US edn pp. 225ff.

12 'Evolution, animals and the basis of morality', *Inquiry*, 22 (1979), p. 91.

13 See Leon Festinger, *A Theory of Cognitive Dissonance* (Stanford, CA: Stanford University Press, 1957). See also below.

14 Compare Karl Marx: 'Each new class which displaces the one previously dominant is forced, simply to carry out its aim, to represent its interest as the common interest of all members of society . . . It has to give its ideas the form of universality and represent them as the only rational, universally valid ones.' *The German Ideology* (New York: International Publishers, 1966), pp. 40–1.

15 Festinger, *A Theory of Cognitive Dissonance*, chapter 1, cited from *The Expanding Circle*, p. 143.

16 From the *Critique of Practical Reason*, trans. L. W. Beck (Chicago: University of Chicago Press, 1949), p. 186; reprinted in Peter Singer, *Ethics* (Oxford: Oxford University Press, 1994), p. 131.

17 *The Methods of Ethics*, p. 498.

18 *Ethics*, p. 275; Immanuel Kant, *Groundwork of the Metaphysic of Morals*, trans. H. J. Paton as *The Moral Law* (London: Hutchinson University Library, 1966), p. 86.

19 *How Are We to Live?* (US edn), p. 218.

20 I am not sure why Crisp thinks that scepticism about moral objectivity should lead me to naturalism, rather than, say, to prescriptivism. Crisp's use (on p. 96) of a quotation from *Democracy and Disobedience* is also not apt, for in that passage I was making a specific point about the possibility of dispensing with the language of 'obligation' as an element of moral discourse, not about dispensing with moral language altogether.

21 For further examples of mysterious moral claims, see my response to Rolston, below.

22 For further details see my *Rethinking Life and Death*, pp. 57–67.

23 London: Mansell, 1989.

24 For examples of this defence of speciesism, see Mary Midgley, *Animals and Why They Matter* (Harmondsworth: Penguin, 1983), chapter 9; Jeffrey Gray, 'On the morality of speciesism', *The Psychologist*, 4 (May 1991), pp. 196–8. For one of my responses see Peter Singer, 'Speciesism, morality and biology', *The Psychologist*, 4 (May 1991), pp. 199–200.

25 Perhaps the most revealing and best documented of these experiments in collective child-rearing is the Israeli kibbutz movement. See Yonina Talmon, *Family and Community in the Kibbutz* (Cambridge, MA: Harvard University Press, 1972), pp. 3–34.

26 *The Methods of Ethics*, p. 489–90.

27 McGinn has a propensity to find utilitarian positions where none is intended. He did the same thing in his review of Peter Unger's *Living High and Letting Die*, to which he refers in his note 6. I at least am a utilitarian, even if in 'Famine, affluence and morality' I was consciously refraining from presenting a utilitarian argument. Unger has vigorously denied not only that the argument of his book is based on utilitarianism, but also that he is himself a utilitarian (personal communication).

28 Jeremy Bentham, *An Introduction to the Principles of Morals and Legislation* (New York: Hafner, 1948; first published 1789), p. 5n.

29 *Practical Ethics*, p. 330; that it is these remarks that led Kamm astray, I know from her.

30 *How Are We to Live?*, US edn p. 185, UK edn p. 219.

31 Ibid., US edn p. 218, UK edn p. 258.

32 See *Practical Ethics*, chapter 1.

33 Ibid., pp. 121ff.

34 New York: New York Review/Random House, 1975, pp. 254–5.

35 Kamm has told me that she drew this inference from two sentences on pp. 22 and 23 of *Practical Ethics*, but she has read something into these passages that I did not intend.

36 'Sidgwick and reflective equilibrium', *The Monist*, 58 (July 1974), pp. 490–517. In calling Rawls's approach conservative, I do not, of course, mean that it is conservative in a political sense, but that of its nature it cannot challenge, as a whole, the prevailing broad consensus of moral opinion in a community.

37 For further discussion, see my *Animal Liberation*, chapter 5; Helga Kuhse and Peter Singer, *Should the Baby Live?* (Oxford: Oxford University Press, 1985), chapters 5 and 6; and my *Rethinking Life and Death* (Melbourne: Text, 1994; New York: St Martin's Press, 1995; Oxford: Oxford University Press, 1995), chapter 8.

38 Dale Jamieson makes a useful distinction between hypothetical and imaginative examples, and argues against relying on our intuitions in the latter cases. See his 'Method and moral theory', in my *A Companion to Ethics* (Oxford: Blackwell, 1991), especially pp. 484–5. See also R. M. Hare, 'The argument

from received opinion', in his *Essays on Philosophical Method* (London: Macmillan, 1971).

39 An important early article was Judith Jarvis Thomson, 'Killing, letting die, and the trolley problem', *The Monist* (1976), reprinted in John M. Fischer and Mark Ravizza (eds), *Ethics: Problems and Principles* (New York: Harcourt Brace Jovanovich, 1992), pp. 70–1, but the problem derives from an earlier paper by Philippa Foot, 'The problem of abortion and the doctrine of the double effect', *Oxford Review* (1967).

40 Peter Unger, *Living High and Letting Die* (Oxford: Oxford University Press, 1996), p. 102.

41 *Animal Liberation* (London: Pimlico, 1995), pp. 113–18.

42 *Behavioral and Brain Sciences*, 13, 1 (1990), pp. 9–12. The references are to Marian Stamp Dawkins, *Animal Suffering: the Science of Animal Welfare* (London: Chapman & Hall, 1980), and Bernard Rollin, *The Unheeded Cry* (Oxford: Oxford University Press, 1989).

43 *Freedom and Reason*, chapter 9; *Moral Thinking*, chapter 10.

44 He can and would stand by the remark Holton and Langton quote about thinking himself into the positions of non-sentient objects (p. 224). Since stoves, mountains, trees, human corpses, brain-dead humans or any other inanimate objects or beings without sentience have no experiences at all, thinking oneself into their position involves blanking out all experiences, and is the same no matter what the nature of the particular object or being in question. I will return to this issue when discussing Holmes Rolston's chapter, but is it really so difficult to imagine what it is like to be dead and without any experiences?

45 For some of my responses to these objections, see 'Philosophical vegetarianism: a reply', *The Humanist*, 37 (July/August 1977); 'The fable of the fox and the unliberated animals', *Ethics*, 88 (January 1978), pp. 119–25; 'Ten years of animal liberation', *New York Review of Books* (17 January 1985), pp. 46–52; 'Bandit and friends', *New York Review of Books* (9 April 1992), pp. 9–13; 'Ethics and animals', *Behavioral and Brain Sciences*, 13 (1990), pp. 45–9; 'The pervasiveness of species bias', *Behavioral and Brain Sciences*, 14 (1991), pp. 759–60; 'Speciesism, morality and biology', *The Psychologist*, 4 (May 1991), pp. 199–200; *Practical Ethics*, 2nd edn, pp. 68–82.

46 London: Vincent Stuart, 1964, p. 3.

47 Derek Parfit shows just how difficult this quest is in his *Reasons and Persons* (Oxford: Clarendon Press, 1984). For an alternative approach see David Heyd, *Genethics: Moral Issues in the Creation of People* (Berkeley: University of California Press, 1992). In my review of this book in *Bioethics*, 7, 1 (1993), p. 64, I tried to explain why Heyd has not solved the problem.

48 *Animal Liberation*, 2nd edn, p. 229; see also *Practical Ethics*, 2nd edn, p. 134.

49 These are not just philosophical speculations. As President of the Australian and New Zealand federation of Animal Societies, an umbrella group for most Australian animal liberation and animal welfare organizations, I have been involved in drafting the organization's policy and lobbying governments along these lines.

Peter Singer: Selected Publications 1970–1998

Books

Democracy and Disobedience, Clarendon Press, Oxford, 1973; Oxford University Press, New York, 1974; Gregg Revivals, Aldershot, Hampshire, 1994.

Spanish translation, *Democracia y Desobediencia*, Editorial Ariel, Barcelona, 1985.

Animal Liberation: a New Ethics for Our Treatment of Animals, New York Review/Random House, New York, 1975; Cape, London, 1976; Avon, New York, 1977; Paladin, London, 1977; Thorsons, London, 1983.

Dutch translation, *Pro Mens, Pro Dier*, Anthos, Baarn, 1977; German translation, *Befrejung der Tiere*, Hirthammer, Munich, 1982; Spanish translation, *Liberación Animal*, ALECA, Lope de Vega, Mexico, 1985; Italian translation, *Liberazione Animali*, Lega Anti-Vivesezione, Rome, 1987; Japanese translation, Gijutsu-to-Ningen, Tokyo, 1988.

Animal Liberation, 2nd edn, New York Review/Random House, 1990; Jonathan Cape, London, 1990; Avon, New York, 1991; Thorsons, London, 1991.

Italian translation, *Liberazione Animali*, Mondadori, Milan, 1991; Finnish translation, *Oikeutta Elaimille*, Werner Soderstrom, Helsinki, 1991; Swedish translation, *Djurens Frigörelse*, Nya Doxa, Stockholm, 1992; French translation, *La Libération Animale*, Grasset, Paris, 1993; Dutch translation, *Dierenbevrzjding*, De Geus, Breda, 1994; Chinese translation, Life Conservation Association, Taipei, 1996; German translation, *Befreiung der Tiere*, Rowohlt, Hamburg, 1996; Spanish translation, *Liberación Animal*, Mexico, 1995; Trotta Sociedad Anonima Editorial, forthcoming; Hebrew translation, Or-Am, forthcoming.

Animal Rights and Human Obligations: an Anthology (co-editor with Thomas Regan), Prentice Hall, Englewood Cliffs, NJ, 1976. Second, revised edition, Prentice Hall, Englewood Cliffs, NJ, 1989.

Italian translation, Edizioni Gruppo Abele, Turin, 1988.

Practical Ethics, Cambridge University Press, Cambridge, 1979.

German translation, *Praktische Ethik*, Reclam, Stuttgart, 1984; Spanish translation, *Etica Práctica*, Ariel, Barcelona, 1984, 1988, 1991, 1995; Italian translation, *Etica Pratica*, Liguori, Naples, 1989; Swedish translation, *Praktisk Ethik*, Thales, Stockholm, 1990; Japanese translation, *Jissen no Rinri*, Showa-do, Kyoto, 1991.

Practical Ethics, 2nd edn, Cambridge University Press, 1993.

Danish translation, *Praktisk Etik*, Hans Reitzels Forlag, Copenhagen, 1993; Portuguese translation, *Ética Prática*, Livraria Martins Fontes, São Paolo, 1994; German translation, *Praktische Ethik*, Reclam, Stuttgart, 1994; Spanish translation, *Ética Práctica*, Cambridge University Press, Cambridge, 1995; Swedish translation, *Praktisk Ethik*, Thales, Stockholm, 1996; Bengali translation, Bangla Academy, Dhaka, 1996; Korean translation, Chul-hak, Seoul, forthcoming; French translation, Bayard Presse, forthcoming.

Marx, Oxford University Press, Oxford, 1980; Hill & Wang, New York, 1980; also included in full in K. Thomas (ed.), *Great Political Thinkers: Machiavelli, Hobbes, Mill and Marx*, Oxford University Press, Oxford, 1992.

Italian translation, *Marx*, Dall Oglio, Milan, 1981; Italian Book Club edition, Club degli Editori, Milan, 1982; Japanese translation, Yushodo Press, Tokyo, 1989; Spanish translation, Harla, Mexico, forthcoming; Chinese translation, in *Great Political Thinkers*, Oxford University Press, Hong Kong, forthcoming.

Animal Factories (co-author with James Mason), Crown, New York, 1980; 2nd, revised, edn, Harmony, New York, 1990.

Japanese translation, Gendai Shokan, Tokyo, 1983.

The Expanding Circle: Ethics and Sociobiology, Farrar, Straus and Giroux, New York, 1981; Oxford University Press, Oxford, 1981; New American Library, New York, 1982.

Korean translation, In Gan Sa Rang, Seoul, forthcoming.

Hegel, Oxford University Press, Oxford and New York, 1982; also included in full in *German Philosophers: Kant, Hegel, Schopenhauer, Metzsche*, Oxford University Press, Oxford, 1997.

Portuguese translation, *Hegel*, Dom Quixote, Lisbon, 1986; Czech translation, Odeon, Prague, 1995; Spanish translation, Harla, Mexico, 1996; Polish translation, Michael Urbanski, Warsaw, 1996; Romanian translation, Humanitas, Bucharest, 1996; Japanese translation, Aoki Shoten, forthcoming.

Test-Tube Babies: a Guide to Moral Questions, Present Techniques, and Future Possibilities (co-edited with William Walters), Oxford University Press, Melbourne, 1982.

Japanese translation, Iwanami Shoten, Tokyo, 1983.

The Reproduction Revolution: New Ways of Making Babies (co-author with Deane Wells), Oxford University Press, Oxford, 1984. Revised American edition, *Making Babies*, Scribner's, New York, 1985.

Dutch translation, *Het Nieuwe Nageslacht*, Anthos, Baarn, 1985; Polish translation, *Dzieci z Probowki*, Wiedza Powszechna, Warsaw, 1988; Japanese translation, Koyo Shobo, Kyoto, 1989.

Should the Baby Live? The Problem of Handicapped Infants (co-author with Helga Kuhse), Oxford University Press, Oxford, 1985; Oxford University Press, New York, 1986; Gregg Revivals, Aldershot, Hampshire, 1994.

German translation, *Müss dieses Kind am Leben Bleiben?*, Harald Fischer, Erlangen, 1993.

In Defence of Animals (ed.), Blackwell, Oxford, 1985, Harper & Row, New York, 1986.

German translation, *Verteidigt der Tiere*, Neff, Vienna, 1986; pb, Ullstein, Frankfurt, 1988; Dutch translation, *Dierenactiboek*, Anthos, Baarn, 1986; Japanese translation, Gijutsu To Ningen, Tokyo, 1986; Italian translation, *In Difesa degli Animali*, Lucarini, Rome, 1987.

Ethical and Legal Issues in Guardianship: Options for Intellectually Disadvantaged People (co-author with Terry Carney), Human Rights Commission Monograph Series, no. 2, Australian Government Publishing Service, Canberra, 1986.

Applied Ethics (ed.), Oxford University Press, Oxford, 1986.

Animal Liberation: a Graphic Guide (co-author with Lori Gruen), Camden Press, London, 1987.

Embryo Experimentation (co-editor with Helga Kuhse, Stephen Buckle, Karen Dawson and Pascal Kasimba), Cambridge University Press, Cambridge, 1990; paperback edition, updated, 1993.

A Companion to Ethics (ed.), Basil Blackwell, Oxford, 1991; paperback edition, 1993.

Spanish translation, *Compendio de Ética*, Alianza, Madrid, 1995; Polish translation, Wydawnictwo Ksiazka I Wiedza, forthcoming; Turkish translation, Yapi Yayinlari, forthcoming.

Save the Animals! (Australian edition, co-author with Barbara Dover and Ingrid Newkirk), Collins Angus & Robertson, North Ryde, NSW, 1991.

The Great Ape Project: Equality Beyond Humanity (co-editor with Paola Cavalieri), Fourth Estate, London, 1993; St Martin's Press, New York, 1994 (hardback); St Martin's Press, New York, 1995 (paperback).

German translation, *Menschenrechten für die Grossen Menschenaffen*, Peter Goldmann, Munich, 1994; paperback, Goldmann, 1996; Italian translation, *Il Progetto Grande Scimmia: Equalianza oltre i confini della species umana*, Theoria, Rome, 1994; Spanish translation, Trotta Sociedad Anonima Editorial, forthcoming.

How Are We to Live? Ethics in an Age of Self-interest, Text Publishing, Melbourne, 1993; Mandarin, London, 1995, Prometheus, Buffalo, NY, 1995, Oxford University Press, Oxford, 1997.

Japanese translation, Horitsu-bunka sha, Kyoto. 1995; German translation, *Wie Sollen Wir Leben?*, Harald Fischer, Erlangen, 1996; Swedish translation, Natur och Kultur, Stockholm, 1997; Spanish translation, *Ética para vivir mejor*, Editorial Ariel, Barcelona, 1997; Korean translation, Sejong Books, Seoul, 1997.

Ethics (ed.), Oxford University Press, Oxford, 1994.

Individuals, Humans and Persons: Questions of Life and Death (co-author with Helga Kuhse), Academia Verlag, Sankt Augustin, Germany, 1994.

Rethinking Life and Death: the Collapse of Our Traditional Ethics, Text Publishing, Melbourne, 1994; St Martin's Press, New York, 1995; Oxford University Press, Oxford, 1995.

Italian translation, *Ripensare la vita*, Ii Saggiatore, Milan, 1996; Dutch translation, *Tussen Dood en Leven*, Jan van Arkel, Utrecht, 1997; Spanish translation, *Repensar la Vida y la Muerte*, Paidos, Barcelona, 1997; German translation, Harald Fischer, Erlangen, forthcoming; Polish translation, forthcoming; Japanese translation, Showa-Do, forthcoming.

The Greens (co-author with Bob Brown), Text Publishing, Melbourne, 1996.

The Allocation of Health Care Resources (co-author with John McKie, Jeff Richardson and Helga Kuhse), Ashgate, Aldershot, 1998.

A Companion to Bioethics (co-editor with Helga Kuhse), Blackwell, Oxford, 1998.

Bioethics: an Anthology (co-editor with Helga Kuhse), Blackwell, Oxford, 1998.

Ethics into Action: Henry Spira and the Animal Rights Movement, Rowman and Littlefield, Lanham, MD, 1998.

Articles in Professional Journals

'Is act utilitarianism self-defeating?', *Philosophical Review*, 81 (January 1972), pp. 94–104.

'Famine, affluence and morality', *Philosophy and Public Affairs*, 1 (Spring 1972), pp. 229–43.

'Moral experts', Analysis, 32 (March 1972), pp. 115–17.

'The triviality of the debate over "is–ought" and the definition of "moral"', *American Philosophical Quarterly*, 10 (January 1973), pp. 51–6.

'Altruism and commerce: a reply to Arrow', *Philosophy and Public Affairs*, 2 (Spring 1973), pp. 312–20.

'Sidgwick and reflective equilibrium', *The Monist*, 58 (July 1974), pp. 490–517.

'All animals are equal', *Philosophical Exchange*, 1 (Summer 1974), pp. 103–16.

'Is racial discrimination arbitrary?', *Philosophia*, 8 (November 1978), pp. 185–203.

'Killing humans and killing animals', *Inquiry*, 22 (Summer 1979), pp. 145–56.

'Animals and human beings are equals', *Animal Regulation Studies*, 2 (1979/80), pp. 165–74.

'Utilitarianism and vegetarianism', *Philosophy and Public Affairs*, 9 (1980), pp. 325–37.

'Animal liberation', *The Connecticut Scholar*, Occasional Papers, no. 3 (1980), pp. 70–88.

'An argument for utilitarianism' *Canadian Journal of Philosophy*, XI (June 1981), pp. 229–39 (with Yew-Kwang Ng).

'Ethics and sociobiology', *Philosophy and Public Affairs*, 11 (1982), pp. 40–64.

'The Oxford vegetarians – a personal account', *International Journal for the Study of Animal Problems*, 3 (1982), pp. 6–9.

'Can we avoid assigning greater value to some lives than to others?', *Community Health Studies*, Supplementary issue, May 1982, pp. 39–44.

'The treatment of newborn infants with major handicaps: a survey of obstetricians and paediatricians in Victoria', *Medical Journal of Australia* (17 September 1983), pp. 274–8 (with H. Kuhse and C. Singer).

'*In vitro* fertilisation: the major issues', *Journal of Medical Ethics*, 9 (December 1983), pp. 192–5, 198–9 (with Deane Wells).

'The ethics of the reproduction revolution', *Annals of the New York Academy of Sciences*, 442 (1985), pp. 588–94.

'Making laws about making babies', *Hastings Center Report*, 15/4 (August 1985), pp. 5–6.

'Ethics and the handicapped newborn infant', *Social Research*, 52 (1985), pp. 505–42 (with Helga Kuhse).

'Resources and hard choices in aged care', *Proceedings of the 20th Annual Conference of the Australian Association of Gerontology* (1985), pp. 38–41 (with Helga Kuhse).

'Animal liberation: a personal view', *Between the Species*, 2 (Summer 1986), pp. 148–54.

'The ethics of embryo research', *Law, Medicine and Health Care*, 14 (1986), pp. 133–8 (with Helga Kuhse).

'For sometimes letting – and helping – die', *Law, Medicine and Health Care*, 14 (1986), pp. 149–54 (with Helga Kuhse).

'Animal liberation or animal rights?', *The Monist*, 70 (January 1987), pp. 3–14.

'Attitudes of Australian neonatal paediatricians to the treatment of extremely preterm infants', *Australian Paediatric Journal*, 23 (1987), pp. 223–6 (jointly with C. De Garis, H. Kuhse and V. Y. H. Yu).

'Which babies are too expensive to treat?', *Bioethics*, 1/3 (July 1987), pp. 275–83.

'Age and the allocation of medical resources,' *The Journal of Medicine and Philosophy*, 13 (1988), pp. 101–16 (with Helga Kuhse).

'IVF and the argument from potential', *Philosophy and Public Affairs*, 17 (1988), pp. 87–104 (with Karen Dawson).

'Doctors' practices and attitudes regarding voluntary euthanasia', *Medical Journal of Australia* (20 June 1988), pp. 623–7 (with Helga Kuhse).

'Allocating resources in perinatal medicine: a proposal', *Australian Paediatric Journal*, 24 (August 1988), pp. 235–9 (with J. Mackenzie and H. Kuhse).

'Whither surrogacy?', *The Medical Journal of Australia* (17 October 1988), pp. 426–9 (with E. Carl Wood).

'Can bioethics be both rigorous and practical?', *Reseaux*, 53–4 (1987–8), pp. 121–30.

'The syngamy debate: when *precisely* does a human life begin?', *Law, Medicine and Health Care*, 17/2 (Summer 1989), pp. 174–81 (with Stephen Buckle and Karen Dawson).

'Australian Commissions and Committees on Issues in Bioethics', *Journal of Medicine and Philosophy*, 144/4 (August 1989), pp. 403–24 (with Pacal Kasimba).

'The quality/quantity-of-life distinction and its moral importance for nurses', *International Journal of Nursing Studies*, 26/3 (1989), pp. 203–12 (with Helga Kuhse).

'To do or not to do?', *Hastings Center Report*, 19/6 (November/December 1989), pp. 42–4.

'Il concetto di morte tra etica filosofica e medicina', *Politeia* (Milan), 5/16 (1989), pp. 4–13.

'Bioetica: dilucidazioni e problemi' ('Bioethics: elucidations and problems'), *Iride* (Rome), 3 (1989), pp. 167–81 (an interview with M. Mori).

'Bioethics and academic freedom', *Bioethics*, 4/1 (January 1990), pp. 33–44.

'Should fertile people have access to in vitro fertilisation?', *British Medical Journal* 300 (20 January 1990), pp. 167–70 (with Karen Dawson).

'The Human Genome Project: for better or for worse?', *Medical Journal of Australia*, 152 (7 May 1990), pp. 484–6 (with Karen Dawson).

'Zwischen Leben entscheiden: eine Verteidigung' ('Deciding between lives: a defence'), *Analyse und Kritik*, 12 (1990), pp. 119–30 (with Helga Kuhse).

'The 'Singer-affair' and practical ethics: a response', *Analyse und Kritik*, 12 (1990), pp. 245–64.

'The ethics of patenting life-forms', *Intellectual Property Forum*, 14 (May 1991), pp. 31–8.

'A philosopher among the test-tubes', *Meanjin*, 50 (1991), pp. 493–500.

'Euthanasia and academic freedom in the German-speaking world', *Kriterion*, 1/2 (1991), pp. 8–10.

'Applied ethics in a hostile environment', *Theoria*, LXVII/1–2 (1991), pp. 111–14.

'Euthanasia: a survey of nurses's attitudes and practices', *Australian Nurses Journal*, 21/8 (March 1992), pp. 21–2 (with Helga Kuhse).

'A German attack on applied ethics', *Journal of Applied Philosophy*, 9/1 (1992), pp. 85–91.

'Xenotransplantation and speciesism', *Transplantation Proceedings*, 24/2 (April 1992), pp. 728–32.

'L'éthique appliquée', *Cahiers antispécistes lyonnais*, 4 (July 1992), pp. 5–12.

'Bioethics at Monash University', *International Journal of Bioethics*, 2/3 (June–July 1992), pp. 111–15.

'The International Association of Bioethics', *Medical Journal of Australia*, 158 (March 1993), pp. 298–9.

'Voluntary euthanasia and the nurse: an Australian survey', *International Journal of Nursing Studies*, 30/4 (1993), pp. 311–22 (with Helga Kuhse).

'More on euthanasia: a response to Pauer-Studer', *The Monist*, 76/2 (1993), pp. 158–74 (with Helga Kuhse).

'Bioethics and the limits of tolerance', *The Journal of Medicine and Philosophy*, 19/2 (1994), pp. 129–45.

'Die Ethik der Embryonenforschung', *Aufklizrung und Kritik*, 1 (1995), pp. 83–7.

'Feminism and vegetarianism: a response', *Philosophy in the Contemporary World*, 1/3 (Fall 1994), pp. 36–9.

'Double jeopardy and the use of QALYs in health care allocation', *Journal of Medical Ethics*, 21/3 (1995), pp. 144–50 (with John McKie, Helga Kuhse and Jeff Richardson).

'Is the sanctity of life ethic terminally ill?', *Bioethics*, 9/3–4 (1995), pp. 327–43.

'William Godwin and the defence of impartialist ethics', *Utilitas*, 7/1 (May 1995), pp. 67–86 (with Leslie Cannold and Helga Kuhse).

'Xenotransplantation: is it ethically defensible', *Xeno*, 3/4 (August 1995), pp. 58–60 (with Alison Hutchinson).

'The legalisation of voluntary euthanasia in the Northern Territory', *Bioethics*, 9/5 (October 1995), pp. 419–24.

'Maximizing health benefits vs. egalitarianism: an Australian survey of health issues', *Social Science and Medicine*, 41/10 (1995), pp. 1429–37 (with Erik Nord, Jeff Richardson, Andrew Street and Helga Kuhse).

'Active voluntary euthanasia, morality and the law', *Journal of Law and Medicine*, 3/1 (November 1995), pp. 129–35.

'The Great Ape Project: premises and implications', *ATLA*, 23 (1995), pp. 626–31 (with Paola Cavalieri).

'Coping with global change', *Critical and Creative Thinking*, 3/2 (1995), pp. 1–12.

'Is there a universal moral sense?', *Critical Review*, 9/3 (Summer 1995), pp. 325–39.

'Who cares about cost? Does economic analysis impose or reflect social values?', *Health Policy*, 34 (1995), pp. 79–94 (with Erik Nord, Jeff Richardson, Andrew Street and Helga Kuhse).

'Coping with global change: the need for different values', *Journal of Human Values*, 2/1 (January–June 1996), pp. 37–48.

'What is the justice–care debate *really* about?', *Midwest Studies in Philosophy*, XX (1996), pp. 357–77 (with Leslie Cannold, Helga Kuhse and Lori Gruen).

'Ethics and the limits of scientific freedom', *The Monist*, 79/2 (April 1996), pp. 218–29.

'Dilemma von Leben und Tod', *Universitas*, 51 (May 1996), pp. 432–7.

'The significance of age and duration of effect in social evaluation of health care', *Health Care Analysis*, 4 (1996), pp. 103–11 (with Erik Nord, Jeff Richardson, Andrew Street and Helga Kuhse.

'Caring and justice: a study of two approaches to health care ethics', *Nursing Ethics*, 3/3 (1996), pp. 212–23 (with Maurice Rickard and Helga Kuhse).

'O naravi bioetike' ('On the nature of bioethics'), *Drustvena Istrazivanja* [Zagreb], 5/3–4 (1996), pp. 523–32.

'Allocating healthcare by QALYs: the relevance of age', *Cambridge Quarterly of Healthcare Ethics*, 5/4 (Fall 1996), pp. 534–45 (with John McKie, Helga Kuhse and Jeff Richardson).

'End-of-life decisions in Australian medical practice', *Medical Journal of Australia*, 166/4 (17 February 1997), pp. 191–6 (with Helga Kuhse, Maurice Richard, Malcolm Clark and Peter Baume).

'Neither human nor natural: ethics and feral animals', *Reproduction, Fertility and Development*, 9/1 (1997), pp. 157–62.

'Partial and impartial ethical reasoning in health care professionals', *Journal of Medical Ethics*, 23/4 (1997), pp. 226–32 (with Helga Kuhse, Maurice Rickard, Leslie Cannold and Jessica van Dyk).

Discussion Notes in Professional Journals

'A note on an objection to determinism', *Philosophy* (April 1970), 45, pp. 156–7.

'Neil Cooper's concepts of morality', *Mind* (July 1971), 80, pp. 421–3.

'Why Nozick is not so easy to refute', *Western Political Quarterly*, XXIX (1976), pp. 191–2.

'Utility and the survival lottery', *Philosophy* (April 1977), 52, pp. 218–22.

'Can ethics be taught in a hospital?', *Pediatrics*, 60 (August 1977), pp. 253–5.

'The fable of the fox and the unliberated animals', *Ethics*, 88/2 (January 1978), pp. 119–25.

'Anglin on the obligation to create extra people', *Canadian Journal of Philosophy*, 8/3 (September 1978), pp. 583–5.

'Regan's critique of Singer', *Analysis*, 39/3 (June 1979), pp. 118–19.

'Advocacy, objectivity and the Draize test', *International Journal for the Study of Animal Problems*, 1 (1980), pp. 212–13.

'Reply to Dr Harris', *Philosophical Books*, XXII (1981), pp. 198–200.

'How do we decide?', *Hastings Center Report*, 12/3 (June 1982), pp. 9–11.

'Sanctity of life or quality of life?', *Pediatrics*, 72 (1983), pp. 128–9.

'A comment on the animal rights debate', *The International Journal of Applied Philosophy*, 1/3 (1983), pp. 89–90.

'Ng and Singer on utilitarianism: a reply', *Canadian Journal of Philosophy*, XIII/2 (1983), pp. 241–2 (jointly with Y.-K. Ng).

'In reply', *Pediatrics*, 73 (February 1984), pp. 261–3.

'The moral status of embryos: response', *Journal of Medical Ethics*, 10/2 (June 1984), pp. 80–1.

'Neonatal intensive care: how much, and who decides', *Medical Journal of Australia*, 142 (18 March 1985), pp. 335–6.

'The expanding circle: a reply to Munevar', *Explorations in Knowledge*, IX/1 (1987), pp. 51–4.

'Australian developments in reproductive technology', *Hastings Center Report*, 18/2 (April/May 1988), p. 4.

'Comment on Frey: "Moral standing, the value of lives, and speciesism"', *Between the Species*, 4/3 (June 1988), pp. 202–3.

'Resolving arguments about the sanctity of life: a response to Long', *Journal of Medical Ethics*, 14 (1988), pp. 198–9 (with Helga Kuhse).

'Experiments on animals', *British Medical Journal*, 299 (18 November 1989), pp. 1238–9.

'The significance of animal suffering', *Behavioral and Brain Sciences*, 13 (1990), pp. 9–12.

'Ethics and animals', *Behavioral and Brain Sciences*, 13 (1990), pp. 45–9.

'An argument for utilitarianism: a defence', *Australasian Journal of Philosophy*, 68/4 (1990), pp. 448–54 (with Yew-Kwang Ng).

'Viel Wind um Nichts' ('A lot of wind about nothing'), *Ethik und Sozialwissenschaften*, 2/3 (1990), pp. 411–14 (with Helga Kuhse).

'Speciesism, morality and biology', *The Psychologist*, 4/5 (May 1991), pp. 199–200.

'Prolonging dying is the same as prolonging living – one more response to Long', *Journal of Medical Ethics*, 17/4 (December 1991), pp. 205–6 (with Helga Kuhse).

'The pervasiveness of species bias', *Behavioral and Brain Sciences*, 14/4 (1991), pp. 759–60.

'How to argue with egg producers', *Behavioral and Brain Sciences*, 17/4 (1994), p. 749.

'Straw men with broken legs: a reply to Per Sandström', *Journal of Medical Ethics*, 21/2 (1995), pp. 89–90.

'Euthanasia: Kuhse and Singer respond', *Australian Nursing Journal* (September 1995), p. 26 (with Helga Kuhse).

'Blind hostility: a response to Russell and Nicoll', *Proceedings of the Society for Experimental Biology and Medicine*, 211/2 (1996), pp. 139–46.

'Double jeopardy, the equal value of lives and the veil of ignorance: a rejoinder to Harris', *Journal of Medical Ethics*, 22/4 (1996), pp. 204–8 (with John McKie, Helga Kuhse and Jeff Richardson).

'Another peep behind the veil', *Journal of Medical Ethics*, 22/4 (1996), pp. 216–21 (with John McKie, Helga Kuhse and Jeff Richardson).

Book Reviews in Professional Journals

'The writings of the young Marx', *The Human Context*, IV/1 (1972).

'Illich's "Deschooling Society"', *The Human Context*, IV/3 (1972).

'"The Gift Relationship" by Richard Titmuss', *The Human Context*, V/3 (1973).

'"Utilitarianism, For and Against" by J. J. C. Smart and B. Williams', *Philosophical Books*, 15 (May 1974).

'"Reason and Violence" ed. by S. Stanage', *Mind*, 85 (October 1976).

'"Human Needs and Interests", ed. by R. Fitzgerald', *Australasian Journal of Philosophy*, 56/1 (May 1978).

'"The Limits of Altruism" by Garrett Hardin', *Hastings Center Report*, 8/1 (February 1978), pp. 37–9.

'"Doing Evil to Achieve Good", ed. Paul Ramsey and Richard McCormick', *Hastings Center Report*, 10/1 (February 1980), pp. 42–4.

'"Violence for Equality" by Ted Honderich', *Philosophical Quarterly*, 31 (1981), pp. 284–5.

'"Karl Marx" by Allen Wood', *Australasian Journal of Philosophy*, 60 (June 1982), pp. 191–2.

'"Animals in Research", ed. D. Sperlinger; "Animal Rights and Human Morality", by B. Rollin; "Animal Suffering", by M. Dawkins', *Quarterly Review of Biology*, 57 (December 1982), pp. 481–2.

'"The American Blood Supply" by A. Drake, S. N. Finkelstein and M. Sapolsky, and "Blood: Gift of Merchandise?", by P. J. Hagen', *Hastings Center Report*, 13/4 (1983), pp. 48–50.

' "The Tangled Wing" by Melvin Konner', *Quarterly Review of Biology*, 58, (1983), pp. 294–5.

' "Triage and Justice" by G. Winslow', *Ethics*, 94 (1983), pp. 142–3.

' "Ethics and Animals", ed. H. Miller and W. Williams', *Quarterly Review of Biology*, 59 (1984), pp. 57–8.

' "The Case for Animal Rights" by Tom Regan', *Quarterly Review of Biology*, 59 (September 1984), p. 306.

' "Biophilia" by Edward O. Wilson', *Biology and Philosophy*, I/3, (1986), pp. 367–71.

' "Ethics of Dealing with Persons with Severe Handicaps: Toward a Research Agenda" by P. Dokecki and R. M. Zaner (eds)', *A&NZ Journal of Developmental Disabilities*, 12 (1986), pp. 273–4.

' "Setting Limits: Medical Goals in an Aging Society" by Daniel Callahan', *Bioethics*, 2/2 (1988), pp. 151–69.

' "Reshaping Life: key issues in genetic engineering" by G. J. V. Nossal and R. L. Coppel', *Medical Journal of Australia*, 152 (5 March 1990), pp. 273–4.

'A refutation of ordinary morality' (review essay on S. Kagan, *The Limits of Morality*), *Ethics*, 101 (April, 1991), pp. 625–33.

' "Factory Farming" by Andrew Johnson', *Nature*, 353 (17 October 1991), pp. 613–14.

' "Encyclopedia of Ethics" by Lawrence C. Becker and Charlotte B. Becker', *Ethics*, 103/4 (July 1993), pp. 807–10.

' "Life's Dominion" by Ronald Dworkin', *British Medical Journal*, 307 (23 October 1993), pp. 1077–8.

' "Monkey Business" by Kathy Snow Guillermo and "In the Name of Science" by Barbara Orlans', *Nature*, 367 (10 February 1994), pp. 523–4.

' "Essays on Henry Sidgwick" edited by Bart Schultz', *Ethics*, 104/3 (April 1994), pp. 631–3.

' "Dangerous Diagnostics" by Dorothy Nelkin and Laurence Tancredi, "Lost Lullaby" by Deborah Golden Alecson, "Time to Go" edited by Anne Hunsaker Hawkins and James O. Ballard', *Bioethics*, 10/1 (January 1996), pp. 88–9.

' "Persons, Animals and Fetuses" by Mary Gore Forrester', *Bioethics*, 11/2 (April 1997), pp. 179–80.

Articles Contributed to Books

'A utilitarian population policy', in M. Bayles (ed.), *Ethics and Population*, Schenkman, Cambridge, MA, 1976.

'Freedoms and utilities in health care', in G. Dworkin, G. Bermant and P. Brown (eds), *Markets and Morals*, Halstead Press, New York, 1977.

'Unsanctifying human life', in J. Ladd (ed.), *Ethical Issues Relating to Life and Death*, Oxford University Press, New York, 1978.

'Reconsidering the famine relief argument', in P. Brown and H. Shue (eds), *Food Policy: US Responsibility in the Life and Death Choices*, The Free Press, New York, 1977.

'Animal experimentation', in W. T. Reich (ed.), *The Encyclopedia of Bioethics*, Macmillan, New York, 1978.

'Life: value of life', in *The Encyclopedia of Bioethics*, ibid.

'Rights and the market', in J. Arthur and W. Shaw (eds), *Justice, and Economic Distribution*, Prentice Hall, Englewood Cliffs, NJ, 1978.

'Animals and the value of life', in T. Regan (ed.), *Matters of Life and Death*, Random House, New York, 1980; revised versions, Random House 1986, McGraw-Hill, 1993.

'Not for humans only: the place of non-humans in environmental issues', in K. E. Goodpastor and K. M. Sayre (eds), *Ethics and Problems of the 21st Century*, University of Notre Dame Press, 1979.

'Preface' to H. S. Salt, *Animal Rights* (first published 1892), reissued 1980, Society for Animal Rights, Clarks Summit, PA, pp. v–x.

'Teaching about human rights', in A. Erh-Soon Tay (ed.), *Teaching Human Rights*, Australian Government Publishing Service, Canberra, for the Australian National Commission for UNESCO, 1981, pp. 95–8.

'Why human rights for humans only?', in ibid., pp. 179–82.

'The moral status of the embryo', in Williams Walters and Peter Singer (eds), *Test-tube Babies*, Oxford University Press, Melbourne, 1982, pp. 57–67 (co-author with Helga Kuhse).

'Conclusions – and costs', in ibid., pp. 128–41 (co-author with William Walters).

'The concept of moral standing', in A. Caplan and D. Callahan (eds), *Ethics in Hard Times*, Plenum Press, New York, 1981, pp. 31–45.

'Contemporary theories of morality: a secularist perspective', in T. J. Connolly (ed.), *Health Care in Crisis: a Bioethical Perspective*, Laurdel Bioethics Foundation, Sydney 1982, pp. 101–15.

'The ethics of animal use', in L. Peel and D. E. Tribe (eds) *World Animal Science, volume A1, Domestication, Conservation and Use of Animal Resources*, Elsevier, Amsterdam, 1983, pp. 153–65.

'The ethics of animal liberation: a summary statement', in *Animal–Human Relationships, Some Philosophers' Views*, RSPCA, West Sussex, 1985.

'Arguments against markets: two cases from the health field', in C. L. Buchanan and E. W. Prior (eds), *Medical Care and Markets*, Allen & Unwin, Sydney, 1985, pp. 2–19.

'Foreword' to Daniel Dombrowski, *Vegetarianism: the Philosophy Behind the Ethical Diet*, Thorsons, Wellingborough, 1985.

'Ethics', *Encyclopaedia Britannica*, 1986 and subsequent printings, pp. 627–48, abridged version, *Encyclopaedia Britannica 1986 Book of the Year*.

'Can the law cope with our increasing ability to preserve life at any cost?', in *Winds of Change: Papers from the 24th Australian Legal Convention*, Law Council of Australia and The Law Book Company, Melbourne and Sydney, 1987 (with Helga Kuhse).

'Creating embryos', in W. B. Weil and M. Benjamin (eds), *Ethical Issues at the Outset of Life*, Blackwell Scientific Publications, Boston, 1987, pp. 43–62.

'Hegel and Marx' (a dialogue with Bryan Magee), in B. Magee (ed.), *The Great Philosophers*, BBC Books, London, 1987, pp. 190–208. Portuguese translation: Presenca, Lisbon, 1989.

'Ethical issues raised by treatment of extremely preterm infants', in V. Y. H. Yu and E. C. Wood (eds), *Prematurity*, Churchill Livingstone, Edinburgh, 1987, pp. 257–73 (with Helga Kuhse).

'Life's uncertain voyage', in P. Pettit, R. Sylvan and J. Norman (eds), *Metaphysics and Morality: Essays in Honour of J. J. C. Smart*, Blackwell, Oxford, 1987, pp. 154–72.

'Ethical issues in reproductive alternatives for genetic indications', in F. Vogel and K. Sperling (eds), *Human Genetics*, Springer, Berlin, 1987, pp. 683–91 (with Helga Kuhse).

'Reasoning towards utilitarianism', in D. Seanor and N. Fotion (eds), *Hare and Critics*, Clarendon Press, Oxford, 1988, pp. 147–59.

'Ethical experts in a democracy', in D. Rosenthal and F. Shehadi (eds), *Applied Ethics and Ethical Theory*, University of Utah Press, Salt Lake City, 1988, pp. 149–61.

'The ethics of refugee policy', in M. Gibney (ed.), *Open Borders? Closed Societies?*, Greenwood Press, New York, 1988, pp. 111–30 (with Renata Singer).

'Some consequences of regulating reproductive medicine in Australia', in C. Byk (ed.), *Procreation artificielle ou en sont l'ethique et le droit?*, Lacassagne, Lyon, 1989, pp. 185–92 (with Karen Dawson).

'Animal liberation?' (interview with Robyn Williams), in Robyn Williams, *The Uncertainty Principle*, ABC Books, Sydney, 1989, pp. 139–50.

'Il dibattito bioetico in Australia' ('The bioethics debate in Australia') in O. Polleggioni and M. Russo (eds), *Il Bambino Bionico*, La Nuova Italia, Florence, 1989, pp. 139–43.

'Geleitwort' (Introduction) to Helmut Kaplan, *Warum Vegetarier?*, Peter Lang, Frankfurt, 1989, pp. 7–10.

'Should all seriously disabled infants live?', in Geoffrey Scarre (ed.), *Children, Parents and Politics*, Cambridge University Press, Cambridge, 1989, pp. 168–81 (with Helga Kuhse).

'When do people begin?', in K. Andrews and M. Stainsby (eds), *Collaborating in Health Care: Proceedings of the 1989 Annual Conference on Bioethics*, St Vincent's Bioethics Centre, Melbourne, 1990, pp. 21–5.

'IVF and Australian law', in D. Bromham, M. Dalton and J. Jackson (eds), *Philosophical Ethics in Reproductive Medicine*, Manchester University Press, Manchester, 1990, pp. 31–47.

'Introduction: the nature of ethical argument', in Peter Singer, Helga Kuhse, Stephen Buckle, Karen Dawson and Pascal Kasimba, *Embryo Experimentation*, Cambridge University Press, Cambridge, 1990, pp. 37–42 (with Helga Kuhse).

'Individuals, humans and persons: the issue of moral status' in Peter Singer, Helga Kuhse, Stephen Buckle, Karen Dawson and Pascal Kasimba, *Embryo Experimentation*, Cambridge University Press, Cambridge, 1990, pp. 65–75 (with Helga Kuhse).

'The new genetics: some ethical issues', in *Advances in Biotechnology: Proceedings of an International Conference*, Swedish Council for Forestry and Agricultural Research and the Swedish Recombinant DNA Advisory Committee, Stockholm, 1990, pp. 213–20 (with Karen Dawson).

'Je mehr wir fuer andere leben, desto zufriedener leben wir', in K. Deschner (ed.), *Woran ich Glaube*, Gerd Mohn, Guetersloh, 1990, pp. 267–71.

'Introduction' and 'Afterword', in P. Singer (ed.), *A Companion to Ethics*, Basil Blackwell, Oxford, 1991, pp. v–vi and 543–5.

'Research into aging: should it be guided by the interests of present individuals, future individuals, or the species?', in Frederic C. Ludwig (ed.), *Life Span Extension: Consequences and Open Questions*, Springer, New York, 1991, pp. 132–45.

'Bioethics and education', in G. Rex Meyer (ed.), *Bioethics in Education*, International Union of Biological Sciences, Commission for Biological Education, Erziehungswissenschaften Bd. 27, Lit Verlag, Munich, 1991, pp. 60–7 (with Helga Kuhse).

'Environmental values', in Ian Marsh (ed.), *The Environmental Challenge*, Longman Cheshire, Melbourne, 1991, pp. 3–24.

'Mir leuchtet nicht ein, wie man so Werte bewahren will', in R. Hegselmann and R. Merkel (eds), *Zur Debatte ueber Euthanasie*, Suhrkamp, Frankfurt a. M., 1991, pp. 153–77 (with C. Fehige and G. Meggle).

'Problems in the legislative regulation of reproductive technology: learning from the Victorian experience', in *The Australian Bioethics Association First Annual Conference: Bioethics and the Wider Community*, Melbourne, 1991, pp. 273–6.

'Hard choices: ethical questions raised by the birth of handicapped infants', in Paul Badham (ed.), *Ethics on the Frontiers of Human Existence*, Paragon House, New York, 1992, pp. 153–77 (with Helga Kuhse).

'Ontogeny of pain and the concept of speciesism: a comment', in T. Kuchel, M. Rose and J. Burrell (eds), *Animal Pain: Ethical and Scientific Perspectives*, Australian Council on the Care of Animals in Research and Teaching, Glen Osmand, SA, 1992, pp. 74–6.

'Embryo experimentation and the moral status of the embryo', in E. Matthews and M. Menlowe (eds), *Philosophy and Health Care*, Avebury, Aldershot, 1992, pp. 81–91.

'Foreword' to Lewis Gompertz, *Moral Inquiries on the Situation of Man and of Brutes*, Centaur Press, Fontwell, Sussex, 1992, pp. 11–15.

'Allocating health care resources and the problem of the value of life', in D. Cockburn (ed.), *Death and the Value of Life*, Trivium, Lampeter, 1992, pp. 7–23 (with Helga Kuhse).

'Foreword' to Richard Ryder (ed.), *Animal Welfare and the Environment*, Duckworth, London, 1992, pp. vii–x.

'Beyond traditional religion', in Georg Feuerstein and Trisha Lamb Feuerstein (eds), *Voices on the Threshold of Tomorrow*, Quest, Wheaton, IL, 1993, pp. 251–2.

'Das gekreuzigte tier', in Edgar Dalil (ed.), *Die Lehre des Unheils: Fundamentalkritik am Christentum*, Carlsen, Hamburg, 1993, pp. 280–9 (with Edgar Dahl).

'Animals, ethics and experimentation' in N. E. Johnston (ed.), *Animal Welfare Conference: Proceedings*, Animal Ethics Unit, Monash University, 1993, pp. 1–8.

'Abortion and contraception: the moral significance of fertilization', in Fritz Beller and Robert F. Weir (eds), *The Beginning of Human Life*, Kluwer, Dordrecht, 1994, pp. 145–61 (with Helga Kuhse).

'Life and death decision: the need for a new approach', in M. Rajaretnam (ed.), *Bioethics and Environmental Education*, UNESCO/Information and Resource Center/Institute for Policy Research, Singapore and Kuala Lumpur, 1994, pp. 81–3.

'The role of ethics' in J. McKie (ed.), *Ethical Issues in Prenatal Diagnosis and the Termination of Pregnancy*, Centre for Human Bioethics, Monash University, 1994, pp. 1–7.

'On the nature of bioethics', in Helga Kuhse and Peters Singer, *Individuals, Humans, Persons*, Academia Verlag, Sankt Augustin, 1994, pp. 21–32.

'Late termination and selective non-treatment of disabled infants – some comparisons', in John McKie (ed.), *Ethical Issues in Prenatal Diagnosis and the Termination of Pregnancy*, Centre for Human Bioethics, Monash University, 1994, pp. 71–9.

'Australia's core values and the next thirty years', in Economic Planning Advisory Commission, *Ambitions for Our Future: Australian Views*, Conference Report 3, Australian Government Publishing Service, Canberra, 1994, pp. 69–71.

'The Great Ape Project' in Raymond Corbey and Bert Theunissen (eds), *Ape, Man, Apeman: Changing Views since 1600*, Department of Prehistory, Leiden University, 1995, pp. 367–76.

'New assisted reproductive technology', in Karen Dawson (ed.), *Reproductive Technology: the Science, the Law, and the Social Issues*, VCTA Publishing, Melbourne, 1994, pp. 99–102.

'Animal research: philosophical issues', in W. T. Reich (ed.), *Encyclopedia of Bioethics*, Macmillan and Simon & Schuster, New York, 1995, I, pp. 147–153.

'Ethical problems in economic evaluation of health care', in C. Selby Smith and M. F. Drummond (eds), *Economic Evaluation in Australian Health Care*, Australian Government Publishing Service, Canberra, 1995, chapter 15, pp. 172–8 (with Helga Kuhse, John McKie, Erik Nord and Jeff Richardson).

'Kirche und Embryonenforschung', in Edgar Dahl (ed.), *Die Lehre des Unheils: Fundamentalkritik am Christentum*, Goldmann, Hamburg, 1995, pp. 276–85.

'Taking sides on the right to die', in Simon Chapman and Stephen Leeder (eds), *The Last Right: Australians Take Sides on the Right to Die*, Mandarin, Melbourne, 1995, pp. 142–4.

'Abortion', in Ted Honderich (ed.) *The Oxford Companion to Philosophy*, Oxford University Press, Oxford, 1995, pp. 2–3.

'Animals', in ibid., pp. 35–6.

'Applied ethics', in ibid., pp. 42–3.

'Dialectic' in ibid., p. 198.

'Fertilization *in vitro*', in ibid., p. 275.

'Hegel', in ibid., pp. 339–43.

'Killing' in ibid., pp. 445–6.

'Owl of Minerva' in ibid., p. 638.
'Vegetarianism' in ibid., p. 897.
'World-soul' in ibid., p. 919.
'State policy and the sanctity of human life', in *Death and the State: Papers Presented to a Conference on Euthanasia at the Centre for Public Policy, University of Melbourne, 23–24 August, 1995*, Centre for Public Policy, University of Melbourne, 1996.
'This I believe', in John Marsden (ed.), *This I Believe*, Random House, Sydney, 1996, pp. 293–6.
'How are we to live?', in Geoff Mulgan (ed.), *Life after Politics: New Thinking for the Twenty-first Century*, Fontana, London, 1997, pp. 49–55.
'QALYs: some methodological and ethical issues', in S. Gindro, R. Bracalenti, and E. Mordini (eds), *Bioethics Research: Policy, Methods and Strategies. Proceedings of a European Conference*, European Commission, Directorate-General XII, 1997, pp. 83–92 (with Helga Kuhse, John McKie, Jeff Richardson and Erik Nord).
'On comparing the value of human and non-human life', in Edgar Morscher, Otto Neumaier and Peter Simons (eds), *Applied Ethics in a Troubled World*, Kluwer, Dordrecht, 1998, pp. 93–104.

Articles in Non-professional Publications (Including Review Articles)

'Animal liberation', *New York Review of Books* (5 April 1973).
'Discovering Karl Popper', *New York Review of Books* (2 May 1974).
'Philosophers are back on the job', *New York Times Sunday Magazine* (7 July 1974).
'Looking backwards', *New York Review of Books* (18 July 1974).
'Should we let them starve?', *New Humanist* (June 1974).
'The right to be rich or poor', *New York Review of Books* (6 March 1975).
'Making monkeys neurotic, dogs shriek, etc. etc.', *New York Times* (27 December 1975).
'The case for animal liberation', *The Age* (Melbourne) (13 March 1976).
'Bio-ethics and the case of the fetus', *New York Review of Books* (15 August 1976).
'Philosophy', *The New York Times* (8 May 1977).
'Philosophical vegetarianism: a reply', *The Humanist*, 37 (July/August 1977).
'Human prospecting', *New York Review of Books* (22 March 1979), pp. 30–2.
'Forswearing secrecy', *Nation* (5 May 1979), pp. 488–91.
'Why the whale should live', *Habitat*, 6/3 (June 1978), pp. 8–9.
'Do animals have equal rights?', *Animal Industry Today*, 2 (July/August 1979), pp. 4–8.
'On your Marx', *New York Review of Books* (20 December 1979), pp. 44–7.
'Dictator Marx', *The New York Review of Books* (25 September 1980).
'The case for prostitution', *The Age* (Melbourne) (18 September 1980).
'Revolution and religion', *The New York Review of Books* (6 November 1980), pp. 51–4.

'How the bunny lobby terrorized Revlon', *The Age* (21 February 1981).

'Genes and dominance', *The Age Monthly Review*, 1/1 (4 May 1981).

'The real Marx', *The Age Monthly Review*, 1/4 (3 August 1981).

'Marx and the real world', *The Age Monthly Review*, 1/5 (September 1981).

'The control of cures', *The Age Monthly Review*, 1/7 (November 1981).

'Conceptions and misconceptions', *Times Literary Supplement* (October 1981).

'Animal liberation and changing the role of the modern zoo', *Thylacinus* (Journal of the Australasian Society of Zookeepers), 7/1 (1982), pp. 26–30.

'Dim seer', *The Age Monthly Review*, 2/4 (August 1982).

'Preferences, pleasure and happiness', *Times Literary Supplement* (27 August 1982).

'Whales and the Japanese: a lesson in ethics', *The Age Monthly Review*, 2/8 (December 1982).

'The Whitlam experiment revisited', *Sydney Morning Herald* (1 December 1982).

'In vitro veritas', *The Age Monthly Review*, 2/12 (April 1983).

'The Horizon Lecture: A covenant for the Ark?', *The Listener* (14 April 1983), pp. 11–14.

'The politics of procreation', *Australian Penthouse* (October 1983), pp. 156–7.

'Thinking about animals', *Habitat*, 11 (October 1983), pp. 15–16.

'The animal liberation movement', *Current Affairs Bulletin*, 60/3 (August 1983), pp. 15–21.

'Misleading arguments on the right to die', *The Age* (15 December 1983).

'The future of Baby Doe', *New York Review of Books* (1 March 1984), pp. 17–22 (co-author with Helga Kuhse).

'Mind over manure: changing thoughts on man and animals' (review of *Man and the Natural World* by Keith Thomas and of *Animal Thought* by Stephen Walker), *The Age Monthly Review* (April 1984), pp. 17–18.

'Ten years of animal liberation: a review of ten recent books', *New York Review of Books* (17 January 1985), pp. 46–52.

'Handicapped babies: a right to life?', *Nursing Mirror* (20 February 1985), pp. 17–20 (co-author with Helga Kuhse).

'Animal rights and wrongs', *Times Higher Education Supplement* (29 March 1985).

'Technology and procreation: how far should we go?', *Technology Review*, 88/2 (February/March 1985), pp. 22–30.

'Ethics and intensive farming', *60 Days*, (October 1985), pp. 7–9.

'After Live Aid: how much is enough?', *The Age Monthly Review* (December 1985/January 1986).

'Luv a duck, I just can't understand it', *The Age* (February 1986).

'Reductio ad embryo', *The Age Monthly Review* (May 1986).

'Animal welfare and scientific inquiry', *Times Higher Education Supplement* (12 September 1986).

'Acting on Karn', *The Age Monthly Review* (October 1986).

'Embryo Report is just the beginning of the debate', *The Age* (17 November 1986).

'Carrying the white man's burden', *The Age* (7 March 1987).

'The Vatican viewpoint on IVF: stop it, you will go blind', *Sydney Morning Herald* (19 March 1987).

'The dog in the lifeboat: an exchange', *The New York Review of Books* (25 April 1987), pp. 57–8.

'As the world's numbers rise, our aid falls', *The Herald* (3 June 1987).

'Public life and private morality', *The Herald* (13 August 1987).

'A question of mice and men', *The Herald* (14 October 1987).

'How many and who? Australia's refugee policy', *The Age Monthly Review* (April 1988), pp. 18–21 (with Renata Singer).

'Migration policy: nasty, brutish and short-sighted', *The Age* (4 August 1988) (with Renata Singer).

'Why anorexics lose their right to die', *The Herald* (9 September 1988).

'Do blacks need extra help?', *The Herald* (15 November 1988).

'Survey shows Australian professionals seek change', *New South Wales Doctor* (20 September 1988) (with Helga Kuhse).

'Defending my right to put pin-ups on my walls', *The Herald* (16 December 1988).

'Your freedom of speech is under threat', *The Herald* (24 January 1989).

'Unkind to animals', *The New York Review of Books* (2 February 1989), pp. 36–8.

'Absence of malice', *The Animals Voice* (February 1989), pp. 8–9.

'Through an IVF glass darkly', *The Age* (8 April 1989) (with Pascal Kasimba).

'Stutters are still good for a laugh', *The Herald* (3 May 1989).

'Salt of the Earth', *New York Review of Books* (15 February 1990), pp. 41–2.

'The great research grant caper', *The Age* (2 July 1990).

'New attitudes needed on animal testing', *New Scientist* (11 August 1990), p. 4.

'Viewpoint: animal experimentation', *Scientific European* (December 1990), pp. 8–9.

'Tutti gli animali sono uguali', *Cenobio* (Lugano, Switzerland and Varese, Italy), XL/1 (January–March 1991), pp. 5–11.

'The philosopher and the future' (interview with Terry Lane), *21C* (Autumn 1991), pp. 43–7.

'Remember: dogs and cats are people too, you know', *Sunday Age* (7 July 1991).

'On being silenced in Germany', *The New York Review of Books* (15 August 1991), pp. 36–42.

'Thinking about suicide', *The Independent Monthly* (October 1991), p. 16.

'Uber das Recht, Fragen zu stellen', *Zitry* (Berlin), 22 (October 1991), pp. 18–19.

'Greed is stupid', *Australian Business Monthly* (March 1992), pp. 78–81.

'Not what you produce, but how much you spend', *Modern Times* (March 1992), pp. 16–17.

'The last rights', *The Age* (6 March 1992).

'That dangerous animal', *Modern Times* (April 1992), pp. 10–12.

'Bandit and friends', *The New York Review of Books* (9 April 1992), pp. 9–13.

'It's all a question of ethics', *The Australian* (4 June 1992), p. 6.

'Can free trade make you happy?', *Australian Business Monthly* (June 1992), pp. 98–100.

'A response to David DeGrazia', *Between the Species*, 8/1 (Winter 1992), pp. 51–3.

'Animal liberation: an exchange', *The New York Review of Books* (5 November 1992), pp. 60–1.

'Has capitalism reached its limits?', *Australian Business Monthly* (November 1992), pp. 112–13.

'Be radical: let's try self-reliance', *Australian Business Monthly* (January 1993), pp. 56–9.

'Animal liberation', *Island*, 54 (Autumn 1993), pp. 62–6.

'Holding back on a question of life or death', *The Australian* (7 May 1993), p. 15 (with Helga Kuhse).

'The rights of ape', *BBC Wildlife* (June 1993), pp. 28–32.

'Cultural clash sets rite against reason', *The Australian* (9 June 1993).

'The Great Ape Project and its implications for scientific and biomedical research', *Genetic Engineering News* (1 November 1993).

'Is there a God?', *The Age* (24 December 1993).

'Address to Council', *RACS Bulletin*, 14/3 (November 1994), pp. 23–6.

'The RACS Code and the patient who asks for help in dying', *RACS Bulletin*, 14/3 (November 1994), p. 29.

'What price a human life?', *The Sunday Age* (8 January 1995).

'To live ethical lives', *The Age* (16 January 1995).

'Brave new territory', *The Sunday Age* (4 February 1995).

'Equality: why it matters', *Australian Business Monthly* (February 1995), pp. 36–9.

'Menschenrechte fur Menschenaffen', *Geo* (April 1995), pp. 176–9.

'Is our changing definition of death for the better?', *USA Today* (18 May 1995), p. 15A.

'Taking note of the quality of the life that chooses death', *The Age* (7 June 1995).

'Final frontiers', *The Times Higher Education Supplement* (18 August 1995), p. 15.

'Killing babies isn't always wrong', *The Spectator* (16 September 1995), pp. 20–2.

'Sentenced to life', *The Sunday Age*, (22 October 1995), p. 14.

'Abortion: a woman's right', *Beat* (1 November 1995), p. 10.

'A Christmas roast' *The Sunday Age* (24 December 1995), p. 10.

'The ethics of commercialising wild animals', *Animals Today*, 4/1 (February–April 1996), pp. 20–3.

'Meaning of life', *Resurgence* (March/April 1996), pp. 14–15.

'Unnatural practices', *The Sunday Age* (7 April 1996).

'Natural classic', *BBC Wildlife*, 14/6 (June 1996), p. 89.

'The Great Ape Project, *Animals' Agenda*, 16/3 (July/August 1996), pp. 12–13.

'Time to bid farewell to the politics of fear', *The Age* (10 October 1996), p. A15.

'Standing for the Greens', *Generation*, 6/1–2 (October 1996), pp. 3–6.

'On authenticity', *Australian Book Review*, 187 (December 1996/January 1997), p. 49.

'Humanismen maste överskrida gränserna', *Dagens Nyheter* (9 February 1997).

'The drowning child and the expanding circle', *New Internationalist* (April 1997), pp. 28–30.

'Euthanasia: no time for hastened conclusions', *The Australian* (24 February 1997) (with Helga Kuhse and Peter Baume).

'Cloning the news', *The Republican* (4 April 1997), p. 16.

' "Muddled" commentary on end-of-life study', *Australian Doctor* (18 April 1997), p. 23 (with Helga Kuhse, Peter Baume and Malcolm Clark).

'Angling for equality of consideration', *Times Higher Education Supplement* (28 February 1997), p. 22.
'Research babies: another case of the stolen children?', *Sydney Morning Herald* (11 June 1997).
'To give or not to give?', *Horizons*, 6/2 (Spring 1997), pp. 10–11.

Other Works

The Animal Liberation Movement, Old Hammond Press, Nottingham, 1985, 20 pp. Italian translation: *Il Movimento di Liberazione Animale*, Sonda, Torino, 1989. French translation: *Le movement de liberation animale*, Françoise Blanchon, Lyon, 1991.
Rats, Patients and People: Issues in the Ethical Regulation of Research, Annual Lecture 1989, Academy of the Social Sciences in Australia, Australian National University, Canberra, 1990, 27 pp.
'Introduction' to the Catalogue of *100 Artists Against Animal Experimentation*, Deutscher Brunswick St Gallery, 1990, pp. 3–4.
'A question of morality', *Australian Wildlife Calendar*, The Wilderness Society, Hobart, 1992.
'Literature, truth and argument', *1995 New South Wales Premier's Literary Awards Address*, NSW Ministry of Arts, Sydney, 1995.
'The significance of age and duration of effect in social evaluation of health care,' *Centre for Health Program Evaluation Working Paper 47*, Monash University and the University of Melbourne, 1995 (with Erik Nord, Jeff Richardson, Andrew Street and Helga Kuhse).

Works Reprinted

Democracy and Disobedience, pp. 86–92, reprinted in J. Rachels (ed.), *Moral Problems*, 2nd edn, Harper & Row, New York, 1975; pp. 84–92, reprinted in H. A. Bedau (ed.), *Civil Disobedience in Focus* (Routledge, 1991).
'Animal liberation' (*New York Review*, 5 April 1973) has been reprinted in: J. Rachels (ed.), *Moral Problems*, 2nd edn 1975, 3rd edn 1979, Harper & Row, New York; P. and K. Struhl (eds), *Ethics in Perspective*, Random House, New York, 1975; *The National Observer* (28 April 1973); *The Match* (Tuscon, AZ) (January 1974); M. Stubbs and S. Barnet (ed.), *The Little Brown Reader*, Little, Brown & Co., Boston, 1977; Vincent E. Barry (ed.), *Personal and Social Ethics*, Wadsworth Publishing Co., Belmont, CA, 1978; F. E. Mosedale (ed.), *Philosophy and Science*, Prentice Hall, Englewood Cliffs, NJ, 1979; K. S. Shrader-Frechette (ed.), *Environmental Ethics*, Boxwood Press, 1981; A. T. Rottenberg (ed.), *Elements of Argument*, St Martin's Press, New York, 1985; D. Vandeveer

and C. Pierce (eds), *People, Penguins and Plastic Trees*, Wadsworth, 1985; J. Sterba (ed.), *Morality in Practice*, Wadsworth, 1987; L. J. Pojman (ed.), *Philosophy: the Quest for Truth*, Wadsworth, 1991; Steven Luper-Foy and Curtis Brown, *The Moral Life*, Harcourt Brace Jovanovich, 1991; J. Ramage and J. Bean (ed.), *Writing Arguments*, 2nd edn, Macmillan, 1992; E. Soifer (ed.), *Ethical Issues*, Broadview Press, Peterborough, Ontario, 1992; E. Gampel (ed.), *Personal Values*, Kendall-Hunt, Dubuque, IA, 1992; M. Zimmerman (ed.), *Environmental Philosophy*, Prentice Hall, Englewood Cliffs, NJ, 1993; R. Abelson and M. L. Friquenon, *Ethics for Modern Life*, St Martin's Press, 5th edn, 1995; Robert Gamer (ed.), *Animal Rights: the Changing Debate*, Macmillan, London 1996. An Italian translation was published in *Communita* (Milan) (October 1973), p. 170; a Swedish translation has been reprinted as a foreword to S. Godlovitch, R. Godlovitch and John Harris (eds), *Djur, Manniskor, Moral*, Aldus, Stockholm, 1976; and a Japanese translation in N. Iida and H. Kato (eds), *Bioethics*, Tokyo, 1988.

'Famine, affluence and morality' has been reprinted in J. Rachels (ed.), *Understanding Moral Philosophy*, Dickenson, 1976; P. and R. Struhl (eds), *Philosophy Now*, 2nd edn, Random House, 1976, 3rd edn, 1980; T. Mappes and J. Zembaty (eds), *Social Ethics*, McGraw-Hill, 1977, 2nd edn 1982, 3rd edn 1987, 4th edn 1992); W. Aiken and H. A. La Follette (eds), *World Hunger and Moral Obligations*, Prentice Hall, 1977; P. Laslett and J. Fishkin (eds), *Philosophy, Politics and Society*, fifth series, Blackwell, Oxford, 1979; J. Feinberg (ed.), *Reason and Responsibility*, 4th edn, Dickenson, 1978; 5th edn 1992; J. Rachels (ed.), *Moral Problems*, 3rd edn, Harper & Row, 1979; Richard Wasserstrom, *Today's Moral Problems*, 2nd edn, Macmillan, 1979; J. Burr and M. Goldinger (eds), *Philosophy and Contemporary Issues*, Macmillan, 1980; E. D. Klemko, A. D. Kline and R. Hollinger (eds) *Philosophy I: the Basic Issues*, St Martin's Press, New York, 1982; Vincent Barry (ed.), *Applied Ethics*, Wadsworth, Belmont, CA, 1st edn 1982, 2nd edn 1985; Milton Goldinger (ed.), *Philosophy and Contemporary Issues*, Macmillan, New York, 4th edn, 1984; S. Cahn, P. Kitcher and G. Sher (eds), *Reason at Work*, Harcourt Brace, New York, 1984; M. Velasquez and C. Rostankowski (eds), *Ethics: Theory and Practice*, Prentice Hall, Englewood Cliffs, NJ, 1984; C. H. Sommers, *Vice and Virtue in Everyday Life*, Harcourt Brace, 1985, 3rd edn 1993; C. R. Beitz, M. Cohen, T. Scanlon and A. J. Sums (eds), *International Ethics*, Princeton University Press, 1985; J. Perry and M. Bratinan (eds), *Introduction to Philosophy*, Oxford University Press, New York, 1986; R. Abelson and M. L. Friquenon, *Ethics for Modem Life*, 3rd edn, St Martin's Press, 1987; 4th edn 1992; 5th edn 1995; George Sher (ed.), *Reason at Work*, 2nd edn, Harcourt Brace Jovanovich, 1988; J. Rachels (ed.), *Moral Theory and Practice*, Random House, 1990; Steven Luper-Foy and Curtis Brown, *The Moral Life*, Harcourt Brace Jovanovich, 1991; J. G. Haber (ed.), *Doing and Being: Introductory Readings in Moral Philosophy*, Macmillan, 1992; T. Fulwiler and A. Biddle (eds), *A Community of Voices: Reading and Writing in College*, Macmillan, 1992; L. Bowie (ed.), *Thirteen Questions in Ethics*, Harcourt Brace Jovanovich, 1992; L. Pojman (ed.), *Environmental Ethics: A Reader*, Jones and Bartlett, Boston, 1994; L. Pojman (ed.), *Life and Death*, Jones and

Bartlett, Boston, 1994; William E. Rivers (ed.), *Issues and Images: An Argument Reader*, Harcourt Brace, 1993; John Cottingham (ed.), *Western Philosophy: an Anthology*, Blackwell, Oxford, 1996.

'Reconsidering the famine relief argument' has been reprinted in Vernon Ruttan (ed.), *Why Food Aid?*, Department of Agricultural and Applied Economics and Center for International Food and Agricultural Policy, University of Minnesota, St Paul, 1990; reissued by The Johns Hopkins University Press, Baltimore, 1993.

'Altruism and commerce: a reply to Arrow' has been reprinted in S. Gorovitz (ed.), *Moral Problems in Medicine*, Prentice Hall, 1976; and in M. Cohen, T. Nagel and T. Scanlon (eds), *Medicine and Moral Philosophy*, Princeton University Press, 1981.

'All animals are equal' has been reprinted in J. Rachels (ed.), *Understanding Moral Philosophy*, Dickenson, 1976, T. Regan and P. Singer (eds), *Animal Rights and Human Obligations, an Anthology*, Prentice Hall, 1976; James White (ed.), *Contemporary Moral Philosophy*, West, 1985, 1997; Robert K. Miller (ed.), *The Informed Argument*, Harcourt, Brace Jovanovich, 1986; (abridged) in Paul Clarke and Andrew Linzey (eds), *Political Theory and Animal Rights*, Pluto Press, London, 1990; (abridged) in Michael Palmer (ed.), *Moral Problems*, Lutterworth Press, Cambridge, 1991; T. Mappes and J. Zembaty (eds), *Social Ethics*, McGraw-Hill, 4th edn, 1992; S. Gold (ed.), *Critical Issues: Race and Gender in Applied Ethics*, Wadsworth, 1992; L. Pojman (ed.), *Environmental Ethics: a Reader*, Jones and Bartlett, Boston, 1994; L. Pojman (ed.), *Life and Death*, Jones and Bartlett, Boston, 1994; J. Arthur (ed.), *Morality and Moral Controversies*, Prentice Hall, Upper Saddle River, NJ, 4th edn, 1995); Gregory Pence (ed.), *Classic Works in Medical Ethics*, McGraw-Hill, 1998, pp. 231–43. Swedish translations have been published in *Djurfront*, no. 2 (1976) and in *Brutus*, 1 (January 1984); an Italian translation in S. Castignone (ed.), *I diritti degli animali*, Il Mulino, Bologna, 1985; and a German translation in Angelika Krebs (ed.), *Naturethik*, Suhrkamp, 1997.

'Discovering Karl Popper' has been translated into Spanish and reprinted in *Revista de Occidente* (Madrid), January 1975.

'Philosophers are back on the job' has been abridged and reprinted under the title 'The new relevance of philosophy', in *Dialogue* (Washington, DC), 8/2 (1975).

Animal Liberation chapter 1 has been abridged and reprinted as *The PETA Guide to Animal Liberation*, People for the Ethical Treatment of Animals, Washington, DC, 1993.

Animal Liberation chapter 2 (extract) has been reprinted in L. Kirszner and Stephen Mandell, *Patterns for College Writing*, 4th edn, St Martins Press, New York, 1989; in Stuart Hirschberg, *Strategies of Argument*, Macmillan, New York, 1990; and in R. Munson (ed.), *Intervention and Reflection: Basic Issues in Medical Ethics*, 5th edn, Wadsworth, 1996.

Animal Liberation chapter 3 has been abridged and reprinted in T. Regan and P. Singer (eds), *Animal Rights and Human Obligations, an Anthology*, Prentice Hall, 1976; and in Lawrence M. Hinman (ed.), *Contemporary Moral Issues*, Prentice Hall, 1996. An Italian translation has been reprinted in *I diritti degli animali*, Il Mulino, Bologna, 1985; an extract from chapter 3 has been reprinted in J. Trimmer (ed.), *Writing with a Purpose*, 10th edn, Houghton Mifflin, 1991.

Animal Liberation chapter 4 has been reprinted in D. Curtin and L. Heldke, *Cooking. Eating, Thinking*, Indiana University Press, 1992.

Animal Liberation chapter 5 has been translated into Swedish and reprinted in *Djurfront*, no. 4, 1976; nos 1 and 2, 1977.

Animal Liberation (revised edn), pp. 7–10, 15–21, 269–71 has been reprinted in Stephen Satris (ed.), *Taking Sides: Clashing Wews on Controversial Moral Issues*, 4th edn, Dushkin, Guildford, CT, 1994; pp. 1–4, 8–9 have been reprinted in Menell and Stewart, (eds), *Environmental Law and Policy*, Little, Brown and Co., 1994; pp. 1–9 and other passages have been reprinted in Barbara Mac-Kinnon (ed.), *Ethics: Theory and Contemporary Issues*, Wadsworth, 1994; and in Thomas Mappes and David De Grazia (eds), *Biomedical Ethics*, McGraw-Hill, New York, 4th edn, 1996.

'Making monkeys neurotic, dogs shriek, etc. etc.' has been reprinted in several US newspapers through the *New York Times* service.

'Freedoms and utilities in health care' has been reprinted in R. Veatch and R. Branson (eds), *Ethics and Health Policy*, Ballinger, Cambridge, MA, 1976, and in *Working Papers for a New Society*, 4/2 (Summer 1976).

'Bioethics and the fetus' has been abridged and reprinted as 'Fetal research', J. Rachels (ed.), *Moral Problems*, 3rd edn, 1979.

'Utility and the survival lottery' has been reprinted in *Bioethics Reporter*, 1/1 (1984).

'The case for animal liberation' has been translated into Dutch and reprinted in H. Smid (ed.), *Dierproeven in de Moderne Samenleving*, Hermes, Deventer, 1979.

'Rights and the market' has been reprinted in T. Beauchamp and N. Bowie (eds), *Ethical Theory and Business*, Prentice Hall, 1979, and (with minor alterations) under the title 'Individual rights and the free market' in M. Sawyer (ed.), *Australia and the New Light*, Allen and Unwin, Sydney, 1982, and in Vincent Barry (ed.), *Moral Issues in Business*, 2nd edn, Wadsworth, Belmont, CA, 1983.

'On your Marx' has been translated into Portuguese and reprinted in *O Estado E S Paulo* (Brazil) (16 March 1980).

'Animals and humans as equals' has been translated into Polish and reprinted in *Etyka*, 18 (1980), pp. 49–61.

Practical Ethics, 1st edn, chapter 8 has been abridged and reprinted in J. Arthur (ed.), *Morality and Moral Controversies*, Prentice Hall, 1981; J. Ramage and J. Bean (eds), *Writing Arguments*, Macmillan, London, 1992; E. Soifer (ed.), *Ethical Issues*, Broadview Press, Peterborough, Ontario, 1992. It has also been translated into German and reprinted in G. Nunner-Winicler, *Weibliche Moral*, Campus, Frankfurt, 1991. Chapter 10 has been abridged and reprinted in C. H. Sommers (ed.), *Vice and Virtue in Everyday Life*, Harcourt Brace, 1985; an abridged version of chapter 1 has been reprinted in G. Brodsky, J. Troyer and D. Vance (eds), *Social and Political Ethics*, Prometheus, 1984; chapter 7 has been abridged and reprinted in J. Arras and R. Hunt (eds), *Ethical Issues in Modern Medicine*, Mayfield, 1983; R. Munson (ed.), *Intervention and Reflection: Basic Issues in Medical Ethics*, 3rd edn, Wadsworth, 1987; J. Arthur (ed.),

Morality and Moral Controversies, Prentice Hall, Upper Saddle River, NJ, 4th edn, 1995). It has been translated into German and reprinted in H. M. Sass (ed.), *Medizin und Ethik*, Reclam, 1989.

Practical Ethics, 2nd edn, chapter 7 has been reprinted in James White (eds), *Contemporary Moral Philosophy*, West, 1997; chapter 8 has been abridged and reprinted in J. Ramage and J. Bean, *Writing Arguments*, 3rd edn, Allyn and Bacon, Boston, 1995, in Lawrence M. Hinman (ed.), *Contemporary Moral Issues*, Prentice Hall, 1996, and in James White (ed.), *Contemporary Moral Philosophy*, West, 1997.

'Conceptions and misconceptions' has been reprinted by *The Age Monthly Review*, 1/8 (1981–2) under the title 'The abortion question'.

'Is racial discrimination arbitrary?', has been reprinted in T. Mappes and J. Zembaty (eds), *Social Ethics*, 2nd edn, McGraw-Hill, New York, 1982, in Jan Narveson (ed.), *Moral Issues*, Oxford University Press, Toronto, 1983, and in James White (ed.), *Contemporary Moral Problems*, West Publishing, 1991, 1997.

'The right to be rich or poor' has been reprinted in Jeffrey Paul (ed.), *Reading Nozick*, Blackwell, Oxford, 1982.

'The Oxford vegetarians – a personal account' has been translated into Swedish and published in *Djurens Ratt!*, no. 6 (1982), pp. 10–13.

'Moral experts' has been reprinted in Wesley Cragg (ed.), *Contemporary Moral Issues*, McGraw-Hill Ryerson, Toronto, 1983; 2nd edn 1988, 3rd edn 1992.

'Not for humans only' has been reprinted in M. Velasquez and C. Rostankowski (eds), *Ethics: Theory and Practice*, Prentice Hall, 1984.

'Sanctity of life or quality of life' has been reprinted in *National Right to Life News* (18 August 1983); G. McCoen and T. Boucher (eds), *Terminating Life*, McCoen, Hudson, WI, 1985; *Perinatal Press*, 7/8 (1983); *Human Life Review* (Fall 1983); B. Szumski (ed.), *Death and Dying: Opposing Viewpoints*, Greenhaven Press, 1984.

'Can we avoid assigning greater value to some lives than to others?' has been reprinted in R. S. Laura and A. Ashman (eds), *Moral Issues in Mental Retardation*, Croom Helm, London, 1985.

'Ethics and sociobiology' has been reprinted in *Zygon*, 19/2 (June 1984), pp. 141–58; and in J. E. Hutchingson (ed.), *Readings in Science and Religion*, Holt, Rinehart and Winston, New York, 1992.

'A covenant for the Ark' has been reprinted in O. Hanfling (ed.), *Life and Meaning: a Philosophical Reader*, Blackwell, Oxford, 1987.

'Technology and procreation: how far should we go?' has been translated into Italian under the title 'La rivoluzione riproduttira' and reprinted in *Prometeo* (Milan) 3/12 (December 1985); and has been translated into Spanish and reprinted in *El Pais* (Madrid) (February 1986).

'Ethics' has been abridged, translated into Japanese and reprinted in the *TBS-Britannica Yearbook* (Tokyo) (1986), pp. 14–20.

'Ten years of animal liberation' has been translated into Italian and reprinted in *Communità* (Milan), no. 188 (December 1986), and abridged, translated into Swedish and published in *Djurens Ratt!*, 3 (1989).

'Luv a duck, I just can't understand it' has been reprinted in Jill Thompson (ed.), *Focus on Writing*, Martin Educational, Hawthorn, 1987; and has been abridged, translated into Swedish and published in *Djurens Ratt!*, 3 (1989).

'IVF technology and the argument from potential' (with Karen Dawson) and 'The syngamy debate: when precisely does a life begin (with Stephen Buckle and Karen Dawson) have been reprinted in Peter Singer, Helga Kuhse, Stephen Buckle, Karen Dawson and Pascal Kasimba, *Embryo Experimentation*, Cambridge University Press, Cambridge, 1990.

Review essay of 'Setting Limits: Medical Goals in an Aging Society' by Daniel Callahan has been reprinted in P. Homer and M. Holstein (eds), *A Good Old Age? The Paradox of Setting Limits*, Simon and Schuster/Touchstone, New York, 1990, pp. 170–81.

Should the Baby Live, chapter 2 (with Helga Kuhse) has been reprinted in E. J. McCullough and R. L. Calder, *Time as a Human Resource*, University of Calgary Press, 1991, pp. 121–50.

'Experiments on animals' has been reprinted in *The Bulletin of the Institute of Animal Technology*, 26/7 (July 1990), pp. 37–9.

'To do or not to do' has been reprinted in *PETA News* (People for the Ethical Treatment of Animals, Washington, DC) (April 1990) and in R. Baird and S. Rosenbaum (eds), *Animal Experimentation: the Moral Issues*, Prometheus, New York, 1991, pp. 57–66. It has been translated into Italian and published as 'Fare o non fare?', *Ethica e Animali*, 2/2 (1989), pp. 96–8; and reprinted in *Cenobio* (Lugano, Switzerland and Varese, Italy), XL/1 (January–March 1991), pp. 77–82.

'The significance of animal suffering' has been reprinted in R. Baird and S. Rosenbaum (eds), *Animal Experimentation: the Moral Issues*, Prometheus, New York, 1991.

'Creating embryos' has been reprinted in T. Mappes and J. Zembaty (eds), *Social Ethics*, 4th edn, McGraw-Hill, New York, 1992; J. Arras and B. Steinbock, *Ethical Issues in Modern Medicine*, 4th edn, Mayfield, New York, 1995; T. Mappes and D. De Grazia (eds), *Biomedical Ethics*, McGraw-Hill, New York, 4th edn, 1996.

'Bioethics and academic freedom' has been translated into German and reprinted in R. Hegselmann and R. Merkel (eds), *Zur Debatte ueber Euthanasie*, Suhrkamp, Frankfurt a. M., 1991, pp. 312–26.

'On being silenced in Germany' has been reprinted in *Australian Jewish Democrat*, 2/3 (Summer 1991), pp. 2–4, 23–6, and has been translated into German and published in *Suhrkamp Wissenschaft Neuerscheinungen*, 2, Halbjahr, 1991, pp. 44–56, and as 'Redeverbot in Deutschland' in *Gaia*, 11 (Summer 1992), pp. 25–7.

'It's all a question of ethics' has been reprinted in Dennis Gastin and Chris Mitchell (eds), *Creating the Future*, Department of Industry, Technology and Commerce and *The Australian*, Sydney, 1992.

'*In vitro* fertilisation: the major issues' (with Deane Wells) has been translated into Italian and reprinted in G. Ferranti and S. Maffetone (eds), *Introduzione alla Bioetica*, Liguori, Naples, 1992.

'Environmental values' has been translated into Italian and reprinted in Laura Marchetti and Peter Zeller (eds), *La Madre, Il Gioco, La Terra*, Laterza, Bari, 1992.

'The rights of ape' has been reprinted under the title 'The Great Ape Project' in *ProAnimal* (Rehovat, Israel), 4 (December 1993), pp. 6–8.

'Has capitalism reached its limits?' has been abridged and reprinted in John Jackson, Ron McIver and Campbell McConnell (eds), *Economics*, 4th edn, McGraw-Hill, Sydney, 1994.

'Is there a God?' has been reprinted in Roslyn Guy (ed.), *English Matters*, Social Science Press, Wentworth Falls, NSW, 1994.

'Late termination and selective non-treatment of disabled infants – some comparisons' has been reprinted in the *Bulletin of The Information Alliance of FNQ Families of Disabled People Inc.*, June 1995.

'Je mehr wir fuer andere leben, desto zufriedener leben wir' has been reprinted in Edgar Dahl (ed.), *Die Lehre des Unheils: Fundamentalkritik am Christentum*, Goldmann, Hamburg, 1995.

'Literature, truth and argument' has been abridged and reprinted as 'Fiction, faction, fact and literature', *Sydney Morning Herald* (16 September 1995), p. 33; and an extract has been reprinted as 'The two Helens in intellectual footy match', *The Age* (19 September 1995), p. 11.

'Animal liberation: an exchange' (from the *The New York Review of Books*, 5 November 1992) has been reprinted in *Animal Husbandry*, 49/8 (August 1995), Yokendo Ltd, Japan, pp. 852–6.

'Sidgwick and reflective equilibrium' has been reprinted in Michael Smith (ed.), *Meta-ethics*, Dartmouth, Aldershot, 1995.

'Animal liberation or animal rights?' has been translated into Italian and reprinted in P. Donatelli and E. Lecaldano (eds), *Etica Analitica*, Edizione Universitarie di Lettere Economia Diritto, Milan, 1996.

'Zwischen Leben entscheiden: eine Verteidigung' has been reprinted in Norbert Diesenbeng and Hans Gerhard Neugebauer, *Unterrichtsideen: Textarbeit im Philosophie-Unterricht*, Ernst Klett, Stuttgart, 1996.

'The ethics of commercialising wild animals' has been translated into German and reprinted in *Moma* (Zurich) (April 1997), pp. 31–6.

'Animal liberation' (from *Island*) has been translated into Swedish and reprinted in Lisa Gälmark (ed.), *Djur & Människor*, Nya Doxa, Nora, 1997.

Extracts from *Making Babies* have been reprinted in Gregory Pence (ed.), *Classic Works in Medical Ethics*, McGraw-Hill, 1998, pp. 83–91.

Index